Perspectives on Accountability at International Financial Institutions

Perspectives on Accountability at International Financial Institutions

Thirty Years after Creation of the World Bank Inspection Panel

Edited by

Daniel D. Bradlow
David B. Hunter
Nicholas Paul
Varsha Iyengar Ramaswamy

BRILL | NIJHOFF

LEIDEN | BOSTON

The Library of Congress Cataloging-in-Publication Data is available online at https://catalog.loc.gov
LC record available at https://lccn.loc.gov/2025029401

Typeface for the Latin, Greek, and Cyrillic scripts: "Brill". See and download: brill.com/brill-typeface.

ISBN 978-90-04-68757-8 (hardback)
ISBN 978-90-04-72973-5 (e-book)
DOI 10.1163/9789004729735

Published by Koninklijke Brill BV, Plantijnstraat 2, 2321 JC Leiden, The Netherlands.
Koninklijke Brill BV incorporates the imprints Brill, Brill Nijhoff, Brill Schöningh, Brill Fink, Brill mentis, Brill Wageningen Academic, Vandenhoeck & Ruprecht, Böhlau and V&R unipress.

For more information: info@brill.com.

This book is printed on acid-free paper and produced in a sustainable manner.

Contents

PART 4
Critiques of IAMs

PART 5
Next Steps on Accountability

Acknowledgements

This book, like all edited volumes, is a collaborative effort and it is important to acknowledge the many people and organizations that contributed to its completion.

First, this book was conceived at a conference commemorating the 30th anniversary of the World Bank Inspection Panel and co-hosted by the Panel, the Program on Environmental and Energy Law (PEEL) at the American University Washington College of Law (AUWCL), and the Centre for the Advancement of Scholarship at the University of Pretoria. We particularly would like to thank the members of the Inspection Panel at the time--Ramanie Kunanayagam (the Chairperson), Mark Goldsmith, and Ibrahim James Pam—for their support of the Conference and this project. The Honorable Kate O'Regan deserves special thanks for making the extraordinary effort to serve as our keynote speaker in what totaled less than a 24-hour visit to Washington, DC. The real burden of putting on the Conference—all the logistics—fell disproportionately on Rupes Dupai, research analyst at the Panel, and Ingrid Lesemann, the PEEL program coordinator. We are eternally grateful to both of them.

Second, we would like to thank the contributors to this book, both for their enthusiastic response in providing their *Perspectives*, as well as their patience and flexibility in working with us in completing this book. Many contributors to this volume also participated in the 30th Anniversary Conference, particularly the morning session facilitated by Gina Barbieri that elicited a diversity of perspectives and sparked the idea of capturing the *Perspectives* in writing.

Third, we would like to thank the students and staff of the American University Washington College of Law who have supported the project in many ways. We particularly thank Access Services Law Librarian, Khelani Clay, and recent graduate, Murphy Chen, for their support of the *Perspectives* web presence, among other things. Also deserving our deepest gratitude is Reagan Ferris, who provided timely research support, editorial skills, and a new-found love of the "that/which" rule to the production of this volume.

Finally, the *Perspectives* project, like much of civil society's advocacy surrounding the Panel and the IAMs over the past thirty years, is supported by the Charles Stewart Mott Foundation. The editors thank the Foundation not only for its generous support of this *Perspectives* Project, but for the decades of support it has given toward enhancing people-centered accountability and reducing the environmental impacts of IFIs more generally. Through this time, the Foundation has been more than just a funder; its program officers and advisors have been true thought partners in the development of the IAMs' community of practice.

Figures and Tables

Figures

Tables

Abbreviations

ADB	Asian Development Bank
AFDB	African Development Bank
AI	Artificial Intelligence
AIIB	Asian Infrastructure Investment Bank
AM	Accountability Mechanism
AMS	Accountability Mechanism Secretariat
APCC	Alexandria Portland Cement Company
BEFT	Bank Executive Trust Fund
BIC	Bank Information Center
CAO	Compliance Advisor Ombudsman
CI	Conservation International
CIEL	Center for International Environmental Law
CM	Complaints Mechanism
COPINH	Consejo Cívico de Organizaciones Populares e Indígenas de Honduras ("National Council of Popular and Indigenous Organizations of Honduras")
CRMU	Compliance Review and Mediation Unit
CSO	Civil Society Organizations
DR	Dispute Resolution
DRS	Dispute Resolution Service
E&S	Environmental and Social
EA	Environmental Assessment
EBRD	European Bank for Reconstruction and Development
ECRF	Egyptian Center for Rights and Freedoms
ECESR	Egyptian Center for Economic and Social Rights
EDF	Environmental Defense Fund
EIB	European Investment Bank
EIPR	Egyptian Initiative for Personal Rights
EPA	Environmental Protection Agency
ESA	Egyptian Survey Authority
ESF	Environmental and Social Framework
ESG	Environmental, Social, and Governance
FCV	Fragility, Conflict, and Violence
FI	Financial Institution
FMO	Netherlands Development FInance Company
GCF	Green Climate Fund
GRM	Grievance Redress Mechanism

GRS	Grievance Redress Service
IAM	Independent Accountability Mechanism
IAMnet	Independent Accountability Mechanism Network
IBRD	International Bank for Reconstruction and Development
IDA	International Development Agency
IEG	Independent Evaluation Group
IDB	Inter-American Development Bank
IFC	International Finance Corporation
IFI	International Finance Institutions
IMF	International Monetary Fund
IPAM	Independent Project Accountability Mechanism
IRM	Independent Review Mechanism
IRM	Independent Redress Mechanism (Green Climate Fund)
JFF	Joint Fact-Finding
MICI	Independent Consultation and Investigation Mechanism (IDB)
MIGA	Multilateral Investment Guarantee Agency
NBA	Narmada Bachao Andolan
NTPC	National Thermal Power Corporation
OGC	Office of General Counsel
OPIC	Overseas Private Investment Corporation
PS	Performance Standard
PCM	Project Complaint Mechanism
SDG	Sustainable Development Goals
SEAH	Sexual Exploitation, Abuse, and Harassment
SOGI	Sexual Orientation and Gender
R&R	Rehabilitation and Resettlement
T&A	Transparency and Accountability
TRI	Toxic Release Inventory
TSDP	Transport Sector Development Project
UNDHR	United Nations Declaration of Human Rights
UNDP	United Nations Development Programme
UNEP	United Nations Environmental Program
UNFAO	United Nations Food and Agricultural Organization
UNFCCC	United Nations Framework Convention on Climate Change
USAID	United States Agency for International Development
WBG	World Bank Group
WDR	World Development Report
WJP	World Justice Project

Notes on Contributors

Editors

Daniel Bradlow
Professor and Senior Fellow at the Centre for Advancement of Scholarship at the University of Pretoria; Professor Emeritus at the American University Washington College of Law; and a Compliance Officer in the Social and Environmental and Compliance Unit of the United Nations Development Programme (UNDP). His publications include many books, including *The Law of the International Financial Institutions* (*OUP, 2023*) and articles focused on international financial law, international financial institutions, foreign investment, and accountability in international financial institutions.

David Hunter
Professor Emeritus of international and comparative environmental law at American University's Washington College of Law. He currently serves on the Boards of Directors of Accountability Counsel, the Center for International Environmental Law, and Friends of Green Advocates–Liberia. His research is focused on international and comparative environmental law, human rights and the environment, and international accountability for environmental and social harm. He is co-author of *International Environmental Law & Policy* (5th ed.) and *Climate Change Law* (2nd ed.).

Nick Paul
Editor and writer with a background in business communications, journalism, and international development organizations. His work is strongly focused on business development, corporate social responsibility, and sustainability.

Varsha Iyengar Ramaswamy
Lawyer and mediator with experience in human rights and sustainability and specializing in dispute resolution and impact-based human rights litigation She currently works on business and human rights issues, while preparing her thesis as an SJD Candidate at American University Washington College of Law.

Contributors

Eduardo G. Abbott

International consultant on Accountability, Institutional and Environmental /Social matters. He has advised a number of institutions on accountability matters, including the European Investment Bank, the Inter American Development Bank, the UNDP and the World Bank as well as NGOs. Prior to his retirement, he was the Executive Secretary of the World Bank's Inspection Panel, a position he held for 12 years. He assisted in the establishment and operation of the World Bank's Inspection Panel.

Scott Adams

Senior Dispute Resolution Officer at the World Bank Accountability Mechanism Dispute Resolution Service. This essay represents the personal views of the authors and should not be attributed to the World Bank Group, its Management, its Executive Directors, or its Member countries.

Camila Jorge do Amarel

Investigation Officer for the World Bank Inspection Panel. Previously, she worked with the government of the State of São Paulo on initiatives related to social protection, sustainable development, child labor issues, and refugees.

Joe Athialy

Experienced grassroots, national and international re advocate and an avid campaigner for the accountability of financial institutions. He worked at the Narmada Bachao Andolon, National Alliance of People's Movements, Amnesty International and Bank Information Center in various senior roles. Currently, he is heading the Centre for Financial Accountability, a Delhi-based research and campaign organization on matters related to the national and international economy, and financial institutions. He is on the Board of Recourse, Focus on the Global South India and Environment Support Group. He has written and published several articles and reports in newspapers and other publications.

Gina Barbieri

South African human rights lawyer and expert in environmental and social accountability systems design and practice. She served as the inaugural Ombudsperson for WWF's global network, and prior to that managed the dispute resolution function for the independent accountability mechanism for the private sector arm of the World Bank Group (CAO).

Dilek Barlas
Adjunct professor of law at Georgetown University and an international consultant on accountability issues to the World Bank. She served as the Executive Secretary of the Inspection Panel from July 2014 to 2021. She was the Panel's Deputy Executive Secretary from 2007 to 2014. She has extensive experience in the field of development. She has served as the Senior Counsel in the World Bank Legal Vice Presidency for the Europe and Central Asia Region. As Senior Counsel she was responsible for the legal aspects of World Bank operations and conducted negotiations in numerous countries.

Gregory Berry
Policy associate at Accountability Counsel. Prior to this, he served two years as a staff attorney for the New York State Supreme Court, Appellate Division. His areas of focus include environmental and human rights, and he has a masters in Environmental Law and Policy with a concentration in Water Resources Law.

Richard E. Bissell
Lead Compliance Officer for the Social and Environmental Compliance Unit at the United Nations Development Programme. He has also served as Chair of the World Bank Inspection Panel, Member of the ADB Compliance Review Panel, and Chair of the AfDB Panel of Experts. The views expressed in his chapter are entirely his personal views, and do not reflect the corporate views of UNDP.

Juan Pablo Bohoslavsky
Researcher at Argentina's National Scientific and Technical Research Council (CONICET), Universidad Nacional de Río Negro (CIEDIS). He has also worked as an independent expert on debt and human rights at the UN and has published numerous articles related to these subjects.

Aldo Caliari
Senior Director of Policy and Strategy at Jubilee USA Network. He previously served as the Senior Advisor at the Intergovernmental Group of 24 on International Monetary Affairs and Development (G–24) and directed the Rethinking Bretton Woods Project at the Center of Concern. With a focus on macroeconomic and sustainable development finance, Caliari has conducted policy research and advocacy on various issues including debt, tax, private finance and investment, international financial architecture, financial regulation, and trade, as well as exploring their respective links to human rights. He holds Master's degrees on economics and finance from George Washington

University and on international legal studies from the Washington College of Law, American University. He earned his first law degree in Argentina, at the Universidad Nacional de Tucuman.

C.P. Chandrasekhar
Senior Research Fellow at the Political Economy Research Institute, University of Massachusetts. His work focuses on the role of finance and industry in development and the impact of economic policy reforms in developing countries. He has published many academic articles on the subject and co-authored several books, including *The Market that Failed: Neo-Liberal Economic Reforms in India.* He has also served as a consultant for international organizations, including UNDP, ILO, and ADB.

Rupes Dalai
Research Analyst for the World Bank Inspection Panel. He manages the Panel's website and social media with the goal to expand awareness about the Panel among stakeholders in affected communities.

Lalanath de Silva
Executive Director of Environmental Law Alliance Worldwide. Previously he served as the Managing Director of Transparentem (an NGO) and Panel Member at the Independent Complaints Mechanism of the International Climate Initiative of the German Government. He also served as the Head of the Independent Redress Mechanism of the Green Climate Fund (2016–2022) and as a Panel Member of the Compliance Review Panel of the Asian Development Banks (2012–2016).

Charles E. Di Leva
Chief Counsel of the Environmental and International Law Practice Group in the World Bank Legal Vice-Presidency and the Bank's Legal Advisor to the Climate Change Solutions Area and the Environment and Natural Resources Global Practice Group. Since 1992 he has worked in all regions, specializing on issues pertaining to sustainable development, such as climate finance, development and implementation of multilateral environmental agreements, and national laws. He has represented the Bank in international treaty negotiations in areas of Climate, Biodiversity, Chemicals and Wetlands. He has also played a key role in the development and implementation of the World Bank's environmental and social policies, as well as activities concerning the Bank's Independent Inspection Panel.

Natalie Bridgeman Fields
Director of International Programs at Earth Justice. Natalie founded, and for fourteen years led, Accountability Counsel, a non-governmental organization that advocates for and supports requests to international accountability mechanisms. Previously, she was a litigator involved in human rights, environmental, and business law cases in U.S. federal and state courts, and a consultant for international institutions on accountability issues.

Jonathan Fox
Professor of development studies at the School of International Service at American University, where he directs the Accountability Research Center – https://accountabilityresearch.org/. His involvement in multilateral development bank accountability agendas dates to the early 1990s. His publications include "Contested Terrain: International Development Projects and Countervailing Power for the excluded," in *World Development.*

Giada Giacomini
Postdoctoral researcher at the International Law Department, Geneva Graduate Institute of International and Development Studies (Switzerland). Giada also served as an Intern at the Independent Redress Mechanism of the Green Climate Fund in the 2020/2021 cohort.

Mark Goldsmith
Former Member and Chair of the Inspection Panel. He possesses over twenty-five years of experience managing projects related to financial services, development, strategy consulting, and energy sectors. He was director of Responsible Investment for Actis and began his own sustainability consultancy, FiveOak, in 2015.

Ayako Kubodera
Investigation Officer for the World Bank Inspection Panel. Prior to the Panel, she worked for the UN with a focus on strategic planning, coordination, monitoring, reporting, and evaluation, including COVID-19 prevention and response..

Ramanie Kunanayagam
Former Member and Chair of the Inspection Panel 2018–2023. She has extensive experience conducting fieldwork in Indonesia and leading sustainability initiatives both in the private and nonprofit sector.

Owen McIntyre

Professor, Director of the Environmental & Natural Resource Law LL.M program, and Co-Director for the Centre for Law and the Environment at School of Law, University College Cork. He serves on the editorial boards of several Irish and international journals and is widely published, particularly in the area of International Water Law. He has served on boards and expert panels on the subject, including as inaugural Chair for the IUCN World Commission on Environmental Law's Specialist Group on Water and the Wetlands. One of his most recent articles, "Environmental activism on plastics through clinical legal education" was featured in *Natural Resources & the Environment.*

Aparna Mukerjee

Lawyer and internationally accredited mediator based in Chennai, India whose experience includes mediating cases for several IAM. She is the former coordinator of the Tamil Nadu and Mediation and Conciliation Centre. She also trains company employees, judges, and lawyers on mediation.

Suzan Nada

Labor lawyer and activist, accountability and resolution expert, human rights lawyer, co-founder of the Bread and Freedom political party in Egypt, and Coordinator of the Coordinating Committee to Support Wadi al-Qamar.

Suresh Nanwani

Professor in Practice at Durham University, United Kingdom and Honorary Research Fellow at Birkbeck University of London. He is also subject expert consultant for environmental and international law in the Green Climate Fund's Independent Redress Mechanism and is accountability expert (Compliance Review Panel and Advisor) with the Caribbean Development Bank. He holds a PhD in Organization Development from SAIDI Graduate School of Organization Development, Philippines. He is co-editor of *The Practice of Independent Accountability Mechanisms: Towards Good Governance in Development Finance* (Brill Nijhoff, 2019) and author of *Organization and Education Development: Reflecting and Transforming in a Self-Discovery Journey* (Routledge, 2022, Open Access). He publishes extensively on international governance and accountability.

Ibrahim James Pam

International lawyer and Chair of the World Bank Inspection Panel. His analyst, investigator, and advocacy work has focused on mass crimes, human rights abuses, fraud, financial crimes, and internal oversight and accountability for international institutions. At the International Criminal Court, he worked as an Analyst and Investigator for the Integrity and Anti-Corruption Department, and also assisted in developing the General Principles for Review of Investigative Offices of the Conference of International Investigators.

Susan Park
Professor of Global Governance in Government and International Relations at the University of Sydney. She focuses on how international organisations and global governance can become greener and more accountable, particularly in the transition to renewable energy. Her most recent books are: *The Good Hegemon* (2022, OUP) and Environmental Recourse at the Multilateral Development Banks (2020, CUP). She is co-lead Editor of the journal Global Environmental Politics.

Dustin Schäfer
Head of the IFI team at Urgewald, Germany. He received his PhD from the University of Kassel. His research runs at the intersection of post development, governance research, and political science organizational research. He holds a BA of Ed. and MA of Ed. in Vocational Education (Political Science and Electrical Engineering).

Serge Selwan
Senior Operations Officer and Adviser for the World Bank Inspection Panel. He has over twenty years of experience in international accountability and has reviewed several projects pertaining to development-induced resettlement, indigenous peoples, core labor rights, and community health and safety.

Hamid Sharif
The inaugural Managing Director of the Complaints-resolution, Evaluation, and Integrity Unit of the Asian Infrastructure Investment Bank (AIIB). Mr. Sharif has held several senior positions at the Asian Development Bank, including as Country Director of People's Republic of China Resident Mission, Head of Procurement, and Assistant General Counsel. Mr. Sharif is also a member of the Expert Committee of the China International Commercial Court under the Supreme People's Court of China.

Christopher H. Stephens
Senior Vice President and General Counsel of the World Bank Group. He has also served as the General Counsel of IFC and ADB.

Lori Udall

International Consultant with over 30 years of experience in the review, design, and functioning of independent accountability mechanisms. She has also extensive experience working directly with communities in the global south who have been forcibly resettled or adversely impacted by top-down development projects and programs funded by development banks, governments, and conservation NGOs. Udall also works in philanthropy, project evaluation, and environmental and indigenous rights policy. Udall has a BA from George Mason University, LLM from Downing College Cambridge University, and an MCL from George Washington University National Law Center.

Luis Vieira

Coordinator of the Bretton Woods Project. Previously, he served as the chief of mission for the International Organisation for Migration and worked with Mercy Corps on a variety of emergency response situations. He also has been a guest lecturer at the Columbia University School of International Public Affairs.

Richard Wyness

Senior Environment Specialist on the World Bank Inspection Panel. He has over thirty years of experience in environmental and social risk management for the oil and gas sector and has conducted similar work around renewable energy.

Introduction

Daniel Bradlow, David Hunter, Nick Paul and Varsha Iyengar Ramaswamy

The creation in 1993 of the World Bank Inspection Panel was an important experiment in the democratization of international law, significantly expanding individual rights in international governance. For the first time, communities and groups of individuals who contended that they had been harmed by the actions of an international organization could bring a complaint against the organization and, after an independent investigation, have their claim considered by the top decision-making body in the organization. Over the ensuing thirty years, the Inspection Panel's general promotion of citizen-based accountability has become the norm for international development finance. Today, "Independent Accountability Mechanisms" (IAMs) have been adopted in one form or another by virtually all International Finance Institutions (IFIs), all the climate finance institutions, nine UN agencies, several bilateral financial or development agencies, and several of the largest international conservation organizations. The most noteworthy exception is the International Monetary Fund, which remains unaccountable to communities and groups of individuals who allege harm from its actions. More than twenty IAMs are members of the IAM Network[1] and nine more are members of the UN Accountability Mechanism Network.[2]

1 The World Bank Inspection Panel, *Independent Accountability Mechanisms Network (IAMnet)-23 Members* (May 13, 2024). https://accountability.worldbank.org/en/iamnet. Members are the following: African Development Bank (AfDB), Asian Development Bank (ADB), Asian Infrastructure Investment Bank (AIIB), Bank aus Verantwortung (KFW), Black Sea Trade and Development (BSTD), Caribbean Development Bank (CDB), European bank for Reconstruction and Development (EBRD), European Investment Bank (EIB), FinDev Canada, French Development Agency AFD), German Development Bank (DEG), Netherlands Development Finance Company (FMO), Green Climate Fund (GCF), Inter-American Development Bank Group (IADB), International Finance Corporation and Multilateral Investment Guarantee Agency (IFC/MIGA), Internationale Klimaschutzinitative (IKI), Japan Bank for International Cooperation (JBIC), Japan International Cooperation Agency (JICA), Nippon Export and Investment Insurance (NEXI), Nordic Investment Bank (NIB), U.S. International Development Financial Corporation (DFC), United Nations Development Program (UNDP), World Bank Inspection Panel (IPN), World Bank Accountability Mechanism.

2 The United Nations Development Programme, *Annual Report Social and Environmental Compliance Unit (SECU)*, 33 (May 8, 2024).

The mechanisms are regularly at the center of controversial cases that put a spotlight on the institutions and the impacts they have on local communities.[3] When the IAMs work as designed, they can offer a pathway to voluntarily resolving disputes between communities and the project proponents—whether member states or private sector companies—or through a compliance review can publicly report on whether the IFI adheres to the IFI's environmental and social standards. But the IAMs do not always work as designed. Despite their widespread adoption, these mechanisms have often fallen short of their initial purpose—neither providing affected communities with an effective means of remedy, nor driving systemic change at the IFIs. The Panel and the other IAMs are still met with persistent (if sometimes hidden) opposition from the IFI management and many borrowing country member states. Access to the IAMs is difficult for affected communities, most of which do not have any knowledge of the IAMs. IFI management and the borrowing states do not always welcome the IAM's brand of oversight, and they frequently work together to introduce barriers to the IAMs' independence and effectiveness.

Given the relatively unique and controversial role of the Inspection Panel and the other IAMs, people active in the accountability ecosystem have a variety of perspectives on the IAMs. This book contains a collection of essays providing new, and sometimes personal perspectives on the evolution, impact, and future of the IAMs at international finance and development institutions.

On the one hand, this collection has been quite literally thirty years in the making, as it coincides with the thirtieth anniversary of the creation of the World Bank Inspection Panel (the Panel), the first of what have become known as IAMs. On the other, the book was an impromptu response to discussions held at a Conference marking the 30th Anniversary of the Panel at American University's Washington College of Law. Sitting at any one of the small group discussion tables at that conference, you might have found the General Counsel of the World Bank, a World Bank Executive Director, a community advocate from a fisherman's collective in India, an international civil society advocate, and an academic , all exchanging views in a dynamic conversation about what it meant for the World Bank to "be accountable," and what the Panel's thirty-year contribution was to that effort. Few issues could attract that disparate a group of World Bank stakeholders, each with their own perspectives, to have

3 *See e.g.*, BBC, *Tanzania Tourism: World Bank Suspends Funding for Ruaha National Park project* (Apr. 23, 2024); Paul Rappaport, *Investigation finds World Bank Failed to Police Abuse at Kenyan Schools,* NY Times (March 14, 2024).

a conversation—particularly one where every perspective was treated with equal respect. Those small groups reflected the fundamental innovation of the Panel and the IAMs; it created a forum where the highest levels of Bank leadership and its member states could be educated about the experience of – and be held accountable to – the people most affected by the Bank's development projects. It was the first, and still the only, mechanism where the interests of affected people could set the agenda for the General Counsel and Executive Directors and possibly influence the way in which operational policies and procedures of the Bank are interpreted and applied.

The *Perspectives* project was born from reflecting on how the experiment of people-centered IAMs had given rise to a diverse, committed and engaged community of practitioners and academicians. To capture the diverse perspectives of this community of practice, the editors solicited relatively short essays from approximately thirty-five potential contributors. We provided only the slightest of prompts for the essays: What do you think about the past experience of the IAMs? What lessons have been learned from them? What is the future potential for effective community-facing accountability mechanisms that provide remedy and drive systemic change? Can we imagine and create more effective approaches for communities to promote their rights in the development context?

Almost every one of the invitees responded enthusiastically. Contributors to this volume include, among others, current and past members of the Inspection Panel (Bissell, Kunanayagam, et al); two former executive secretaries of the Panel (Abbott and Barlas); the current World Bank General Counsel (Stephens); the first environmental lawyer ever hired by the Bank (DiLeva); civil society advocates who both support and criticize the IAMs (Berry, Bridgeman Fields) and leading academics who have studied and written about the IAMs (Park, Bradlow) since their beginning. The chronological experience of the contributors spans more than the thirty years of the Panel, including those external advocates who pushed for the Panel before it existed (Bradlow, Hunter, and Udall) and the Bank lawyer responding to those proposals (DiLeva) back in 1993, all the way to a new generation of advocates (Schäfer and Berry) and researchers (Giacomini). The contributors also draw on their experience as past or current employees or consultants to the IAMs from thirteen different IFIs other than the World Bank Group: Barbieri (CAO, UNDP, & WWF), Bissel (UNDP, AFDB), Bradlow (AFDB, UNDP), da Silva (GCF), Hunter (ADB, OPIC, UNDP, UNEP), McIntyre (EBRD), Nanwani (GCF and Caribbean Development Bank), Sharif (AIIB), and Lori Udall (ADB, IDB).

1 The Organization of the Book

The book is organized into five parts. Part one explores the conceptual framework for understanding what is meant by accountability, generally, and with respect to the accountability of IFIs, specifically. Part one also presents accountability from the social sciences, political, and legal perspectives.[4]

Part two focuses on the creation, operation, and impact of the Inspection Panel. Much has been written about the Inspection Panel, but this book includes more personalized accounts from insiders that have not heretofore been published. In this regard, the perspectives of two executive secretaries of the Panel (Abbott and Barlas) are particularly noteworthy.[5] The contributions of Charles Di Leva and David Hunter also provide internal and external perspectives from the time when the Panel was created.[6] Part three explores current operational issues facing the IFIs and the IAMs. Some of these issues, such as the continued support of projects causing massive involuntary resettlement, the persistent claims of immunity by the IFIs, and the responsibility of the IFIs to provide effective remedies for the impacts their projects cause, are part of the contextual background within which the IAMs operate. Others emerged only as we gained experience with the IAMs, including questions relating to the management of dispute resolution processes with parties that have such disparate power and access to information, the responsible exit of the IFIs from a project that is subject to a pending IAM case, and the protection of complainants against retaliation.[7] Part four provides critiques of the

4 *See* Jonathan Fox, *What Counts as Accountability, infra* Chapter 1; Susan Park, *Are the MDBs Accountable? Reflecting on the Independent Accountability Mechanisms of the Multilateral Development Banks, infra* Chapter 2; Owen McIntyre. *The Critical Contribution of Independent Accountability Mechanisms (IAMs) to the Global Governance Paradigm, infra* Chapter 3; Daniel Bradlow, *The Inspection Panel and International Law, infra* Chapter 4.

5 *See* Eduardo Abbott, *The Inspection Panel Early Years (An Inside Story), infra* Chapter 5; Dilek Barlas, *Thirty Years of Community-Centered Accountability in International Development: Key Developments at the World Bank Inspection Panel, infra* Chapter 6.

6 *See* Charles Di Leva, *"Reflections on the Role of the Panel in Strengthening Environmental and Social Accountability: A View from a Former Chief Counsel," infra* Chapter 7.

7 *See* Richard Bissell, *Three Decades of Seeking Elusive Remedies, infra* Chapter 10; Suzan Nada. *Exiting the Disaster, Evading the Responsibility? Wadi al-Qamar- The Moon Valley, infra* Chapter 11; Lori Udall, *Unacceptable Means: The Inspection Panel Action on World Bank Forcible Resettlement, infra* Chapter 12; Athialy, *The World Bank, the Inspection Panel & Immunity, infra* Chapter 13; Greg Berry. *Ending Violence in Development Finance Actions to Affirmatively Prevent and Stop Reprisals Against Rights Defenders, infra* Chapter 14; Scott Adams and Aparna Mukerjee, *Collaborative Dispute Resolution: Five Essential Questions, infra* Chapter 15; Gina Barbieri. *The Promise of Collaborative Problem Solving in Enhancing IAM Effectiveness, infra* Chapter 16.

IAMs and their approach to accountability. These criticisms include a full range of critical views based on a variety of frameworks, including the failure to fully consider human rights, the risk of "accountability washing" a flawed international development system, and broad questions of whether the IAMs work well enough to warrant the risks taken by the affected people who use them.[8] Part five includes different visions of future steps that could support the positive evolution of IAMs and the continued search for people-centered accountability in the development process. These include a variety of visions, including some that favor the expansion of IAMs to new institutions, particularly the IMF, and others favoring consolidation.[9]

Each of the parts has its own introduction that draws together the essays it contains. These introductions also identify interconnections between essays in different parts. Because contributors were allowed to choose their own topics and approaches, the resulting essays could be organized in multiple ways. For example, in addition to several essays focused only on the Panel, other essays draw heavily from their authors' experience with accountability in other development institutions, including the Asia International Infrastructure Bank (Sharif), the European Bank for Reconstruction and Development (McIntyre), the Compliance Advisor and Ombudsman (Adams & Mujareen, Barbieri, and Wada), and the International Monetary Fund (Viera and Caliari). The parts could also have been organized more explicitly by past, present, and future. Two of the editors (Bradlow and Hunter) and four of the contributors (Abbott, Bissell, DiLeva, and Udall) have been engaged since the conception of the Panel and its earliest years of operation. Their contributions bring the historical arc of the IAMs into focus. Another approach could have included a part highlighting fundamental but aspirational principles: accessibility (Barlas), transparency, independence (Abbott), sequencing between compliance and

8 Juan Bohoslavsky and C.P. Chandrasekhar, *World Bank's Roadmap and the Inspection Panel's Human Rights Responsibilities*, *infra* Chapter 17; Natalie Fields, *'Use and Improve' is My Accountability Mantra, Despite Thirty Years of Eye-Opening Disappointments*, *infra* Chapter 18; Dustin Schäfer, *Between Disruption and Legitimation of Development: A Critical Perspective on the Inspection Panel and a Call for More Radical Thinking within the Accountability Community*, *infra* Chapter 19; Lalanath De Silva and Giada Giacomini, *Should Decisions of Independent Accountability Mechanisms be Binding?*, *infra* Chapter 20.

9 Christopher Stephens, *Strengthening Accountability in Challenging Times: Insights from the General Counsel of the World Bank Group*, *infra* Chapter 21; Aldo Caliari, *IMF Human Rights Accountability: A Pragmatic Way to Break the Deadlock*, *infra* Chapter 22; Luiz Vieira, *Ending Thirty Years of IMF Exceptionalism: A Call for an Accountability Mechanism at the International Monetary Fund*, *infra* Chapter 23; Hamid Sharif, *An Increased Normalization of IAMs Faces Ground Realities: Lack of Transparency Impedes Access to IAMs*, Chapter 24; Suresh Nanwani, *The River of Accountability: Then and Now*, *infra* Chapter 25.

dispute resolution functions (Barbieri), and remedy (Bissell). The wide range of perspectives provides a variety of ways to experience the book.

2 The Perspectives Project

This book is part of a broader IAM Project aimed at chronicling the creation of the IAMs and capturing the lessons learned over the past thirty years of people-centered accountability at IFIs. In addition to this book, the IAM Project launched the *Perspectives* website, where earlier versions of most of the chapters in this book have been available since 2023.[10] At the IAM Project website you can learn about other parts of the project, including other *Perspectives,* several interviews with key contributors to the history of the IAMs, a comprehensive bibliography including hundreds of publications on the IAMs, and a timeline with access to relevant historical documents from the archive. A second book is also anticipated in 2026—this one focusing on the innovations sparked by the creation of the CAO and marking its 25 years of operation providing community-based accountability for IFI-funding of private sector sponsored development projects.

We hope this *Perspectives* project will serve not only as a valuable reflection on how far we have come in democratizing and humanizing international development, but also as an expression of our collective imagination of what the future of accountability should be in international development finance and international organizations in particular, and in international law, more generally.

---

10 https://digitalcommons.wcl.american.edu/accountability/.

PART 1

Reflections on Accountability

Introduction to Part 1: Conceptual Frameworks

The four perspectives in this first part explore four different conceptual frameworks for understanding what accountability means in general and more specifically with respect to International Financial Institutions (IFIs). The first two chapters (Fox and Park) present accountability from a social sciences perspective and the second two (McIntyre and Bradlow) review the Inspection Panel (Panel) from a transnational and international law perspective. These different frames will allow readers of the book to understand the IAMs in different ways, hopefully facilitating new insights for readers as they approach later chapters in the book.

In the first chapter, Professor Jonathan Fox critically explores the general concept of accountability. He argues that the idea of accountability is malleable, ambiguous, and contested. The resulting "fuzziness" makes it difficult to answer many of the questions about accountability that others struggle with in later chapters of the book. For example, if we are not clear accountability means or what its ultimate purpose is, how do we know which strategies bolster accountability? How do we know, for example, whether increased transparency leads to greater accountability? "Sunshine is the best disinfectant" is not just a slogan, but also a longstanding theory of change for many civil society organizations (CSOs), and one that is reflected in the public-facing nature of the Independent Accountability Mechanisms (IAMs). Even if we increase accountability, under what conditions does that either improve (IFI) performance or mitigate the adverse impacts of their operations? By raising these questions, Fox invites all of us to test the basic assumptions underlying our theories of change, ultimately enabling us to strengthen the impact of our work on accountability.

The second chapter, authored by Professor Susan Park, focuses on the IAMs' records and assesses them according to the standard questions about accountability: who is accountable; to whom; for what are they accountable; and what are the standards, processes, and sanctions employed to demonstrate that the MDBs are accountable. This framework helps clarify the IAMs' approach to accountability, including the limits of issues for which the IAMs can and cannot hold the MDBs to account. It also helps us identify the extent to which the IAMs are effective in their particular context, and how to promote accountability in other international contexts. This is particularly relevant for people seeking to defend their lives, livelihood, and land in the context of a globalized economy, climate breakdown, and species extinction.

DANIEL D. BRADLOW ET AL., 2026 | DOI:10.1163/9789004729735_003

The third chapter by Professor Owen McIntyre explores the IFI accountability systems, consisting of the environmental and social safeguard policies and related accountability frameworks, in the context of emerging conceptions of transnational or global law. He defines global law, in this context, as consisting of the standards, principles, and processes that apply to activities taking place across borders or in international settings. He distinguishes global law from international law, which regulates activities between States. He argues that the IFI accountability systems were at the forefront of the global movement to apply good environmental and social governance standards to the corporations and organizations active in economic globalization, and that the process of developing the IFI accountability systems was itself a major contributor to global administrative law.

Professor Daniel Bradlow also addresses the IAMs' contributions, but from the perspective of international law. His chapter argues that the creation of the Inspection Panel was an important development in international law, because it was the first time that an international organization established a mechanism that enabled individuals and communities, who have no contractual relationship with a particular international organization but that they claim to have been harmed by its decisions and actions, to hold the organization accountable. Rather than framing the IAMs as something other than international law as McIntyre's chapter does, Bradlow identifies the Panel's focus on non-state actors who have been harmed by IFIs as critical innovations in international law.

These four chapters and their conceptual frameworks for understanding the IFI accountability systems hint at how innovative the creation of the Panel was. It represented a new form of accountability, running from an international organization directly to affected people. The unprecedented nature of its role triggered new ways of thinking about law, accountability, and global governance, attracting great interest from international practitioners and academics in the IAMs.

CHAPTER 1

Rethinking "What Counts" as Accountability

*Jonathan Fox**

1 Introduction**

The creation of International Accountability Mechanisms (IAMs) three decades ago represented the cutting edge of a broader wave of transparency and accountability reforms. Their focus on avoiding and mitigating environmental and social harm associated with projects funded by Multilateral Development Banks (MDBs) joined a broader stream of accountability reforms at the local, national, and international levels.[1] This broader set of reforms was driven by motives that also included democratization, anti-corruption, corporate social responsibility, and improved public service provision. Global multistakeholder initiatives to address both public and private sector accountability multiplied, ranging from extractive industries, open contracting, open budgeting, and open government, as well as a wide range of social and environmental certification initiatives focused on global supply chains. Yet many of these initiatives have limited institutional mandates to tangibly address accountability failures. Their institutional design relies heavily on the assumption that investigations of claims will have a deterrent effect. This limited reach raises practical, analytical, and conceptual questions about what it means to deliver accountability.

About a decade and a half ago, during a period of great optimism about reform initiatives at the local, national, and international level, private

* Jonathan Fox is a professor of development studies at the School of International Service at American University, where he directs the Accountability Research Center – https://accountabilityresearch.org/. His involvement in multilateral development bank accountability agendas dates to the early 1990s. *See* https://jonathan-fox.org/publications/world-bank-accountability-campaigns/ (last visited Nov. 27, 2024).

** This essay draws from a keynote talk presented virtually to the XX World Congress of Sociology (June 28, 2023) as well as a working paper and blog series called Accountability Keywords (Jan. 2022), at https://accountabilityresearch.org/publication/accountability-keywords/ (last visited Nov. 27, 2024).

1 For an early independent overview of the World Bank Inspection Panel's dynamics, see Dana Clark et al., Demanding Accountability: Civil Society Claims and the World Bank Inspection Panel (2003).

foundation funders and other international practitioners began to call this broad governance reform agenda "transparency and accountability" (T&A).[2] In practice, a big bet on the power of data led many reforms in this field to focus much more on transparency than on accountability – with the notable exception of the spread of grievance redress mechanisms (GRMs) at the international, national, and local levels. Voluntary initiatives were the order of the day, with institutional "teeth" few and far between.[3]

Yet institutionalization marched on. As the range of IAMs has broadened and deepened, so have local and national GRMs. The World Bank 2016 revised Environmental and Social Framework mandated that all of its investment projects include their own governmental GRMs.[4] This institutional commitment was backed by an internal tracking system that produced the appearance of high rates of compliance by counting project *plans* to create GRMs years in the future; how many address grievances practice is not measured.[5] Internal MDB advocates of project-level GRMs explicitly recognized their limited effectiveness with the evocative title of a report "Gaining Traction or Spinning Wheels," while also implicitly managing expectations of actual redress by dropping that word from a new acronym: "GM."[6]

The capacity of GRMs to redress grievances in practice remains an open question, whether at the local, national or international levels.[7] After all, most GRMs are limited to documenting (and only sometimes disclosing) accountability failures, with the expectation that their findings will lead *other* actors to deliver tangible sanctions or redress. This constraint on most GRMs long predates IAMs and is a problem even where the rule of law is ostensibly institutionalized – consider the very limited track record of more than half a century of civilian police review board efforts in the United States. Recently, the World Bank Inspection Panel, the first IAM, recognized its incapacity to

2 *See* Transparency and Accountability Initiative, *Who Are We*, https://transparency-initiative.org/ (last visited Nov. 27, 2023).

3 On the relationship between voice and teeth in the context of accountability initiatives, see Jonathan Fox, *Social Accountability: What Does the Evidence Really Say?* WORLD DEVELOPMENT 72:346 (2015).

4 The World Bank, *Environmental and Social Framework*, approved Aug. 4, 2016 (2017), https://thedocs.worldbank.org/en/doc/837721522762050108-0290022018/original/ESFFramework.pdf (last visited Jan. 17, 2025) [hereinafter WB Envtl & Social Framework].

5 *Id.*

6 The WORLD BANK, GAINING TRACTION OR SPINNING WHEELS?: FACTORS INFLUENCING THE EFFECTIVENESS OF GRIEVANCE MECHANISMS IN WORLD BANK-FINANCED PROJECTS (2021).

7 *See, e.g.*, Naomi Hossain et al., *The Politics of Complaint: A Review of the Literature on Grievance Redress Mechanisms in the Global South*, POLICY STUDIES, at 1 (May 2023).

protect complainants from reprisals – a remarkable constraint on "the right to be heard."[8] While functioning GRMs have a potential to deter abuse that could at least partly compensate for their limited capacity for redress, whether and how this works in practice is not clear. This combination of weak capacity to deliver redress with potential for prevention raises the question of 'what counts' as accountability.

2 Rethinking "what counts" as Accountability

Taking stock in 2023, the primary trend in the global accountability field seems to be one of stalemate or rollback rather than the 'onwards and upwards' trend that many advocates and reformers expected not so long ago. This *accountability impasse* suggests that it is time for a rethink of core concepts, as well as of the field's underlying theories of change.

The point of departure here is the recognition of the profound *fuzziness* of the concept of accountability. *We know it when we see it.* Consider the many different ways that the idea of accountability is understood, deployed, and often captured. The accountability idea is often treated as an all-purpose solution to a wide range of problems. The concept has become shorthand to refer to disparate efforts to address problems with the exercise of power. Yet the idea turns out to be *malleable, ambiguous, and contested.* This fuzziness poses challenges for both theory and practice – how do we know what strategies bolster accountability – or whether accountability produces its expected effects?

A conceptual rethink suggests disentangling two different questions that bridge analysis and strategy. One issue is what drives transitions to accountability. In other words, how to get answerability? Another question is whether and how *bits* of accountability can leverage improved institutional performance – for example, by deterring abuse, bolstering policy reform, or incentivizing positive change. We often assume the two go together, but these are distinct questions – what are the *causes* of accountability versus what are the *effects*? Instances of accountability (such as IAM reports that validate citizen claims) may or may not change institutions. Plus, there are plenty of other pathways to institutional change that do not involve accountability. Here is a preview of this essay's punchline: there is a difference between *how to deliver accountability – and whether accountability delivers.*

8 The World Bank Inspection Panel, *Right to be Heard: Intimidation and Reprisals in World Bank Inspection Panel Complaints* (Dec. 2021).

The following are three brief takes on the issues facing GRMs:

- Recognize the challenge of defining 'what counts' as accountability;
- Unpack one long-standing theory of change – that sunshine is the best disinfectant;
- Consider some information-based reform initiatives to identify missing links in the causal chain between transparency and accountability.

2.1 *Conceptual Stretching*

Why should we worry about conceptual stretching? Admittedly this is an arcane political science term, but fuzziness about 'what counts' as accountability is not just a problem of scholarly hair-splitting. For example, if coalitions for change are trying to find common ground among diverse actors, then clearly shared goals are needed to sustain joint action. In addition, vagueness about "what counts" as accountability can enable powerful actors *to resist* systemic change, as when authorities claim that institutional abuse is just the result of a few bad apples rather than a systemic problem. This problem of deflection of accountability claims takes an extreme form when accountability agendas get fully hijacked. Around the world, corrupt and authoritarian actors have shown they can win elections by co-opting anti-corruption discourse, sometimes followed by weaponizing the law to criminalize political opponents. For one more illustration, fuzziness about 'what counts' as accountability makes it hard for strategists to know whether their efforts to achieve accountability are effective.

2.2 *Defining Accountability*

In the accountability field, definitions vary, but they tend to involve some combination of answerability, consequences or sanctions, and redress. Answerability refers to a requirement to explain or justify actions, as when executives report to legislatures. For some analysts, answerability is enough to 'count' as accountability while for others some kind of sanction or redress needs to be involved. What kind of sanction is *enough* to count is an open question. For example, recall Nixon and Pinochet, who both faced limited degrees of procedural accountability but never had to answer or be sanctioned for their most notorious crimes.

One could begin to address these differences by adding adjectives – answerability alone could be considered "soft accountability," while meaningful sanctions or redress would count as "hard accountability." Plus, we can have one without the other.[9] This "hard-soft" question turns out to be just the beginning of the definitional challenges.

9 *See* Jonathan Fox, *The Uncertain Relationship Between Transparency and Accountability*, Development in Practice, 17(4): 663 (Aug. 2017).

Consider the difference between "upwards accountability," as with workers to managers, or "downwards accountability," as with elected officials to voters. Meanwhile, political scientists refer to institutions of checks and balances as "horizontal accountability." How do we disentangle accountability as a process versus an outcome? Consider abusers of power who may be charged (or impeached even) with no sanctions to follow, even where the process was followed. Scholars of environmental governance refer to procedural formalities without tangible institutional change as an "accountability trap."[10] Some institutions prefer to focus on so-called "bad apples" rather than systemic problems, underscoring the difference between holding individuals versus institutions accountable. Ironically however, IAMs studiously avoid focusing on individual responsibility. The question of accountability relates to the distinction between crimes of commission versus omission, since the rule of law is titled towards holding immediate perpetrators accountable, rather than those who gave the order or looked the other way.

Then there is the relationship between public and private sector accountability. Violations of environmental or labor laws by ranchers in the rainforest or transnational corporate factories indicate failure of *both* public and private accountability, insofar as laws are not enforced. Plus, the boundary between public and private spheres is itself contested, since the criminalization of abuses of power needs to be politically constructed in the first place – whether they involve the idea of occupational safety, gender-based violence, or the invasion of indigenous territories.

Perhaps the most challenging conceptual question is *where* preventative approaches to accountability failures fit in. The core of the accountability concept is fundamentally *ex post facto*, as actors are held accountable *after* their actions or inaction. Yet clearly, an ounce of prevention is worth a pound of cure. Many preventative approaches to improve institutional performance do not involve accountability institutions or processes such as answerability and sanctions. Policy reforms or changes in recruiting and training staff may be more likely to have systemic preventative effects than answerability and sanctions that are rarely applied in practice; those kinds of systemic institutional changes do not necessarily involve accountability per se. This recognition underscores the problem with conceptual stretching of the accountability idea – it's no magic bullet.

10 *See* SUSAN PARK & TERESA KRAMARZ, EDS, GLOBAL ENVIRONMENTAL GOVERNANCE AND THE ACCOUNTABILITY TRAP (2019).

3 Unpacking the Causal Chains That Link Transparency and Accountability

Transparency is key to this rethink, because it is so closely associated with one of the most time-honored, widely-accepted theories of change in the accountability field: Louis Brandeis' idea that "sunshine is the best disinfectant."[11] His original 1913 proposition also had a less widely-cited clause, "electric light [is] the best policeman."[12] The sunshine idea is that exposure *remedies,* while the electric light idea is that visibility *deters* because streetlights increase the *likelihood of detection.* This is another way to describe the distinction between preventative and reactive approaches to accountability. For practitioners, the synergy between these two approaches is obvious, yet researchers have so far shed little light on how and when they reinforce each other. That said, recognizing the distinction between preventative and reactive approaches to accountability can spotlight both how they differ and where they can overlap to produce synergy. Figure 1.1 depicts this conceptual exercise by mapping examples of different kinds of causal mechanisms.

The role of information disclosure is central to both preventative and reactive accountability strategies. Sunshine can be seen as referring to the public results of investigations by accountability mechanisms. Electric light can be understood as encompassing the perceived risk of exposure – if powerful institutions were to fail to comply with their own environmental or social

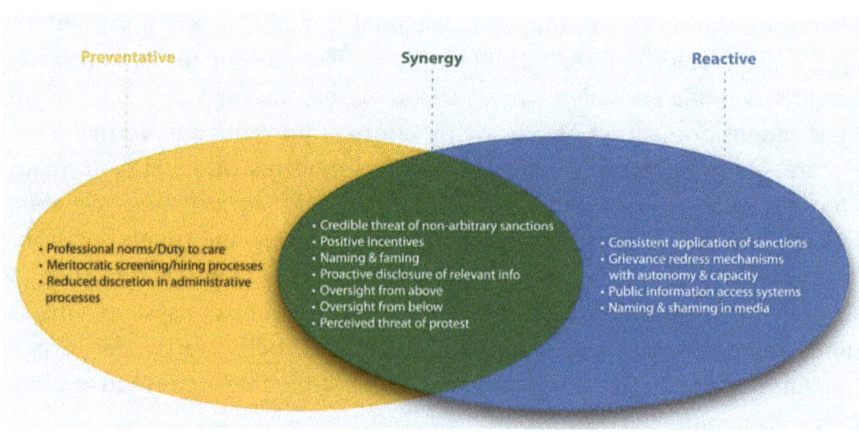

FIGURE 1.1 Synergy between preventative and reactive accountability strategies

---

11 Louis Brandeis, *What Publicity Can Do*, HARPER'S WEEKLY 10 (Dec. 20, 1913).

12 *Id.*

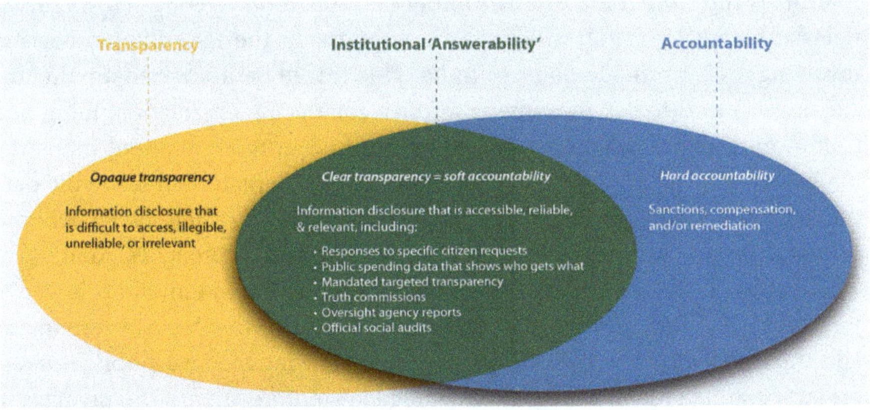

FIGURE 1.2 Answerability is in a zone of overlap between transparency and accountability.

standards. Yet as powerful institutions have increasingly recognized the necessity of transparency reforms, the incentives for generating merely the appearance of transparency have also grown.

This risk of "open-washing" leads to the production of two distinct kinds of institutional transparency – *opaque* (or fuzzy) vs *clear*. Clear transparency involves authorities answering to the public by disclosing reliable, relevant information about what they actually do. Fuzzy transparency involves disclosure of *data* that does not add up to usable, accessible, relevant or reliable *information* – sometimes going as far as *openwashing*, or deliberate dissembling.

This underscores a related distinction – between *soft* and *hard* accountability. Soft accountability is limited to answerability (reporting, explaining or justifying actions), while hard accountability involves sanctions or redress, with or without answerability. When that answerability is especially thin, or sanctions and redress are especially weak, one could begin to speak of "accountability-washing." In this view, *clear transparency and soft accountability overlap*. This in turn complicates efforts to identify the causal relationship between them. Figure 1.2 provides examples that illustrate this zone of conceptual overlap.

3.1 *What Kinds of Transparency Deliver Accountability? Cases for Discussion*

A few case examples spotlight some of the challenges involved in trying to pin down whether and how transparency delivers accountability. After all, institutional reforms that produce opaque transparency will not drive the expected causal chain towards accountability. One of the classic cases of information-led reforms is the United States Environmental Protection Agency's (EPA's) Toxic Release Inventory (TRI), which was a response to the 1984 Bhopal disaster involving a US pesticide plant in India. This tragedy empowered an already-existing US anti-toxics movement to push for the Emergency Planning and Community Right-to-Know Act. The law, passed in 1986, required industrial plants to report their emissions to the government, which then made the data public in the TRI.[13] This became a widely-cited case of *regulation by information*, contrasted with so-called 'command and control' approaches. Analysts of TRI data were thrilled to report a 46 percent reduction in emissions between 1988 and 1999. Researchers puzzled over the links in the causal mechanism. Did the information – once made accessible and legible by a public interest group – enable citizen action to encourage law enforcement? Did changes in real estate values get homeowners to take action? Did information influence companies via stock prices? Did companies learn they could save money by using fewer expensive chemical inputs? Those intermediate links in the causal chain are still not clear. One bit of evidence comes from an environmental watchdog organization in Houston, a center of the petrochemical industry. Their independent estimate of emissions was four times the volume reported to the government's database. So, there is another possible explanation for the drop: companies learned how to evade reporting requirements. To sum up, at least during its first couple of decades, the TRI relied on self-reporting, with no consequences for under-reporting.[14]

Consider also the vast world of global multistakeholder initiatives, which set voluntary social and environmental standards and brought together some combination of government, CSO, and private sector actors. The initial pioneers were the World Commission on Dams, followed by the Extractive Industries Transparency Initiative, the Open Government Partnership, the Open Contracting Partnership, and many private sector-led initiatives for supply chains (e.g., seafood, timber, apparel). Certification became a transparency-for-accountability tool, sometimes with a race-to-the-top theory of change. Yet these approaches can also incentivize both greenwashing and openwashing. Consider the independent watchdog reports on the Roundtable for Sustainable Palm Oil's tolerance for repeated, systematic violations of its own standards.[15] Do such exposés count as transparency or accountability?

---

13 United States Envtl. Protection Agency, *Original TRI Regulations*, EPA.GOV, https://www.epa.gov/toxics-release-inventory-tri-program/original-tri-regulations (last visited Nov. 27, 2024).

14 For sources, see Fox, *supra* note 9.

15 Environmental Investigative Agency & Grassroots, *Who Watches the Watchmen: Auditors and the Breakdown of Oversight in the RSPO* (Nov. 2015).

Similarly, exposés of sweatshop conditions in global factory supply chains led to consumer campaigns in northern countries that posed brand risk to corporations, especially in apparel. While workers' rights organizations called for independent monitors to do unannounced inspections to certify that factories were not sweatshops, many corporations outflanked them by promoting known private sector consultants and accounting firms to do the certification. Such collusion turned out to be a systemic problem.

For a last illustration of the limits of transparency-for-accountability approaches, consider a recent case of questionable self-reporting from the World Bank. The Bank has been emphasizing its current climate funding practices to bolster its role as a leader in future global climate funding. Yet independent monitoring found that hundreds of projects categorized as climate-related – many in poorer countries – "appear to have little to do with climate change mitigation or adaptation."[16]

All these cases have something in common – powerful institutions use self-reporting ostensibly to incentivize higher social and environmental standards. This 'information-for-regulation' strategy is appealing to policy-makers looking for a light touch approach that does not involve accountability with teeth. These cases also suggest that many 'information for regulation' initiatives share a lack of verification of the reliability of the information – with little accountability for unreliable reporting.[17] Some within powerful institutions lead conscientious efforts to report on whether they meet social and environmental standards – as with the IAMs of many MDBs – yet evidence of their impact on those institutions remains unclear, especially if one is looking for signs of preventative rather than reactive actions.

4 Summing Up

Even robust Independent Accountability Mechanisms are often designed to deliver answerability but not redress or sanctions. This underscores the fuzziness of 'what counts' as accountability. The dual role of answerability – in the zone of overlap between transparency and accountability – complicates efforts to pin down the relationship between transparency and accountability. When

16 Vijaya Ramachandran & Scott Morris, *How Does the World Bank Spend its Climate Money?*, Center for Global Development (June 14, 2023).

17 The World Bank has also hired mainly private firms to carry out third party monitoring, to take stock of government performance in its payment-for-results projects. Yet the results of such monitoring are not publicly disclosed, so validating or acting on them is left to the discretion of World Bank staff.

we connect that ambiguity with a recognition of the incentives for openwashing, that further disrupts the expected causal chain linking information disclosure to improved institutional performance. To sum up, taking stock of the power of sunshine, sometimes transparency and accountability reforms fail to deliver, in the sense of improved institutional performance. Yet the problem is often a *failure to deliver enough transparency and accountability* in the first place.

Bibliography

Brandeis, Louis. "What Publicity Can Do." *Harper's Weekly*, 10, December 20, 1913.

Environmental Investigative Agency and Grassroots. *Who Watches the Watchmen: Auditors and the Breakdown of Oversight in the RSPO*. Washington: Environmental Investigative Agency, 2015.

Fox, Jonathan. "Social Accountability: What Does the Evidence Really Say?" *World Development* 72 (2015): 346.

Fox, Jonathan. "The Uncertain Relationship Between Transparency and Accountability." *Development in Practice* 17, no. 4 (2017): 663.

Hossain, Naomi, et al. *"The Politics of Complaint: A Review of the Literature on Grievance Redress Mechanisms in the Global South." Policy Studies* (2023): 1.

Park, Susan, and Teresa Kramarz. Eds. *Global Environmental Governance and the Accountability Trap* (Cambridge: The MIT, 2019).

Pfeil, Hélène, and Sanjay Agarwal. *Gaining Traction or Spinning Wheels?: Factors Influencing the Effectiveness of Grievance Mechanisms in Bank-Financed Projects*. Washington DC: World Bank, 2021.

Ramachandran, Vijaya and Scott Morris. "How Does the World Bank Spend its Climate Money?" *Center for Global Development*. 14 June, 2017.

Thorne, Michelle. "Openwashing." *Michelle Thorne*. 14 March 2009.

Transparency and Accountability Initiative. "Who Are We." Accessed November 27, 2023. https://transparency-initiative.org/.

United States Environmental Protection Agency. "Original TRI Regulations." Last visited November 27, 2024. https://www.epa.gov/toxics-release-inventory-tri-program/original-tri-regulations.

World Bank, *Environmental and Social Framework*. Washington DC: World Bank, 2016.

World Bank Inspection Panel, *Right to be Heard: Intimidation and Reprisals in World Bank Inspection Panel Complaints*. Washington DC: World Bank, 2021.

CHAPTER 2

Are the MDBs Accountable? Reflecting on the Independent Accountability Mechanisms of the Multilateral Development Banks

*Susan Park**

1 Introduction

Taken from domestic democratic political systems, accountability is a concept that is increasingly applied to international organizations (IOs).[1] This perspective evaluates the nature of the accountability the International Accountability Mechanisms (IAMs) provide to the Multilateral Development Banks (MDBs or Banks) according to the six standard questions of accountability: (1) who is accountable; (2) to whom are they accountable; (3) for what are they accountable; (4) to what standards are they being held accountable; (5) what is the process for holding them accountable; and (6) what sanctions are employed.[2] Doing so sheds light on how the IAMs, as part of the governance of the MDBs, can hold the institution to account for their environmental and social impacts, particularly in light of global processes of production and exchange, climate breakdown, and species extinction.

2 Who Do the IAMs Seek to Hold to Account?

A common definition of "accountability" is that it is "when some actors have the right to hold other actors to a set of standards, to judge whether they have filled their responsibilities in light of those standards, and to impose sanctions

* Susan Park is Professor of Global Governance in Government and International Relations at the University of Sydney.

1 Susan Park, The Good Hegemon: US Power, Accountability as Justice, and the Multilateral Development Banks (2022).

2 Jerry Louis Mashaw, *Accountability in Institutional Design: Some Thoughts on the Grammar of Governance,* in Michael D. Dowdle, ed., Public Accountability: Designs, Dilemmas and Experiences 115–16 (2006); Teresa Kramarz & Susan Park, *Identifying Multiple Accountabilities in Global Environmental Governance,* in Susan Park & Teresa Kramarz, eds., Global Environmental Governance and the Accountability Trap (2019).

© Susan Park, 2026 | DOI:10.1163/9789004729735_005

if they determine that those responsibilities have not been met."[3] The concept of accountability comes from democratic political systems where people have the right to hold those they elect to account for their actions and to vote them out should politicians not meet certain standards and responsibilities for governing. This transfers to the international context through representative models of accountability. This is where states are held responsible by their political communities for their decisions, and international organizations are responsible to the member states that create them.[4] This is built into the Articles of Agreement comprising the MDBs constitution or charter. In the case of the MDBs, the member states collectively oversee the Banks through the Board of Governors, who then delegate to a smaller group of member states on the Board of Executive Directors. The MDBs are relatively autonomous technical agencies, where the President manages the staff and has been given discretion to present policies, development project, and program loans to the Board of Executive Directors for their approval. The 'governors dilemma' is to ensure that Bank management does as requested by the member states, which maintain control over the Bank as an international organization, despite the member states having neither the expertise nor information to ensure their directives are carried out.[5]

The IAMs are viewed as presenting both 'vertical' and 'horizontal' forms of accountability.[6] Vertically, the IAMs were introduced, after sustained transnational and national activism, by member states to hold the MDBs to account for their actions. This represents a hierarchical relationship between those in authority (the member states) to their subordinates (Bank management to staff). The IAMs themselves also represent a form of horizontal accountability in that they investigate whether the operations staff of the Banks are meeting the institution's environmental and social policies in project financing. Thus, the IAMs investigate whether the Banks are accountable for their actions to their member states while identifying where in the project lending process they have failed to fulfil their environmental and social responsibilities. While the Banks

3 Ruth W. Grant & Robert O Keohane, *Accountability and Abuses of Power in World Politics*, 99(1) AMERICAN POL. SCI. REV. 29–43 (2005).

4 Ngaire Woods, *Making the IMF and the World Bank More Accountable*, 77(1) INTERNATIONAL AFFAIRS 83–100 (2001).

5 *See* Kenneth W. Abbott, et al., *Competence versus control: The governor's dilemma*, 14 REGULATION & GOVERNANCE 619–36 (2020) (describing the "governor's dilemma," a theory based on the trade-off between governing control and technical competence); *see also* DARREN G. HAWKINS, ET AL., EDS, DELEGATION TO INTERNATIONAL ORGANIZATIONS (2006).

6 Alexandru Grigorescu, *Horizontal Accountability in Intergovernmental Organisations*, 22(3) ETHICS AND INTERNATIONAL AFFAIRS 285–308 (2008).

can be held accountable for not meeting those standards to their member states, staff are notably not sanctioned for working on projects that contribute to environmental and social harm. No real negative consequences exist for staff if they are investigated, although there is a great deal of fear that they may be investigated.[7] An investigation may contribute to project delays and increased costs, leading to borrower opposition.[8] But the IAM's aim is to ensure the accountability of the MDBs, not of borrowers nor of individual staff.

3 To Whom Are MDBs Rendered Accountable?

As outlined above, the aim of the IAMs is to render an account of the MDBs' compliance to their member states, not to those affected by the projects financed by the MDBs. Over time, almost all of the IAMs have transitioned from only undertaking compliance investigations to determine whether the Banks contributed to environmental and social harm, to offering problem-solving that seeks to address people's grievances. The IAMs are now bifurcated mechanisms that provide the opportunity for 'problem-solving' where the Bank, the borrower member state, company (for non-sovereign loans), and claimants in the project area, can come together to discuss the grievance and determine whether they can be addressed. Should they remain dissatisfied, they may choose to make a claim to have the issue formally reviewed through a compliance investigation (or they may choose to skip the problem-solving stage altogether and go straight to an investigation).

4 For What Are the MDBs Accountable?

The IAMs seek to hold the MDBs accountable for their environmental and social impacts, for example, where their projects lead to the loss of land or livelihoods for local communities, loss of biodiversity, damage to cultural heritage, and other impacts. Initially, the complaints had to identify the specific environmental and social standards according to which claimants were seeking recourse for Bank transgressions, such as the World Bank's Indigenous Peoples Policy or its Resettlement Policy. The MDBs specify the environmental and social standards against which they are to be held to account–for example, their

7 Susan Park, *supra* note 1.

8 Filho Walter Leal & Angel Rene Rios, Accountability Issues in International Development Projects (2007).

environmental and social frameworks. These policies have evolved since the first attempts to instill environmental impact assessments in the World Bank in the late 1970s. They are updated periodically, increasingly with stakeholder input. There are some sectors in the Banks' portfolios that are more likely to lead to claims from people in project areas, primarily where there are more sensitive projects with a larger impact; these sectors include the extractive oil, gas and mining sectors, as well as infrastructure (transport) and energy (such as hydropower).[9]

Under the policies, Bank projects are classified according to four categories, into which they are placed based on assessment of their "likely type, location, sensitivity and scale of the project and the nature and magnitude of its potential environmental impacts."[10] Thus, Category A includes projects with *significant* environmental and social impacts, Category B describes projects with *substantial* environmental and social impact, Category C features low-risk environmental and social impacts, and the Financial Intermediary (FI) category describes projects whose impacts should be mitigated by a third party under their own environment and social management system.

The IAMs can only investigate claims that pertain to projects being financed by the Banks, with technical criteria to determine if a claim is *bona fide*. This means that the IAMs cannot investigate claims that lie outside this scope, and cannot accept claims by people outside the project area unless authorized by affected people in the project area–for example where project-affected people fear state or company reprisal, they may ask for a group to act on their behalf.[11] The IAMs seek to ascertain whether the Banks contributed to harm. If there is no link between the harm and Bank operations, then the IAMs will not investigate, even if harm is occurring. Increasingly, however, the IAMs have chosen not to investigate even where there is harm resulting from Bank practices. In the cases of both the World Bank Group and the European Bank for Reconstruction and Development (EBRD), the IAMs increasingly focus on claims that demonstrate evidence of substantial harm arising from Bank practices, or harm that comes from practices by the Banks that are considered

9 Kristen Lewis, *Citizen-Driven Accountability for Sustainable Development: Giving Affected People a Voice 20 Years On: A Paper by the Independent Accountability Mechanisms Network* (July 5, 2012); Violet Benneker, et al., *Glass Half Full: The State of Accountability in Development Finance* (Jan. 1, 2016) (report by eleven non-governmental organizations).

10 The World Bank, *Environmental and Social Framework,* approved Aug. 4, 2016, at 6 (2017), https://thedocs.worldbank.org/en/doc/837721522762050108-0290022018/original/ESFFramework.pdf (last visited Jan. 17, 2025) [hereinafter WB Envtl & Social Framework].

11 This excludes the European Bank for Reconstruction and Development's IAM that does allow claims from people outside the project area.

systemic.[12] This raises questions as to the processes, standards, and sanctions that the IAMs use to demonstrate that the MDBs are accountable for their actions.

5 By What Processes Do the MDBs Demonstrate That They Are Accountable?

The IAMs were established as last resorts for project-affected people to seek recourse for environmental and social harm. People must first take their concerns to Bank management to have their issues addressed. If there is no response within a reasonable timeframe, or claimants are dissatisfied with the Banks' response, they can then file a claim with the IAMs. In this regard, the IAMs are "citizen-driven" in that they are triggered by claims from people in the project area or their representatives.[13] The creation of the IAMs was very much a product of negotiations among member states and the Banks, with significant involvement from national and transnational activists in shaping the structure of the IAMs. The processes followed by the IAMs to determine how they will hold the Banks to account are detailed in the resolutions creating them. Over time, the MDBs have become more transparent with information about the claims submitted to the IAMs and how they are processed. The IAMs increasingly have converged on similar stages for the progression for claims. These include the filing of claims, the determination of whether they are bona fide claims under the assessment criteria, and the evaluation of whether they should progress through the consultation (the problem-solving phase) or through the compliance investigation phase. In the problem-solving phase these are followed by stages of mediation, agreement of the parties, and monitoring. Publicly available data demonstrates how and why claims do not progress through the stages for consultation or investigation. For example, few claims end up with a facilitated settlement between stakeholders during the consultation process, most often because stakeholders are unwilling to undertake or continue with the process,[14] usually due to a lack of trust or communication breakdown between the parties.

In relation to the compliance investigations process, the IAMs have very clear procedures for undertaking investigations, determining whether it was a Bank's actions or inactions contributing to harm, and making recommendations to

12 Susan Park, *supra* note 1.
13 Kristen Lewis, *supra* note 9.
14 Susan Park, *supra* note 1.

the Board and management as to how this may be corrected. Over time, the IAMs have been given monitoring powers to ascertain whether Bank management have addressed the violations and, where possible, bring the project into policy compliance. The IAMs have established regular reporting requirements and oversight in relation to monitoring the MDBs; the resulting material is now publicly available. Increasingly, there is demonstrable evidence that MDB management is being held to account once it has been found to have contravened their own policies, although there is variation amongst the Banks.

The IAMs however, have no capacity to determine whether, in terms of stopping environmental and social harm and rectifying damage, people are better off after making a claim.[15] While the IAMs provide recourse for affected people, it remains the purview of the Banks' boards and management to ensure remedy. A recent United Nations report highlights the ways in which the MDBs could include remedy throughout the Banks' operations to embed accountability in the development project process.[16] Some argue that the IAMs represent a corrective norm to the Banks' activities, rather than a means to pre-empt harm.[17]

6 To What Standards Are the MDBs Being Held Accountable?

In order to assess whether the IAMs are able to hold the MDBs to account, it is worth understanding the extent to which the standards against which the MDBs are being held to account are substantive commitments or merely vague assurances. As mentioned above, the policies of the MDBs include environmental and social impact assessments, involuntary resettlement, Indigenous Peoples, biodiversity, and waterways.[18] These are increasingly converging with other standards, most notably the UN Guiding Principles for Business and Human Rights in relation to transnational corporations and other business enterprises.[19]

15 Daniel Bradlow & Andria Naudé Fourie, *Independent Accountability Mechanisms at Regional Development Banks*, in THOMAS HALE & DAVID HELD, EDS., HANDBOOK OF INNOVATIONS IN TRANSNATIONAL GOVERNANCE 122–38 (2011).

16 United Nations Office of High Commissioner for Human Rights, *Remedy in Development* (2022).

17 SUSAN PARK, *supra* note 1.

18 SUSAN PARK, ENVIRONMENTAL RECOURSE AT THE MULTILATERAL DEVELOPMENT BANKS (2020).

19 Radu Mares, *Securing Human Rights through Risk-Management Methods: Breakthrough or Misalignment*, 32 LEIDEN J. OF INT'L L. 517 (2019).

While policy adherence may seem easily verifiable, there are two points to bear in mind. First, throughout the history of the Panel its findings of violations by the World Bank of its own environmental and social safeguard policies have been challenged by Bank Management, with environmental specialists involved in a "he said, she said" style of conflict between technical experts. Second, there is difficulty in implementing standards in challenging environments; some scholars have argued that it is difficult to implement such standards on the ground.[20] The aim of the Panel is not, therefore, just to demonstrate whether harm has occurred, but also to investigate staff deliberations for implementing the policy and monitoring it.

7 What Sanctions Are Used to Enforce Compliance?

The creation of the IAMs was very much a product of transnational campaigns demonstrating large-scale environmental and social harm resulting from World Bank lending to developing countries. Transnational campaigns relied on four means to change the World Bank's behaviour: information politics, symbolic politics, leverage politics, and accountability politics.[21] Accountability politics in this regard is to name and shame those undertaking the harm to halt it; by shaming actors, transnational activists can draw attention to MDB operations to change them. Over the decades, the MDBs have strengthened their environmental and social policies, become more transparent, improved their monitoring of project implementation and post-hoc reviews of their portfolios. In no instance, including during IAM findings of MDB violations contributing to harm, is use made of hard sanctions such as fines or firings that would be found in public or corporate settings. Some scholars argue that hard sanctions are needed to ensure compliance.[22] Although the IAMs lack hard sanctions, they are increasingly able to monitor the MDB's actions on behalf of member states, who do have the authority to determine how to control these international organizations.

---

20 Jessie Connell, *Is 'Good' Resettlement Policy Unimplementable?: Learning from Advocacy in Cambodia*, 25(5) DEVELOPMENT IN PRACTICE 655–72 (2015).

21 MARGARET E. KECK & KATHRYN SIKKINK, ACTIVISTS BEYOND BORDERS: ADVOCACY NETWORKS IN INTERNATIONAL POLITICS (1998).

22 Marcel Kaba, *NGO Accountability: A Conceptual Review across the Engaged Disciplines*, 23 INT'L STUDIES REV. 958 (2021).

8 Conclusion

In reviewing the IAMs against the six standards of accountability, we find that they are able to hold the MDBs to account. This is evidenced by the ability of IAMs to show when the Banks have not met their own policies through compliance investigations. They hold the MDBs accountable for environmental and social impacts resulting from whether their actions do or do not meet the Board-adopted environmental and social standards, thus seeking to hold the MDBs to account to their member states, not necessarily to those affected. The IAMs have detailed procedures for undertaking their problem-solving and compliance investigations. Over time, the IAMs have been given the power to monitor whether the MDBs have sought to address the harm and bring the projects back into compliance, although implementation remains uneven. Nonetheless, many scholars argue that without hard sanctions it is very difficult to ensure that the accountability of the MDBs contributes to a change in MDB operations. Although it is common for the MDBs to highlight the role of the IAMs as contributing to institutional learning, the IAM cases routinely demonstrate the same policies being violated over time. Furthermore, in only a few instances have findings from case violations contributed to changing World Bank policies.[23] Accordingly, the lack of hard sanctions may indicate that accountability is not fully realized and might be difficult to implement in the MDBs.

Bibliography

Abbott, Kenneth W., et al. "Competence versus control: The governor's dilemma." *Regulation & Governance*, 14 (2020): 619–36.

Benneker, Violet, et al. "Glass Half Full: The State of Accountability in Development Finance." *Somo*. January 1, 2016.

Bradlow, Daniel, and Andria Naudé Fourie. "Independent Accountability Mechanisms at Regional Development Banks," in *Handbook of Innovations in Transnational Governance*, edited by Thomas Hale and David Held, 122–38. Polity, 2011.

Connell, Jessie. "Is 'Good' Resettlement Policy Unimplementable?: Learning from Advocacy in Cambodia." *Development in Practice*, 25, no. 5 (2015): 655–72.

23 Susan Park, *supra* note 1. One positive example is a high-profile Inspection Panel investigation from 2009 into the forced movement of people in Cambodia relating to a Bank-financed land management project. The Panel's involvement led to the creation of a Bank-wide Natural Resource Management Framework to address land tenure rights.

Dowdle, Michael D. *Public Accountability: Designs, Dilemmas and Experiences.* 115–116. Cambridge: Cambridge University Press, 2006.

Grant, Ruth W., and Robert O Keohane. "Accountability and Abuses of Power in World Politics." *American Political Science Review*, 9, no. 1 (2005): 29–43.

Grigorescu, Alexandru. "Horizontal Accountability in Intergovernmental Organisations." *Ethics and International Affairs*, 22, no. 3 (2008): 285–308.

Hawkins, Darren G., et al. *Delegation to International Organizations.* Cambridge: Cambridge University Press, 2006.

Kaba, Marcel. "NGO Accountability: A Conceptual Review across the Engaged Disciplines." *International Studies Review*, 23 (2021): 958.

Keck, Margaret, and Kathryn Sikkink. *Activists Beyond Borders: Advocacy Networks in International Politics* Ithaca: Cornell University Press, 1998.

Kramarz, Teresa, and Susan Park. "Identifying Multiple Accountabilities in Global Environmental Governance," in *Global Environmental Governance and the Accountability Trap*, edited by Susan Park and Teresa Kramarz. Cambridge: MIT Press, 2019.

Leal, Filho Walter, and Angel Rene Rios, *Accountability Issues in International Development Projects.* Switzerland: Peter Lang Publishing, 2007.

Lewis, Kristen. "Citizen-Driven Accountability for Sustainable Development: Giving Affected People a Voice 20 Years On: A Paper by the Independent Accountability Mechanisms Network." Washington DC: World Bank, July 5, 2012.

Mares, Radu. "Securing Human Rights through Risk-Management Methods: Breakthrough or Misalignment." Leiden Journal of International Law, 32 (2019): 517.

Mashaw, Jerry Louis. "Accountability in Institutional Design: Some Thoughts on the Grammar of Governance," in *Public Accountability: Designs, Dilemmas and Experiences*, edited by Michael D. Dowdle, 115–116. Cambridge: Cambridge University Press, 2006.

Park, Susan. *Environmental Recourse at the Multilateral Development Banks.* Cambridge: Cambridge University Press, 2020.

United Nations Office of High Commissioner for Human Rights. "Remedy in Development Finance: Guidance and Practice." Switzerland: The United Nations, February 23, 2022.

Woods, Ngaire. "Making the IMF and the World Bank More Accountable." *International Affairs*, 77, no. 1 (2001): 83–100.

World Bank. "The World Bank Environmental and Social Framework." Washington DC: The World Bank, 2017.

CHAPTER 3

The Critical Contribution of Independent Accountability Mechanisms (IAMs) to the Global Governance Paradigm

*Owen McIntyre**

1 Introduction

For several decades now, the environmental and social safeguard policies adopted by International Financial Institutions (IFIs), along with the related accountability frameworks provided by the Independent Accountability Mechanisms (IAMs) each IFI has established, have been at the very forefront of a global movement to extend good environmental and social governance values to the practice of international development finance. The complex substantive and procedural standards of institutional conduct required under Multilateral Development Bank (MDB) safeguard policies in respect of the assessment and implementation of bank-funded development projects or activities exemplifies the phenomenon of so-called "transnational" or "global" law, the rich and extensive variety of traditional and novel forms of transnational environmental and social regulatory activity that have proliferated in recent years. Such regulation comprises an almost endless assortment of codes, standards, and assessment and certification processes, many of which are non-State-led and essentially voluntary in nature, though they tend generally to reflect the values enshrined in more formal national and international legal frameworks.

At the same time, the institutional and procedural rules governing the work of IAMs in ensuring the banks' accountability for compliance with such safeguard policies epitomize the phenomenon of "global administrative law," converging around a set of good governance principles, standards, and practices commonly employed in national administrative law systems with a view to protecting the rights of those impacted by administrative decision-making. Such principles and standards, which reflect the strict procedural character of

* Owen McIntyre is a Professor, Director of the Environmental & Natural Resource Law LL.M program, and Co-Director for the Centre for Law and the Environment at School of Law, University College Cork.

national administrative law systems, such as regulatory licensing or permitting regimes, serve to enhance the credibility and legitimacy of each accountability mechanism and include, *inter alia*, guarantees of transparency, participation, legality, rationality, proportionality, reviewability, and accountability. It has been noted that "the procedural rigor of administrative law is a critical tool for refining international governance and legitimizing the exercise of supranational authority."[1] Of course, the primary, overarching function of administrative law has always been to protect the rights of individuals by checking the unauthorized, excessive, arbitrary, or unfair exercise of public power and, by so doing, to give legitimacy and direction to the practices of administrative bodies, particularly in their responsiveness to broader public welfare interests.[2] As bodies such as MDBS and their associated IAMS take on what is essentially a regulatory role, their legitimacy and authority in doing so is supported and enhanced by rules guaranteeing their administrative integrity.

Following the example of MDBS, a wide range of other actors and agencies active in funding development–including export credit agencies,[3] United Nations agencies,[4] and major private-sector providers of development project finance[5]–have in recent years adopted similar standards of environmental and social protection applicable to the financing of developmental projects, along with supporting accountability mechanisms.

It is becoming increasingly apparent that informal regulatory rules and standards, including those set out under the safeguard policies of IFIS, enjoy a complex, symbiotic relationship with formal legal frameworks at the international, regional, and national levels.[6] The standards applied under informal normative frameworks are undoubtedly informed by those established in formal legal

---

1 Daniel C. Esty, *Good Governance at the Supranational Scale: Globalizing Administrative Law*, 114 YALE L. J. 1490, 1495 (2006).

2 *See* Owen McIntyre, *Transnational Environmental Regulation and The Normativisation of Global Environmental Governance Standards: The Promise of Order From Chaos?*, 10(2) JOURNAL OF PROP., PLANNING & ENVTL. L. 92, 97 (2018).

3 *See, e.g.*, U.S. International Development Finance Corporation, *Independent Accountability Mechanism*, https://www.dfc.gov/our-impact/transparency/independent-accountability-mechanism (last visited Dec. 15, 2024).

4 *See, e.g.*, UNDP, *Social and Environmental Standards* (*SES*), https://www.undp.org/accountability/social-and-environmental-responsibility/social-and-environmental-standard (last visited Dec. 15, 2024) (adopted in 2014, along with the related Social and Environmental Compliance Unit (SECU) and Stakeholder Response Mechanism (SRM)).

5 *See The Equator Principles* (EP4) (July 2020), https://equator-principles.com/app/uploads/The-Equator-Principles_EP4_July2020.pdf (last visited Jan. 17, 2025).

6 *See generally* Daniel D. BRADLOW & DAVID HUNTER, EDS., INTERNATIONAL FINANCIAL INSTITUTIONS AND INTERNATIONAL LAW (2010).

systems, but such influence can run in both directions. In addition to filling lacunae and addressing deficiencies in formal legal frameworks, informal regulatory standards increasingly influence the evolution of formal law, especially in the developing world, improving its responsiveness, flexibility, and accessibility. One commentator notes, for example, that informal frameworks can function to improve the quality of formal legal rules, "[b]y generating competing policy perspectives, assumptions, analyses, options, and assessments, global governance institutions provide a supplemental set of policymaking laboratories."[7]

Most significantly, MDB standards might apply, even if only indirectly, to economic actors and activities where formal national and international law frameworks have consistently proven ineffective. Consider, for example, a 2016 compliance investigation by the Office of the Compliance Advisor Ombudsman (CAO), the IAM of the International Finance Corporation (IFC), into investments in a palm oil refinery in Ukraine that made a finding of non-compliance with respect to IFC's obligation to supervise the environmental and social risks associated with the refinery's palm oil supply chain.[8] The complaint that gave rise to this investigation was brought by local communities in Indonesia and related to unresolved land disputes with IFC's client.

2 Transnational / Global (Environmental and Social) Law

Commentators routinely include MDB safeguard standards amongst examples of environmental and social regulatory regimes that typify global law. Indeed, one leading expert observed more generally that "[s]ome entities are given roles in global regulatory governance which they may not wish for or be particularly designed or prepared for,"[9] bringing to mind the reluctant initial adoption of safeguard policies by MDBs in the wake of controversial lending decisions in the 1990s. Broadly similar safeguard standards for determining, assessing, and managing environmental and social risk are also applied now by a majority of private-sector project-finance providers that have signed on to the Equator Principles (EPs).[10] A previous iteration of the EPs recognized

7 Daniel Esty, *supra* note 1, at 1501–02.

8 Compliance Advisor/Ombudsman, *Delta Wilmar Ltd., Report* (Aug. 2016), https://documents1.worldbank.org/curated/ar/952231488275543553/pdf/112844-NEWS-CAO-News-Issue4-PUBLIC.pdf (last visited Jan. 17, 2024).

9 Benedict Kingsbury, *The Concept of 'Law' In Global Administrative Law*, 20(1) EUROPEAN J. OF INT'L L. 23, 25 (2009).

10 Equator Principles, *supra* note 5.

growing "convergence around common environmental and social standards" and acknowledged the seminal importance of IFC's Performance Standards in such convergence, noting that "[m]ultilateral development banks, including the European Bank for Reconstruction and Development, and export credit agencies, through the OECD Common Approaches, are increasingly drawing on the same standards as the EPS."[11] One reason for such convergence around a common set of environmental and social standards and principles, and broadly similar IAMS rules of procedure, is the established practice of MDBS in periodically reviewing and revising their policies on the basis of a thorough benchmarking exercise. Of course, the review exercise itself tends to be subjected to robust standards of administrative scrutiny and integrity, requiring transparency and broad stakeholder consultation and participation, thereby typifying the guarantees of global administrative law. In addition, MDB environmental and social safeguard policies inevitably tend to be based upon international best practice, which is often exemplified in international conventions and established national legal practice.

The European Bank for Reconstruction and Development (EBRD), for example, adopted its first Environmental Policy in 1991, but it currently applies its 2019 Environmental and Social Policy (ESP), which sets out the ways in which the Bank is to implement in practice its commitment to promote environmentally sound and sustainable development in the full range of its investment and technical cooperation activities.[12] The scope and ambition of the ESP has grown considerably over time, largely owing to the regular periodic review of the Policy that, in later iterations, has resulted in greater emphasis on compliance with international human rights values and requirements. Such periodic review processes tend to include, *inter alia*, benchmarking against the policies of peer institutions and, more generally, against the international legal commitments of a bank's member states. Modelled on the format of the safeguard policies adopted by the IFC, the private-sector lending institution of the World Bank Group, the EBRD's 2019 ESP contains detailed procedural and substantive requirements for the avoidance or mitigation of project-related harm set out under ten detailed Performance Requirements (PRS), each relating to a

11 *See* Owen McIntyre, *Independent Accountability Mechanisms as Agents of 'Global Good Governance, in* OWEN MCINTYRE & SURESH NANWANI, EDS., THE PRACTICE OF INDEPENDENT ACCOUNTABILITY MECHANISMS (IAMS): TOWARDS GOOD GOVERNANCE IN DEVELOPMENT FINANCE 21, 23 (2020).

12 *See* European Bank for Reconstruction and Development, *Environmental and Social Policy* (April 25, 2019) [hereinafter 2019 EBRD Envtl. & Social Pol'y].

particular type of environmental or social impact, a type of lending, or good governance practice.

Illustrating the close interlinkage of global or transnational standards with formal legal frameworks, in stipulating applicable environmental governance standards, the EBRD's ESP relies heavily upon, and operates to ensure compliance with, formal environmental standards set out under applicable national, EU, or international law. For example, it expressly commits the EBRD to ensuring that projects meet "EU environmental principles, practices and substantive standards, where these can be applied at the project level, regardless of their geographic location," and to refraining from financing projects that would "contravene national laws or country obligations under relevant international treaties, conventions and agreements."[13]

As regards social protections, the ESP also reiterates that "[t]he EBRD is committed to the respect for human rights in projects financed by EBRD" and "will require clients, in their business activities, to respect human rights, avoid infringement on the human rights of others, and address adverse human rights risks and impacts caused by the business activities of clients."[14] It includes further general commitments in respect of, *inter alia*, gender equality, protection of vulnerable people and groups, and climate change,[15] each of which is likely to be informed by continuing legal developments. More specifically, in respect of the rights of workers, the ESP lists eight core International Labour Organisation (ILO) Conventions setting out the applicable standards of protection.[16] Similarly, Performance Requirement 6 (Biodiversity Conservation and Sustainable Management of Living Natural Resources), expressly refers to concepts and standards employed under the Convention on Biological Diversity and the IUCN Red List of Threatened Species,[17] though the more normatively imperative and directly applicable assessment and conservation requirements of the EU Habitats Directive are likely to prove more relevant pursuant to the general commitment in the ESP to "EU environmental principles, practices and substantive standards."[18] Somewhat controversially, the Habitats Directive requirements have proven decisive in a number of complaints.[19]

---

13 *Id.*, at paras. 2.2., 2.3.

14 *Id.*, at paras. 2.4.

15 *Id.*, at paras. 2.5, 2.6, 2.7.

16 *Id.*, at Performance Requirement 2, para. 2.

17 *Id.*, at Performance Requirement 6, paras. 1, 13.

18 *Id.*, at paras. 2.2., 2.3.

19 *See, e.g,* EBRD Project Complaint Mechanism (PCM), Request No. 2011/06 *Ombla Hydropower Project*, Compliance Review Report (Dec. 10, 2013), https://www.ebrd.com/downloads/integrity/Ombla_CRR.pdf (last visited Jan. 17, 2025). For the complete register of

Taking the specific example of projects implemented in international watercourses is illustrative of the dynamic interaction between MDB safeguard policies and relevant international law. The World Bank has a long history of involvement in the cooperative management and development of international water resources, issuing its first policy in 1956.[20] It has since adopted a special policy instrument, Operational Policy (OP) 7.50, most recently revised in 2012, that is specifically dedicated to "Projects on International Waterways" and is of particular and direct relevance to the development and operation of projects in international watercourses.[21] Likewise, hydropower projects have featured prominently among the complaints submitted to MDB IAMs alleging non-compliance with the relevant environmental and social policies.[22]

In this way, IAMs will sometimes assume, often inadvertently, the role of informal enforcement agents, as regards a bank's clients' projects, for international, regional, or national environmental and social norms that might not otherwise be directly applicable to their clients' operations or effectively enforced by the relevant state-established regulatory agencies. IAMs increasingly play a critical role in assessing compliance with formal legal requirements where complainants allege non-compliance with related MDB safeguard standards. There is obvious utility in such indirect enforcement of formal international environmental, social, and human rights norms, especially in the case of private-sector borrowers, against whom such norms might not otherwise apply, at least directly. Though this indirect enforcement function is undoubtedly of greater significance in the case of MDBs that lend exclusively or principally to the private-sector, such as the IFC or EBRD, it should be borne in mind that private-sector borrowings make up an ever-greater proportion of overall international development lending.

PCM Complaints see EBRD, *PCM Registry*, https://www.ebrd.com/work-with-us/project-finance/project-complaint-mechanism/pcm-register.html (last visited Dec. 15, 2024) [hereinafter PCM Registry].

20 Operational Memorandum No. 8: Projects on International Inland Waterways (Feb. 8, 1956); *see also* S.M.A. SALMAN, THE WORLD BANK POLICY FOR PROJECTS ON INTERNATIONAL WATERWAYS: AN HISTORICAL AND LEGAL ANALYSIS 31–36, App. 1 (2009).

21 The World Bank, *Operational Policy 7.50, Projects on International Waterways* (Oct. 1994, rev. Aug. 2004 & Mar. 2012).

22 For example, even though the restricted geographical scope of EBRD's lending mandate would suggest that it funds relatively few major water-related projects, hydropower projects have featured prominently among complaints submitted to EBRD's successive complaints mechanisms, including: Boskov Most – FYR Macedonia (2011); Ombla – Croatia (2011); Paravani – Georgia (2012); Dariali – Georgia (2014); Shuakhevi HPP – Georgia (2018 & 2019); Nenskra HPP – Georgia (2018). *See* PCM Registry, *supra* note 19.

3 IAMs and Global Administrative Law

The procedurally rigorous operating rules adopted by IAMs both reflect and contribute to the steady accretion of a broad range of universally accepted standards of administrative good governance that are increasingly put forward by a diverse community of global or transnational regulatory actors as representing formal or informal legal or quasi-legal requirements. Such standards are designed to promote the core good governance values prevalent in almost all national systems of administrative law and increasingly applied to global actors. These values generally include, in one form or another, transparency of decision-making processes, broad public or stakeholder participation in decision-making, delivery of reasoned decisions, accountability of decision-makers, respect for proportionality in decision-making, and general respect for human rights. This organic and decentralized movement towards recognition of a set of universally accepted good governance standards, applying to both public and private actors operating at the global, transnational, regional, national, and local levels of administrative regulation, is the very epitome of the "global administrative law" phenomenon. Thus, the trend in international development banking practice towards the adoption of accountability mechanisms and procedures that accord with the legally recognized practices of sound administration suggests that the international development banking sector might be regarded as a key driver of this gradual, cross-sectoral evolution of global standards of good administrative governance.

In this regard, the EBRD's 2019 Environmental and Social Policy places clear emphasis on general good governance values and practices, reaffirming that the EBRD "is committed to the principles of transparency, accountability and stakeholder engagement" and to "promoting adoption and implementation of these principles by its clients."[23] More specifically, the rules governing the operation of the Independent Project Accountability Mechanism (IPAM),[24] the latest iteration of EBRD's independent accountability mechanism, typify the practical application of such standards of administrative good governance in the investigation of complaints from project-affected persons and civil society concerning EBRD-funded projects. The 2019 Project Accountability Policy prominently declares that one of its key purposes is "to enhance transparency and accountability, improve discourse with affected stakeholders, and

23 2019 EBRD Envtl. & Social Pol'y, *supra* note 12, para. 2.9.

24 Independent Project Accountability Mechanism, Project Accountability Policy (2019) [hereinafter IPAM Policy]; *see also* Independent Project Accountability Mechanism, Guidance on Case Handling (2019); PCM Registry, *supra* note 19.

foster good governance,"[25] and lists the following among its guiding principles: independence and impartiality, transparency, predictability, equitability, and accessibility.[26] This commitment to administrative good governance is evident throughout the detailed procedural rules contained in the Project Accountability Policy. In the conduct of the IPAM's compliance review function, for example, the Mechanism is required to keep Requesters informed about the status of requests in a timely manner,[27] and to engage actively "with the Requesters, Bank management, the Client and other relevant stakeholders."[28] More generally, the IPAM is required to maintain an online public Case Registry to provide internal and external stakeholders with up-to-date information on the nature and status of each registered Request[29] and to cooperate with other IAMs in respect of a project at issue in a registered Request that is co-financed by other institutions.[30]

4 The New Landscape of Global Governance

One could hardly dispute that the environmental and social safeguards imposed by MDBs provide a clear illustration of transnational or global law, as they constitute transnational regulatory activity in a "global administrative space" that "marks a departure from those orthodox understandings of international law in which the international is largely inter-governmental and there is a reasonably sharp separation of the domestic and the international," and that reflects the practice of modern global governance, whereby "transnational networks of rule-generators, interpreters and appliers cause such strict barriers to break down."[31] Such frameworks have an important role to play, especially where "[w]eak regulation or exclusion from relevant governance institutions of non-state actors needs to be superseded by an inclusive system of participation and responsibility."[32] In addition, such "[m]ulti-tier governance may also promote welfare-enhancing regulatory competition ... By generating competing policy perspectives, assumptions, analyses, options, and

25 IPAM Policy, *supra* note 24, at Part 1.
26 *Id.*, at Part 3, para. 1.3.
27 *Id.*, at Part 3, para. 3.1(a).
28 *Id.*, at Part 3, para. 2.7(c)(i).
29 *Id.*, at Part 3, para. 3.1(b).
30 *Id.*, at Part 3, para. 3.1(e).
31 Benedict Kingsbury, *supra* note 9, at 25.
32 ELENA BLANCO & JONA RAZZAQUE, GLOBALISATION AND NATURAL RESOURCES LAW: CHALLENGES, KEY ISSUES AND PERSPECTIVES 3–4 (2011).

assessments, global governance institutions provide a supplemental set of policymaking laboratories."[33] Thus, MDB safeguard policies and IAMs practice can significantly supplement the effective functioning of formal legal frameworks for environmental and social protection, especially in the light of the immense challenges posed for traditional, state-led regulatory frameworks by transnational patterns of developmental lending and investment.[34]

Not only do IAMs contribute to global environmental and social governance by interpreting, applying, and elaborating upon such transnational rules. At the same time, the institutional and procedural rules that have evolved to govern the operation of IAMs are firmly based upon certain "[g]eneral principles of public law [which] combine formal qualities with normative commitments in the enterprise of channeling, managing, shaping and constraining political power."[35] Taken together, these constitute a set of administrative principles and values that provide "a refined system of procedures [which] can promote decision-making based upon the rule of law, participation, rationality, clarity, stability, neutrality, fairness, efficacy, deliberation, efficiency, and accountability."[36] Esty argues convincingly that "[i]f properly developed and implemented, administrative procedures promote careful rulemaking, efficient delivery of public goods, and fair treatment of both individuals and economic entities."[37] These are precisely the values and aims that IAMs ought to pursue.

5 Conclusion

Commentators increasingly recognize that new globalized financial and trade flows represent a critical challenge for traditional legal frameworks to effectively regulate the environmental and social impacts of a range of significant economic sectors.[38] While traditional, state-centered mechanisms for elaborating and enforcing such legal protections are ever more frequently proving inadequate due to the transnational character of much economic activity, as well as to their own inherent lack of responsiveness, flexibility, and accessibility, a wide range of novel forms of rules and standards, often informal, that function to normativize a broad and progressive understanding of environmental, and

33 Daniel Esty, *supra* note 1, at 1501–02.
34 *See* Owen McIntyre, *supra* note 11, at 40.
35 Benedict Kingsbury, *supra* note 9, at 32.
36 Daniel Esty, *supra* note 1, at 1496.
37 *Id.*
38 *See* NEIL WALKER, INTIMATIONS OF GLOBAL LAW (2014); ELENA BLANCO & JONA RAZZAQUE, *supra* note 32.

social governance, play an increasingly important role. Thus, a new conception of legal order is emerging, based on "the processes, practices, institutions, doctrines, values and aspirations through which law becomes less centered upon the jurisdiction and less dependent on the organs of the modern state, and instead gradually comes to assume a 'global' significance."[39] It becomes necessary, therefore, "to re-situate the state on a multipolar densely connected legal map in a complex relationship with other economic, political and cultural globalising forces."[40] This vision of a rapidly evolving, de-territorialized global legal order neatly captures and explains the normative governance structures established by MBD environmental and social safeguard policies and accountability mechanisms, situating them among the myriad emerging requirements to apply governance standards, often informal, to a wide range of potentially harmful economic activities, including to the provision of development project finance. It is immediately apparent that, as intergovernmental institutions involved in transnational regulatory activity, MDBs and their respective IAMs belong among the "global administrative bodies" operating in the "global administrative space" that generate global governance norms and to which such norms might apply.[41] In the case of certain multilateral lenders that focus on lending to private sector clients, such as the EBRD or IFC, MDB standards of environmental and social governance, often reflecting the most progressive standards in international and/or national law, are imposed, albeit indirectly, upon private corporate entities, against which many formal legal requirements could never be applied effectively. The 2016 IFC-CAO compliance investigation into IFC's investments in Delta Wilmar Ltd. provides a case in point.[42] The investigation focused on the improper use of customary lands in Indonesia, activity that might not otherwise have been effectively regulated, and clearly illustrates the potential impact of MDB safeguard policies and related IAM enforcement in curtailing the worst excesses of multinational actors in certain sectors, such as the palm oil industry, with a traditionally poor record of environmental and social governance.

Thus, MDB environmental and social safeguard standards can fill lacunae where formal law-making institutions, at either the national, regional,

---

39 WALKER, *supra* note 38, at 2.

40 *Id.*, at 8.

41 Benedict Kingsbury et al., *Foreword: Global Governance as Administration – National and Transnational Approaches to Global Administrative Law*, 68(1) LAW AND CONTEMPORARY PROBLEMS 3, 5 (2005).

42 *See* CAO, *Indonesia / Wilmar Group-03/Jambi*, https://www.cao-ombudsman.org/cases/indonesia-wilmar-group-03jambi (last visited Dec. 15, 2024); *see also* Charles Di Leva, *infra* Chapter 7.

or international levels, have failed to elaborate, adopt, or enforce appropriate binding rules. Alternatively, the non-legal rules and standards imposed by MDBs can function to enhance the effectiveness, formation, and scope of application of formal rules that can take a considerable time to emerge, especially in less developed jurisdictions and at the transnational level.[43] Of course, concerns have inevitably arisen in respect of such novel forms of regulatory activity regarding, *inter alia*, their lack of democratic foundations and reduced policy control at the national and local levels, the distance of transnational decision-makers from the public or regulated community, and their lack of effective accountability.[44] In order to address such concerns regarding the legitimacy of their norm-creating regulatory activities, transnational agencies have almost universally adopted the principles inherent to national systems of administrative law as central tenets of their operation.[45] Such a proceduralized approach, based on robust standards of transparency and stakeholder participation, is now everywhere evident in processes for legal and non-legal regulatory decision-making, as exemplified by the ubiquitous corresponding requirements found in MDB safeguard policies[46] and in IAM rules of procedure.[47]

Bibliography

Blanco, Elena, and Jona Razzaque, *Globalisation and Natural Resource Law: Challenges, Key Issues and Perspectives*, 3–4. Cheltenham: Edward Elgar Publishing, 2011.

Bradlow, Daniel, and David Hunter, *International Financial Institutions and International Law*. Netherlands: Kluwer Law International, 2010.

International Finance Corporation [IFC] Compliance Advisor/Ombudsman [CAO]. *CAO Update*, 4. Washington DC: CAO, 2016.

43 *See* Joost Pauwelyn, *Is It International Law or Not and Does It Even Matter*, in JOOST PAUWELYN, ET AL., EDS., INFORMAL INTERNATIONAL LAWMAKING 125 (2012).

44 *See* Armin Steinbach, *The Trend Towards Non-Consensualism in Public International Law: A (Behavioural) Law and Economics Perspective*, 27(3) EUROPEAN J. OF INT'L L. 643, 645 (2016); Nico Krisch, *The Decay of Consent: International Law in an Age of Global Public Goods*, 108(1) AMERICAN J. OF INT'L L., (2014).

45 Daniel Esty, *supra* note 1, at 1494–95, 1503.

46 *See, e.g.*, EBRD Envtl. & Soc. Pol'y, Performance Requirement 10, Information Disclosure and Stakeholder Engagement (2019).

47 *See, e.g.*, text accompanying notes 24–30 (describing the IPAM's 2019 Project Accountability Policy).

CAO. *Indonesia / Wilmar Group-03/Jambi.* Accessed December 15, 2024. https://www.cao-ombudsman.org/cases/indonesia-wilmar-group-03jambi.

European Bank for Reconstruction and Development [EBRD]. *Environmental and Social Policy.* London: European Bank for Reconstruction and Development, April 25, 2019. https://www.ebrd.com/environmental-and-social-policy.pdf.

EBRD. "PCM Registry." Accessed December 15, 2024. https://www.ebrd.com/project-finance/independent-project-accountability-mechanism/ipam-policies.html.

EBRD Project Complaint Mechanism (PCM). Request No. 2011/06 *Ombla Hydropower Project*, Compliance Review Report (Dec. 10, 2013) https://www.ebrd.com/downloads/integrity/Ombla_CRR.pdf.

EBRD Independent Project Accountability Mechanism. *Project Accountability Policy.* London: Independent Project Accountability Mechanism, 2019. https://www.ebrd.com/documents/occo/ipam-policy.pdf.

EBRD Independent Project Accountability Mechanism. *Guidance on Case Handling.* London: Independent Project Accountability Mechanism, 2019. https://www.ebrd.com/documents/ipam/guidance-on-case-handling.pdf.

EBRD. *PCM Registry.* Accessed December 15, 2024. https://www.ebrd.com/work-with-us/project-finance/project-complaint-mechanism/pcm-register.html.

Etsy, Daniel C. "Good Governance at the Supranational Scale: Globalizing Administrative Law." *Yale Law Journal*, 114 (2006): 1490, 1495.

Kingsbury, Benedict, et al. *Forward:* "Global Governance as Administration-National and Transnational Approaches to Global Administrative Law." *Law and Contemporary Problems* 68, no. 1 (2005): 3, 5.

Kingsbury, Benedict. "The Concept of 'Law' in Global Administrative Law." *European Journal of International Law*, 20, no. 1 (2009): 23, 25.

Krish, Nico. "The Decay of Consent: International Law in an Age of Global Public Goods." *American Journal of International Law.* (2014).

McIntyre, Owen. "Transnational Environmental Regulations and the Normativisation of Global Environmental Governance Standards: The Promise of Order From Chaos?" *Journal of Property, Planning & Environmental Law.* (2018): 92, 97.

McIntyre, Owen. "Independent Accountability Mechanism as Agents of 'Global Good Governance,'" in *The Practice of Independent Accountability Mechanisms (IAMS): Toward Good Governance in Development Finance*, edited by Owen McIntyre and Suresh Nanwani, 21, 23. Netherlands: Brill Nijoff, 2020.

Pauwelyn, Joost. "Is It International Law or Not and Does it Even Matter," in *Informal International Lawmaking*, edited by Joost Pauwelyn, et al. 125. Oxford: Oxford University Press, 2012.

Salman, Salman M.A. *The World Bank Policy for Projects on International Waterways: An Historical and Legal Analysis.* Washington DC: World Bank Publishing, 2009.

Steinbach, Armin. "The Trend Towards Non-Consensualism in Public International Law: A (Behavioural) Law and Economics Perspective." *Environmental Journal of International Law*, 27, no. 3 (2016): 643, 645.

The Equator Principles (*EP4*). July 2020.

Walker, Neil. *Intimations of Global Law*. Cambridge: Cambridge University Press, 2014.

World Bank. *Operational Policy 7.50, Projects on International Waterways*. Washington DC: The World Bank, October 1994, revised August 2004 and March 2012.

United Nations Development Programme. "Social and Environmental Standards (SES)." Accessed December 15, 2024. https://www.undp.org/accountability/social-and-environmental-responsibility/social-and-environmental-standard

United States International Development Finance Corporation. "Independent Accountability Mechanism." Accessed December 15, 2024.

CHAPTER 4

The Inspection Panel and International Law

*Daniel D. Bradlow**

1 Introduction

This essay discusses the impact that the creation of the World Bank Inspection Panel (Panel) had on the development of international law, its impact on the accountability of international organizations, international law making and the role of non-state actors in international law.

2 The Panel and the Accountability of International Organizations

A general characteristic of international organizations is that, unless they specifically give consent, they are immune from being sued in any national court. Historically, they have only been willing to give this consent in cases arising from their commercial contracts. For example, the World Bank (the Bank) waives its immunity in the debt instruments that it uses to finance its operations.[1] However, it has not waived its immunity in any case brought by a party that does not have a contractual relationship with the Bank.

The Bank's position is unsurprising. The Bank's founding member states understood that the design, construction, and operation of new infrastructure projects could have significant social and environmental impacts and political implications. However, they maintained that it was each sovereign state's prerogative to decide, through its political and administrative processes, how to allocate the costs and benefits of the projects and how to manage their impacts. The Bank, as an external funder, was expected to respect these sovereign decisions. This meant that the Bank should take these decisions as given and only assess the economics and technical and financial feasibility of the projects that it financed. This division of labor was formalized in the International Bank

* Daniel Bradlow is Professor/Senior Research Fellow, Centre for Advancement of Scholarship, University of Pretoria; Compliance Officer, Social and Environmental Compliance Unit, UNDP; Emeritus Professor of Law, American University Washington College of Law.

1 *See, e.g.*, International Bank for Reconstruction and Development, *Articles of Agreement of the IBRD*, Art. VII (3) (Jul. 22, 1944) [hereinafter IBRD Articles of Agreement].

 | DOI:10.1163/9789004729735_007

for Reconstruction and Development's (IBRD's) Articles of Agreement, which prohibited the Bank from taking the political character of the member state or any other political considerations into account in its decisions.[2]

It followed from this division of responsibility that the IBRD concentrated on engaging with its borrower governments, financing technically and economically feasible projects, and ensuring that the loans were being repaid in a timely manner. Any necessary interactions with affected communities or the project contractors about the projects were the responsibility of the borrowing states.

The establishment of the Panel[3] challenged this division of responsibility. It was the first time that an international organization had created a mechanism that was independent of the organization's management, and that could receive and investigate complaints from external stakeholders who claimed they had been harmed by the organization's failure to comply with its own policies and procedures. The Panel would report these findings to the Bank's Board of Executive Directors (EDs), who could require the management to take corrective action.

The establishment of the Panel was an important milestone in the law applicable to international organizations in five ways. First, it was a formal acknowledgement that the decisions and operations of international organizations, like the Bank, were in fact directly affecting individuals and communities, and that these impacts had consequences for which they could be held accountable. Second, it clarified that these organizations' internal operational policies and procedures[4] were the standards that external stakeholders could use to determine if the organization's actions were the cause of their harm. Third, it demonstrated that international organizations like the Bank had a responsibility to provide these individuals and communities with some mechanism that they could use to hold the organization accountable. Fourth, it established that this mechanism should enable the individuals and communities who are most directly impacted by its projects to communicate their

2 *See id.* at Art. III (5)(b), Art. IV (10).

3 *See* International Bank for Reconstruction, World Bank Inspection Panel, *Resolution No. IBRD 93–10* (Sept. 22, 1993); International Dev. Association World Bank Inspection Panel, *Resolution No. IDA 93–6* (Sept. 22, 1993) [hereinafter, together, 1993 Inspection Panel Resolutions]; *see also* International Bank for Reconstruction, World Bank Inspection Panel, *Resolution No. IBRD 2020–0004* (Sept. 8, 2020); International Dev. Association World Bank Inspection Panel, *Resolution No. IDA 2020–0003* (Sept. 8, 2020) [hereinafter, together, 2020 Inspection Panel Resolutions].

4 World Bank, *Operations Manual*, https://policies.worldbank.org/en/policies/operational-manual (last visited Nov. 27, 2024).

experiences and concerns to the organization's supervisory organs, for example the Bank's Executive Directors, without the mediation of the organization's staff and management, and without directly implicating the sovereignty of the member state. Fifth, the findings of mechanisms like the Panel imposed on the international organization some responsibility to respond to their investigations and findings and, when appropriate, to take actions to correct the harm that the organization's non-compliance had caused.

The establishment of the Panel also had a broader significance for international development financing institutions like the Bank. It represented, in effect, an acknowledgement by the Bank and its member states that the original view of the division of responsibility between the international financial institutions (IFIs) and their member states was no longer tenable. Several factors contributed to this realization. One was the entry into force in the 1970s of the international human rights treaties. They meant that the sovereignty of the state even in its domestic affairs was no longer absolute and that it was legitimate, at least in some circumstances, for external actors to express an interest in the way in which the state interacted with its own subjects. This raised the issue of whether the Bank, while not a signatory to these human rights treaties, had any responsibility to take human rights considerations into account in its operations. This was particularly pertinent because the projects that it funded often gave rise to important human rights issues. These issues ranged from providing financing to governments that were generally engaged in wide-spread human rights violations[5] to funding specific projects that had human rights impacts such as the involuntary resettlement of communities or the destruction of sites that had cultural and religious importance for the local communities.

A second pressure arose from the rising concerns around the world about the social and environmental impacts of large development projects. The first manifestations of this concern were protests in borrower countries about particularly controversial projects funded by the World Bank. In addition, citizens in non-borrower countries, often cooperating with protesters in borrower countries, began to express concern about the way in which their taxes were being used to support controversial and environmentally damaging projects. They also began to object to the lack of transparency and participation of affected communities in Bank-funded projects.

These pressures and the Bank's failure to adequately respond to them highlighted the problem that its immunity posed to communities seeking relief

---

5 *See, e.g.*, Samuel A. Bleicher, *UN v IBRD: A Dilemma of Functionalism*, 24(1) INT'L ORGANIZATION 31 (1970).

from the adverse impacts of Bank-funded projects. It demonstrated how limited their chances of getting relief were. Their only options were either to lobby their governments to take up their case, or to create enough political noise about the organization's operations that it was forced into giving them redress.

The Panel was a principled response to the Bank's failings for two reasons. First, it is a mechanism that focuses only on the Bank's compliance with its own operational policies and procedures.[6] This means that the Panel focuses only on the conduct of Bank staff and, if relevant, on the consequences of their non-compliance with the Bank's operational policies and procedures. Second, the Panel is precluded from investigating the actions and decisions of the borrower state. In this way, the Panel both demonstrates respect for and avoids undermining the sovereignty of the borrower state.

3 The Panel and International Law Making

An important consequence of the Panel's operations is that it has become a maker of soft international law. In this context, "soft" international law refers to international norms and standards that are non-binding and do not satisfy the formal requirements of "hard", or binding, international law. Nevertheless, soft international law can still exert a compliance pull on its target's conduct.[7]

The Panel's role as a maker of soft international law arises from the way in which it interprets and applies the World Bank's operational policies and procedures in its investigations and reports, and the consequences that flow from this.

The World Bank's operational policies and procedures are intended to provide guidance to Bank staff on how they should conduct the Bank's business. These policies cover all aspects of Bank operations, including how the staff should deal with the social and environmental aspects of Bank operations. It is important to note that they do not bind the Bank's borrowers, member states, or contractors, unless they are specifically incorporated into the relevant loan agreements or related contractual documents.

While any of the Bank's operational policies and procedures can be the focus of a Panel complaint, most Panel cases involve the Bank's environmental

6 *See* 1993 Inspection Panel Resolutions, *supra* note 3.

7 *See generally* Daniel D. Bradlow & David B. Hunter, eds., Advocating Social Change Through International Law: Exploring the Choice Between Hard and Soft International (2020).

and social policies.[8] These policies tend to be written in general terms because their subject matter is complex, and they are applicable across the full range of the Bank's operations. This means that Bank staff and management, and the Panel must interpret the policies when they apply them in their work. The Panel's interpretations can influence its decisions about which issues are eligible for investigation, the scope of the investigation, and its findings regarding staff compliance with the applicable policies in particular Bank operations.

While the Panel does not have the power to make binding decisions on how these policies should be interpreted, the management and staff cannot afford to completely ignore its interpretations of the applicable policies. Firstly, the Board will expect them to develop and implement a plan for correcting any acts of non-compliance identified by the Panel and accepted by the Board. Second, the Panel can be expected to follow its own precedents in future Panel cases. Consequently, the Bank's staff, its borrowers, and potential Panel complainants can be expected to pay close attention to the Panel's interpretations of Bank policies.

The operational policies and procedures also inform the Bank's member states, particularly the borrower states, and non-state stakeholders, about how the Bank organizes its operations and the standards of conduct with which its staff should comply in these operations. These policies and procedures therefore help shape the expectations of these external actors and establish the standards of conduct on which they can rely in their dealings with Bank staff. They also help guide the Bank's clients and stakeholders in understanding the norms and standards with which the Bank will expect them to comply in their transactions with the Bank. It is important to note that even though the operational policies and procedures are not binding and enforceable against borrowers, they understand that if their conduct diverges too markedly from the policies, they risk the Bank either declining to fund them or denying them access to loan proceeds. In addition, both the Bank staff and the borrowers understand that communities and other external stakeholders will rely both on the policies and the way in which the Panel has interpreted and applied them in formulating their complaints to the Panel.

A useful illustration of the Panel's law making role is a Panel case dealing with a land administration project in Honduras.[9] In this case, the Panel,

8 The World Bank, *Environmental and Social Framework,* approved Aug. 4, 2016 (2017), https://www.worldbank.org/en/projects-operations/environmental-and-social-framework (last visited Nov. 27 2024) [hereinafter WB Envtl and Social Framework].

9 World Bank Inspection Panel, *Honduras: Land Administration Case,* Case No. 38, Request 06/0 (Jan. 3, 2006).

in the course of its investigation, had to interpret and apply the Bank's policies regarding the adequacy of its consultations with affected communities, the implications of the proposed land titling scheme for the rights of indigenous people, and the adequacy of the protection granted to the rights of local communities when designating environmentally protected areas. While later cases[10] interpreting the same Bank policies do not explicitly refer to the Honduras case, the Panel's findings and reports need to be consistent with its policy interpretations in the Honduras case. If they are not, they risk undermining the credibility of later Panel reports and the Panel's reputation as being independent and competent. They also risk undermining the predictability of Bank policies and generating confusion among Bank staff and external stakeholders about the requirements of Bank policies and procedures.

The result is that Bank staff and management should take the precedents set by the Panel into account in their interpretation of the operational policies and procedures, and in how they prepare their projects. It is also noteworthy that other MDBs and even private companies look to the Bank and how it interprets and applies its operational policies in developing their own policies and applying them in their operations. Similarly, borrowers may look at these precedents when preparing project proposals for the Bank.

The second way in which the Panel has affected the development of soft international law is in its impact on rulemaking in the Bank. This can be seen for example in the effort the Bank made in 1999 during its second review of the Panel procedures. In this case, the Board of the Bank decided that it would not complete the second review without first consulting with interested stakeholders in the Panel.[11] In fact, to ensure that it had consulted with affected communities and the civil society organizations that represent them, it paid for some of these representatives to travel to a meeting in Washington, DC that was jointly chaired by the most senior Board member and an official from one of the organizations. During this meeting, the Board presented its proposed amendments and listened to the views of these representatives. In the end, it adopted amendments that were more acceptable to these external stakeholders.

---

10 *See, e.g.*, World Bank Inspection Panel, *Cambodia; Land Management and Administration Project*, Case No.60, Request 09/08 (Sept. 4, 2009); *see also*, World Bank Inspection Panel, *Panama; Land Administration Project* (First Request), Case No. 53, Request: 09/01 (Feb. 25 2009).

11 Daniel D. Bradlow, *Precedent-Setting NGO Campaign Saves the World Bank's Inspection Panel*, 6 (3) HUMAN RIGHTS BRIEF 71 (1999).

Another example of this impact is the Bank adoption of an open and consultative process for developing its Environmental and Social Framework. It circulated its draft of the Framework for public comment and arranged a series of consultative meetings around the world at which the draft was presented and discussed. The result was that the finalization of the Framework was slower than anticipated, but that it ultimately had more credibility than if it had been merely adopted by the Bank without adequate consultation. The framework, which took almost 4 years to complete, was adopted in 2016 and became fully operational in 2018.[12]

The Panel has had a third, perhaps less anticipated but perhaps more profound, impact on international law. Because it is driven by complaints from affected communities, the Panel has opened a channel through which these communities can have an influence in the way Bank operational policies are interpreted and applied. In this sense, the Panel has become a mechanism for making international law from below.

This process of lawmaking from below can be seen, for example, in connection with human rights. Given that the Bank policies on environmental and social issues address such issues as impacts on Indigenous Peoples, involuntarily resettled people, and communities; access to land, water, health care and educational facilities, and livelihoods, it is inevitable that human rights issues arise in Panel cases. These issues pose a significant challenge for both the Panel and the Bank because, pursuant to the political prohibition in its Articles of Agreement,[13] the Bank is reluctant to explicitly take human rights issues into account in its operations. Nevertheless, Panel cases involving these issues require Bank management and staff, at least implicitly, to explain how they interpreted and applied the applicable policies to these human rights issues.[14] Similarly, the Panel in its compliance review reports must apply its operational policies to these human rights issues. In this way, the Panel's cases are helping to produce a form of jurisprudence on how human rights apply in the development financing context.[15]

---

12 WB Envtl and Social Framework, *supra* note 8. For an analysis of the process leading to its adoption and of its content, see Philipp Dann, et al., *The World Bank's Environmental and Social Safeguards and the Evolution of Global Order* 32 LEIDEN J. INT'L L. 537 (2019).

13 *See* IBRD Articles of Agreement, *supra* note 1, Art. (10).

14 *See, e.g.*, World Bank Inspection Panel, *Uganda: Transport Sector Development Project-Additional Financing,* Case No. 98, Request No. 14/07, (Dec. 19, 2014) (dealing with, *inter alia*, gender-based violence).

15 *See, e.g.*, Kelebogile Zvogbo, et al., *The World Bank as an Enforcer of Human Rights*, 19(4) J. HUMAN RIGHTS 425 (2018).

4 An Assessment of the Panel's Contribution to International Law

Thirty years of Panel operations have convincingly demonstrated the benefits that follow when operational international organizations become more accountable, transparent, and participatory. It has helped make the Bank responsive to the individuals and communities that are most affected by Bank-financed projects and operations. In addition, the Panel has made a positive and creative contribution to the development and interpretation of the soft international law applicable to international development finance.

The work of the Panel and other independent accountability mechanisms is also influencing the development of soft international norms and standards applicable to responsible business conduct.[16] It is impacting the evolution and interpretation of such international human rights principles as the rights of indigenous people to free, prior, informed consent and the adequacy of the compensation given to communities involuntarily resettled because of large infrastructure projects.

However, the experience of the last thirty years has also helped to underline some of the Panel's shortcomings. The most significant of these arises from the failure of the Bank to fully meet its customary international law obligation to offer an effective remedy to those who have been harmed by its actions and decisions. This obligation is expressed in the Universal Declaration on Human Rights (UDHR), in the core international human rights conventions, and in all regional human rights conventions; further, it has been recognized by international human rights bodies and is acknowledged by all states.

While the principle on remedies is clear, the precise contents of the obligation are not easily determined. The European Court of Human Rights has stated that it must be a remedy that is functionally equivalent to that awarded by a court.[17] The Panel does not meet this standard in two respects. First, while the Panel is independent of Bank management, it is not fully independent of the Bank. Second, the Panel does not offer complainants anything comparable to the remedy that they could obtain from a court.

While it will be challenging for the Bank to meet these two requirements, it could be more creative in trying to meet them. For example, to improve the Panel's independence, it could enhance the Panel's ability to make remedial recommendations based on its findings and to limit the grounds on which the

---

16 *See, e.g., The Equator Principles*, https://equator-principles.com/ (last visited Dec. 15, 2024).

17 European Court of Human Rights, *Waite and Kennedy v. Germany*, App. No. 26083/94 (Feb. 18, 1999).

Board and management could reject these recommendations. Alternatively, it could work with other IFIs to establish one truly independent IAM for all IFIs.[18]

To meet the second requirement, the Bank must identify a remedy that it can offer the complainants that does not unduly penalize the Bank's other member states. If the Bank used its own resources to compensate the complainants it would mean that the Bank has less resources available to lend to other member states, thus unfairly penalizing them. However, this does not preclude the Bank from seeking to devise, either on its own or in collaboration with its member states and other IFIs, meaningful financial or non-financial remedies for complainants who have been harmed by the Bank's non-compliance.

Bibliography

Bleicher, Samuel A. "UN v IBRD: A Dilemma of Functionalism." *International Organizations*, 24, no. 1 (1970): 31.

Bradlow, Daniel D. and Hunter, David B. (eds) *Advocating Social Change Through International Law: Exploring the Choice Between Hard and Soft International Law*, DD Bradlow and DB Hunter (eds) (Brill, 2020).

Bradlow, Daniel D. "Precedent-Setting NGO Campaign Saves the World Bank's Inspection Panel." *Human Rights Brief*, 6, no. 3 (1999): 71.

Bradlow, Daniel D., "Multilateral Development Banks, Their Member States and Public Accountability: A Proposal", 11 Indian Journal of International Economic Law (2019).

Dann, Philipp, et al., "The World Bank's Environmental and Social Safeguards and the Evolution of Global Order." *Leiden Journal of International Law*, 32 (2019): 537.

European Court of Human Rights, *Waite and Kennedy v. Germany*, App. No. 26083/94, (Feb. 18, 1999).

International Bank for Reconstruction and Development. *Articles of Agreement of the IBRD*, art. VII (3). Washington DC: International Bank for Reconstruction and Development, July 22, 1994.

The Equator Principles (*EP4*). July 2020. https://equator-principles.com/.

World Bank Inspection Panel. *Resolution No. IBRD 93–10, Resolution No. IDA 93–6*. Washington DC: The World Bank, September 22, 1993. https://www.inspectionpanel.org/sites/default/files/documents/Resolution1993.pdf.

18 Daniel David Bradlow, *Multilateral Development Banks, Their Member States and Public Accountability: A Proposal*, 11 INDIAN J. INT'L ECON. LAW (2019) (reprinted, *infra*, Chapter 26).

World Bank Inspection Panel, *Honduras: Land Administration Case*, Case No. 38, Request 06/0, (Received 3 January 2006), https://www.inspectionpanel.org/Panel-cases/land-administration-project.

World Bank Inspection Panel *Panama; Land Administration Project* (First Request), Case No. 53, Request: 09./01, (Received Feb. 25 2009), https://www.inspectionpanel.org/Panel-cases/land-administration-project-first-request.

World Bank Inspection Panel, *Cambodia; Land Management and Administration Project*, Case No.60, Request 09/08, (Received Sept. 4, 2009), https://www.inspectionpanel.org/Panel-cases/land-management-and-administration-project.

World Bank Inspection Panel *Uganda: Transport Sector Development Project-Additional Financing,* Case No. 98, Request No. 14/07, (received Dec. 19, 2014). https://www.inspectionpanel.org/Panel-cases/transport-sector-development-project-additional-financing,

World Bank. "Operations Manual." Accessed November 27, 2024. https://policies.worldbank.org/en/policies/operational-manual.

World Bank. "The World Bank Environmental and Social Framework." Accessed November 27, 2024. https://www.worldbank.org/en/projects-operations/environmental-and-social-framework.

World Bank Inspection Panel. *Resolution No. IBRD 2020–0004 and Resolution No. IDA 2020–0003*. Washington DC: The World Bank, September 8, 2020. https://www.inspectionpanel.org/sites/default/files/documents/InspectionPanelResolution.pdf.

Zvogbo, Kelebogile, et al. "The World Bank as an Enforcer of Human Rights." *Journal of Human Rights*, 19, no. 4 (2018): 425.

PART 2

Perspectives on the Inspection Panel Experience

Introduction to Part 2: The Panel Experience

This part is focused on the establishment, operation, and effectiveness of the World Bank Inspection Panel (the Panel). Each of the contributions brings a unique perspective based on long-standing engagement with the Panel. This includes a perspective from current Panel members (Kunanayagam et al.) as well as the two longest serving executive secretaries (i.e. chiefs of staff) (Abbott and Barlas). The perspectives also include two voices external to the Panel (Di Leva and Hunter) who were engaged in the give-and-take that led to the establishment of the Panel in 1993. Di Leva was the chief environmental lawyer at the Bank at the time of the 1993 Resolution and represented Management in several of the early Panel cases. Hunter lobbied for creation of the Panel as an attorney at the Center for International Environmental Law (CIEL) and assisted requesters in several of the early requests to the Panel. Taken one at a time, each of the contributions in this part offer a personal and interesting account; taken as a whole, the part reveals the rich and diverse perspectives that can be found in the accountability community-of-practice.

Eduardo Abbott was the first executive secretary of the Panel, and the first person employed as a staff member of the Panel. He offers a unique perspective on the challenges that Ernst Broder, the first chair of the Panel, faced in positioning the Panel as an important voice that Bank management and staff needed to take seriously. His contribution highlights the measures that Mr. Broder and the other initial Panel members took to establish the Panel's presence in the Bank and ensure its independence in the face of efforts by management and staff to undermine the Panel's ability to investigate complaints effectively. Abbott also highlights the tensions that Panel cases created between Executive Directors from Part 1 (donor) and Part 2 (borrower) countries when the Board had to make decisions on Panel cases. This, in part, is attributable to the fact that the establishment of the Panel was seen as an imposition by Part 1 countries, particularly the United States, on Part 2 countries. This division persists to this day and still contributes to many of the Panel's current challenges.

Dilek Barlas worked for the Panel for thirteen years, first as the Deputy Executive Secretary (2007–2014) and then the Executive Secretary (2014–2020). She writes about her experiences in some of the more than 100 specific Panel cases in which she was involved, as well as the Board's effort to update the Panel's toolkit. This effort led ultimately to the establishment of the Accountability Mechanism that includes both the Panel and a dispute resolution function for the Bank. Barlas explains why the structure of the Accountability Mechanism was flawed from the beginning, not least because it effectively eliminated the role of the Executive Secretary, which had an adverse impact on the administrative independence of the Panel. This view is shared by Eduardo Abbott in his chapter.

The third perspective in this part is that of Charles Di Leva, the chief of the Environmental and International Law Division in the World Bank's legal department at the time of the Panel's launch and later head of the environmental and social framework division at the Bank. DiLeva places the Inspection Panel in the broader context of accountability for MDBs. He argues that the Panel is one of several forms of environmental and social accountability at work in the context of IFI lending, including in addition to the Panel the more recently established project-level grievance mechanisms (PLGMs) and management-led grievance redress mechanisms (GRMs), such as the World Bank's Grievance Redress Service (GRS). Di Leva sees promise in the GRS, which can ensure that Bank management responds to project-related complaints more quickly and often through a less formal process than the Panel process. Di Leva also reminds us that the first line of accountability for projects must be stronger implementation of environmental and social standards in national law. His is an important reminder that the Panel should be viewed as a last resort for ensuring environmental and social accountability of Bank-financed projects–and is meant to fill the gaps when other systems fail. A focus on these other systems is also necessary in ensuring that Bank-financed projects are held accountable for their environmental and social performance. Although he sees the trends in expanding GRMs and PLGMs as positive, he rightly raises concerns about weakening commitments to the environmental rule of law in many borrower countries.

The fourth contribution in this part is that of Professor David Hunter. He provides a somewhat personal account and interpretation of the Panel's creation, its "legislative history," and its early implementation. Although his chapter touches on issues of independence and effectiveness, his main focus is on the struggle of CSOs to maintain the people-centered, public facing aspect of the Panel. He highlights some of the fissures in the negotiations over the initial Resolution, including some insights based on transcripts of the key Board discussions not made public until 2014. The account also describes his impressions and experiences in bringing some of the first cases to the new Panel, once it was launched. His chapter covers some of the same ground of Eduardo Abbot's Chapter, but from the outside CSO perspective.

The fifth piece in this part is a contribution by a group of authors who were either Panel members or staff of the Panel at the time of the 30th anniversary. It provides useful data and insights on the caseload of the Panel over the thirty years of its existence; on the contributions that the Panel's cases have made to the Bank's learning; on improvements in Bank policies; and on measures to provide relief to complainants in at least some cases. However, it also shows that the Panel has been less effective in providing remedy to complainants than the creators of the Panel may have expected. The contribution also briefly discusses some of the challenges that the Panel is currently having to deal with – for example the risk of reprisals to complainants.

The five contributions in this part, collectively, demonstrate three things. First, they show that the Panel has come a long way from its shaky start. It is now a well-established and well-respected entity inside and outside the Bank. Second, the contributions also suggest the need for continued vigilance to ensure IAM independence and effectiveness, as evidenced by the concerns noted by both Abbott and Barlas over the Board's decision to establish the Accountability Mechanism that would include both the Panel and a new dispute resolution unit. The Board had to revisit the IAM structure and announced in January 2025 revisions that appear to confirm the Panel's independence. Third, these contributions show that the Panel has a long way to go before it can be said to be a truly effective accountability mechanism capable not only of making independent findings on compliance, but in turning those findings into both corrective action by Bank Management and remedy for the complainants. To be sure, this is not only the fault of the Panel; Bank management must take responsibility for how the Bank responds to Panel claims. In this context, the Panel experience needs to be considered in the broader context of the entire "accountability system." DiLeva's concerns about weakening environmental and social commitments within the member states, for example, speaks to new challenges for strengthening the broader accountability system.

CHAPTER 5

The Inspection Panel Early Years: (An Inside Story)

*Eduardo G. Abbott**

1 Introduction

Almost thirty years have passed since the World Bank established its Inspection Panel.[1] At the time, according to the Bank, it was,

> an unprecedented means for increasing the transparency and accountability of the Bank's operations. This was a first of its kind for an international organization-the creation of an independent mechanism to respond to claims by those whom we are most intent on helping that they have been adversely affected by the projects we finance.[2]

When it was established, the Panel was a long-awaited breakthrough in the accountability of International Financial Institutions (IFIs), but also a tentative and experimental one. The Resolution provided that *"The Executive Directors shall review the experience of the inspection function established by this Resolution after two years from the date of the appointment of the first members of the Panel."* In fact, the letters of appointment of the first Panel Members reflected this reality – they would be let go after two years if the Bank decided

* Eduardo G. Abbott is an international consultant on Accountability, Institutional, and Environmental/Social matters.

1 International Bank for Reconstruction, World Bank Inspection Panel, *Resolution No. IBRD 93–10* (Sept. 22, 1993); International Dev. Association World Bank Inspection Panel, *Resolution No. IDA 93–6* (Sept. 22, 1993) [hereinafter, together, 1993 Inspection Panel Resolutions] (Twin resolutions of the International Bank for Reconstruction and Development (IRBD) and International Development Association (IDA) establishing the World Bank Inspection Panel). In this article the International Bank for Reconstruction and Development (IBRD) and the International Development Association (IDA) are collectively referred to as the "World Bank" or "the Bank." Much has been written about the establishment and operation of the World Bank's Inspection Panel and other IAMs. *See* David Hunter & Reagan Ferris, Comprehensive Bibliography Relating to Independent Accountability Mechanisms (2024), available at the https://digitalcommons.wcl.american.edu/accountability/) (last visited Dec. 22, 2024).

2 James Wolfensohn, *Accountability at the World Bank: The Inspection Panel 10 Years On*, World Bank Group vii (2003).

DOI:10.1163/9789004729735_009

to terminate its Inspection Panel.[3] The world has changed a great deal since the Panel was established – in science, technology, and politics, in advances (and setbacks) in the rights of individuals, and in the field of accountability. And the Panel has evolved – for better or for worse – during this period. In looking to the future, it is worth revisiting some of the issues and challenges that helped shape the IFIs' first accountability mechanism in its early days, to ensure continued progress in accountability.

In considering the Panel's early days, its establishment, structure, early operations, and especially the challenges it faced during this initial period to make it independent and credible to all parties, both inside and outside the World Bank Group, it is appropriate to reflect upon (a) expectations of and about the Panel; (b) the strive for independence; (c) the use of its operating and administrative procedures to ensure that independence; (d) changes in its enabling environment; and (e) the initial operating challenge it faced.

2 Great Expectations amid Great Concerns

Academics and members of civil society had for years been demanding more transparency and accountability in Bank operations. They were delighted to learn of the Panel's establishment and anticipated that as an accountability mechanism it would improve the Bank's transparency and performance, while providing redress for people negatively affected by Bank-financed projects. More importantly, they were encouraged by its precedent-setting impact on the rights of citizens under international law.[4]

However, the same academics and members of civil society had serious misgivings about the Bank's intentions. Was the Panel just "window dressing" in the face of external and internal pressures? What was the role of the Panel and its authority? How were the Panel Members and the Executive Secretary selected, and how was their commitment to accountability measured? Statements by leading NGO representatives before the United States Congress effectively summarized these misgivings and concerns.[5]

---

3 1993 Inspection Panel Resolutions, *supra* note 1, at para. 27.

4 *See* Ellen Hey, *The World Bank Inspection Panel: Towards the Recognition of New Legally Relevant Relationship in* INTERNATIONAL LAW: HOFSTRA LAW AND POLICY SYMPOSIUM, 2, 61–74 (1997); *see also* IBRAHIM SHIHATA, THE WORLD BANK INSPECTION PANEL: IN PRACTICE 261-67 (2d ed. 2000).

5 Lori Udall, *Statement of Lori Udall on Behalf of International Rivers Network, Friends of the Earth, Bank Information Center, Environmental Defense Fund, Greenpeace, Sierra Club, in* WORLD BANK DISCLOSURE POLICY AND INSPECTION PANEL: HEARING BEFORE

World Bank Management, staff, and even members of the Board of Executive Directors (the Board) also had serious misgivings about the Panel. Although there were no articles or public manifestations of these concerns, they surfaced soon after the Panel began operations; sadly, many remain to this day.

Even supportive members of the Board shared some of civil society's concerns. Shortly after I was – to my big surprise – appointed as the Panel's Executive Secretary, I met with Executive Director Nicolás Flaño.[6] He told me that his support for the Panel was twofold. First, he was acutely aware of the need for transparency and accountability in the operation of IFIs like the Bank. Second, he regarded the Panel as an instrument that would support/assist the Board in discharging its fiduciary duties. In supporting the Panel's establishment, he shared his experience of visiting, with other Executive Directors, a Bank-financed problem project where, assisted by Bank staff, they were provided with considerable information about the project's technical aspects and problems. The project company provided a somewhat different version of the same issues, while local people offered yet another view of the situation. The visit had convinced him of the Board's need for independent expert advice when making decisions related to civil society complaints about Bank-financed projects. However, he was now concerned about the selection process of the first Panel Members, and whether the hard-won Resolution would allow the Panel to carry out its duties with independence.

Mr. Flaño also mentioned many of his colleagues' concerns about the Panel. In the view of many, it was a political imposition by Part 1 (donor) countries, and it had the potential not only to be detrimental to the sovereignty of borrowers, but also to give certain local groups such as requesters and NGOs political clout that they would not otherwise have. This, they felt, would alter the "political

THE SUBCOMMITTEE ON INTERNATIONAL DEVELOPMENT, FINANCE, TRADE, AND MONETARY POLICY OF THE COMMITTEE ON BANKING, FINANCE, AND URBAN AFFAIRS-HOUSE OF REPRESENTATIVES. 103RD CONGRESS, SECOND SESS. (JUNE 21, 1994); Durwood Zaelke & David Hunter, *Statement of Durwood Zaelke, President and David Hunter, Senior Staff Attorney of the Center for International Environmental Law, in* WORLD BANK DISCLOSURE POLICY AND INSPECTION PANEL: HEARING BEFORE THE SUBCOMMITTEE ON INTERNATIONAL DEVELOPMENT, FINANCE, TRADE, AND MONETARY POLICY OF THE COMMITTEE ON BANKING, FINANCE, AND URBAN AFFAIRS- HOUSE OF REPRESENTATIVES. 103RD CONGRESS, SECOND SESS. (JUNE 21, 1994).

6 Nicolas Flaño was the Executive Director from Chile, whose office represented a group of South American countries. More importantly, he was a member of a group of four "accountability champions" at the Board who supported the Panel's establishment. The other members of this group were Fritz Fisher (Germany), Eveline Herfkens (the Netherlands) and Aris Othman (Malaysia).

equilibrium" of the country in question.[7] Another significant concern was that Panel investigations had the potential to substantially increase the cost of project implementation–-although Bank policies apply to borrowers only to the extent that they are incorporated in the respective financing agreements. Later, this concern resurfaced in Management's reactions to some requests for inspection.[8]

Many staff members and managers welcomed the establishment of a forum, run by independent experts, where they could defend themselves from allegedly unwarranted accusations about errors in the design, appraisal, and implementation of Bank-financed projects. They felt that the Panel would bring an end to "irresponsible complaints." Others rejected the idea of what they saw as an external body "looking over their shoulders" in their professional work. In general, project staff were worried about the impact that negative Panel findings could have on their standing and careers in the Bank. In fact, the first staff interviewee during the eligibility phase of the Arun III request for inspection asked to bring a personal lawyer to the meeting with the Panel. She ultimately accepted my explanation that there was no reason to be concerned, because every important step in the project cycle required multiple "clearances" (approvals) within the Bank, the Panel was looking at institutional, not personal, responsibilities. On the other hand, safeguards and legal staff appreciated that their comments about project activities and documents would be more carefully considered by their colleagues, now that affected people could demand compliance with the Bank's Operational Policies and Procedures.

---

7 For some, this was apparently a real concern. During a Board discussion a couple of years later, an Executive Director stated that in his country members of a Panel mission could be prosecuted for "traffic of influence." Although this statement was somehow lost in the tense discussion of a Panel recommendation, after the Board meeting, I met with this Executive Director in his office to explain the actual purpose and extent of Panel visits. At the end, I also referred to the immunities and privileges accorded to its officers and employees by the Bank's Articles of Agreement. He smiled and replied that his statement was made in the heat of the discussion and that only a lawyer would take issue with it.

8 For the cost of borrowers' "action plans" regarding requests for inspection see, for example, The World Bank, *Rondônia Natural Resources Management Project,* https://www.inspectionpanel.org/panel-cases/rondonia-natural-resources-management-project (last visited Dec. 14, 2024); The World Bank, *Yacyretá Hydroelectric Project,* https://www.inspectionpanel.org/panel-cases/yacyreta-hydroelectric-project (last visited Dec. 14, 2024); The World Bank, *Itaparica Resettlement and Irrigation Project*, https://www.inspectionpanel.org/panel-cases/itaparica-resettlement-and-irrigation-project (last visited Dec. 14, 2024). Based on these management-developed plans, the Board of Executive Directors rejected the Panel's investigation recommendations.

The Bank's Management, especially the President Lewis T. Preston, was cautiously welcoming of the Panel's establishment. But, again, Management revealed its sentiment in its responses to the first requests for inspection, which were quite aggressive and sometimes clearly outside the procedures provided in the Board Resolution.

3 Staffing and Logistics – Operationalizing Independence

The members of the Inspection Panel and the Executive Secretary were appointed on April 21, 1994, and started to work with the aim to open the Panel to the public on August 1 of the same year. The Panel Members had impressive personal, academic, and professional backgrounds.[9] Although they did not know each other and were unsure of each other's commitment to the task ahead, after a few meetings they came together as a team with similar goals and aspirations. To operationalize the new, unprecedented accountability mechanism, they were to count only upon the part-time assistance of a staff member of the Legal Department, whom they had not met.[10]

On short notice, I was told to meet Mr. Ernst-Günther Bröder who was traveling to the Bank to assume the position of Chair of the Inspection Panel. When he arrived, he was taken aback. He had no office or secretarial support and was only able to work with an office and support provided by an Executive Director's office. I joined him in several meetings where we requested logistical and administrative support. We learned that the Secretary's Vice Presidency was to provide support to the Panel, as it did for Board Committees. Mr. Bröder found this arrangement unacceptable and requested a meeting with the Bank's President immediately. Before the meeting was even set, he told me to prepare myself because "tomorrow we are seeing the President."[11]

The following day, in our meeting with the President, Mr. Bröder demanded that the position of Executive Secretary (my position) be made independent and full time and that proper arrangements be made to ensure the Panel's

9 The first Panel members were Mr. Ernst-Günther Bröder, Chairperson (Germany), Richard E. Bissell, appointed for three years (United States), and Alvaro Umaña-Quesada (Costa Rica), appointed for four years. After the first year, they rotated as Chairperson of the Panel.

10 The first Executive Secretary was Eduardo G. Abbott (Chile), at the time Principal Counsel, Operational Policy in the Bank's Legal Department.

11 Actually, he said "tomorrow you wear your blue suit because we are seeing the President." He used this phrase every time that we had some problem that, according to him, required intervention by the Bank's President.

overall administrative independence. When the President inquired what the Panel needed, Mr. Bröder replied: appropriate office space, two staff assistants, and another professional staff to support the Executive Secretary.[12] He was very emphatic that the Panel's total and complete independence was essential. He insisted that he had the full support of his fellow Panel members who wholeheartedly felt the Panel could not be regarded as independent from Management unless it controlled its own staff and budgetary resources. This, to the Panel Members, was not negotiable.

Concerned of a possible "revolt" by the Panel members, Mr. Preston instructed then-Secretary and Vice President Mr. Timothy Tahane to provide the staff and logistical support the Panel required. Although the issues appeared resolved, the process of staffing the Panel's Secretariat and obtaining offices and a file room with reliable, restricted access–viewed as essential safeguards to ensure integrity of the Panel process–took weeks of persistent and difficult negotiations.

In a subsequent meeting, Mr. Preston agreed upon the administrative status of Panel Members. According to the Resolution, only the Chairperson would work full time, but the rank of his or her staff position required definition. As an experienced manager of international institutions, Mr. Bröder insisted that to be respected internally, the Panel Chair position needed to be equivalent to that of Senior Management. A ranking of Vice President was agreed upon, which benefited the Panel in terms of office space and administrative support, including staff assistants and logistics. Administratively, the non-full-time Panel Members were considered Senior Consultants, a status like that of the Members of the Bank's Administrative Tribunal.

4 Asserting the Panel's Independent Interpretation of the Resolution

The Panel members had other pressing problems. Their role, status, procedures, and mission were defined by a Resolution that was rather vague in many aspects. It was obviously the result of protracted and intense negotiations and compromise at the Board that had left several matters poorly defined. Although eventually the Operating Procedures (OPs) reflected the Resolution, the Panel took the liberty of clarifying or adding important elements. Indeed, faced with external and internal misgivings about the Panel's role and the commitment

12 The first "recruit" of the Panel was Antonia Macedo, a lawyer from New Zealand, at the time a research assistant in the Legal Department. She later became the Panel's Assistant Executive Secretary.

of its members, drafting the OPs presented a unique opportunity to assert the Panel's independence and add helpful details to the Resolution.

Due to time constraints, the Panel opted to limit consultations on the draft Operating Procedures. The Panel's opening was to occur shortly after its members took office. Broad consultations with the public, Management, and member governments would potentially bury the drafting process in delay and potentially undermine the Panel's ownership of its own OPs.[13] The Panel's lack of transparency in formulating the OP Draft was not reflected in the substance of the OPs.

The OPs included a detailed explanation of all steps in the Panel process, their requirements and timing, and, as elaborated below, the OPs introduced a number of innovations into the Panel not included in Resolution, but in the Panel's view consistent with its spirit. Many of these innovations expanded the independence, accessibility, and transparency of the Panel process.

The Resolution, for example, only loosely defined who could submit requests for inspection as "an affected party in the territory of the borrower which is not a single individual (i.e., a community of persons such as an organization, association, society or other grouping of individuals.) ..." This definition and the confidentiality of requesters' names was put to the test with the Panel's first request for inspection, involving the Nepal Arun III dam and submitted by two requesters who asked that their names remain confidential.[14] Mr. Ibrahim Shihata, the Bank's General Counsel–and main drafter of the Resolution–was asked by an Executive Director to issue an opinion regarding the request's eligibility, in which he disagreed with the Panel's definition of "affected party".[15] The Panel's recommendation to investigate was nonetheless approved, and the Panel's "affected party" definition became not only the Panel's standard, but

13 Personally, I think that many features added by the Panel would not have survived a consultation process including Management, Civil Society, the Legal Department, and the Board. In fact, when the Panel tried to update the OPs to reflect the 1996 and 1999 amendments to the Resolution, the Legal Department insisted that the amendments should be cleared by Board and Legal. The Panel Chair felt the proposed approval process was detrimental to the Panel's independence and dropped this initiative.

14 The World Bank Group, *Nepal – Arun III Hydroelectric Project: Request for Inspection (English)*. (Oct. 24, 1994).

15 IBRAHIM SHIHATA, *Legal Opinion of the Senior Vice President and General Counsel of January 3, 1995, The Role of the Inspection Panel in the Preliminary Assessment of Whether to Recommend Inspection, in* THE WORLD BANK IN A CHANGING WORLD (1995) (issued in connection with the Panel's "recommendation that the Arun III Project be investigated."). SHIHATA, *supra* note 4, at 329–337.

the standard widely accepted by almost all other Independent Accountability Mechanisms (IAMs).[16]

The OPs also introduced a process for registering requests for inspection and a Registry of Panel activities regarding the processing of requests, both to be available to interested parties and the public.[17] The Registration Notice would include: an identification of the project; the requesters names (unless they asked for confidentiality); a summary of the request including reference to which Bank policies were allegedly violated or the Panel identified as related to the factual allegations made in the request; and a notice specifying the date when Management's response was due. The Registry also recorded all relevant actions and dates in connection with processing requests, including dates on which documents or notifications were received or sent by the Panel.[18]

Further, the OPs incorporated provisions to facilitate access and make the Panel process more transparent, including advice on how to prepare and submit requests, the ability of requesters and third parties to submit additional relevant information during the investigation process, and priority information throughout the process to requesters and the public.

The OPs made small, but as it later turned out significant, additions to the processes for receiving a request and launching an investigation. For example, the OPs allowed the Panel to request additional information from the requesters and Management before acting upon a request or Management Response; introduced a "preliminary review" for cases where the Panel was not satisfied with the information contained in the request and/or Management Response; and made reference to an "initial study," including a desk study and visits to the project site.

The Panel immediately realized the importance of these country visits, not only to confirm the existence and eligibility of the requesters, but also to obtain *prima facie* information about the existence or possibility of harm, a

16 World Bank Inspection Panel, *Review of The Resolution Establishing The Inspection Panel, 1996 Clarification Of Certain Aspects Of The Resolution*, (Oct. 17, 1996), https://www.inspectionpanel.org/sites/default/files/documents/ReviewResolution1966.pdf (last visited Feb. 19, 2025) [hereinafter 1996 Clarification of Panel Resolution] ("It is understood that the "affected party" which the Resolution describes as "a community of persons such as an organization, association, society or other grouping of individuals includes any two or more persons who share some common interests or concerns.").

17 *See* World Bank Inspection Panel, *The Inspection Panel at the World Bank: Operating Procedures*, 17–21, 64–65, (Apr. 2014).

18 Given the communications technology available at the time, the publicity accorded to these documents was rather limited, but the Panel made efforts to have them widely distributed.

key element for recommending an investigation. In addition to interviews with local staff, requesters, and local authorities, the OPs included provision for visiting project sites and holding public hearings in the project area. These site visits became increasingly relevant as management and some Board members objected strongly to the eligibility of virtually every Panel request. The Board took the position that field visits related to Panel investigations required prior consent of the country's government, usually provided through the respective Executive Director, but country visits for eligibility purposes[19] did not require prior approval.[20] The Panel's only opportunity to visit the site in such cases was during the eligibility review.

5 The Delicate Dance with the General Counsel

The Panel also used the OPs to try to clarify its relationship with the General Counsel. The OPs reproduced paragraph 15 of the Resolution that provides that the "Panel shall seek, through the Vice President and General Counsel of the Bank, the written advice of the Bank's Legal Department on matters related to the Bank's rights and obligations with respect to the Request under consideration." The Panel questioned the extent to which this advice would impact its independence given that the Legal Department was closely involved in project preparation and implementation and drafting Management Responses, creating an obvious conflict of interests. The Panel decided it would seek the General Counsel's advice with regard to the Bank's legal relations with third parties, but not in connection with Management's obligations to follow its own Operational Policies and Procedures. To confirm this interpretation, the Panel was quite active in requesting legal opinions in relation to remedies available to the Bank, enforceability of contract clauses, etc. For example, the Panel requested an opinion about the remedies available to the Bank under credit

19 SHIHATA, *supra* note 4, at 84–85.

20 During a courtesy meeting announcing an "eligibility visit" of the country in question, the Executive Director stated that he had to consult the government before granting his approval. I informed him that such approval was not necessary because the Panel members, as Bank officials, had the right to visit the project pursuant to the General Conditions incorporated in all Bank financing agreements. For projects under preparation, I added, the fact that Bank officials were not allowed to visit a proposed project area would negatively affect the processing of the loan. During my time at the Panel this issue was raised only a couple of times again.

agreements for a sector adjustment financing credit.[21] The resulting legal opinion formed the Panel's basis for rejecting Management's claim that the word "project" in the Resolution did not include adjustment operations.[22]

In another instance, Management's Response claimed that a request for inspection was ineligible because the amount remaining undisbursed of the two loans financing the project was equivalent to just 2.5%; the Resolution barred requests filed "after the loan financing the project has been substantially disbursed," i.e., 95% of the loan amount.[23] The problem was that although both loans were financing the same project items, they were granted at separate times and had different amortization schedules. Legally, they were not one loan, and the remaining loan had disbursed less than 95%. The General Counsel's opinion confirmed the Panel's position.[24] The Panel declared the request eligible, but, perhaps not surprisingly, the Board rejected the Panel's recommendation to investigate.

In yet another example, a Management Response to a request for inspection involving Uganda's Bujagali Dam[25] stated that the World Bank Group concluded that a site close to the area to be inundated by the project "must be conserved in perpetuity for its spiritual, natural habitat, environmental, tourism and cultural values." Adding that such "site will be preserved in its present state as per the agreement between the Government, IFC and International Development Association (IDA) as an environmental off-set" pursuant to a Mitigation for Loss and Indemnity Agreement related to the project in question. The Panel was concerned about the "perpetuity" of such an agreement and requested a legal opinion, which confirmed that the provisions of such

21 *See* World Bank Group, *Bangladesh- Jute Sector Adjustment Credit Project*, https://documents.worldbank.org/en/publication/documents-reports/documentdetail/746401468013776331/bangladesh-jute-sector-adjustment-credit-project (last visited Feb. 19, 2025).

22 The legal opinion was issued by Mr. Andrés Rigo, Acting VP and General Counsel on January 29, 1997. The meaning of "project" in the Resolution as it stands now, was afterwards agreed in a meeting between the Panel and Senior Management and ratified by the 1996 Clarifications. The Panel ultimately declined to recommend an investigation in that case since the Credit was canceled because, inter alia, of the policy violations claimed in the request.

23 SHIHATA, *supra* note 4, at 127–128; *see also* World Bank Inspection Panel, *Brazil: Itaparica Resettlement and Irrigation Project, Case No. 9, Request No. 97/1* (Apr. 28, 1997) [hereinafter Brazil: Itaparica Resettlement and Irrigation Project]; World Bank Inspection Panel, *Management Response for Request for Inspection Panel Review of Itaparica Resettlement and Irrigation Project*, 21–22 (Oct. 24, 2002) (about Management Action Plan).

24 SHIHATA, *supra* note 4, at 338–344.

25 World Bank Inspection Panel, *Bank Management Response to Request for Inspection Panel Review of the IDA-financed Uganda Third Power Project (Credit 2268–Ug) and the Proposed Bujagali Hydropower Project*, paras. 141–142 (Dec. 13, 2002).

Agreements "do not give rise to a valid, binding and enforceable obligation" of the country to conserve in perpetuity the site "as an environmental and cultural offset." The General Counsel (Mr. Ko-Yung Tung) thus supported the Panel's interpretation of the Agreement, but he also added an interpretation of the underlying policy: that "the lack of any obligation to conserve [the site] in perpetuity" was "not inconsistent" with the provisions of OP/BP 4.04 on Natural Habitats.[26]

6 A Change in Management – More Challenges

In November 1999, the Panel Chair and I were invited to meet the Bank's new General Counsel, Mr. Ko-Yung Tung.[27] It was a cordial meeting where he inquired after the Panel's work and how the Legal Department could support it. Towards the end of the meeting, he told us that, as legal counsel for the Board, he intended to participate more actively in the Panel's work, adding that the Panel would freely and independently establish the facts while he would decide whether there was any violation of the Bank's rights and obligations regarding inspection requests. We were stunned. The Panel Chair flatly rejected this "proposal" stating that he considered it a challenge to the integrity of the Panel process. Further, if needed, the Panel would ask for the Board's and civil society's support, and the Panel would resign if Management supported this stance. The General Counsel retracted, saying that he was only exploring how the Legal Department could better support the Panel. In his view, an opinion of the General Counsel on whether policy violations occurred would carry much weight with the Board and the public. To my knowledge, the matter was never raised again.

7 The Administrative Procedures – an Instrument to Support Independence

The Panel's Administrative Procedures (APs) were issued with the purpose of reaffirming its control over its administration. The APs set out rules for the Panel's management and internal operations, and also included several provisions related to its independence. These included:

26 Legal Opinion from Mr. Ko-Yung Tung, Vice President and General Counsel of World Bank (Dec. 14, 2001).

27 Mr. Ko-Yung Tung replaced Mr. Ibrahim Shihata as General Counsel in November, 1999.

- Article 10: "[T]he Panel is an independent forum. Any attempt to interfere with the functioning of the Panel for political or economic reasons or exert political or other influence on the Panel shall be made public."
- Article 12: "[R]ecommendations and findings of the Panel shall be strictly impartial: only facts relevant to the Request or investigation under consideration shall be relevant to their decisions. Consideration of political factors shall be strictly prohibited."
- Article 19: "[A] Panel member shall not participate in the preliminary review and investigation of any Request related to a matter in which he/she has a personal interest or had significant involvement in any capacity. A Panel member shall disclose to the Chairperson any circumstances, which might be deemed to affect his/her impartiality or independence."
- Article 34: "[T]he Executive Secretary and the staff of the Secretariat shall be committed to the functions and role of the Panel. Any attempt by Bank member countries, non-governmental and other organizations, the Executive Directors, or Bank staff to interfere with or influence staff of the Secretariat in the discharge of their functions shall be reported to the Panel."

The Administrative Rules were clear, and none of these situations ever happened during my time at the Panel. Some Bank staff may have been upset with the Panel's existence or actions, but they always were professional and respectful in their dealings with Panel members and staff.

8 Publication of the Panel's Procedures

Ten days before their distribution to Bank staff and the public, the Panel submitted its Operating and Administrative Procedures to the Board of Executive Directors. No comments or observations were received from Board members, and the Panel's authority to issue its own procedures was, thus, confirmed.

In 1996, the Board met to discuss the continuity of the Panel function, pursuant to Article 27 of the Resolution and issued some "clarifications" to the Resolution that made it consistent with the Panel's OPs.[28] Elements like the definition of affected party and project, the possibility of a preliminary review during the eligibility phase, and the role of the Board, *inter alia*, were confirmed.

28 1996 Clarification of Panel Resolution, *supra* note 16.

9 Looking Back, the Panel in Retrospect

When the Panel started operations, it was anyone's guess whether it was going to be flooded with requests for inspection (legitimate or not) or was going to be ignored by affected people in developing countries because of lack of information about its existence. In 1993 when the Panel was launched, email and the internet were only just emerging and rarely available to people where Bank-financed projects were implemented. Within its limited means, the Panel tried to make people aware of its existence but relied upon the Bank and civil society to help. In the 1996 Clarifications, the Board instructed Management to make significant efforts to raise awareness of the Inspection Panel in borrowing countries, but they were not to provide technical assistance or funding to potential requesters.

The feared flood of requests never materialized, and the number of requests were less than expected in the Panel's initial years, but this did not prevent the surprisingly antagonistic reactions by Management and some Board members to virtually every one of the initial requests for investigation. From the very first request, management started with *ex parte*, outside-the-Resolution procedures, lobbying Board members about requests without the Panel's presence and questioning the eligibility, seriousness, and legitimacy of the claims before the Panel acted on them.[29] To the Panel, it appeared that Management was resorting to a three-pronged strategy to avoid investigations (i.e., accountability): deny eligibility of the request; almost always claim full compliance with Bank policies and procedures; and when it appeared the first two tactics may not succeed, try to preempt the investigation by unilaterally offering action plans to address the harm that the alleged policy violations had or would cause.

Management's preemptive use of action plans, in particular, raised subtle but critical challenges to the Panel. First, although in theory the "action plans" were supposed to bring the Bank into compliance with applicable policies, Management's plans almost always did so at the expense of the borrowing country. Second, because Management's plans were trying to preempt the Panel's investigation, their plans had to be drawn up expeditiously with little

29 This practice was formally banned by the Board in the context of a second review of the Panel. Paragraph 2 of the 1999 Clarifications, provides that "Management will follow the Resolution. It will not communicate with the Board on matters associated with the request for inspection, except as provided for in the Resolution." World Bank Inspection Panel, *Conclusions of the Board's Second Review of the Inspection Panel,* para. 2 (April, 1999).

time for consultation. Third, the lack of consultation exacerbated the affected people's dissatisfaction with the Management's response to social and environmental problems that had become internationally well-known thanks to the Panel's involvement. This would bring more pressure (and expenses) on national and local governments. This, plus the unpleasant sensation of being "inspected" in their own territories, negatively impacted the borrower countries' view of the Panel, who increasingly formed blocs in opposition to Panel recommendations. This, in turn, created a difficult environment in Board meetings, where the usual decision making by consensus was replaced by dramatic, conflictive vote counting.[30] Both donor and borrower countries disliked this new tension at the Board.[31]

The divided environment in Board discussions also sent conflicting messages to the Panel. For example, the Executive Directors agreed in one case that "before a decision could be made by the Board on the Panel's recommendation [to investigate] ... the Panel should conduct an additional review to further substantiate the materiality of the damages and to establish whether such damages were caused by a deviation from Bank policies and procedures."[32] As instructed, the Panel submitted an additional review containing a detailed description of the "materiality of damages" and included an assessment of harm – quite apparent during the eligibility visit – that was similar to what would have been included in the full investigation, but the request for inspection was not approved.[33] Understanding this experience to mean that the Board now required a more detailed description of harm to determine eligibility, the Panel in its next case included in its eligibility report a discussion on "preliminary evidence of material harm" – only to be criticized by Board members for including information that belonged in an investigation report.[34]

Management's "attack" strategy seemed to work initially; in the period immediately following its first investigation,[35] most of the Panel's recommendations

30 For an excellent description of Board dynamics, especially regarding Panel matters, see Jonathan Fox, "The World Bank Inspection Panel: Lessons from the First Five Years", 6 *Global Governance* 301–305 (2000).

31 The Board resorted to "informal meetings" to discuss Panel cases, apparently to leave out of official records these contentious discussions. The official meeting would only take place after Board members agreed on the outcome. Sometimes Panel members were verbally mistreated in the course of their appearances before the Board.

32 The World Bank Inspection Panel, *Brazil: Rondônia Natural Resources Project*, Case No. 4, Request No. 95/03, (received June 16, 1995).

33 *Id.*, at Additional Review Report (Dec. 8, 1995).

34 Brazil: Itaparica Resettlement and Irrigation Project, *supra* note 23.

35 The World Bank Inspection Panel, *Nepal: Arun III Proposed Hydroelectric Project and Restructuring of IDA Credit*, Case No. 1, Request No. 94/1 (Oct. 24, 1994); World Bank

for full investigations were rejected. In one exception, the Panel's investigation could continue but it was limited to a desk study. In rejecting the Panel's recommendation to investigate another case, the Board authorized the Panel to conduct some degree of oversight regarding the implementation of Management's preemptive action plan.[36]

This unfortunate situation continued until the Board passed the *1999 Clarifications to the Resolution,* which granted the Panel's eligibility findings greater deference and largely clipped Management's use of preemptive action plans. After this clarification, Board's consideration of some Panel recommendations have been contentious but, in my experience, never reached the level of animosity of the early days.

10 Back to the Future: the Continuing Fight for the Panel's Independence

The Panel, as of this writing, has received 165 requests for inspection. It continues to be an accountability mechanism of worldwide reach. Despite the often-criticized selection procedures, the Bank has recruited many very capable Panel members who, together with a dedicated Secretariat, have maintained its independence and its standing as a leading accountability mechanism.

In retrospect, the push to establish the Panel came mostly from civil society and some enlightened member governments. The expectation that the Panel would create a "win-win" situation, opening the Bank to the communities it served, improving projects for stakeholders' benefit, while making the Bank more accessible and transparent and governments more responsive to their citizens, has faded in many quarters. Borrowing countries, Board Members, and staff have felt attacked by those whose livelihoods they work to improve. But these are just people raising their voices out of concern related to actual or potential harm, often the "unintended side effects" of development assistance.

Notwithstanding numerous public statements generally supporting the Panel and its mandate, Bank Management and some Member governments have continued to look for ways to undermine the Panel's independence and

Inspection Panel, *The Inspection Panel Report on Request for Inspection- Nepal: Proposed Arun III Hydroelectric Project and Restructuring of the Arun* (June 21, 1995).

36 Management's approach to these first cases and the hostile environment facing the early Panel Members has been well documented. *See, e.g.*, Lori Udall, *The World Bank Inspection Panel: The First Three Years* (Bank Information Center), Oct. 1997 (evaluating the Inspection Panel's first ten claims).

effectiveness. In recent years, other IFIs have established accountability mechanisms that have expanded upon the Panel's people-centered, compliance-focused model by adding problem-solving alternatives and the monitoring of remedial actions.[37] In the name of modernizing the Panel's functions, the Bank sought to expand the Panel's toolkit and improve its cost-effectiveness. Some in the Bank used the opportunity to undermine the Panel, by first weakening and later removing the position of Executive Secretary.[38] Subsequently, under the guise of introducing a dispute resolution function, the Bank created an Accountability Mechanism with a Secretary that would provide administrative oversight to the Panel. The Panel has been effectively deprived of managing its staff and budgetary resources – the very principle that initial Panel members fought for so diligently and what is, perhaps, the most essential criterion for effective independence.

The fact that a third party – no matter how well intentioned and independent from management she or he may be – administers the Panel's resources, evaluates its staff, makes budgetary decisions, and decides who to hire and fire, would be simply unthinkable for the original Panel members and many of their successors. Was this change needed? Was the Panel's management inefficient or ineffective? While some may point to minor adjustments that would help improve its administration, it is very difficult to understand this fundamental change in the Panel's organization and responsibilities – to repeat, one that goes straight to the heart of what made the Panel independent.

To many observers, the creation of the Accountability Mechanism and the constraints placed on the Panel's operations was an unacceptable attack on its independence, and the Board called for a review of the structure just two years after the changes came into effect. The Bank has been widely praised for establishing and maintaining the Inspection Panel – an unprecedented accountability mechanism that has had a major impact on the fields of accountability and international law. That impact was made possible by the Panel members' diligent attention to maintaining its operational independence since its very first days. There are again great expectations that the forthcoming review of the accountability function at the World Bank will restore the Panel's

37 There are now twenty members of the international Independent Accountability Mechanisms Network (IAMNet), an initiative promoted by Professor Edith Brown Weiss while she was Chair of the Inspection Panel.

38 This decision took away the continuity of a function that most Panel Members have valued greatly over the years because it was the source of institutional memory and instrumental in ensuring the effectiveness of the Panel's work, and lasting relations with external and internal stakeholders.

independence. Hopefully, the review will serve to respect and honor the hard-fought achievements of the Panel's early years.[39]

Bibliography

Hey, Ellen. "The World Bank Inspection Panel: Towards the Recognition of New Legally Relevant Relationships in International Law." 2 *Hofstra L. & Policy Symp.* 61–74 (1997).

Shihata, Ibrahim. *The World Bank Inspection Panel: In Practice*. Oxford: Oxford University Press, 2nd ed., 2000: 261–267.

Udall, Lori, Durwood Zaelke & David Hunter. "Statement of Lori Udall on Behalf of International Rivers Network, Friends of the Earth, Bank Information Center, Environmental Defense Fund, Greenpeace, Sierra Club," in "*World Bank Disclosure Policy and Inspection Panel: Hearing before the Subcommittee on International Development, Finance, Trade, and Monetary Policy of the Committee on Banking, Finance, and Urban Affairs—House of Representatives. 103rd Congress, Second Session (June 21)*." Washington DC: Government Printing Office, 1994.

Udall, Lori. "The World Bank Inspection Panel: The First Three Years." Washington DC: Bank Information Center, October 1997.

Wolfensohn, James. "World Bank. Accountability at the World Bank: The Inspection Panel 10 Years On." Washington, DC: World Bank Group (2003): viii.

World Bank Inspection Panel. *Nepal: Arun III Proposed Hydroelectric Project and Restructuring of IDA Credit*, Case No. 1, Request No. 94/1. Washington DC: World Bank, October 1994.

World Bank Inspection Panel. *Brazil: Rondônia Natural Resources Project*, Case No. 4, Request No. 95/03. Washington DC; World Bank, June 16, 1995. https://www.inspectionpanel.org/panel-cases/rondonia-natural-resources-management-project.

World Bank Inspection Panel. *Review of The Resolution Establishing The Inspection Panel – 1996 Clarification of Certain Aspects of The Resolution*. Washington DC: The World Bank, May 14, 1996. https://www.inspectionpanel.org/sites/default/files/documents/ReviewResolution1966.pdf.

39 The final outcome of this Review of the Panel's function was not yet concluded as this chapter went to press. Please visit the World Bank Accountability Mechanism's website, https://accountability.worldbank.org/en/home, or that of the Perspectives Project, https://digitalcommons.wcl.american.edu/accountability-perspectives/, for additional information on the Review process.

World Bank Inspection Panel. *Brazil: Itaparica Resettlement and Irrigation Project, Case No. 9, Request No. 97/1*. Management Response. Washington DC: World Bank, April 28, 1997.

World Bank Inspection Panel. *The Inspection Panel at the World Bank: Operating Procedures*. Washington DC: The World Bank, April 2014: 17–21, 64–65.

World Bank Inspection Panel. *Management Response for Request for Inspection Panel Review of Itaparica Resettlement and Irrigation Project*. Washington DC: World Bank, October 24, 2022: 21–22.

https://www.inspectionpanel.org/sites/default/files/ip/PanelCases/9-Management%20Response%20%28English%29.pdf.

World Bank Inspection Panel. *Bank Management Response to Request for Inspection Panel Review of the IDA-financed Uganda Third Power Project (Credit 2268–Ug) and the Proposed Bujagali Hydropower Project*. Washington DC; World Bank, December 12, 2022: paras. 141–142. https://www.inspectionpanel.org/sites/default/files/ip/PanelCases/24-Management%20Response%20%28English%29.pdf.

Zaelke Durwood and David Hunter, Statement of Durwood Zaelke, President and David Hunter, Senior Staff Attorney of the Center for International Environmental Law," in "*World Bank Disclosure Policy and Inspection Panel: Hearing before the Subcommittee on International Development, Finance, Trade, and Monetary Policy of the Committee on Banking, Finance, and Urban Affairs—House of Representatives. 103rd Congress, Second Session (June 21)*." Washington DC: Government Printing Office, 1994.

CHAPTER 6

People-Centered Accountability in International Development: Key Developments at the World Bank Inspection Panel (2014–2023)

*Dilek Barlas**

1 Introduction

Established more than thirty years ago, the World Bank Inspection Panel (the Panel) was the first independent complaints mechanism for environmental and social accountability in international development. The Inspection Panel aims to promote accountability at the International Bank for Reconstruction and Development and the International Development Association (collectively known as "the World Bank" or "the Bank"), to give affected people a greater voice in activities supported by the Bank that affect their rights and interests, and to foster remedy when warranted. The Panel is widely viewed as the leading accountability mechanism for investigating the compliance of Bank Management with the institution's policies and procedures, and related harm.

This essay reflects on major developments at the Panel through the lens of important cases that occurred during my tenure as Executive Secretary and shows how the Panel has evolved to improve accessibility, influenced overall development policies, and become a catalyst for institutional change. The Panel's success has largely been due to its structural and operational independence, reporting as it does directly to the Bank's Board of Executive Directors. The essay also discusses how the Panel faces some of the same issues today, including the challenge to its independence resulting from the 2020 creation of the new Accountability Mechanism Secretariat (AMS).

2 Ensuring Safe and Secure Access to the Panel

Accessibility has been one of the core principles and strengths of the Panel since its creation. The Panel has recognized that it cannot be effective as a

* Dilek Barlas served as the third Executive Secretary of the Panel (2014–2020) and before that as the Deputy Secretary (2007–2014).

complaints mechanism if affected people either do not know about its existence or are unable or unwilling to access it.

2.1 *Expanding Knowledge of the Panel*

Although some modest progress has been made over time, enlisting Bank Management to help inform project-affected people of the Panel's existence has been a constant challenge. Working with Bank Management, the Panel has introduced measures to make its existence better known to project-affected people. The Panel was included on the World Bank website, in project appraisal documents, and in the Environmental and Social Framework ("ESF"). Outreach activities, either online or face-to-face, are an integral part of the Panel's work program. However, the main project safeguard documents disclosed to the affected people, including environmental and social assessment reports, resettlement action plans, and Indigenous Peoples' plans, still lack information regarding the availability of the Panel.

The lack of knowledge about the Panel is particularly acute in cases where the Bank is engaged in supporting policy changes through development policy financing or the program-for-results. Policy lending is usually not visible to project-affected people, and understanding the link between actual or potential harm and the policies and activities supported by these operations is often less clear. The growing use of financial intermediaries in investment project financing creates similar challenges for project-affected people due to the difficulty of understanding the ultimate source of financing for these operations.

2.2 *Reducing Barriers to Access*

Since its conception, the Panel has taken considerable steps, including independently updating its operating procedures, to provide easier access to affected people. The process for lodging a complaint with the Panel is simple and user-friendly; a minimum of two individuals or their representative can file complaints by simply sending a letter to the Panel in any language, as long as it contains their name, a description of the harm or potential harm, and a description of attempts to resolve the issue with Bank management. The complaint does not have to reference specific Bank policies in describing the complaint. The Panel Secretariat staff works with the complainants to clarify any issues and assist them, if needed, to meet these simple requirements.

When requested, the identities of the complainants are kept confidential and not shared outside of the Panel, but the Panel recognizes that confidentiality alone has not been enough in some environments to protect the complainants and the people helping them. Early on in its operation, the Panel learned about intimidation and retaliation of complainants in some of its cases. The Panel has put in place measures to ensure the protection of its internal and external communications, and visits to project areas are independently and carefully planned so as not to compromise the identity of the complainants.

An example of the dangers was the imprisonment of a facilitator hired by the Panel after its investigation in the 2012 Ethiopia Promoting Basic Services case, in which the Anuak Indigenous peoples from the Gambella region submitted a complaint alleging serious human rights violations arising from block grants financed by the Bank to improve basic services in the region.[1] The complaint claimed that the grants were contributing directly to the government's villagization program that forced the Anuak indigenous people to leave their ancestral land to relocation sites where their livelihoods deteriorated due to less fertile land, lack of other income-generating opportunities, and lack of public services. After the Panel investigation, the facilitator was first detained without charges for six months and then charged with terrorism.

Once the Panel learned of the arrest, it immediately informed Bank Management, although the Panel no longer employed the facilitator. The regional team, the Bank President, and relevant Executive Directors then reached out to government authorities, and the Panel issued two press releases expressing its concern. It was almost three years after the arrest before all charges were dropped, and the facilitator was released. As a result of this case, the Panel became the first Independent Accountability Mechanism (IAM) to adopt anti-retaliation guidelines.

Bank Management maintains a strong commitment against reprisals. Although Bank Management and other financial organizations' decisive actions influence the situation, once reprisal occurs the relevant government authorities ultimately decide how to address the issue. While the Panel guidelines introduced measures to identify and prevent the risk of intimidation, reprisal, and retaliation in its cases, bringing a complaint to an international forum like the Panel requires courage by the project-affected people, regardless of the protections offered. The risk of intimidation, reprisal, and retaliation remains a significant deterring factor for project-affected people in accessing the Panel, and requires the continued attention of the Panel, Bank Management, Civil Society Organizations, and the development community at large.

---

1 International Bank for Reconstruction and Development & International Development Association, *First Progress Report on the Implementation of Management's Action Plan in Response to the Inspection Panel Investigation Report (Report No. 9184–ET) on the Ethiopia Promoting Basic Services Project (Credit No 51620)* (Feb. 11, 2016).

3 Influencing International Development and Policies

Compliance investigations are the core activities of the Panel. The Panel consists of three members of different nationalities and backgrounds and a permanent professional secretariat staff that assists and advises the Panel. The Panel independently hires expert consultants who provide technical expertise for its cases. Panel investigations have led to strong institutional accountability, and significantly improved the compliance of the Bank with its own environmental and social safeguards policies; although all operational policies and procedures are under its purview, environmental and social safeguard policies are often the main policies raised in Panel cases.[2] Numerous lessons have emerged from Panel cases that have improved the application of policies on environmental assessment, resettlement, indigenous peoples, and consultation and disclosure of information. The Panel's publication series on "emerging lessons" captures and documents many of these examples.[3]

Through the Panel's independent, impartial, and comprehensive fact-finding, it has been able to expose important development issues, giving a strong voice to people affected by these issues to the extent that the Bank has taken steps to address them. As a result, important contributions have been made to the World Bank's overall development agenda; although the Panel does not have policy-making authority, these cases have influenced the Board and Management's adoption of new policies on the issues.

The Uzbekistan Second Rural Enterprise Support[4] and the Uganda Transport Sector Development[5] cases provide powerful examples of how the Panel advances development by paving the way to a response to its potentially severe and widespread consequences. The Uzbekistan case highlighted child and forced labor issues, and the Uganda case involved gender-based violence

2 The Environment and Social Framework is only applicable to the World Bank's investment project financing, and the environmental and social provisions that apply to development policy lending are much more limited in scope.

3 For the Panel's Emerging Lessons series, see World Bank Inspection Panel, *Publications*, https://www.inspectionpanel.org/publications (last visited Oct. 16, 2023).

4 World Bank Inspection Panel, *Uzbekistan-Second Rural Enterprise Development Project*, https://www.inspectionpanel.org/panel-cases/second-rural-enterprise-support-project (last visited Jan. 15, 2024).

5 World Bank Inspection Panel, *Uganda Transport Sector Development Project*, https://www.inspectionpanel.org/panel-cases/transport-sector-development-project-additional-financing (last visited Jan. 15, 2025); *see also* Elana Berger, *How a Community-Led Response to Sexual Exploitation in Uganda Led to Systemic World Bank Reform*, ACCOUNTABILITY NOTE NO. 3 (June 2018) (published jointly by the Bank Information Center and the Accountability Research Center).

(GBV). Even without an explicit policy of the Bank on these issues at the time of the complaints – through the Panel's eligibility process in the case of Uzbekistan and its investigation in the Uganda case – important policy and institutional changes took place not only at the World Bank but also in other international development organizations.

3.1 *Addressing Forced Labor in the Uzbekistan Cotton Sector*

A complaint from Uzbekistan in 2013 on the Bank-financed project that included support to the country's cotton sector reforms, noted that the project neither identified nor safeguarded against the child and forced labor prevalent in the cotton sector, thus contributing to harm. While there was then no Bank policy on labor issues, child and forced labor was prohibited under the national legislation together with the International Labour Organization (ILO) Conventions ratified by Uzbekistan. In its initial response, Bank Management disagreed that the project was contributing to child and forced labor, but later acknowledged the seriousness of the issues and the project's shortcomings in dealing with them. Bank Management committed to pursuing a range of measures to combat these practices; on this basis, the Panel postponed its decision on whether a full investigation was warranted for a year to provide Bank Management with time to report on the implementation of its initiatives.

During this period, the Bank took important steps to support the modernization of the cotton sector, including mechanizing harvesting, to eliminate child and forced labor in the sector. The Bank included labor issues as an integral part of its dialogue with the government of Uzbekistan on agricultural sector reforms. Most importantly, the Bank signed a Memorandum of Understanding with the ILO to undertake third party monitoring of Bank-financed projects for the use of child and forced-labor during the 2015 and 2016 cotton harvesting seasons. Following these developments, the Panel decided not to conduct an investigation. The Bank adopted its ESF in 2016, including its policy on labor and working conditions; prevention of the use of all forms of forced labor and child labor is one of the objectives of this policy.

3.2 *Addressing Gender Based Violence in Uganda's Transport Sector*

Another groundbreaking complaint received by the Panel in 2014 stemming from a road rehabilitation project in Uganda raised the issue of Gender-Based Violence in a Bank-financed project for the first time. The complainants alleged that the project had caused serious harms, including many cases of child sexual abuse and teenage pregnancies by road workers, an increased presence of sex workers, the spread of HIV/AIDS, sexual harassment of female employees, inadequate resettlement practices, lack of road safety, and negative construction impacts. The Panel's investigation confirmed these allegations. The Panel found the environmental and social impact assessment neither adequately estimated the risks from the influx of workers into the project area nor proposed sufficient mitigation measures. The Panel also found that Bank Management's oversight was insufficient, and that supervision missions did not effectively address these problems.

Bank Management acknowledged the Panel's findings and undertook several initiatives to address issues raised in the Panel's investigation at both the community and institutional levels. Bank Management canceled the project due to the borrower's failure to implement appropriate social standards and practices. Notwithstanding these steps, the government and Bank Management continued to address and supervise outstanding issues, and to support several remedial actions, including assisting victims of abuse and strengthening child protection in project communities. A program was implemented to offer sexually abused girls psycho-social counseling, help with school reintegration, provide additional training, assist with pre- and post-natal care, and offer a monthly stipend to help meet basic needs.

The Bank's institutional initiatives included the establishment of a Global Gender-Based Violence Task Force to provide recommendations for preventing and addressing Gender-Based Violence in Bank operations, a guidance note for staff on how to handle labor influx and related issues in Bank projects, and a report on lessons learned and actions to address internal systemic issues. The Bank became the first International Financial Institution to disqualify contractors for failing to comply with GBV-related obligations. A requirement was included for Bank staff to conduct due diligence on the risks to individuals and groups who might be adversely affected or excluded from project benefits due to gender, sexual orientation, or gender identity.

4 Challenges in Providing Project Remedies

Institutional accountability, including improvements in the application of Bank policies and procedures, is an important role of the Panel, but the Panel recognizes that project-affected people who bring their claims to the Panel seek remedy for their harms. The Panel, following its independent investigation, reports its findings to the Bank's Board of Executive Directors, and Bank Management must prepare a response, including actions to address Panel findings of policy non-compliance and related harm. While Bank Management, on its own, can propose actions to address institutional issues to improve policy application, Bank Management's proposed remedial actions to address harm need to be agreed upon with the borrower.

Project-affected people have been able to secure remedies in many cases that they have brought to the Panel. However, there have been some cases where this was not possible. When borrowing governments do not agree on remedial actions, the impact of the Panel process is dependent on the effective use of the Bank's leverage to compel the borrower to agree and implement these measures. Sometimes this is not enough. In two cases – the Albania Integrated Coastal Zone[6] and Cambodia Land Management investigations[7] – the Panel showed serious non-compliance in the application and implementation of Bank policies. As a result, affected communities were harmed and needed remedies. However, the governments in both cases refused to agree on remedial actions. These investigations were important for enhancing the internal accountability within the Bank, but this was of little or no consolation to the affected people.

4.1 *Albania Integrated Coastal Zone Project*

Families living in the small community of Jale brought the complaint about the Albania Integrated Coastal Zone Management and Cleanup Project following the demolition of their houses by the local construction police because the residents lacked building permits. Bank Management initially denied any link between the demolitions and the Bank-supported project. Bank Management stated that the government had agreed to a demolition moratorium in the coastal area covered by the project until safeguards for affected people were in place.

The Panel investigation established direct links between the Bank-financed project and the demolitions. The Panel also uncovered that the Board approved the project based on the premise that there was a moratorium on future demolitions – and Bank Management failed to inform the Board that the government had not agreed to such a moratorium. After the Panel's report was issued, the Bank took important steps to improve safeguards in the context of land-use

6 World Bank Inspection Panel, *Albania: Integrated Coastal Zone Management and Clean-Up Project* (*First Request*) https://www.inspectionpanel.org/panel-cases/integrated-coastal-zone-management-and-clean-project-first-request (last visited Jan. 23, 2025).

7 World Bank Inspection Panel, *Investigation Report-Cambodia: Land Management Administration Project* (*Credit No. 350-KH*), (Nov. 23, 2010), https://documents.worldbank.org/en/publication/documents-reports/documentdetail/183101468229739528/cambodia-land-management-and-administration-project-inspection-panel-investigation-report (last visited Jan. 23, 2025).

planning projects. A Bank-wide review identified and examined safeguards aspects of more than 1,500 projects either under preparation or supervision, and an accountability review of staff was undertaken. The Bank introduced procedures to strengthen the oversight of quality assurance measures, clarified the application of safeguard policies to land-use planning projects, and issued a guidance note on social risks involved in such projects.

As a remedial measure, Bank management proposed compensation to the families for damages to their houses. However, the government maintained that the demolitions were in line with its laws and that it never agreed to a project design that included a moratorium to its ongoing demolition program. Thus, the government did not agree to compensate the affected families. The only support government agreed to was Bank financing for legal services for the families to bring their cases before the Albanian courts and an independent observer to report to the Bank on the review process. Of the nine cases pursued by the families, only two were successful and resulted in compensation.

4.2 *Cambodia Land Management and Administration Project*

In a complaint about the Cambodia Land Management Project, more than 4,000 families living around Boeung Kak Lake in Phnom Penh claimed they had been forcefully evicted and denied the right to have their property claims considered under the project. The Panel investigation found serious non-compliance with the Bank's involuntary resettlement and supervision policies, and confirmed harm suffered by the community. While Bank Management accepted the Panel's findings and tried to put in place remedial measures to address the issues raised, the government rejected the proposed actions. Due to the government's position, the Bank eventually suspended all lending to Cambodia for five years. After the investigation, which was claimed to be independent of the Panel case, the government issued a sub-decree granting title to approximately 700 project-affected families from the Boeung Kak Lake.

4.3 *Expanding Pathways to Remedy*

As noted above, the Panel, being the first accountability mechanism, only has the compliance function; the majority of IAMs established after the Panel eventually included a dispute resolution function to facilitate or mediate a resolution between the parties. In light of this emerging practice at other IAMs, the Panel began to explore ways in less contentious and more focused cases to facilitate the early resolution of issues. When Bank Management proposed substantial time-bound actions to address the issues raised in a complaint, the Panel, with the Board's approval, deferred its decision on whether to recommend an investigation to create additional opportunities for Bank Management, implementing agencies, and complainants to agree to an early resolution of the case during its eligibility phase.

Later, the Panel amended its operating procedures to introduce a pilot to delay registration when Bank Management initiates measures to address alleged harms, and complainants support this approach. Although these approaches to supporting early resolution either during the registration or eligibility phase led to some successful outcomes, they were roundly criticized by Civil Society Organizations and others in the accountability field, as they were led by Bank Management and arguably outside the Panel's procedures. According to the critics, the inherent power imbalance between Bank Management and implementing agencies on the one hand and the usually vulnerable complainants on the other present the threat of skewed outcomes if dispute resolution is continued without a clearer mandate and procedures.

The first independent dispute resolution case for the Bank followed a Panel investigation related to the Kenya Electricity Expansion Project.[8] The project was co-financed with the European Investment Bank (EIB), and the Panel and the EIB's Complaint Mechanism both received complaints and agreed to cooperate during their separate investigations. Following the Panel investigation, the Board approved for the first time that Bank management cooperate with the EIB Complaints Mechanism's mediation process between the complainants and the implementing agency to agree on remedial actions. The Board asked Bank Management to return to the Board within one year to present the results of the mediation and an action plan for its approval. The dispute resolution process resulted in a detailed plan with remedial actions.

5 Implications of the 2020 Review

The Bank approved its new Environmental and Social Framework (ESF) in 2016, with its application to projects to start in 2018. During the same period, the lack of an independent dispute resolution service and other gaps in the Panel's mandate repeatedly came up during different Panel cases. These include the lack of a monitoring function to follow up on remedial actions, the lack of a formal advisory service, unavailability of Panel's investigation reports to the complainants before action plan consultation, and a time limit to submit complaints. A comparative study reviewing the functions and trends

8 World Bank Inspection Panel, *Panel Cases- Kenya: Electricity Expansion Project*, https://www.inspectionpanel.org/panel-cases/electricity-expansion-project (last visited Dec. 5, 2024).

in other accountability mechanisms, mainly focusing on dispute resolution, monitoring and advisory functions, underscored the availability of these functions in other IAMs.

Consequently, the Board of Executive Directors embarked on a review of the Panel to ensure that the Panel has adequate tools compared to other IAMs, to operate effectively under the new ESF. As the interlocutor of the Panel, the Board's Committee on Development Effectiveness spearheaded the process of the Panel's review in 2017.

All the stakeholders agreed not to open the Panel Resolution[9] for a general review but to select the most important issues to improve accountability and focus only on those. The understanding was that the Panel as an independent accountability mechanism has been instrumental in providing access to project-affected people, ensuring accountability, and improving compliance with the World Bank's policies and procedures, and should continue to operate as such. In order to indicate the limited scope of the review, it was named the "Review of the Panel's Toolkit" (the Toolkit Review). The Board decided to limit the scope of the Toolkit Review to seven areas aimed at exploring potential expansion of the Panel's operations: (i) advisory services; (ii) monitoring action plans; (iii) dispute resolution; (iv) the cut-off date for filing complaints; (v) communication with complainants after investigations; (vi) assessing the extension of Panel case eligibility to Bank-Executed Trust Funds (BEFTs); and (vii) determining whether accountability gaps may exist in the context of Bank co-financing operations as a result of differences between the respective institutions' accountability mechanisms.

Due to the Board's interest in the Inspection Panel, the working group established for the review included representatives from the offices of all Board members. The review started with an external qualitative assessment of these seven focus areas and continued with working group deliberations of issues. The Panel, Bank Management, and the Bank's Legal Vice Presidency provided support to the Board.

9 Rather than a Bank policy, the Panel was established through a Board Resolution and went through two Board-governed reviews in 1996 and 1999, prior to the 2020 review. Although approved by the Board, Bank policies are initiated, drafted, and their amendments prepared by Bank management. In order to keep the Board's full authority on the Panel, including initiating and preparing amendments to its main legal document, the Panel Resolution was not converted to a Bank policy. It was kept separate from the Bank's policy and procedure framework that retrofitted the existing policies and procedures in 2014.

5.1 *Updates on the Panel's Mandate*

Four of the seven issues were quickly resolved between the Panel and Bank Management. In 2018 the Board approved measures to:

(i) formally recognize the Panel's advisory role in its mandate;
(ii) have Bank Management issue clarifications on the use of BEFTS;
(iii) formalize the Panel's current practice to coordinate with the accountability mechanism of co-financier(s) to process the complaints in the most efficient and effective way possible; and
(iv) update the procedures for sharing the Panel investigation report with complainants before it is considered by the Board.

The deliberations on the remaining areas continued for another two years, and in 2020 the Board approved:

(i) independent and proportionate, risk-based verification of the implementation of Bank Management action plans developed in response to Panel investigation reports by the Panel and independent Audit Group, when approved by the Board;
(ii) an extension to the time limit under which complaints can be submitted to the Panel to fifteen months beyond project closure; and
(iii) the establishment of an Accountability Mechanism (AM) housing both the Panel and a new dispute resolution function.

The dispute resolution function would be conducted by a new Dispute Resolution Service (DRS) and offered to the complainants and borrowers following the approval by the Board of the Panel's eligibility determination and recommendation for investigation.

5.2 *A New Structure Impacting the Panel's Independence*

All these measures were important advancements to the Panel's mandate and the Bank's overall accountability framework. However, the structure created with the new AM significantly limited the Panel's authority over its budget and staff. Despite the initial intention to preserve the Panel as is, the new AM has limited the Panel's operational independence.

According to the new AM's structure, the mechanism houses both the Panel and the DRS, and the newly established AM Executive Secretary is the head and manager of the mechanism. Similar to the Panel members, the AM Executive Secretary is independent, appointed by and reporting directly to the Board with a five-year term limit. The staff of the AM, both those responsible for the Panel's compliance review and its dispute resolution service report to the AM Executive Secretary. The AM Executive Secretary is also responsible for managing the budget of the AM, including that of the Panel.

The new structure limited the powers of the AM Executive Secretary vis-a-vis the Inspection Panel. The Inspection Panel members continue to be independent and report directly to the Board. The compliance staff report to the AM Executive Secretary on administrative matters, but to Inspection Panel members on technical matters related to compliance. The AM Executive Secretary "consults" with the Panel Chairperson on the appointment and performance reviews of technical and administrative staff of the Panel. Finally, the AM Secretary "works" with the Inspection Panel Chairperson on the allocation and oversight of the Panel budget.

There were several considerations in the creation of this unusual structure. The perceived need to avoid any conflict of interest between the dispute resolution and compliance functions arguably required that the dispute resolution function be organizationally separate from the Panel. However, establishing a separate independent oversight and accountability mechanism for dispute resolution was not favored. As a result, the Panel and DRS were put under the accountability mechanism umbrella. The Panel members do not have administrative responsibility; the Panel's administrative functions were the responsibility of the Panel Chairperson and its executive secretary reporting to the Panel. Therefore, it was decided to have an Executive Secretary to head the mechanism, the newly created DRS, and to provide administrative support to the Panel. Since the administrative functions of the Panel's own executive secretary were largely transferred to the AM Executive Secretary, this position reporting to the Panel was declared redundant.

The structure created with the new AM is different from several other accountability mechanisms, including the International Finance Corporation's Compliance, Advisor/Ombudsman (CAO). The CAO has a Vice President who heads both compliance and dispute resolution functions. The AM Executive Secretary heads the dispute resolution function, but the Panel with its compliance function will continue to operate independently.

Although the review was about possibly adding new tools to the Panel without altering its independence or functioning, the new structure significantly changed the operational independence of the Panel. As a result of the new structure, the Panel has lost its independence over its staff and budget and has to negotiate these issues with the AM Secretary who does not report to the Panel. Namely, the independence of the Panel over its staff and its budget are left to the good faith of the AM secretary. It is well known that functional independence cannot be achieved without administrative autonomy. Keeping only the Panel members' independence is not enough to ensure the functional independence of the Panel, which is fundamental to its credibility and legitimacy.

6 Conclusion

The Panel has and will continue evolving to adapt to new development challenges. However, the Panel's evolution should not jeopardize fulfilling its accountability function and bringing remedy to project-affected people. Independence has been its core strength in gaining the trust of project-affected people, assisting the Board in its oversight function over projects, and contributing to the overall development agenda. Ensuring the Panel's independent authority over its staff and budget were hard-won battles in its early years. It is important that these attributes of the Panel are protected and enhanced.

[*Editors' note:* On January 9, 2025, the World Bank issued a press release announcing that the Board of Directors had decided to change the structure of the Accountability Mechanism. In the new structure, both the Panel and the DRS will report directly to the Board. A new AM Executive Secretariat will be established that reports to both the Panel Chair and the head of the DRSD. Although more details were not available at the time this book went to press, the new structure appears to have responded to many of the concerns regarding the AM's potential to diminish the Panel's independence. *See World Bank Board Approves Changes to the Structure of the World Bank's Accountability Mechanism,* Press Release No. 2025/050/SEC (Jan. 9, 2025).]

Bibliography

World Bank Group. *Uganda Transport Sector Development Project.* Accessed December 15, 2024. https://projects.worldbank.org/en/projects-operations/project-detail/P092837.

World Bank Group. *Uzbekistan-Second Rural Enterprise Development Project.* Accessed December 15, 2024. https://documents.worldbank.org/en/publication/documents-reports/documentdetail/174251648048345344/uzbekistan-second-rural-enterprise-development-project.

World Bank Inspection Panel. *Investigation Report- Albania: Integrated Coastal Zone Management and Clean-Up Project* (*IDA Credit No. 4083–ALB*). Washington DC: The World Bank, November 24, 2008.

World Bank Inspection Panel. *Investigation Report-Cambodia: Land Management Administration Project* (*Credit No. 350-KH*). Washington DC: The World Bank, November 23, 2010.

World Bank Inspection Panel. "Publications." Accessed October 16, 2023.

World Bank Inspection Panel. *Panel Cases- Kenya: Electricity Expansion Project.* Accessed December 5, 2024. https://www.inspectionpanel.org/panel-cases/electricity-expansion-project.

CHAPTER 7

Reflections on the Role of the Inspection Panel: View from a Former Chief Counsel

*Charles Di Leva**

1 Introduction

Over the past thirty years, the World Bank (the Bank) and the Inspection Panel (the Panel) have had a supportive relationship applying the principle of accountability, particularly regarding development finance operations and the role and responsibility of the Bank as a multilateral public sector financial institution. This relationship appears in at least three aspects: (i) following the Bank's lead, many development institutions have established Independent Accountability Mechanisms (IAMs) modeled on the Panel; (ii) the Bank and other development institutions have supported stronger environmental and social policies/requirements; and (iii) the steady growth in effective grievance mechanisms, at the management and project level, to help implement policy requirements and resolve issues for affected people.

These initiatives to strengthen accountability are consistent with the understanding of the importance of the "rule of law" and Bank efforts to support it. Unfortunately, while the Bank's own systems for accountability have grown over the years, the trends regarding accountability and the rule of law in many of the Bank's member states have been disappointing. This trend is but one of the reasons why the role of the Panel and other IAMs remains vital.

2 The Panel's Origins – a Personal Perspective

The creation of the Panel dovetailed with my career goals when I joined the Bank in 1992. I entered the Bank's Legal Department after serving in Washington DC for the US Department of Justice, Environmental Enforcement Section,

* Charles E. Di Leva was Chief Counsel of the Environmental and International Law Practice Group in the World Bank Legal Vice-Presidency and the Bank's Legal Advisor to the Climate Change Solutions Area and the Environment and Natural Resources Global Practice Group.

and in Nairobi for the United Nations Environmental Program Environmental Law Unit. With my background, I expected to help countries develop their environmental law and capacity, and to help ensure borrower projects were in compliance with applicable Bank environmental and social policies.

My Bank assignment was with the newly formed Environmental Law Unit, (later, the Environmental and International Law Unit) under Chief Counsel W. Paatii Ofosu-Amaah. Among many matters, our office assisted Ibrahim F.I. Shihata, General Counsel and Senior Vice President, in the drafting of the proposed Resolution to establish the Panel. Throughout this process there was extensive engagement with the Bank's Board of Executive Directors and civil society. As the first IAM, the drafting process was intense and challenging. It was also precedent-setting in that lawyers representing civil society, such as Professors Hunter and Bradlow, would have a role in the process of drafting a World Bank Resolution.

Throughout this period, the Bank was, and remains, the largest multilateral financier of infrastructure projects in developing countries, and issues surrounding compliance with Bank environmental policies were attracting increasing attention. This issue became especially prominent with the release in 1992 of the Morse Commission Report on the Sardar Sarovar Project in India.[1] The Report identified how the Bank had failed to ensure that environmental and social policies were properly applied, and was a major impetus in civil society groups calling for the establishment of the Panel.

The Morse Commission Report findings resonated during one of my first assignments when I differed with a Bank task team member working on another large hydro project about whether certain aspects were mandatory or optional in the Bank's Environmental Assessment Operational Directive on Environmental Assessment (EA). That disagreement highlighted accountability challenges, given the lack of clarity in the then-existing environmental and social directives. It was logical that the Morse Commission Report would have made evident the need for a stronger system for accountability. Bank Management also understood that some major donors were uncomfortable with a lack of clarity on what was required to avoid harm associated with Bank projects. Thus, to Bank Board members representing a majority of its shares, the launch of the Panel was both necessary and timely, and on September 22, 1993, the Bank's Executive Directors established the independent Inspection Panel.

---

1 Bradford Morse & Thomas Berger, Sardar Sarovar: The Report of the Independent Review, xi–xx, 349–58 (1992).

The crux of the Panel's role on compliance is laid out as follows:

> The affected party must demonstrate that its rights or interests have been or are likely to be directly affected by an action or omission of the Bank as a result of a failure of the Bank to follow its operational policies and procedures with respect to the design, appraisal and/or implementation of a project financed by the Bank (including situations where the Bank is alleged to have failed in its follow-up on the borrower's obligations under loan agreements with respect to such policies and procedures) provided in all cases that such failure has had, or threatens to have, a material adverse effect.[2]

Once in place, requests to this new, independent fact-finding body could be filed alleging two or more people had been harmed due to the Bank's actions. The ability to investigate compliance also meant that task teams would understand that there was a new system of accountability to take into consideration during project preparation and the Borrower's implementation of the project.

3 The Panel and Evolution of Environmental and Social Concerns

With the creation of the Panel, it was important for the Panel, borrowers, civil society, and Bank staff to understand which Bank policies were mandatory and reviewable by the Panel, to ensure, *inter alia*, clarity between the role and responsibility of the Bank and the borrower.[3] However, as some investigations revealed, including the high visibility Western China Poverty Reduction

2 While there have been several revisions to the Panel Mandate, the most recent Resolution continues to keep in effect the crux of the requirements for a complaint being eligible; namely potential threat or actual material harm to two or more persons due to the Bank's failure to adhere to its mandatory policies and procedures. *See* International Bank for Reconstruction, World Bank Inspection Panel, *Resolution No. IBRD 2020–0004* (Sept. 8, 2020); International Dev. Association World Bank Inspection Panel, *Resolution No. IDA 2020–0003* (Sept. 8, 2020), https://www.inspectionpanel.org/sites/www.inspectionpanel.org/files/documents/InspectionPanelResolution.pdf (last visited Dec. 25, 2024) [hereinafter, together, 2020 Inspection Panel Resolutions].

3 It was particularly true then, and remains true today, that these policies would almost always be concerned with environmental and social issues. In those cases where the policies were not environmental or social, such as allegations of harm due to poor supervision or failure to properly disclose information, the alleged related impact of those failings was inevitably environmental or social harm.

Project, even post-Morse Berger, the policies were still not clear enough to define roles and responsibilities.[4] Thus, following the Panel's establishment, "Operational Directives" were redrafted to more clearly assign responsibilities, and "safeguard" training courses were launched to help teams follow Bank policies, particularly around EA, involuntary resettlement, and Indigenous Peoples. These efforts included a steady growth in environmental and social staff and redrafting the directives into "operational policies and Bank procedures" to better distinguish mandatory requirements from aspirational goals, and between Bank and Borrower responsibilities.[5]

Thus, the creation of the Panel with its investigatory role helped compel a much-needed management-supported process of organizing and clarifying the then-existing suite of environmental and social instruments. In addition to the influence of the Panel in the move toward improved environmental and social safeguards/standards, the Panel's investigation reports to the Board also had an impact on the application of those policies. One relatively recent example concerns incidents of Gender-Based Violence (GBV) uncovered in the Panel's investigation of the "Uganda Transport Sector Project – Additional Financing." The Panel's investigation led the Bank's Board and Bank Management to enhance existing Bank policies by putting in place provisions to protect against GBV and sexual exploitation, sexual abuse, and sexual harassment (SEAH).[6] Other institutions have followed the Bank and taken similar steps to address these important developments. Thereafter, the Panel captured some of the lessons learned from this investigation in its Emerging Lessons series.[7]

In addition, investigation into projects such as Uganda Transport flagged concern that some projects classified as risk level Category B (as opposed to Category A for "significant risk") may have underestimated the degree of risk posed by potential social impacts. Thus, along with the launch of the 2018 Environmental and Social Framework (ESF), the Bank introduced social risk management tools like the Good Practice Notes that address GBV and SEAH, security personnel, labor influx, sexual orientation and gender identity (SOGI),

4 World Bank Inspection Panel, *China: Western Poverty Reduction Project*; Request No. 99/3, (rec'd June 18, 1999), https://www.inspectionpanel.org/panel-cases/western-poverty-reduction-project.

5 For example, the Directive on Environmental Assessment became effective as the new Environmental Assessment Operational Policy (OP 4.01) and Bank Procedures (BP 4.01) (1999).

6 *See* World Bank, *Uganda Transport Sector Project – Additional Financing,* Project No. P121097, https://projects.worldbank.org/en/projects-operations/project-detail/P121097 (last visited Dec. 10, 2024).

7 World Bank Inspection Panel, *Responding to Project Gender Based Violence through Independent Accountability Mechanisms*, Emerging Lessons Series, no. 6 (2021).

race, and gender across the Bank portfolio, and contributed to changing the risk classification from a three-pronged listing of "A, B, C" to a more nuanced and comprehensive approach that includes contextual and social analysis. This risk-tiering approach requires placing into risk classification of four categories: High, Significant, Moderate and Low.

4 Development of a Management-Led Grievance Redress Service

The founding 1993 Panel Resolution recognized that eligibility should be conditioned on Management having an opportunity to help resolve a complaint before the Panel would have to exercise its competence. Thus, the Resolution included this condition:

> The Panel shall satisfy itself before a request for inspection is heard that the subject matter of the request has been dealt with by the Management of the Bank and Management has failed to demonstrate that it has followed, or is taking adequate steps to follow the Bank's policies and procedures. The Panel shall also satisfy itself that the alleged violation of the Bank's policies and procedures is of a serious character.[8]

In other words, eligibility was intended to be in line with an approach akin to exhaustion of administrative remedies, under which the Panel process should not gear up if Management can resolve the matter on its own. Unfortunately, in some instances, the Panel and Management had different views on whether Management had been given an opportunity to respond to a complaint. There were some complaints that were registered for which Management felt they had not been notified, though the Panel had indications of the opposite. Indeed, there were some instances where Management wanted to engage with requesters, only to find out that there were staff members who failed to respond to requesters, or, even more frustrating, requests that went to staff mailboxes who were no longer employed at a duty station.

Finally, in 2015 Management established the Grievance Redress Service (GRS). The establishment of the GRS also satisfied a recommendation of the Bank's Internal Evaluation Group following a review of the Bank's safeguard policies. While the GRS cannot impede a requester from attempting to go to the Panel with their request, it helps fulfill in a centralized and coordinated

8 World Bank Inspection Panel, *supra* note 2, at para. 14.

role the function that the Panel Resolution had long encouraged. Moreover, given the extensive number of matters it has been handling, GRS can be seen as allowing the Panel to conserve its resources for the more serious matters that deserve its attention. Indeed, the GRS notes it has processed an average of 302 cases annually over the last three years.[9] Moreover, because of the nature of its access to Project teams and Borrowers, the GRS may be able to help resolve some concerns more quickly. Further, other developing institutions appear to have seen the benefit of providing a service like the GRS and have developed similar offices.[10]

5 The Strengthening of Project-Level Grievance Mechanisms

Another positive evolution associated with the drive for accountability and the evolution of the Panel is the enhancement of project-level grievance mechanisms. Notably, the ESF mandates that all Bank-financed investment projects include grievance mechanisms. Today's embrace of grievance mechanisms can be contrasted with that encountered during one of the Panel's more difficult, early investigations. The Yacyretá hydroelectric project was a binational effort between Paraguay and Argentina that required large-scale resettlement of low-income workers and communities on both sides of the Parana River.[11] In recognition that this project would be controversial, the project design called for conflict resolution services to be provided by the Green Cross.

The Panel's investigation established that the Green Cross service was never made effective at the hydropower site. This failure may have been due to lack of a clear policy for a project-based grievance mechanism. Indeed, even when the relevant Bank policy on Environmental Assessment was updated in 1999, the requirement of a project-level grievance mechanism remained unclear.

---

9 World Bank Group, *Grievance Redress Service, https://www.worldbank.org/en/projects-operations/products-and-services/grievance-redress-service* (last visited Dec. 10, 2024).

10 *See, e.g.*, Inter-American Development Bank Group, *Management Grievance Mechanism*,) https://idbinvest.org/en/how-we-work/engagement-and-response-platform (last visited Dec. 10, 2024). The World Bank Group private sector arm, IFC, has also created a Stakeholder Grievance Response team to provide a similar complaint resolution service.

11 The World Bank Inspection Panel *Argentina, Paraguay: Yacyreta Hydroelectric Project*; Case No. 7, Request No. 96/2 (received Sep. 30, 1996).

Today, it is accepted that well-designed and functioning project-level grievance mechanisms[12] are essential where projects carry potential environmental and social risks for project-affected people. Almost thirty years after Yacyretá, every investment project designed under the ESF should have access to at least one grievance mechanism, process, or procedure. The Bank is required to help the Borrower ensure project design includes grievance mechanism(s) that can handle any relevant aspect of the ESF's ten environmental and social standards, as well as a separate one to address grievances pertaining to labor and working conditions and to address risks related to GBV/SEAH . The design must include elements that ensure the mechanism(s) is flexible, transparent, maintains a log and database, advertises its procedures, and has an appeals process.[13]

Moreover, because past projects often had non-functioning grievance mechanisms, Bank supervision reports for all Bank investment projects are now required to include information on whether the mechanism is up and running. The ESF also provided an opportunity to address the Panel's long-standing request that the Bank increase the visibility of the Panel to affected stakeholders. Thus, the ESF'S Environmental and Social Policy section on "Grievance Mechanism and Accountability" spells out how communities can be informed about access to the Panel and the GRS.[14]

During the ESF consultation process, some civil society voices expressed concern that moving from the "do no harm" approach associated with the safeguard policies to the ESF would lead to a weakening of environmental and social protection. Six years after the ESF became effective, there is probably enough data now to make such a comparison. The ESF's broader scope of environmental and social risks and impacts, its uniform and comprehensive drafting, and the added capacity the Bank brought on board to address the ESF demands, makes the new system superior at providing opportunities for improved development outcomes and accountability.

12 World Bank, *The World Bank Environmental and Social Framework* (*ESF*), para. 60–61 (2018) ("The Bank will require the Borrower to provides a grievance mechanism, process, or procedure to receive and facilitate resolution of concerns and grievances of project-affected parties arising in connection with the project, in particular about the Borrower's environmental and social performance.") (Informing that project-affected parties can also file complaints with the GRS and, "After bringing their concerns directly to the World Bank's attention and giving Bank Management a reasonable opportunity to respond, … may submit their complaint to the Inspection Panel.").

13 The World Bank, Environmental and Social Framework, approved Aug. 4, 2016, para. 26, 27, Annex 1: Grievance Mechanism. (2017).

14 *Id.* at para. 61.

6 Recognition of the Importance of the Rule of Law

Despite the Bank's internal advancements in accountability and environmental and social standards, accountability and rule of law at the country level often remains weak. In this light, it is worth recalling the 1992 Rio Conference on Environment and Development and the role foreseen for the international community, including the Bank, in helping fulfill the "Rio Principles."[15] Key to the theme of this essay and its perspective on accountability are Principle 10 on "effective access to judicial and administrative proceedings;" Principle 11 on States "enacting effective environmental legislation;" and Principle 13 on States developing "national law on liability and compensation."

Thirty years after Rio, to what extent have those principles been fulfilled? The World Justice Project's (WJP) Rule of Law Project recently noted declines for the fifth year in a row in 61% of countries surveyed as part of the WJP Rules of Law Project.[16] According to the Report: "[s]ince 2015, the rule of law has weakened in 64% of countries studied in the WJP Index and overall scores have declined by an average of 2.6% globally over this period. This deterioration has been driven by authoritarian tendencies, including weaker checks and balances, diminished accountability, and eroded protection of fundamental rights." These concerns are not necessarily due to the absence of environmental and social legislation, which in many cases was strengthened due to the influence of the Bank and other multilateral financial institutions, though there have been some countries, developed and developing, that have weakened EIA laws relevant to development finance. For the most part, these WJP concerns are about weakening independence of the judiciary and enforcement capacity. These sobering facts bring home that the development community faces a continued uphill climb in helping client countries offer access to justice.

7 Conclusion

Because of the aforementioned challenges in achieving the Rule of Law and because development finance, especially for large infrastructure or policy interventions, continues to pose complex environmental and societal challenges,

15 Rio Declaration on Environment and Development, U.N. Doc. A/CONF.151/26 (Vol. 1), 12 August 1992.

16 World Justice Project, *World Justice Project Rule of Law Index: Between 2022 and 2023, Rule of Law Once Again Weakened in a Majority of Countries*, https://worldjusticeproject.org/rule-of-law-index/insights (last visited Dec. 10, 2024).

the need will continue for effective accountability and grievance mechanisms at all levels of the development finance world. Further, this need remains prominent because civil society often feels hopeless to challenge government agencies responsible for implementing those financial institution-funded projects that cause harm. And even as multilateral financial institutions like the World Bank Group make progress in dealing with accountability issues,[17] it is important to address the number of issues affecting communities concerning projects financed by large sovereign or commercial institutions that do not require environmental and social standards such as the ESF or access to an IAM such as the Panel. While continuing to focus on improving MDB accountability systems, these institutions, their shareholders, and civil society should also shed light on and motivate closing of any gaps that pertain to the due diligence and monitoring required for all financial investments that pose environmental and social risks.

Bibliography

Inter-American Development Bank Group. "Management Grievance Mechanism." Washington DC: IDB Invest, December 10, 2024.

Morse, Brandford, and Thomas Berger. *Sardar Sarovar – Report of the Independent Review*, XI-XXY, 349–58 Ottawa: Resource Futures International, 1992.

United Nations Development Programme. *Rio Declaration on Environment and Development.* (1992).

World Bank. *Environmental and Social Framework.* Washington DC: World Bank, May 25, 2017. https://thedocs.worldbank.org/en/doc/837721522762050108-0290022018/original/ESFFramework.pdf.

World Bank, *Uganda Transport Sector Project – Additional Financing,* Project No. P121097. https://projects.worldbank.org/en/projects-operations/project-detail/P121097.

World Bank Group. *Grievance Redress Service. https://www.worldbank.org/en/projects-operations/products-and-services/grievance-redress-service* (*last visited* Dec., 10, 2024

World Bank Inspection Panel *Argentina, Paraguay: Yacyreta Hydroelectric Project*; Case No. 7. Request No. 96/2. Washington DC: World Bank, September 30, 1996. https://www.inspectionpanel.org/panel-cases/yacyreta-hydroelectric-project

---

17 *See, e.g.,* Int'l Finance Corp., *IFC's Approach to Responsible Exit* (Oct. 4, 2024), https://www.ifc.org/content/dam/ifc/doc/2024/ifc-approach-to-responsible-exit.pdf; Int'l Finance Corp., *IFC/MIGA Framework for Remedial Action* (Oct. 31, 2022), https://www.ifc.org/content/dam/ifc/doc/2023/ifc-miga-proposed-approach-remedial-action-en.pdf.

World Bank Inspection Panel. *China: Western Poverty Reduction Project*; Case No. 3, Request No. 99/3. Washington DC: World Bank, June 18, 1999. https://www.inspectionpanel.org/panel-cases/western-poverty-reduction-project.

World Bank Inspection Panel. *International Bank for Reconstruction and Development & International Development Association: Resolution No. IBRD 2020–0004 and Resolution No. IDA 2020–0003*. Washington DC: World Bank, September 8, 2020. https://www.inspectionpanel.org/sites/www.inspectionpanel.org/files/documents/InspectionPanelResolution.pdf.

World Bank Inspection Panel. *Responding to Project Gender Based Violence through Independent Accountability Mechanisms*. Emerging Lessons Series, no. 6. Washington DC: World Bank, 2021. https://www.inspectionpanel.org/sites/default/files/publications/Emerging%20Lessons%20Series%20No.%206-GBV.pdf.

World Justice Project. "World Justice Project Rule of Law Index: Between 2022 and 2023, Rule of Law Once Again Weakened in a Majority of Countries." Accessed Dec. 10, 2024. https://worldjusticeproject.org/rule-of-law-index/insights.

CHAPTER 8

Reflections on the Launch of the Inspection Panel and People-Centered Accountability

*David Hunter**

1 Introduction

When the World Bank established the Inspection Panel in 1993, it also established an important precedent in international law. It became the first international organization (IO) to enable individuals to complain about the organization's impacts on their lives without going through their governments. The implications of creating a people-centered mechanism that could trigger compliance investigations reverberated well beyond the World Bank. Over thirty development and finance institutions have since adopted independent accountability mechanisms (IAMs) that are accessible to affected people.[1] These people-centered mechanisms have challenged basic assumptions about how the public can engage and participate in the traditionally state-centered international order.

This chapter revisits the Panel origin story from the perspective of this people-centered norm. Given all of the attention and emulation, it is tempting to take the people-centered, public-facing characteristics of the Panel for granted. The question of who could submit requests to the Panel was the most innovative – and divisive – aspect of the Panel proposal, but it did not spark significant direct debate. The primary alternative to the Panel presented to the Board would not have been open to public complaints, nor would the results of the investigations been made public – but even the proponents of that option recognized that any mechanisms had to be accessible to the public. Because the US Congress had conditioned further Bank funding on the adoption of an inspection function that would respond to complaints from affected people,

* David Hunter is professor emeritus of international and comparative environmental law at the American University Washington College of Law and serves on the Boards of Directors of Accountability Counsel, the Center for International Environmental Law, and Friends of Green Advocates–Liberia.

1 *See* Reagan Ferris & David Hunter, Comprehensive Bibliography on Independent Accountability Mechanisms at International Development Finance Institutions (1993–2024) (Feb. 2025), available on the *Perspectives* website.

any mechanism would have to be accessible to public complaints. The debate would not be about *whether* to allow people to file claims, but rather about *how* to define and narrow the impact of that decision. Issues over standing, screening for eligibility, powers of the Panel, and transparency were all debated under the assumption that affected people were going to be able to file – the debate was about what limitations would effectively restrain that power.

This history of the Panel's formation is helpful to understanding many of the recurring tensions between the Panel and its critics, who continue to seek ways to limit access to, and the effectiveness of, the Panel. Bank Management and some countries have gone – and continue to go – to great lengths to control the impact of giving people a greater voice. The history also reminds us that the Panel's independence and power comes from its ability to receive requests from affected people. The most fundamental source of an independent accountability mechanism's independence comes from the fact that its work plan is initially, at least, decided by third-party complaints from outside the institution – what projects it looks at, what issues it raises, which borrowers' projects become the center of Board oversight – are at least partly outside of the institution's control. Reflecting on this past can ground us in what makes the Panel so innovative, and potentially powerful now and into the future.

This chapter reflects my active participation in advocating for accountability at international financial institutions (IFIs) while I was at the Center for International Environmental Law (CIEL). CIEL was launched in 1989 to use international law to protect the global environment. I joined CIEL in 1991, having just returned from a year working with nascent environmental organizations in then-Czecho-Slovakia. My experience in post-Soviet societies hardened my view that the direct participation and advocacy of locally affected people was necessary for protecting the environment. The state could not be trusted with protecting the environment, and this seemed equally true for the state-centered orientation of international law and governance. CIEL shared the same philosophy, as it explicitly sought to expand opportunities for the public to participate directly in the international order, including in international organizations that were actively harming the environment. The creation of a people-centered accountability mechanism at the World Bank aligned perfectly with CIEL's mission.

By the time I started to work on the World Bank, the basis of civil society's considerable influence had already been set. That strategy combined bringing the voices of affected people to Washington to speak with the highest decision makers at the World Bank, as well as the US government and Congress.[23] I barely understood the political strategy when Lori Udall asked me to co-author a draft "resolution" creating a people-centered Independent Appeals Commission at the World Bank – a classic case of being in the right place at the right time. Key members of Congress essentially endorsed our proposal, which became the outline of the US position for a three-member, people-centered investigation mechanism and, ultimately, for the Panel itself.

2 The Creation of the Inspection Panel

The Inspection Panel would not exist in its current form had the US Congress not made an independent mechanism a condition of future funding for the Bank.[4] But the Inspection Panel was also a product of more general trends then at play around development finance generally, and the World Bank more specifically. Consensus was emerging inside and outside the Bank that many of the Bank's projects were not meeting the current needs of the world's poor, or were visiting too much harm on one set of poor communities to benefit others. The Bank was being pushed to approach development differently and, in particular, to take on new roles and responsibilities. The Inspection Panel would be among the highest-profile responses to this shifting environment.

---

2 The US Congress threatened that it would hold up IDA-10 funding to the Bank (and redirect that funding to more "democratic" institutions), if the Bank did not take two major reforms: (1) substantially increase transparency through a complete revision of the Bank's access to information policy and (2) create an independent mechanism to investigate claims brought by local communities that they were unreasonably harmed by Bank-financed projects. See *infra* text accompanying notes 14–16.

3 For an excellent account of the campaigning that led to the Inspection Panel, see Lori Udall, *The World Bank and Public Accountability: Has Anything Changed*, in JONATHAN A. FOX & L. DAVID BROWN EDS., THE STRUGGLE FOR ACCOUNTABILITY: THE WORLD BANK, NGOS, AND GRASSROOTS MOVEMENTS, 391–403 (1998); The World Bank General Counsel Ibrahim Shihata's account from the World Bank's perspective is also excellent and largely consistent with the Udall account. *See* IBRAHIM F. S. SHIHATA, THE WORLD BANK INSPECTION PANEL: IN PRACTICE, 1 – 27 (2d ed. 2000).

4 The role of the US Congress in catalyzing the creation of the Panel has been well documented. *See* Lori Udall, *supra* note 2, at 401–03; SUSAN PARK, THE GOOD HEGEMON: US POWER, ACCOUNTABILITY AS JUSTICE, AND THE MULTILATERAL DEVELOPMENT BANKS (2022).

2.1 *The Conceptual Ferment: Sustainability, Democratization, and Globalization*

Established in 1993, the Panel reflected three major political or social trends that were challenging the status quo in international governance. First, as reflected in the 1992 Earth Summit, the world was shifting at least rhetorically to embrace the goal of sustainable development. No matter the term's considerable ambiguity, *sustainable* development at a minimum had to be different from development as it was practiced in the past. Core to this difference was the integration of environmental and social impacts and the opinions of locally affected people into development decisions.[5] Second, the world was embracing democracy and associated values, as seen in Post-Soviet Central and Eastern Europe and virtually every other region in the World. Principle 10 of the *Rio Declaration* required countries to democratize national governance through expanding rights to information, public participation, and access to judicial review.[6] Although Principle 10 was clearly focused on national governance, the increasingly global call by CSOs for democratization also extended to international institutions and their policies.

For decades, developing country governments had called for democratizing international institutions – but their focus was primarily on increasing their own voice and vote in IFIs and other institutions.[7] In the context of sustainable development, however, democratizing international institutions required international institutions to be more transparent and responsive to affected people. For Part II (borrower) governments, the empowerment of their citizens to raise claims against their projects potentially infringed on their sovereign right to development. With Part I (lender) countries pushing IAMs to highlight the voices of project-affected people, the IAMs tended to reduce the influence of the Part II governments, both over their citizens and over the Part I countries. Moreover, because conditions on Bank lending only applied

5 *See, e.g.*, UNCED Declaration on Environment and Development, Principle 4 (1992) ("In order to achieve sustainable development, environmental protection shall constitute an integral part of the development process and cannot be considered in isolation from it.").

6 *Id.* at Principle 10 ("Environmental issues are best handled with participation of all concerned citizens, at the relevant level. At the national level, each individual shall have appropriate access to information concerning the environment that is held by public authorities, including information on hazardous materials and activities in their communities, and the opportunity to participate in decision-making processes. States shall facilitate and encourage public awareness and participation by making information widely available. Effective access to judicial and administrative proceedings, including redress and remedy, shall be provided.").

7 In the World Bank context, countries are divided into Part I countries (lenders) and Part II countries (borrowers).

to borrowing countries, the IAMs were, in their view, an inappropriate vehicle for promoting a global norm of citizen empowerment as part of the global commitment to sustainable development. Where would similar citizen participation be required in Part I countries? This is partly why the Part II countries insist that the Panel investigate only the Bank's non-compliance.

Third, with the fall of the Soviet Union in 1991, the world could, for the first time, conceive of a global economy that was not dominated by East-West politics. The response was the creation of the World Trade Organization (WTO) and the expansion of bilateral and multilateral investment agreements. The resulting age of economic globalization was embraced as a vehicle for spreading more equitable and democratic development. But just as importantly, globalization included global socialization, which included the emergence of global environmental networks and global advocacy campaigns, like the ones discussed below regarding the Narmada projects and the IDA-10 reforms.[8]

The confluence of these trends put new pressure on IFIs to reform. Not only were they expected to deliver higher-quality, more sustainable projects, but they were also expected to increase their engagement with non-state actors in a new governance model that elevated people as direct constituents.

2.2 *Civil Society's Expanding Engagement with the Bank*

As the economy globalized, so too did the ambitions of environmental and development advocacy CSOs. High-profile anti-globalization protests in Cancun, Prague, and Seattle met calls for economic globalization with calls for global equity and justice, and protection of the global environment. These protests and associated global campaigns were successful in stopping the Multilateral Agreement on Investment and further expansion of the WTO framework. The *50 Years is Enough* campaign – a global campaign targeting the World Bank – documented the massive impacts of project after project financed by the World Bank, including thousands of people being forced from their lands by the massive Sardar Sarovar dam and associated drainage projects on the Narmada River; thousands more being removed from their homes and land in Indonesia's Transmigration Project; thousands of acres of Amazonian forest burning due to the Polonoroeste Project; and hundreds of urban poor resettled to make way for a luxury hotel complex so that Thailand could host the World Bank's own annual meetings.[9]

---

8 *See supra* text accompanying notes 10–17.

9 For a discussion of various controversial projects and the reform campaigns that emerged around them, see THE STRUGGLE FOR ACCOUNTABILITY: THE WORLD BANK, NGOS, AND GRASSROOTS MOVEMENTS (Jonathan A. Fox & L. David Brown eds., 1998); CATHERINE

Initial efforts to engage the Bank directly in discussions about the massive impacts of their projects generally yielded little substantive response from senior Bank Management or the Board of Directors. The IFIs did not see the public as their constituents and operated primarily through country representatives at the Board of Executive Directors. That began to change in the latter part of the 1980s as a growing number of US and European environmental groups started to engage the Bank as a way of influencing development in the Global South. As part of that effort, four US environmental groups hired a leading peace organizer, Chad Dobson, to run a new coordinating organization, the Bank Information Center (BIC). BIC's name reflected its strategic theory of change – get information about Bank-financed projects into the hands of national and local organizations who could then engage with their own governments in trying to shape their own development paths. If their efforts were blocked at home, BIC would help them engage with Bank Management as well as the Executive Directors and the US government. The Bank was no longer able to hide behind its member states – it was being seen as an independent actor with its own responsibilities towards a widening group of constituents.

Emblematic of this increasing CSO engagement was the campaign and debate around the Sardar Sarovar projects in India's Narmada Valley.[10] The Bank approved a $450 million loan in 1985 for the project, which was planned to displace 150,000 people, among other impacts. The project was poorly managed from the outset, with thousands of villagers given little notice or information about their pending displacement. A strong Indian grassroots movement, the Narmada Bachao Andolan (NBA) emerged to resist the project. The NBA garnered the attention and support of an international network of World Bank reformers, including Urgewald in Germany and the Environmental Defense Fund (EDF) in the United States. Lori Udall of EDF arranged for Medha Paktar, a leader of the NBA, to testify before the US Congress about the harms and mismanagement occurring in the Narmada Valley. Medha asked the US Congress to defund the Bank in solidarity with the villagers soon to be displaced. Medha's powerful testimony had an almost immediate impact. Not only did the US government start to raise questions, Japanese and Dutch officials also

---

Caufield, Masters of Illusion: The World Bank and the Poverty Of Nations (1997); Bruce Rich, Mortgaging the Earth: The World Bank, Environmental Impoverishment, and the Crisis of Development (1994); Raymond F. Mikesell & Larry Williams eds., International Banks and the Environment: From Growth to Sustainability: an Unfinished Agenda (1992). For criticism of development institutions more generally, see Graham Hancock, Lords of Poverty: The Power, Prestige, and Corruption of the International aid Business (1989).

10 For a full discussion of the Narmada campaign, see Udall, *supra* note 3, at 394–95.

saw the testimony and their governments would raise concerns with the Bank's Board of Directors. Japan would pull its bilateral funding for Narmada. Pressure grew for the World Bank to authorize an independent "assessment" of the Sardar Sarovar projects, with a particular focus on resettlement and environmental impacts "with reference to existing Bank operational directives and guidelines."[11]

Ultimately, the Bank established a three-person commission headed by Bradford Morse, the former Director of the UN Development Programme. After an intense investigation, the so-called Morse Commission issued unequivocal findings that the Bank was responsible for significant failures and impacts of the Project. In their letter conveying the report, the Morse Commission stated:

> We think the Sardar Sarovar Projects as they stand are flawed, that resettlement and rehabilitation of all those displaced by the Projects is not possible under prevailing circumstances, and that the environmental impacts of the Projects have not been properly considered or adequately addressed. Moreover, we believe that the Bank shares responsibility with the borrower for the situation that has developed.[12]

The body of the report:

> made findings that reveal a failure to incorporate Bank policies into the 1985 credit and loan agreements and subsequent failure to require adherence to enforceable provisions of these agreements. Much of what has gone wrong with Sardar Sarovar Projects is the result of such failures over a range of resettlement and rehabilitation and environmental matters.

The report further concluded that:

> [t]here should be a review of Bank procedures to ensure that the full reach of the Bank's policies is being implemented. The Bank should establish whether the problems we have found in the case of Sardar Sarovar are at issue in other projects in India and elsewhere. Our findings on this project may well indicate a need on the part of the Bank to strengthen quality control.[13]

---

11 Shihata, *supra* note 3, at 6 (citing the terms of reference for the Morse Commission).

12 Letter from Bradford Morse (Chairman) and Thomas R. Berger (Deputy Chairman) to Lewis T. Preston (President, The World Bank) (June 18, 1992).

13 Bradford Morse & Thomas Berger, Sardar Sarovar: The Report of the Independent Review (1992). Independent Review of the Sardar Sarovar Projects.

The Morse Commission Report made three important contributions to the creation of the Panel. First, its findings confirmed CSO criticisms that the Bank and borrowers were not complying with the environmental and social safeguard policy framework that the Board of Directors had passed. Second, the Report highlighted areas where the Bank Management had not provided complete information to the Board. This helped to convince the Board they needed an independent source of information for what was happening on the ground, at least for controversial projects. The Board also believed it would be better to have a permanent mechanism rather than handle controversial cases with ad-hoc commissions. Their view was that the Morse Commission was more expensive, attracted more attention, took longer, and was less controllable than would be the case if they created a permanent mechanism. Third, the Morse Commission's structure, terms of reference and operation served as proof-of-concept for the CSO's proposed "Independent Appeals Commission" that would ultimately serve as the blueprint for the Inspection Panel.

Many of the environmental and social concerns raised by CSOs, and confirmed by the Morse Commission, were further corroborated by the Bank's own internal findings on project quality. Shortly after the release of the Morse Commission Report, an internal review of the Bank's loan portfolio (known as the Wapenhans Report) found that the Bank was not fully enforcing 78 percent of financial conditions in the loan agreements. Using the Bank's own criteria, the reviewers discovered that 37.5 percent of recently evaluated projects were unsatisfactory, up from 15 percent in 1981. The report linked the decline in project quality to a "pervasive" "culture of approval" for loans, whereby Bank staff members perceive the appraisal process as merely a "marketing device for securing loan approval" and the pressure to lend overwhelmed all other considerations. For many inside and outside the Bank, this confirmed the need for a greater emphasis on environmental and social safeguard policies and stronger engagement with, and accountability to, affected communities. Once the Wapenhans Report was leaked to the public, the Bank had serious difficulty defending the status quo against CSO calls for reforms to ensure project quality. Reforms were inevitable; the only question was – which reforms?

The CSOs – or more precisely the US Congress – provided at least part of the answer to which reforms were necessary. Taking their lead from BIC, EDF, and other US-based CSOs, the US Congress agreed to withhold funding to the Bank (and redirect that funding to more "democratic" institutions) if the Bank did not adopt two major reforms: (1) substantially increase transparency through a complete revision of the Bank's access to information policy; and (2) create a citizen's appeal panel to give affected people access to an independent mechanism to investigate their complaints.[14]

2.3 *The Proposal for a People-Centered Mechanism*

In May of 1993, Lori Udall and I drafted proposed terms of reference for an Independent Appeals Commission (IAC) and attached it to Lori's testimony before the House Subcommittee on International Development, Trade, Finance and Monetary Policy, chaired by Congressman Barney Frank. That draft included certain broad principles to ensure the mechanism was fair and credible. These included:

- The IAC had to be permanent and operationally independent from the Bank's project management team;
- The IAC must be empowered to receive and investigate public complaints;
- The IAC must be granted access to all relevant documents and personnel in carrying out an investigation;
- The IAC findings and recommendations should be implemented by Bank operational staff, unless reversed by two-thirds of the Executive Directors; and
- The IAC must be transparent. All findings, recommendations, and underlying documents must be made available to the Executive Directors, Bank Management, the complainant, and the public simultaneously.[15]

Authorization for the $3.7 billion US contribution to IDA-10 had to go through Congressman Frank's Sub-Committee, but he let it be known that the money was not moving without the Bank committing to the reforms. The US Treasury understood at this point that an independent inspection panel generally consistent with the above principles would be necessary for IDA-10 support, and this message was carried to the Bank. As the Bank's General Counsel and author of the Panel resolutions, Ibrahim Shihata, wrote shortly after the Panel's creation:

> the discussion of [the IAC] gave a clear indication of an emerging trend in the US Congress to favor strongly the establishment of a Commission or

14 Every three years the International Development Association (IDA), the part of the World Bank Group that gives no-interest loans to the poorest countries, seeks "replenishment" from the donor countries. In 1993, Congress was being asked to authorize expenditures for the US portion of the Tenth Replenishment (or IDA-10). An international coalition of CSOs formed the "IDA-10" campaign and asked that funding be shifted to other development organizations if the Bank did not reform.

15 Peter Bossherd, David Hunter & Lori Udall, *Creating an Independent Appeals Commission at the World Bank* 5 (Aug. 26, 1993).

> Panel of inspectors in the World Bank and in other international financial institutions. This obviously influenced the position of the U.S. Administration in the Banks' Board discussions.[16]

He was more to the point some years later in an interview, when asked about the forces behind the Panel's creation: the US Congress had said "No Panel, no replenishment."[17] Such was the choice facing the Bank's Board of Executive Directors in 1993.

2.4 *The "Legislative History" of the Panel*

One of the unique, and frankly somewhat unhelpful, features of IFI policy-making is that the Executive Directors representing member states only rarely negotiate amongst themselves. The Board tries to avoid acting politically; instead it relies heavily on the technical analysis and recommendations provided by Management. Rather than negotiating to reach consensus, the IFI's Board typically comments on and discusses proposed policy frameworks, and then sends the draft policy back to Management for revisions. Management makes what revisions it believes will be responsive to the needs of the various Board constituencies, and then submits a revised draft, hoping to have responded to the Board views. Then the process repeats itself. In most instances, Board members do not formally negotiate face-to-face, nor does the Board typically solicit any public input.

The process was no different for the resolutions creating the Panel. The development of the Panel resolution was the result of a series of meetings and written submissions between Executive Directors, representing their government constituencies and the technical experts of the Bank staff. Despite the substantial role of CSOs in conceiving of the Inspection Panel and in setting the political agenda for its adoption, neither the Board nor Management ever invited CSOs to a collective briefing or formally solicited our input. This left CSOs to conduct their own form of "shuttle diplomacy." We submitted detailed comments, including mark-ups of specific text to each draft emanating from the Bank, and then met separately with those Executive Director offices that would agree to meet with us.[18]

---

16 SHIHATA, *supra* note 3, at 21.

17 The World Bank Group, *Transcript of Interview with Ibrahim F.I. Shihata, May 23 & 24, 2000*, 33 (May 2000) [hereinafter WB Oral History: Interview with Ibrahim Shihata].

18 *See* Lori Udall, et al., *Memorandum to the Clinton Administration regarding Comments on World Bank Draft Paper on "Functions and Operations of an Inspection Function* (August 23, 1993) (providing comments on behalf of EDF, Friends of the Earth (FoE), National Wildlife Federation (NWF), the Bank Information Center (BIC), the Sierra Club, and CIEL

At the same time, Professor Daniel Bradlow, then at the American University Washington College of Law, was promoting an ombudsman that would report to the Board, have powers to investigate, and report annually to the public.[19] Importantly, Bradlow's proposed ombudsman would also be people-centered and authorized to review complaints from affected people. Bradlow originally presented the proposal in testimony to the Canadian Parliament, which forwarded it to the Canadian Executive Director who also happened to be the Dean of the Board. He, in turn, invited Bradlow to present the proposal to all the Executive Directors at a Board seminar. The ombudsman proposal was favored by some Bank staff and some governments, in part because it clearly limited the ombudsman's role to investigating only the Bank's conduct. In the end, US support for a Panel structure left little political opportunity for the ombudsman model to prevail at the Board. Nonetheless, Bradlow's proposal was critical in building support for some accountability reform generally, and lent a scholar's credibility specifically to the idea of a people-centered mechanism.

Hoping to forge a better compromise between the aggressive US position and a 'no action' alternative, four Executive Directors – Eveline Herfkins (Netherlands), Franz Fischer (Germany), Nicolás Flaño (Chile), and Aris Othman (Malaysia) – proposed an inspection function on February 10, 1993. They proposed an in-house evaluation unit to investigate environmental and social issues relating to ongoing projects that would be similar to other independent, internal audit functions, and would presumably be housed inside the Bank's Operations Evaluation Group. The proposed unit, as initially presented, would have responded to complaints from borrowers or Executive Directors, but not from affected parties. Later, in an effort to respond to US demands, the proponents of this option would add the possibility of taking claims from affected parties. The proposal garnered significant support from both Part I and Part II countries throughout the Board's consideration of the Panel.[20]

Bank Management, for its part, favored the less-intrusive options of either an ombudsman or an internal evaluations unit, but its paramount concern was securing IDA-10 funding. That meant meeting the expectations of the US

---

on the Bank's August 6, 1993 paper); Bossherd, et al, *supra* note 15 (including detailed comments on the Bank's August 6, 1993 proposal); Lori Udall, et al., *Memorandum to the Clinton Administration regarding Comments on the World Bank's Draft Resolution for Creating an Independent Inspection Panel* (Sept. 20, 2024) (providing comments on behalf of EDF, FoE, CIEL, and BIC on the Bank's September 10 paper and draft resolution).

19 Daniel D. Bradlow, The Cases for a World Bank Ombudsman, Testimony submitted to the Subcommittee on International Development, Finance, Trade and Monetary Policy of the Bank Finance and Urban Affairs Comm., U.S. House of Rep. (May 1993).

20 *See* SHIHATA, *supra* note 3, at 17–18.

Congress. With this in mind, the Bank released a working paper to the Board on June 10, 1993, entitled *Operations Inspection in the Bank: Issues and Options*. The working paper compared the internal evaluations unit proposed by the four directors (named Option A) and an Option B that more closely tracked the US call for an independent inspection panel accessible by project-affected people. Not surprisingly given the politics, Bank Management's paper concluded that the "most effective arrangement would be the establishment of an independent, in-house Inspection Panel."[21]

The Board met to discuss the options paper on July 9, 1993, in the first of three meetings leading up to the September approval of the Panel. The transcripts of those discussions, which were not released until 2014, revealed divisions and compromises that remain today.[22] Most of the Board members that spoke on July 9 supported either doing nothing or the in-house evaluation unit (Option A). Only a few Board members explicitly supported Option B, including the US representative and the Swiss Executive Director. The US intervention was relatively detailed and aimed at addressing some of the specific concerns that other members had raised, including an emphasis on the need to preserve the Board's role as the Bank's top decision-maker.

The July 9 discussion moved the debate beyond *whether* an inspection function would be established, to *what* the function would do and *how* it would operate. It also helped to clarify some of the major concerns going forward. The Executive Directors and Management remained concerned that the proposed panel would interfere with the Board and Management's roles and sought ways to make the panel operate within the current structures of the Board and Management. The Board was also concerned that an autonomous panel might generate its own demand, escalating the costs of the panel and effectively interfering with the Bank's business operations. Interestingly, many countries raised questions about allowing a group of Executive Directors to file a complaint with the panel. They criticized that provision as allowing a small minority of countries to investigate another, potentially creating substantial conflict at the Board.

Although no consensus was actually evident at the Board on July 9, and indeed, several Executive Directors voiced clear objections to any inspection

---

21 *Operations Inspection in the Bank: Issues and Options,* para. 3 (June 10, 1993).

22 *See* International Bank for Reconstruction and Development & International Development Ass'n, *Transcript of Meeting of the Executive Directors, Friday, July 9, 1993* (on Agenda Item 2; "Operations Inspection in the Bank: Issues and Options" [hereinafter Transcript of July 9, 1993 WB Board Meeting].

function at all, Ernest Stern, the Senior Vice President of Operations who presided over the July 9 meeting, directed the staff, to develop a proposal in light of the discussion and any written submissions of the Directors. Given the Bank's focus on securing IDA-10, it was no real surprise when the Bank's next paper, entitled *Functions and Operations of an Inspection Function,* included a draft resolution prepared by Shihata that endorsed a three-member panel accessible by external claimants. It was released to the Board on August 6, 1993 by the President, and circulated to the full Board for subsequent discussions. In the August 27 discussion, the German Executive Director, Franz Fischer, still favored his original proposal of an internal evaluation unit, but expressed the task facing the Board as the following:

> I think our concept in February was leaner and simpler. The problem we have now, Mr. Chairman, is that we are trying to reconcile things which are very difficult to reconcile; a panel with the right to complaint for outsiders, and at the same time as an instrument for oversight by the Board. I mean, this is difficult to reconcile, and it takes all our energies and our innovativeness to reconcile it to some degree.[23]

Shihata saw his role in drafting the resolution the same way: he was to develop a compromise between the internal investigations unit proposed by the four directors and the external investigation panel championed by the United States – a "proposal that could be sustained in between the two proposals; a unit independent from Management, yet not too detached from the Bank."[24]

Shihata's approach to this task had been suggested at the July 9 Board discussion. The chairperson asked Shihata to address the risks that an externally-driven inspection unit would result in "the intrusion of an outsider or the inspection unit itself ... in the responsibilities of the Board or the management." Shihata assured the Board that the:

> risks can be substantially reduced through precise requirements related to eligibility of the complainant who can make a complaint, screening mechanism, how the complaints will be processed, the composition

23 *See* International Bank for Reconstruction and Development & International Development Ass'n, *Transcript of Meeting of the Executive Directors in a Committee of the Whole, Friday, August 27, 2019*, 84 (Aug. 27, 2019) [hereinafter Transcript of Aug. 27, 1993 WB Board Meeting].

24 WB Oral History: Interview with Ibrahim Shihata, *supra* note 17, at page 32–33.

> and the personality of the inspectors, what type of persons, how they are chosen, et cetera, and the procedures. … So through precise and tight requirements, perhaps these risks can be substantially reduced.[25]

Seen in this light, the basic compromise in Shihata's draft resolution becomes clear. The price for allowing a people-centered, public-facing mechanism was to constrain the mechanism through tight, procedural restrictions and limited authority. Ultimately, this trade-off is the root of the legalistic and conflictual relationship between the Panel and Management.

From the CSO perspective, the tight, legalistic approach of the resolutions made it difficult for complainants to access the Panel without legal support, but the rules also gave some protection and procedural predictability to the complainants. Tight procedures also offered claimants some protection if the Panel members became captured by Bank Management or otherwise abused their discretion. CSOs engaged on the various draft submissions advising Congress and the US government on what legal restrictions were too cumbersome for the Panel's effectiveness. Within the give-and-take of the process, CSOs were guided by the principles that the solution should be independent, transparent, and people-centered. From those principles, some priorities emerged as non-negotiable: the Panel had to be accessible to affected people, it could not report to Management, Panel members had to be prohibited from ever working for the Bank again, and the Panel had to have ultimate control over releasing their reports to the public.

3 What Did the Board Create?

There are probably as many different perspectives on what the primary goal of the Panel was meant to be, as there are stakeholders. Bank President Lewis Preston did not mention redress or remedy explicitly when describing the Panel to staff two days after the Resolution passed. Preston described the Panel mandate as: "to look into claims that the Bank may have failed to adhere to its operational policies and procedures in the design, appraisal and/or implementation of its operations, and to carry out a full inspection in those cases, where the Board decides that an investigation is needed."[26]

---

25 Transcript of July 9, 1993 WB Board Meeting, *supra* note 22, at pages 125–27.

26 Memo from Lewis T. Preston, President, The World Bank, to All Staff (Sept. 24, 1993) (announcing the Inspection Panel).

He went on to emphasize that the Panel:

> has been designed to complement the responsibilities and functions of the existing systems for quality control in project preparation and implementation. … [T]he Panel will provide a safety net for use in exceptional circumstances where, because our own policies and procedures have not been followed, there have been or could be adverse consequences for people in developing countries. Such circumstances are rare. But we must ensure that, if they arise, we have in place an objective and efficient means of dealing with them.[27]

Preston assured staff the Panel was not intended to "second guess" staff or to lower the institution's appetite for risk, but merely to ensure the institution followed its own policies and procedures. He also noted that establishing the Panel was "part of a series of changes that we have made recently to improve the development impact of the operations we help finance and to enhance the transparency and outside understanding of our work by increasing public access to Bank information."[28]

As reflected in the "legislative history" of the Panel, the governments were most concerned with ensuring that any accountability mechanism did not disrupt the Bank's normal operations (i.e., flow of loans) nor disrupt the traditional roles and responsibilities of the Bank staff, Management, and executive directors. The country's representative to the Bank acted as the formal intermediary between the Bank and the Member State; all concerns with the Bank were expected to come through their Executive Directors' office. The borrowing countries resisted the people-centered approach because it had the potential to give communities that were critical of their government a voice at the highest levels of the Bank. Not only did this challenge a government's monopoly over the channel of communications between the country and the Bank, but it politicized their relationship with the Bank in ways that could reverberate politically back home.

Shihata's approach of using the rules to limit the Panel's autonomy and authority meant there were plenty of areas for disagreement. Primary disagreements during debate over the Panel resolution could be grouped around the following issues: (1) eligibility or the ease of access to the Panel; (2) the aspects of structural and functional independence of the Panel; and (3) the Panel's

27 *Id.*
28 *Id.*

authorities and expected outcomes of the Panel process. To some extent the same battle lines persist today.

(1) *Accessibility and the Eligibility Criteria.* The major issue of accessibility was whether affected people could access the mechanism at all. Because this was an inherent part of the Congressional conditions, that initial question was settled, and was a huge victory for CSOs. Moreover, CSOs argued that access to the Panel was a right of affected people to be heard in decisions that affected their lives. Efforts to restrict access only to claimants that reflected mainstream views or were part of an association or organized group were rejected. The Bank did not want any one person to be granted such a right, so the final rule required a "group of any two or more people" that could be "an organization, association, society or *grouping* of individuals." This essentially eliminated the Bank's effort to create a barrier for standing, as the requirement was quickly interpreted to mean any two people. Similarly, in an effort to block international CSOs' direct access to the Panel, the claimants had to be "in the country where the project is located." Although the Bank thought this was a severe blow to the international CSOs, they never wanted the ability to file a claim directly, but were more focused on securing the rights of affected people to be heard themselves. Even the efforts to limit international CSOs' representation of affected people misunderstood the CSO approach. The Bank could not prevent them from providing advice to the claimants, and our visible presence on claims was used by the Bank to delegitimize the claimants anyways. In the end, the Bank imposed a few technical restrictions on eligibility that did not appear to present a significant barrier to most legitimate complaints. That assumed, of course, that the Panel would be interpreting the criteria itself – an assumption that has since been frequently tested.

(2) *Structural independence.* The Board, the Management and the CSOs were all concerned about the structural independence of the Panel – although with decidedly different goals. The Board and Management both feared the Panel members would go rogue, with little commitment to the Bank's mission. Management concerns of Board over-reach also manifested themselves in this discussion; Management would have preferred for the Panel to report solely to the President – not the Board. The CSOs were more concerned that the Panel would be captured by the Management than by the Board. The general compromise was that the President would nominate and the Board would approve the Panel members; the Panel would report to the Board; and a number of conditions would be placed on Panel members to make it more likely that they would operate independently. Most critically, this included the two-year period between any Bank employment and Panel service and the requirement that Panel members are prohibited from working at the Bank after serving as

a Panel member.[29] Overall, except for the selection process that had no transparency and no external participation, CSOs were satisfied with the markers for independence.

(3) *The Panel's Powers.* The area where the most serious constraints were adopted was with respect to the powers of the Panel. The primary concerns, voiced by multiple Board members, was that the Panel would not usurp the Board's role as the key decision maker of the Bank, and that the Panel not infringe on the sovereignty of the borrowing countries. The Board was almost unanimous that any Panel that was open to third-party claims could not also make decisions that would be binding on the Board. The ultimate power to take action regarding any project had to remain with the Board. CSO's had proposed (unsuccessfully) that a Panel decision should be considered binding unless two-thirds of the Board votes to overturn it. For the most part, the Board viewed the Panel primarily as a tool for it to monitor Management's activities, and it saw no particular reason to give the Panel any powers that it could otherwise retain for itself. Thus, the Panel could not unilaterally make changes in projects, suspend projects, discipline staff, or require Management to take any action. Recognizing how hard it would be to ignore a Panel recommendation, the Panel was limited to fact-finding.

A further constraint was that the borrowing countries would not accept the Bank taking on an enforcement role vis-à-vis a borrowing country's implementation of the project. Developing countries had long opposed the adoption of any binding international environmental standards that would interfere with their sovereign rights to pursue development as they chose – and this was particularly true at the Bank, where those standards only ever applied to developing countries. Any investigations would have to be restricted to reviewing Bank actions. To soften the practical impact of this limitation, CSOs obtained a clear statement that the Panel could look into the Bank's failure to supervise implementation of the project – which, in the CSO view, *de facto* required investigating the project's implementation.

The limitations on the Panel's power were significant, but CSOs believed that if the Panel's decisions were not going to be binding, then most decisions would have to be taken up to the Board anyway. Relying on the Panel to win conflicts with Management through better technical arguments was necessary

29 International Bank for Reconstruction and Development & International Development Ass'n, Resolution, Panel Resolution, at paras 2–10 (The CSOs argued for transparency in the selection process, including a period of time where Panel nominees could be vetted publicly.).

but it was unlikely to be sufficient. The Panel had to be seen as one tactic in a broader political strategy.

In the end, the Panel resolution reflected many compromises, but none of them fundamentally undermined the basic goals CSOs had set out to achieve. The Panel would provide a formal process whereby locally affected people could get their concerns addressed by an independent body that reported publicly and to the top level of the Bank. The Panel's entire workplan would be driven by locally affected people who would determine at least initially what projects the Panel investigated, what issues it addressed, and which projects in which member states would become the center of Board attention.

By focusing on the impacts of particular cases, locally affected people could set the Board's agenda as well, with the hope of shifting the Board toward taking local impacts more into account – to drive development priorities from the bottom up. From the Part II governments' perspective, however, the Panel was providing dissenting voices with a high-profile avenue to complain about their country's official development policy without going through the traditional intermediaries – their representatives in the Executive Directors' offices. This citizen empowerment was being pushed by Part I countries in the name of achieving sustainable development, but in a context that limited the condition only to Part II countries. The Panel was thus seen as yet one more way wealthier countries interfered with poorer countries' sovereign right to control their own development path. In the face of those somewhat legitimate complaints, framing the Panel explicitly as part of the Bank's (or borrowers') human rights obligations only invited deeper opposition. The Panel could be accepted as a way to improve the Bank's performance and development impact – but not as a back-door way to enable people to enforce their human rights exclusively in poorer countries. CSOs, by contrast, saw the Panel (and the safeguards) as providing a binding, rights-based approach, but they chose not to highlight this view – at least until the Panel was established.

Given the controversial nature of the Panel, CSOs geared up to defend what were expected to be significant challenges from Management and some Board members to gain greater control over the new Panel.[30] And what better place to start than with the appointment of the first Panel members?

30 The Washington-based CSOs who were most often engaged with the early years of the Panel, included Dana Clark and me at CIEL, Chad Dobson and Kay Treakle at BIC, Lori Udall at EDF, and Andrea Durbin at Friends of the Earth. Even CSOs' modest request that the name of any nominee be made public three weeks before the Executive Directors vote on their nomination has not been accepted. *See* David Hunter & Lori Udall, *Proposed Rules for the WBIP, June 17, 1994, App. IV to Statement of Lori Udall*, Subcomm. On Int'l Dev.

4 The First Five Years: Making It Work

4.1 *The Sheep in Wolf's Clothing: Mr. Broder*

After being critical to the limitations of the panel, CSOs were essentially locked out of the selection process for the Panel members. The Bank solicited names from the Member States, and CSOs gave names to our Board allies, but never knew for certain that those names were being seriously considered. The selection of the Panel members remained opaque right up until they were named. CSOs were encouraged by the selection of Alvaro Umana, the former Environment Minister of Costa Rica, who had conducted a highly regarded evaluation of the Global Environment Facility. Richard Bissell's background was similarly encouraging and came with strong US assurances.

When Ernst Gunther Broder was named the first Chairperson, however, I thought the Board had just buried the Panel. As the former President of the European Investment Bank, nothing in Mr. Broder's background suggested he had any experience or sensitivity to the concerns of affected communities. His three-piece suits and formal, somewhat imperious, white-haired bearing did not change my initial impressions. Making matters worse were rumors that Broder had demanded the title of senior Vice President, a parking space next to the President's, and offices near the top floor. In my mind, he was a caricature of an elitist, international banker. I could not have been more wrong.

I first met Mr. Broder at the initial, rather formal, reception held at the Panel's temporary offices. As he welcomed the crowd with a speech praising the Bank's leadership in creating such an accountability mechanism, he gave little sign that he saw the Panel as anything different than the internal evaluations unit that the Germans had been promoting all along. The only hint that he might share the CSOs' vision of the Panel was when he mentioned, offhandedly, that the Panel's permanent office space was being remodeled in order to ensure the entire suite could be locked. At least he appeared to be serious about protecting the Panel's ability to operate confidentially – and hopefully that included the confidentiality of the complainants.

After his speech, he found me sulking in the corner, put his arm on my shoulder, and rather patronizingly (I thought) guided me out of the room for a quiet chat. After thanking me for my work on creating the Panel, he looked at me with a wry grin and an unmistakable twinkle in his eye, and said, "You know, the Board has no idea what they have created here. I postponed my retirement for this because I believe it will force the Board to take its job more

Finance, Trade and Urban Affairs, U.S. H. Rep. (June 24, 1994) (regarding Bank's information policy and inspection panel).

seriously and pay closer attention to the impact of its decisions." When I asked him about the parking space, the twinkle returned, and he confided that he did not even own a car. He insisted on a parking space near the President, so that staff walking into the institution would know the Inspection Panel's position in the hierarchy, reporting as it did to the Board of Directors. Mr. Broder was playing chess, while I was playing checkers.

Mr. Broder and the other two original panel members, as well as the first executive secretary, Eduardo Abbott, were all politically astute, technically capable, and highly ethical. They quickly earned the trust of the CSOs and created a safe and welcoming space for us and the communities we represented. Early on, I accompanied Cristian Opasu from the Chile campaign on the BioBio to the Bank. He and I agreed we would test the ability of community representatives to meet with the Panel confidentially. We refused to give Cristian's name to the Bank's security and explained our need to keep his name confidential for fear of reprisals back home. Security refused our entry, and so we had them call the Panel. The Panel's Executive Secretary came down and berated the security, demanding that we be allowed to enter without giving our names. Security would not budge and neither would the Panel. So, the Panel went and got their things and met us off-site. It was a little test of the system; the Bank failed, but the Panel passed – it was one of many early signs that the Panel stood with the communities. Over time, the Panel offices became the only place within the Bank where CSOs were guaranteed that affected community members would always feel heard and valued.

4.2 *Lawyering Up: the Struggle for Independence and Effectiveness*

The Bank's opposition to a people-centered mechanism did not end with the establishment of the Panel, nor were they ready to let Mr. Broder and his colleagues operate unchecked. As described by Eduardo Abbott in Chapter 5, having been forced to accept a Panel that accepted external claims, Management resorted to other tactics for obstructing or controlling the Panel.[31] Management opposed the eligibility of many of the first claims to the Panel. They cited various provisions, in particular a failure of the claimants to consult first with Management. The Panel had a liberal interpretation of this provision, so Management did not prevail initially.

A more effective tactic was their adoption of announcing a Management action plan at the eligibility stage. The Bank would then argue there was no need to have an investigation because they had already addressed any problem

31 *See* Eduardo Abbott, *supra* Chapter 5 (discussing the lead-up and impact of these clarifications).

that might have existed. This became a major point of conflict, which was partly responsible for two Board clarifications to the Panel resolutions (in 1997 and 1999).[32] In the resolutions, the Panel agreed to keep facts supporting eligibility to a minimum, Management agreed not to issue a pre-emptive unilateral action plan, and the Board agreed to review the Panel's request for investigations on a "no objection" basis. Most of the Panel's subsequent eligibility recommendations have been approved by the Board.

Management's legalistic and confrontational approach was a continuation of Shihata's compromise in drafting a resolution with technical eligibility criteria intended to narrow accessibility to the Panel. Although the Washington-based CSOs shared a vision that anyone should be able to file a simple letter to access the Panel, when asked to represent potential claimants in the early cases we could not risk a bare-bones approach. CIEL represented communities in five of the first six cases brought by affected communities, and we owed it to those communities to anticipate what objections Management would raise. The Panel, besieged by legal arguments on both sides, also took a legalistic approach in setting out its initial procedures and in investigating the various cases.

The legalistic and confrontational tone of those first cases was an extension of Shihata's strategy in drafting the resolution; open the door for project-affected people to have unprecedented access to an investigation arm and then narrow the entrance to admit only those who pass through technical screens – and if the Panel does not enforce the screens adequately then, Management will do so in their response.

To this day, this legalistic and confrontational approach permeates the relationship between the Panel and the Bank, with significant and unfortunate impacts on the accessibility, independence, and effectiveness of the Panel and other IAMs. First, the legalistic nature of the process has disadvantaged and disempowered communities using the Panel process. Communities cannot easily translate their lived experiences into the technical language of policy violations and environmental or social impacts – and they should not have to. The process does not make room to hear them but rather favors interventions by their CSO representatives. As a result, claims brought with the assistance of international CSO support are significantly more likely to result in positive outcomes for the community.[33]

---

32 *Id.*

33 *See* Sara Jaramillo, *Making IAMs Accessible for All Communities*, ACCOUNTABILITY COUNSEL NEWSLETTER (Aug. 7, 2023) (https://www.accountabilityconsole.com/newsletter/articles/making-iams-accessible-for-all-communities/ (last visited Feb. 16, 2025).

Second, the legalistic and confrontational tone impedes constructive institutional learning; Bank Management puts its effort into trying to marginalize and discredit (or otherwise dismiss) most Panel findings. Management has never in practice looked for ways to learn from Panel findings, let alone integrate them into future decision-making at the Bank. The project teams have frequently sought to drive a wedge between the environmental and social (E&S) staff and the Panel, rallying E&S teams to defend decisions that at times they made only because of institutional pressure to "get along" and move the money. The shared goal of improving the Bank's E&S performance should make E&S staff natural allies of the IAMs, but this has never materialized. The IAMs and CSOs may bear some of the blame, but mostly it is a direct outcome of Management's interest from the beginning in narrowing the impact of any independent, people-centered Panel.

4.3 *The Impact of People-Centered Advocacy on the Institutional Culture*

Despite the obstacles it faced, the Panel under Broder was having a significant impact inside the Bank – not necessarily through formal case recommendations, but by creating a debate about the role of E&S standards and, even more so, of affected people. Broder understood how creating space for affected people to be heard could profoundly disrupt the Bank's traditional culture and governance. CSOs understood at a certain level that the Panel would help shape the political narrative at the institution. But CSOs did not fully understand how the Panel would reverberate at many different levels throughout the Bank. For example, the Panel created a lot of concern among the staff who were not accustomed to significant oversight. Soon, we would hear about Panel proofing – a process encouraged by the E&S staff at the Bank to make sure that projects were fully compliant with the safeguard policies to avoid the Panel. This was mostly positive, but the motivation was to avoid the Panel – and not necessarily because of a belief that Panel proofing would improve the projects. At the same time, Management began expressing concerns that the Panel would make the Bank too risk-averse to support the largest projects; this was unsettling in the Bank, which never fully embraced the value of averting risks to the community as a way to improve its overall development effectiveness.

The profound impact that the people-centered approach of the Panel was having on the Bank was brought home to me in two meetings in the early years of the Panel.[34] The first illustrated the novelty of centering people at the Bank, and the second illustrated how the power of local "voice" could be harnessed by

34 These accounts previously appeared in David Hunter, *Lawyers' Voices, Peoples' Stories, and Narrative Justice: Lessons from the Global Financial Accountability Movement, in*

the highest levels of Management. First was a meeting in 1994 with Mr. Ibrahim Shihata, the General Counsel and principal author of the Resolution creating the Panel. After writing an open letter arguing that the Office of the General Council (OGC) should not be the interpreter of the Panel Resolution as it represented Management, Lori Udall and I were summoned to our first meeting with Mr. Shihata. I expected the meeting to be contentious, but I did not expect to be greeted with questions like, "[d]o you know how rare it is for someone in my position to meet with somebody like you?;" "[a]re you even lawyers?;" "[w]here did you attend law school?" I literally did not know whether to be insulted or to laugh. Before long, I realized that what came across as insulting was really just a reflection of the state of affairs. In more than a decade as WB General Counsel, Shihata had *never* before had reason to meet somebody who represented fishermen or bricklayers or an affected community. Such was the state of international law at the time – that one of the most well-respected and influential international lawyers working at one of the most important international organizations had never had reason to meet with affected people or their lawyers. He only met with governments, and only governments represented the interests of their people at the Bank. And so, if a fisherman wanted to be heard at the top level, they went through their government's official representative. And Mr. Shihata was just curious about what kind of lawyer represented them.

Second, we were also fortunate that the early years of the Panel coincided with James Wolfensohn's term as President of the World Bank. Wolfensohn was trying to reform the Bank in his own way, which included centering the Bank's impact on affected people to further his vision of the Bank as a moral force for good. He understood and largely supported the Panel, because it was a connection to people on the ground.

This was clear in a meeting in Wolfensohn's office high atop the World Bank building soon after he became President in 1995. I had arranged the meeting between Mr. Wolfensohn and representatives of artisanal fishermen and brickmakers who lived in small Paraguayan villages about to be flooded by the massive Bank-financed Yacyreta dam. The reception area for the meeting was also filled with suit-clad senior management, including the Bank's Vice-President for Latin America, the Inspection Panel chair, and two or three other Bank officials. Dressed in neat but worn jeans and plain, collared shirts, the fishermen confided that they were nervous about not having a suit and embarrassed by

---

KATIE REDFORD & MARK GEWISER EDS.,THE REVOLUTION WILL NOT (ONLY) BE LITIGATED (2022).

their poor English. I assured them the best I could, but I was also uncertain how we would be received.

As we all walked together into the President's internal office, Mr. Wolfensohn ignored everyone else and moved directly to greet the two fishermen, sticking out his hand and guiding them to the two seats closest to him. Mr. Wolfensohn directed nearly all his attention to the fishermen, who told him of their concerns. At one point, a Senior Vice President of the Bank interrupted to object that, contrary to the fishermen's claims, certain project documents had been translated and were widely available in Paraguay. Mr. Wolfensohn turned abruptly toward him and asked, "[w]hy would these men travel all this way just to lie to me?" Turning back to the fishermen, he said they "would have the documents translated and in their hands by the end of the week or," signaling toward the Vice-President, "he won't have a job."

Mr. Wolfensohn continued to listen respectfully to the fishermen, promised to look into their issues, and thanked them for coming. The meeting went well because Wolfensohn valued the lived experience of the fishermen, but also because their presence provided a tactical opportunity to advance his message inside the Bank. He did not want to hear a filtered voice; he wanted to hear directly from the affected people. Even more, he wanted to send a message to the Bank that his focus was on what was happening on the ground, and he wanted to hear it directly. He sent the same message to me, to Elias Diaz Pena – the co-director of a national Paraguayan environmental group – and to Panel member Alvaro Umana. We had not said a word, and we got everything we wanted, but not because of my legal education. Wolfensohn made it clear that he wanted to be – along with senior management – in the room to hear the fishermen's stories, unfiltered by their professional handlers. Wolfensohn fully understood the novelty and value that bringing voices from affected people could have in shaking up the institution he had just joined.

5 Conclusion: Acceptance of the People-Centered Accountability Norm, if Not Accountability

If asked thirty years ago to describe my aspirations for the Panel, I would have focused on the hope that the Panel would provide a widely respected forum for affected people and communities to vindicate their rights as reflected in a strong and clear set of rights-based environmental and social safeguards. I would have hoped that the safeguards would be more integrated into the culture and operations of the IFIs, resulting in projects today that reflected greater community engagement and protections. That vision is at best a work in progress. The wide-spread acceptance of the norm of accountability, including both IAMs and safeguard policies, at least as a matter of general IFI governance, has been a huge and somewhat surprising achievement. I never would have thought the Panel model would have spread to more than thirty IFIs, UN agencies, and private conservation groups. Also completely unforeseen to me, has been the rise of dispute resolution as a complement to the compliance review function of the Panel. By providing another window for affected people to be heard and empowered, the rise of people-centered dispute resolution has revolutionized IFIs as much as the Panel's people-centered compliance.

On the other hand, thirty years ago I did expect – or at least hope – that the Panel would not be as important today as it was then. I expected other parts of the accountability system surrounding development projects would be stronger in protecting affected people's rights and the environment. I would have expected the Bank's environmental and social staff to have more influence in project design and implementation – but that does not appear to be the case, at least in the World Bank Group. "Safeguards" have turned into "performance standards," the pressure to lend identified in the Wapenhans report has not abated, and job performance evaluations still do not appear to reflect project quality. In general, I would have hoped that the Bank would be at a stage where the institution more fully integrated local community perspectives into development priorities and had an active, constructive process for learning from Bank decisions. Perhaps most critically, I expected the trends reflecting stronger national law protections of human rights and the environment to continue, so that projects were better implemented, with less local harm than in the past. Unfortunately, we have seen a decline in the rule of law in many countries, including, most notably and most recently, in the United States. This makes the need for the Panel and the other IAMs more critical, but it also assures more conflicts with the borrowing countries.

Thirty years later, the IAMs remain a rare example of citizen-based accountability mechanisms in international law and organizations. Allowing citizens more rights in the Bank's governance did not, as many of the Bank's Executive Directors feared and many CSOs hoped, disrupt the normal conduct of the World Bank's business. The Panel and other IAMs have broken down the monopoly that borrowing country governments held in the interactions between their societies and the World Bank by creating a permanent, high-profile direct dialogue between the World Bank and affected citizens of their member states. Unfortunately, this has not resulted in any discernible shift in how the Bank operates nor in the harm its projects ultimately cause to local communities. The Bank still engages in a top-down development model with finance ministries that prioritizes large-scale centralized infrastructure projects. Local impacts are still sacrificed for the greater good. The IAMs in their individual cases raise the profile of those local impacts and force a discussion about whether the local community has been asked to sacrifice too much for the common good. The outcome of these discussions, however, results too rarely in adequate remedy for the community, or in positive systemic shifts in the way the Bank does business. The Panel and the other IAMs are here to stay, but accountability has not yet arrived.

Bibliography

Bossherd, Peter, David Hunter, and Lori Udall. *Creating an Independent Appeals Commission at the World Bank*. August 26, 1993.

Caufield, Catherine. *Masters of Illusion: The World Bank and the Poverty of Nations*. New York City: Henry Holt & Co., 1997.

Fox, Jonathan A. and L. David Brown, *The Struggle for Accountability: The World Bank, NGOs, and Grassroots Movements*. Cambridge Massachusetts: The MIT Press, 1998.

Hancock, Graham. *Lords of Poverty: The Power, Prestige, and Corruption of the International Aid Business*. New York City: Atlantic Monthly Press, 1989.

Hunter, David. "Lawyer's Voices, People's Stories, and Narrative Justice: Lessons from the Global Financial Accountability Movement." In *A Revolution Will Not (Only) Be Litigated*, edited by Katie Redford & Mark Gevisser. New York City: OR Books, 2022.

Jaramillo, Sara. "Making IAMs Accessible for All Communities." *Accountability Counsel Newsletter*, August 2023.

Mikesell, Raymond and Larry Williams. *International Banks and the Environment—From Growth to Sustainability: An Unfinished Agenda*. San Francisco: Sierra Club Books, 1992.

Morse, Bradford and Thomas R. Berger. Bradford Morse and Thomas R. Berger to Lewis T. Preston, June 18, 1992.

Park, Susan. *The Good Hegemon: US Power, Accountability as Justice, and the Multilateral Development Banks*. Oxford, England: Oxford University Press, 2022.

Preston, Lewis T. Lewis T. Preston to all World Bank Staff, September 24, 1993.

Rich, Bruce. *Mortgaging the Earth: The World Bank, Environmental Impoverishment, and the Crisis of Development*. Boston Massachusetts: Beacon Press, 1994.

Shihata, Ibrahim F. S. *The World Bank Inspection Panel*. Washington DC: World Bank, 2000.

Udall, Lori. "The World Bank and Public Accountability: Has Anything Changed." In *The Struggle for Accountability: The World Bank, NGOs, and Grassroots Movements*, edited by Jonathan A. Fox and L. David Brown. Cambridge, Massachusetts: MIT Press, 1998.

United Nations. *United Nations Conference on Environment and Development*. 1992.

CHAPTER 9

The Inspection Panel's Thirty Years of Impact: What the Data Tell Us

Ramanie Kunanayagam, Mark Goldsmith, Ibrahim James Pam, Serge Selwan, Richard Wyness, Ayako Kubodera, Camila Jorge do Amarel, and Rupes Dalai

1 Introduction*

"A stroke of a genius,"[1] *"a bold experiment in transparency and accountability that has worked to the benefit of all concerned,"*[2] *"a precedent under international law,"*[3] and a *"citizen-based accountability mechanism"*[4] are some of the ways in which close observers have described the World Bank Inspection Panel, which celebrated its thirtieth anniversary in 2023.

The Inspection Panel's creation in 1993 was a milestone in the field of international development. It was the first independent, citizen-driven accountability mechanism at any international organization. The Inspection Panel is accessible to persons who are negatively affected by World Bank-financed projects to request an investigation to be heard and seek recourse for actual or potential environmental and social harm. The Panel brings the voices of communities, often marginalized, to the highest levels of the World Bank and therefore provides a conduit for even the most vulnerable to be heard by the Executive Directors of the Bank.[5]

---

* The authors include the three panel members as of October, 2023 and several staff members of the World Bank Inspection Panel: Ramanie Kunanayagam, Chairperson; Mark Goldsmith, Panel Member; Ibrahim James Pam, Panel Member; Serge Selwan, Senior Operations Officer and Adviser; Richard Wyness, Senior Environment Specialist; Ayako Kubodera, Investigation Officer; Camila Jorge do Amarel, Investigation Officer; Rupes Dalai, Research Analyst.

1 Werner Kiene, *An Introduction from the Panel Chair*, in Accountability at the World Bank: The Inspection Panel at 15 Years, Inspection Panel, ix–xiv (2009).

2 James Wolfensohn, *Forward, in* Alvaro Umaña, ed.,The World Bank Inspection Panel: The First Four Years (1994–1995), vii–viii (1998).

3 Susan Park, The Good Hegemon- US Power, Accountability as Justice, and the Multilateral Development Banks (2022).

4 World Bank Inspection Panel, *Accountability at the World Bank: The Inspection Panel at 15 years*, 3 (2009) (quoting David Hunter).

5 Since September 2020, the Inspection Panel has been housed within the World Bank Accountability Mechanism, which was created in September 2020.

Over the years, the Inspection Panel has inspired the establishment of more than two dozen similar accountability mechanisms at multilateral and bilateral development agencies globally. Many of its practices – such as promoting transparency, enhancing predictability of the process, taking precautionary measures such as upholding confidentiality to protect requesters, developing policies and processes against intimidation and reprisals, and sharing lessons from its cases – have become standard among other independent accountability mechanisms (IAMs).

The Inspection Panel has a dual objective: (i) functioning as a redress mechanism for those affected by World Bank-financed operations; and (ii) holding the World Bank accountable to its own policies through its independent, fact-finding compliance investigations. The Panel's work has brought transparency to the projects it has investigated, and it has generated lessons that have influenced the adoption of policies and guidelines to strengthen the World Bank's assessment of environmental and social risks, and the mitigation of related impacts.

This essay reflects both quantitatively and qualitatively on the Panel's work during its first thirty years. It includes the number, origin, and types of cases it has received, identifies emerging trends among them, and examines the impact of the Panel's work within its mandate, while also considering the limitations of the Panel.

2 Case Levels Have Remained Constant

The Inspection Panel assesses the admissibility of the requests it receives based on criteria defined in its legal framework. The admission criteria are: (i) the affected party consists of any two or more persons (the 'requesters') who are affected by a Bank-supported project; (ii) the request is not frivolous, absurd or anonymous; (iii) the project that is the subject of the request and the alleged harm claimed by the requesters can be plausibly linked to a World Bank-funded project; (iv) less than 95 percent of the loan has been disbursed or, for projects approved on or after September 8, 2020, fifteen months have not passed since the project closed; (v) the subject matter of the request does not concern issues of procurement; and (vi) the request is not the same as a previous one, unless there is new evidence or circumstances. Complaints regarding procurement or corruption are reviewed by other specialized offices of the World Bank.

An important additional criterion is that the request's subject matter must have been known to the World Bank Management, allowing it a reasonable opportunity to address the concerns before approaching the Inspection Panel. In that sense, the Panel is often the last opportunity for recourse for requesters, when previous attempts to resolve their concerns with the Bank have not resulted in positive outcomes.

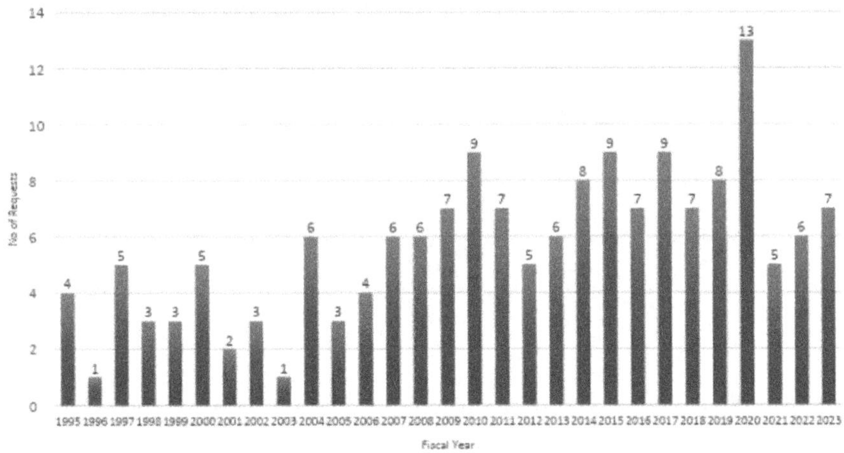

FIGURE 9.1 Cases received by fiscal years (June 30, 2023)

The Panel's caseload is driven by the requests that it receives, which varies from year to year.

The average number of cases per year has been increasing slightly in recent years. Over the thirty years of the Panel's existence, the Panel has registered an average of 4.03 cases per year; in the last five years, it has registered 5.6 cases per year (see Table 9.1).

The geographic distribution of cases has been diverse; over the past thirty years, the Inspection Panel has received 165 admissible requests from 57 countries (see Figure 9.2 below). Note that fewer cases from a particular region do not necessarily correlate to fewer issues in that region. Conversely, once requests are registered from a certain country or region, they are often followed by others.

TABLE 9.1 Inspection panel cases: Registration (June 30, 2023)

5 Year FYs	Cases received	Registered	Registration percentage	Annual average
1994–1998	13	11	85%	2.2
1999–2003	14	13	93%	2.6
2004–2008	25	22	88%	4.4
2009–2013	34	29	85%	5.8
2014–2018	40	18	45%	3.6
2019–2023	39	27	72%	5.6
Total	165	120	73%	4.03

FIGURE 9.2 Geographical distribution of requests for inspection (June 30, 2023)

Admissible requests are those requests that meet the criteria for admission identified earlier. Civil society and academic critics of the Inspection Panel argue that the mechanism's remit for admission is too narrow. They express concern that the Inspection Panel cannot initiate cases on its own, that the Panel needs to establish the plausibility of a link between harm and a Bank-supported project, and that there is a pre-condition for the requesters to ensure that Management is made aware of the concerns and has a reasonable opportunity to address these concerns. The Inspection Panel cannot unilaterally expand its remit for admission of cases. Only the World Bank Board of Directors has the power to make such a change. (See Figure 9.3 below).

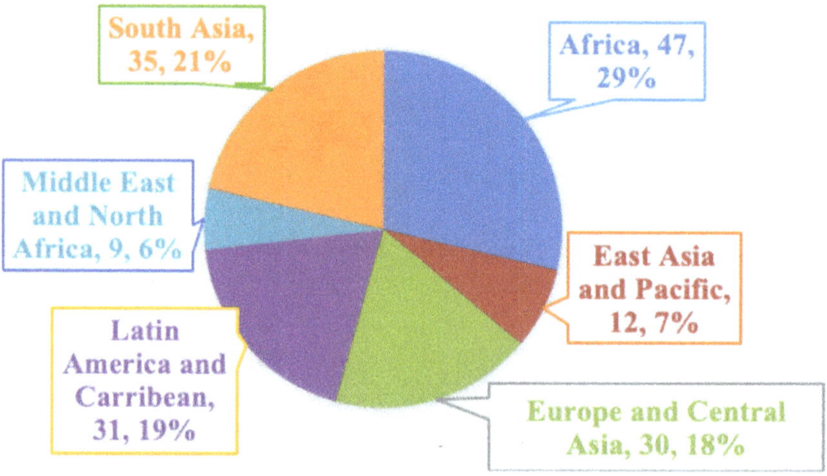

FIGURE 9.3 Case registration by region (June 30, 2023)

A number of factors may deter affected persons from submitting a request for inspection, including shrinking civil society space; lack of information and transparency on project financing; lack of information about the existence of the Panel; fear of intimidation and reprisals; and claims that requesters are undermining progress or working against the national interest are all. When requesters fear reprisals and/or intimidation, they can request that their identities be kept confidential by the Inspection Panel.

On average, as noted, the Inspection Panel registered 4.03 cases per year over its thirty years of existence; it recommended an investigation in 1.6 cases per year. The number of investigations conducted has remained relatively constant over time. Interestingly, the number of investigations did not decline during the peak years of the Covid-19 pandemic, despite widely imposed lockdowns and social distancing measures that curtailed the ability of people to mobilize. (See Table 9.2 below).

TABLE 9.2 Investigations recommended (June 30, 2023)

5 Year FYs	Cases received	Investigation recommended	Recommendation percentage	Annual average
1994–1998	13	6	46%	1.2
1999–2003	14	8	57%	1.6
2004–2008	25	12	48%	2.4
2009–2013	34	9	26%	1.8
2014–2018	40	6	15%	1.2
2019–2023	39	8	21%	1.6
Total	165	49	30%	1.6

The number of projects that reach the Inspection Panel represent a very small fraction of the projects that the World Bank finances each year. Since the Inspection Panel was established, the number of requests received has been equivalent to only about 1.5 percent of the total number of World Bank-financed projects over the same period. Investigations by the Inspection Panel represent less than 0.5 percent of approved World Bank-financed projects.

While the Panel has received requests during the early stages of project design, a large majority of requests are received well after Project approval. This may explain why, although the World Bank's Environmental and Social Framework (ESF) reached its five-year milestone in October this year, the Panel has yet to register a single case on a project that was approved since adoption of the new ESF approach.

As shown in Table 9.3 below, the Inspection Panel has conducted forty-one investigations, corresponding to 34 percent of the registered requests. During the five years between FY 2019 and FY 2023, the Inspection Panel recommended an investigation for 30 percent of its registered requests (eight out of twenty-seven). This is in line with the trend over the past fifteen years. However, since the introduction of the dispute resolution option as part of the Bank's Accountability Mechanism in 2021, three of the investigations that the Panel recommended were addressed instead through dispute resolution.

TABLE 9.3 Registered cases and investigations (June 30, 2023)

5 Year FYs	Cases registered	Investigation recommended (Percentage of registration)	Investigation conducted (Percentage of registered)	Annual average of investigation recommended	Annual average of investigations conducted
1994–1998	11	6 (55%)	2 (18%)[a]	1.2	0.4
1999–2003	13	8 (62%)	8 (62%)	1.6	1.6
2004–2008	22	12 (55%)	12 (55%)	2.4	2.4
2009–2013	29	9 (31%)	8 (28%)[b]	1.8	1.6
2014–2018	18	6 (33%)	6 (33%)	1.4	1.2
2019–2023	27	8 (30%)	5 (19%)[c]	1.6	1
Total	120	**49 (41%)**	**41 (34%)**	1.7	1.37

a Prior to the 1999 clarification of the Panel's resolution, the Board did not have a set of technical criteria to decide on the approval of an investigation. This was introduced in the 1999 clarification. Hence, between 1994 and the 1999 clarification, four of the Panel's recommendations for investigations were not approved.

b The Board did not approve the Panel's investigation recommendation in the case of the Lebanon – Greater Beirut Water Supply Project.

c Since September 8, 2020, the Board requires that a dispute resolution process be offered to parties following the Board's approval of the Panel's investigation. In five out of the eight cases, the parties opted for the Panel to conduct an investigation; and in three cases the parties opted for the dispute resolution service.

3 Rising Trends

As shown in Figure 9.3, below, environmental assessment and consultation have been two of the three most common policy issues cited in requests received by the Inspection Panel since it was created. Environmental assessment has been cited in 135 requests and consultation or disclosure in 112. (See Figure 9.4 below.)

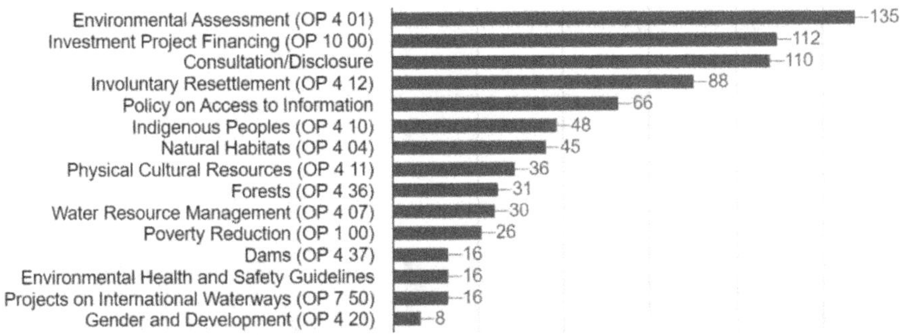

FIGURE 9.4 Major policy issues raised in requests (June 30, 2023)

Since the beginning of 2022, involuntary resettlement issues and livelihood restoration became the most prominent aspects raised in requests. While this seems indicative of a rise in the number of cases received, with resettlement issues at the core of the complaint (and indeed resettlement has consistently remained in the top four of the issues raised throughout the history of Panel cases), drawing any conclusions about trends on issues raised is difficult, given the small number of requests received within less than two years. (See Figure 9.5 below.)

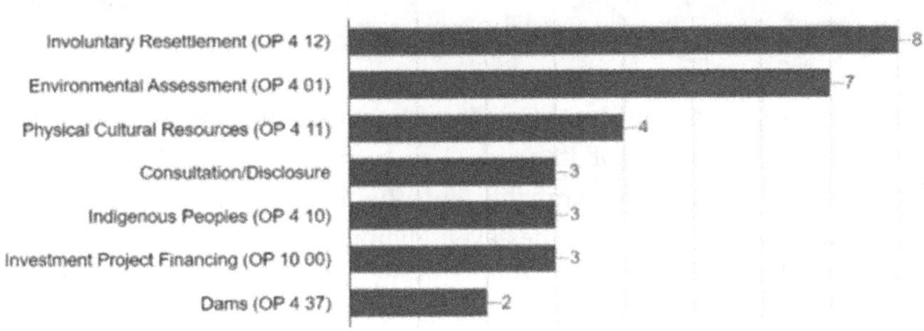

FIGURE 9.5 Major policy issues raised in requests-fiscal year 2022–2023

An issue of growing concern for the Inspection Panel is the upward trend in reports on intimidation and reprisals, and requests for confidentiality due to a fear of retaliation. This can be seen in Figure 9.5 above. In thirteen out of the sixteen projects connected with requests for inspection between FY2021 and FY2023, 81 percent of requesters asked for confidentiality. In half of the related projects, there were allegations of intimidation and reprisals.

The Inspection Panel is the first international accountability mechanism to issue guidelines for reducing retaliation risks to community members during the investigation process and to take a zero-tolerance approach to intimidation and reprisals. Despite this, there are unfortunately limitations as to what the Panel can practically do when requesters face actual retaliation. In 2021, The Panel issued an advisory report, *Right to be Heard: Intimidation and Reprisals in World Bank Inspection Panel Complaints* to raise awareness of the subject.[6]

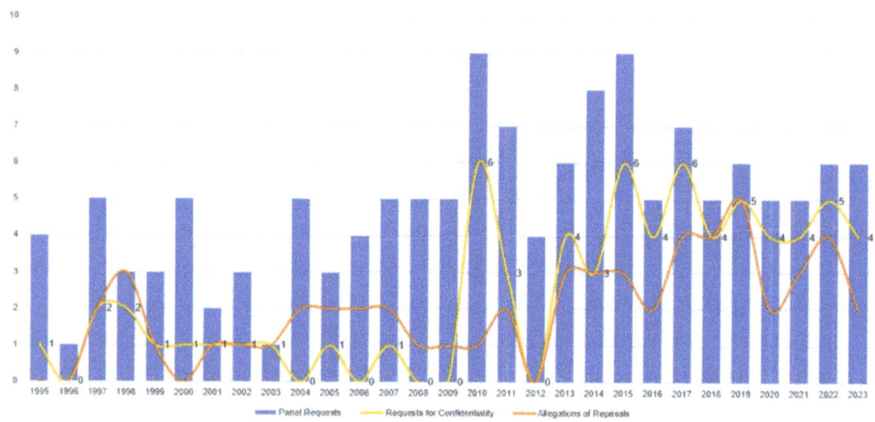

FIGURE 9.6 Inspection panel cases: Record on confidentiality and reprisals (June 30, 2023)

4 The Panel – a Force for Positive Outcomes?

Throughout its history, the Panel has simultaneously been respected for and questioned on the impact of its work. The Inspection Panel investigations carry weight and strength that arguably few other mechanisms can match. The Panel investigations, and sometimes even eligibility reports, have alerted the World Bank to harm or potential harm to the environment and project-affected persons, instances of policy non-compliance, and other important issues that had otherwise been overlooked.

The Panel uses several indicators to measure positive outcomes from its investigations:

6 *See* World Bank Inspection Panel, *Right to be Heard: Intimidation and Reprisals in World Bank Inspection Panel Complaints* (Dec. 2021).

1. Redress of harm to affected people through Management and Borrower actions designed to address or mitigate a project's adverse impact;
2. Identifying systemic issues within the institution, leading to the Bank clarifying policies, improving guidance to staff, and strengthening capacity to address environmental and social safeguard issues;
3. Lessons for improving future Bank operations;
4. Review of broader issues, such as on labor influx risks and gender-based violence; and
5. Publishing advisory reports in its *Emerging Lessons Series,* on topics such as environmental assessment, Indigenous Peoples, involuntary resettlement, biodiversity offsets, gender-based violence, land, and livelihoods, etc.

4.1 *Project-Level Outcomes – Redress of Harm*

At the conclusion of a Panel investigation, Management develops an action plan in response to the investigation findings. This action plan is consulted upon with the requesters, agreed to by the government of the borrowing country, and approved by the World Bank Board of Directors. The action plan is intended to provide remedies to the harms and to bring the project into compliance with World Bank policies. Bank Management provides regular updates to the Board on the progress in the implementation of each action plan, usually on a yearly basis, and these progress reports are published on the Panel's website. Since April 2016, Bank Management has submitted a biannual consolidated report on the implementation of ongoing action plans to the Board of Directors. The Inspection Panel also publishes these reports on its website. Investigation outcomes at the project level have included improvements in resettlement plan design and compensation, the creation of project-level grievance mechanisms, improved information disclosure, and strengthened project supervision.

For example, in an investigation completed this year in Togo,[7] on a climate resilience project that aims to strengthen coastal resilience against severe coastal erosion, the Panel found that the Project proponents did not adequately identify the potential environmental risks and socioeconomic impacts of the

7 *See* World Bank Inspection Panel, *Inspection Panel Investigation Report, Republic of Togo, West Africa Coastal Areas Resilience Investment Project (P162337), Additional Financing (P176313) and Global Environment Facility* (GEF) *(P092289)* (April 20, 2023), https://www.inspectionpanel.org/sites/default/files/cases/documents/153-Inspection%20Panel%20Investigation%20Report-%2020%20April%202023.pdf (last visited Jan. 26, 2025).

project's physical interventions on local fishing communities, especially those fishers and *mareyeuses* practicing traditional beach seine fishing.[8] In response to this finding, in their action plan, Management stated that the Project earmarked $6 million for community activities, including the provision of livelihood support, which will specifically include and target the individuals and groups involved in this fishing activity.[9]

In the Democratic Republic of Congo (DRC) –Transitional Support for Economic Recovery Credit investigation, the Inspection Panel investigated and found that there was a failure during project design to carry out the necessary initial screening to identify risks and trigger the safeguard policies so that crucial steps would be taken to address the rights and needs of the Pygmy Indigenous Peoples.[10] The management action plan approved by the Board emphasized staying engaged in the DRC forest sector, continuing to monitor a moratorium on future logging concessions, and strengthening the enforcement of the implementation of the government forest code. The management action plan was aimed at integrating forest-dependent communities – the Pygmies – more widely into the Bank's activities in DRC and supporting critical activities such as capacity building, recognition of customary rights, law enforcement, and independent monitoring in forthcoming forest-related operations. The Bank with the government and certain development partners, and after consultation with key stakeholders, including the Requesters, developed a *Framework for a National Development Strategy for Pygmy Communities in DRC*. The Framework analyzed factors that threaten the cultural identity of

8 In Togo, beach seine fishing is a land-based fishery, where men, women, and children haul a long fishing net. The nets are two-to-five-kilometer-long; one end is roped to a stick and the other end is taken by a pirogue towards the other side of the beach. The hauling of the net lasts several hours. Mareyeuses are wholesale traders, typically women, also known as fish transformers. They buy and prepare fish, crustaceans, and shellfish for resale. They play an important role in the distribution and transformation of fishery products.

9 World Bank Inspection Panel, *Management Report and Recommendation in Response to the Inspection Panel Investigation Report*, vii (June 2, 2023), https://www.inspectionpanel.org/sites/default/files/cases/documents/153-Management%20Report%20and%20Recommendations-2%20June%202023.pdf (last visited Jan. 26, 2025).

10 *See* World Bank Inspection Panel, *Investigation Report, Democratic Republic of Congo: Transitional Support for Economic Recovery Grant* (*TSERO*) (*IDA Grant No. H 1920–DRC*) *and Emergency Economic and Social Reunification Support Project* (*EESRSP*) (*Credit No. 3824–DRC and Grant No. H 064-DRC*) (Aug. 31, 2007), https://www.inspectionpanel.org/sites/default/files/ip/PanelCases/37-Investigation%20Report%20%28English%29.pdf (last visited Jan. 26, 2025).

Pygmy populations and contribute to their impoverishment, and developed a set of proposed actions to mitigate these factors.[11]

In another project, the Uzbekistan – Rural Enterprise Support Project (Phase II), based on the Panel's eligibility report, Management outlined several actions responding to the request for an investigation.[12] In particular, it ensured the revision of the Rural Enterprise Investment Guidelines to include provisions that require the beneficiaries of loans to comply with national labor legislation as well as international laws on forced and child labor in the cotton sector. The Bank continued to maintain an intensive dialogue with the government of Uzbekistan on issues related to child and forced labor in the cotton sector; the government also engaged in a public campaign about the rights of children and adults, and established a national monitoring plan for the eradication of child and forced labor.

4.2 *Institutional Outcomes – Systemic Learning and Improvement*

Inspection Panel investigations have also led to various commitments by Bank Management with institution-wide implications. In some instances, investigations have encouraged better institutional approaches to environmental and social performance, with improved identification of affected people, protection of livelihoods, and biodiversity outcomes. For example, Inspection Panel investigations on land administration and management projects, such as the Albania Integrated Coastal Zone Management and Clean-Up Project, revealed the existence of a policy gap in the application of the World Bank's Policy on Involuntary Resettlement in the context of land-management projects.[13] Acknowledging the lack of clarity in the application of the Policy to land-use

11 World Bank Inspection Panel, *Second Progress Report to the Board of Executive Directors on the Implementation of Management's Action Plan In Response to the Democratic Republic of Congo Inspection Panel Investigation Report on Transitional Support for Economic Recovery Project and Emergency Social and Economic Reunification Project*, 11 (March 2011), https://www.inspectionpanel.org/sites/default/files/ip/PanelCases/37-Second%20Management%20Progress%20Report%20%28English%29.pdf (last visited Jan. 26, 2025).

12 World Bank Inspection Panel, *Second Progress Report to the Board of Executive Directors in the Implementation of the Management Actions in Response to the Request for Inspection of the Uzbekistan Rural Enterprise Support Project- Phase 2 (P109126) and Additional Financing for Second Rural Enterprise Support Project (P126962)*, v (July 2016), https://www.inspectionpanel.org/sites/default/files/ip/PanelCases/89-Second%20Management%20Progress%20Report%28English%29.pdf (last visited Jan. 26, 2024).

13 World Bank Inspection Panel, *Investigation Report, Albania: Integrated Coastal Zone Management and Clean-Up Project (IDA Credit No. 4083–ALB)*, 30 (Nov. 24, 2008), https://www.inspectionpanel.org/sites/default/files/ip/PanelCases/47-Investigation%20Report%20%28English%29.pdf (last visited Jan. 26, 2025).

planning projects, the Bank issued two guidance documents for staff. The first was to clarify the policy application regarding land-use planning projects; the second was an interim guidance concerning the identification and management of risks intrinsic to land use planning projects.

In investigations on two projects (Uganda – Private Power Generation Project (Bujagali) and Ghana – Second Urban Environment Sanitation Project), the Panel identified that the time lag between data collection and project implementation meant project implementation was based on out-of-date information, and not modified to consider changing conditions.[14] As a result of these investigations, the Bank prepared interim guidelines to provide guidance to staff on addressing legacy issues. These guidance notes pertain to how the Bank re-engages in a project that has been delayed for some time, or when there is a long gap between the collection of data and implementation.[15]

In response to the Panel's investigations into two transport and road sector projects–one in Uganda and one in the DRC[16]--the Bank took a number of actions to prevent Gender-Based Violence (GBV) and other challenges that arise when there is a large influx of project-labor at Bank-financed projects. The Bank developed and published good practice notes on assessing and managing the risks and impacts of using security personnel, and a GBV task force has been established to provide recommendations for the institution on how

14 World Bank Inspection Panel, *Investigation Report, Ghana: Second Urban Environmental Sanitation Project (UESP II) (IDA Credit No. 3889–GH)*, XXVII (March 13, 2009), https://www.inspectionpanel.org/sites/default/files/ip/PanelCases/49-Investigation%20Report%20%28English%29.pdf (last visited Jan. 26, 2025); World Inspection Panel, *Investigation Report, Uganda: Private Power Generation (Bujagali) Project (Guarantee No. B0130-UG)*, LVII (Aug. 29, 2008), https://www.inspectionpanel.org/sites/default/files/ip/PanelCases/44-Investigation%20Report%20%28English%29.pdf (last visited Jan. 26, 2025).

15 World Bank Inspection Panel, *Management Report and Recommendation in Response to the Inspection Panel Investigative Report, Ghana Second Urban Environment Sanitation Project (IDA Credit No. 3889–GH)*, VIII (April 24, 2009),https://www.inspectionpanel.org/sites/default/files/ip/PanelCases/49-Management%20Report%20and%20Recommendation%20%28English%29.pdf (last visited Jan. 26, 2025).

16 *See* World Bank, *International Development Association Project Appraisal Document on a Proposed Credit in the Amount of US $427.98 million to the Democratic Republic of Congo for a Transport and Connectivity Support Project* (May 2022), https://documents1.worldbank.org/curated/en/141991655916124024/pdf/Congo-Democratic-Republic-of-Transport-and-Connectivity-Support-Project.pdf (last visited Jan. 26, 2025); World Bank, *Uganda Transport Sector Development Project-Additional Financing, Lessons Learned and Agenda for Action*, 9 (Nov. 11 2016), https://documents1.worldbank.org/curated/en/948341479845064519/pdf/110455-BR-PUBLIC-LESSONS-LEARNT-IDA-SecM2016-0204.pdf (last visited Jan. 26, 2025).

to prevent and respond to GBV in Bank projects.[17] The Bank also generated a report on lessons learned and actions to address internal systemic issues. In addition, the Bank now requires the personnel of large contractors to sign a code of conduct that explicitly details the prohibition of, and penalties for, any sexual relations with minors, and has become the first international financial institution to disqualify contractors for failing to comply with GBV-related obligations.

4.3 *Country-Level Outcomes* (*Wider and Broader Improvements*)

At the country level, some Panel cases have contributed to improvements in country frameworks and capacity, which are agreed upon between the Bank and borrowers or voluntarily undertaken by the borrower. In some cases, these improvements have expanded well beyond the footprint of the project. For example, in a recent investigation into the Uganda – North Eastern Road-Corridor Asset Management Project, the Panel noted in its findings that the lack of analysis or guidance in the project's framework documents on the acquisition of quarries contributed to a subcontractor leasing the land from the community without applying the Involuntary Resettlement policy provisions and protections, causing harm to the community.[18] In recognition of this gap, before the completion of the Panel's investigation, the Uganda National Roads Authority prepared on a voluntary basis a set of guidelines on the acquisition of quarries.

In some cases, the World Bank has exercised its right to suspend the financing of projects, pending the completion of agreed-upon actions. Such was the outcome in the India – Mumbai Urban Transport Project, where the World Bank suspended disbursement to the road and resettlement component of the Project, in response to a request pertaining to the resettlement of almost

---

17 *See* World Bank, *Environment & Social Framework for IPF Operations, Assessing and Managing the Risks and Impacts of the Use of Security Personnel*, (Oct. 2018), https://documents1.worldbank.org/curated/en/692931540325377520/Environment-and-Social-Framework-ESF-Good-Practice-Note-on-Security-Personnel-English.pdf (last visited Jan. 26, 2025); World Bank, *Global Gender-Based Violence Task Force: Action Plan for Implementation* (Nov. 8, 2017), https://documents1.worldbank.org/curated/en/206731510166266845/pdf/121031-WP-PUBLIC-Gender-Based-Violence-Task-Force-Action-Plan.pdf (last visited Jan. 26, 2025).

18 *See* World Bank Inspection Panel, *Report and Recommendation on a Request for Inspection, Uganda North Eastern Road-Corridor Asset Management Project* (*NERAMP*) (*P125590*) (Feb. 26, 2021), https://www.inspectionpanel.org/sites/default/files/cases/documents/149-Inspection%20Panel%20Report%20and%20Recommendation-26%20February%202021.pdf (last visited Jan. 26, 2025).

20,000 households and shops in a dense and complex urban setting.[19] In this case, the State of Maharashtra agreed to a ten-condition strategy for lifting the suspension of disbursements; once the State had substantially met these conditions, the Bank lifted the suspension. Subsequently, the Mumbai Metropolitan Region Development Authority mainstreamed the application of the resettlement and rehabilitation policy to resettlement activities beyond the project. It applied the project's resettlement and rehabilitation entitlements framework to all of its resettlement projects beyond those supported by the Bank and expanded the post-resettlement support strategy to all the resettlement sites irrespective of funding sources.

The Panel's investigation report on the India – Rural Water Supply and Sanitation Project for Low Income States highlighted the need for the project's frameworks to be implemented through a rigorous system that ensures on-the-ground, risk-based analysis to be followed with detailed, site-specific assessments and mitigation plans.[20]In its action plan, Bank Management acknowledged the Inspection Panel's finding that the construction of the Bagbera and Chhota Govindpur Multi-Village Schemes financed under the project proceeded without the preparation of the required, site-specific environmental and social assessments and environmental management plans. As a result, the analysis of the potential environmental, social, and cultural impacts of these schemes was not considered or factored into project design; required consultations did not happen; and steps to avoid and mitigate harm were not taken. Bank Management performed a comprehensive review, together with the borrower, of the environmental and social safeguards documentation available for specific water schemes funded under the project to inform steps to comply with the policies going forward. Management reviewed and contributed to the improvement of 977 environmental data sheets, 305 environment management plans, and 795 cultural resources screenings of the areas covered by the project.[21]

---

19 *See* World Bank Inspection Panel, *Investigation Report, India: Mumbai Urban Transport Project (IBRD Loan No. 4665–IN; IDA Credit No. 3662–IN)* (Dec. 21, 2005) https://documents1.worldbank.org/curated/en/645491468283447968/pdf/34725.pdf (last visited Jan. 26, 2025).

20 World Bank Inspection Panel, *India Rural Water Supply and Sanitation Project for Low Income States (P132173) Inspection Panel Investigation Report* (Jan. 15, 2020), https://www.inspectionpanel.org/sites/default/files/cases/documents/128-129-Investigation%20Report-15%20January%202020_0.pdf (last visited Jan. 26, 2025).

21 World Bank Inspection Panel, *Management Report and Recommendation in Response to the Inspection Panel Investigation Report, India Rural Water Supply and Sanitation Project for Low Income States (P132173) (IDA Credit-53450)* (Dec. 21, 2022), https://www.inspection

5 The Conundrum of the Panel

The Inspection Panel is simultaneously revered for what it stands for and criticized for not doing enough. It has inspired and informed the creation of independent accountability mechanisms at other multilateral development banks and bilateral agencies. The function and work of the Panel is taught in law schools around the world and is the focal topic of numerous academic articles and post-graduate theses on accountability and multilateral development banks. Since its creation, the Inspection Panel has played an important role in promoting accountability, transparency, and good governance in World Bank operations.

The Panel's prestige and reputation results in part from its structure as a sitting panel, rather than ad hoc as in some other systems. The Inspection Panel is composed of three members of different nationalities, who are at a certain level of seniority in their careers, have distinct and complementary subject matter expertise, and the ability to deal thoroughly and fairly with the requests brought to them. Panel Members serve non-renewable terms and cannot work for the Bank after their term is over, guaranteeing their independence. They are selected based on their integrity and their independence from Bank Management. The structure, term limit, prohibition against future work at the Bank, and other conditions provide confidence that the Panel will exercise their independent, objective judgment in determining whether a violation of Bank policies has resulted in harm to the requestors.

It is for these very reasons that requesters come to the Panel with high expectations and hope that their voices will be heard, their cases will be admitted, their issues will be investigated, harm will be identified, and remedies will be provided. The Panel is often for them a place of last resort.

The Panel is however bound by its Resolution, which is the legal framework within which it operates. In some cases, requests are not admitted because the complaint is submitted after the project is closed, the Bank did not have prior knowledge of the issues, the Panel had previously considered the request and no new evidence or change in circumstances was presented, or the request reflects only unfulfilled expectations of benefits from the project without any other harm. In some cases, the Panel is unable to recommend an investigation because there is a lack of prima facie evidence of harm or a lack of a plausible link between the harm and the project. In addition, the Panel has no monitoring authority; its verification function is highly restrictive and requires Board

panel.org/sites/default/files/cases/documents/128-129-Management%20Report%20and%20Recommendation-21%20December%202022_0.pdf (last visited Jan. 26, 2025).

approval, which means that the Panel may not be able to verify the implementation of management action plans as it sees fit.

As discussed previously, the lack of transparency on project financing and lack of knowledge about the Inspection Panel create barriers to its accessibility. In addition, requesters often take big personal risks submitting these requests to the Panel and have to invest significant time and effort to build and engage with their cases over time. Their fear of reprisals and the Panel's inability to guarantee protection if there is retaliation can also be a barrier to accessibility.

The conundrum for the Panel is balancing these limitations while at the same time maintaining the legitimacy and influence of the impact of its cases, which stems from the rigor of its work and its legal framework. This framework is the imprimatur of the World Bank Board of Executive Directors. The same mandate, that lends credibility and legitimacy to the Panel's work, including its ability to stand up to the highest level of scrutiny both at the World Bank and in the public domain, also imposes limitations on how far the Panel can extend its reach.

6 Conclusion

Analysis of the Inspection Panel data shows a certain constancy over its first three decades of existence. Panel investigations have generated a rich collection of learning, helped redress harm, and provided some level of justice to those affected by Bank-financed projects. At a minimum, the rigor and transparency of the Panel's work has helped to shine a light on people and issues that may not have otherwise surfaced.

Revered or not, the Panel remains a pioneer among the international financial institutions. It has not only broken new ground but has over time maintained its leading reputation as an independent, impartial fact-finder. It continues to work for its hard-won independence as this can never be taken for granted, and is critical to the role it occupies as both a symbolic and actual leader of accountability.

Bibliography

International Bank for Reconstruction & Development and International Development Association. *Management Report and Recommendation in Response to the Inspection Panel Investigative Report, Ghana Second Urban Environment Sanitation Project* (*IDA Credit No. 3889–GH*). Washington DC: World Bank, April 24, 2009.

International Bank for Reconstruction and Development and International Development Association. *Second Progress Report to the Board of Executive Directors in the Implementation of the Management Actions in Response to the Request for Inspection of the Uzbekistan Rural Enterprise Support Project- Phase 2 (P109126) and Additional FInancing for Second Rural Enterprise Support Project (P126962)*. Washington DC: World Bank, July 2016.

International Bank for Reconstruction and Development & International Development Association. *Management Report and Recommendation in Response to the Inspection Panel Investigation Report, India Rural Water Supply and Sanitation Project for Low Income States (P132173) (IDA Credit-53450)*. Washington DC: The World Bank, December 21, 2022.

International Bank for Reconstruction and Development & International Development Association. *Inspection Panel Investigation Report, Republic of Togo, West Africa Coastal Areas Resilience Investment Project (P162337), Additional Financing (P176313) and Global Environment Facility (GEF) (P092289)*. Washington DC: World Bank, April 20, 2023.

Kiene, Werner. "An Introduction from the Panel Chair," in *Accountability at the World Bank: The Inspection Panel at 15 years*. Washington, DC: International Bank for Reconstruction and Development, 2009.

Park, Susan. *The Good Hegemon – US Power, Accountability as Justice, and the Multilateral Development Banks*. New York: Oxford University Press, 2022.

Wolfensohn, James. "Foreword," in *The World Bank Inspection Panel: The First Four Years (1994–1998)*, edited by Alvaro Umaña, VII–VIII. Washington, DC: International Bank for Reconstruction and Development, 1998.

World Bank. *Uganda Transport Sector Development Project-Additional Financing, Lessons Learned and Agenda for Action*. Washington DC: World Bank, November 11, 2016.

World Bank. *Global Gender-Based Violence Task Force: Action Plan for Implementation*. Washington DC: The World Bank, November 8, 2017.

World Bank. *Environment & Social Framework for IPF Operations, Assessing and Managing the Risks and Impacts of the Use of Security Personnel*. Washington DC: The World Bank, October 2018.

World Bank. *International Development Association Project Appraisal Document on a Proposed Credit in the Amount of US $427.98 million to the Democratic Republic of Congo for a Transport and Connectivity Support Project*. Washington DC: World Bank, May 2022.

World Bank Inspection Panel. *Investigation Report, India: Mumbai Urban Transport Project (IBRD Loan No. 4665–IN; IDA Credit No. 3662–IN)*. Washington DC: World Bank, December 21, 2005.

World Bank Inspection Panel. *Investigation Report, Democratic Republic of Congo: Transitional Support for Economic Recovery Grant (TSERO) (IDA Grant No. H 1920–DRC) and Emergency Economic and Social Reunification Support Project* (*EESRSP*) (*Credit No. 3824–DRC and Grant No. H 064-DRC*). Washington DC: World Bank, August 31, 2007.

World Bank Inspection Panel. *Investigation Report, Albania: Integrated Coastal Zone Management and Clean-Up Project* (*IDA Credit No. 4083–ALB*). Washington DC: World Bank, November 24, 2008: 30.

World Inspection Panel. *Investigation Report, Uganda: Private Power Generation* (*Bujagali*) *Project* (*Guarantee No. B0130-UG*). Washington DC: World Bank, August 29, 2008: LVII.

World Bank Inspection Panel. *Accountability at the World Bank: The Inspection Panel at 15 years*. Washington, DC: International Bank for Reconstruction and Development, 2009: 3.

World Bank Inspection Panel. *Investigation Report, Ghana: Second Urban Environmental Sanitation Project* (*UESP II*) (*IDA Credit No. 3889–GH*). Washington DC: World Bank, March 13, 2009: XXVII.

World Bank Inspection Panel. *Second Progress Report to the Board of Executive Directors on the Implementation of Management's Action Plan In Response to the Democratic Republic of Congo Inspection Panel Investigation Report on Transitional Support for Economic Recovery Project and Emergency Social and Economic Reunification Project.* Washington DC: World Bank, March 2010: para 11.

World Bank Inspection Panel. *India Rural Water Supply and Sanitation Project for Low Income States* (*P132173*) *Inspection Panel Investigation Report.* Washington DC: World Bank, January 15, 2020. I

World Bank Inspection Panel. *Report and Recommendation on a Request for Inspection, Uganda North Eastern Road-Corridor Asset Management Project* (*NERAMP*) (*P 125590*). Washington DC: World Bank, February 26, 2021.

World Bank Inspection Panel. *Right to be Heard: Intimidation and Reprisals in World Bank Inspection Panel Complaints.* Washington DC: World Bank, December 2021.

World Bank Inspection Panel. *Management Report and Recommendation in Response to the Inspection Panel Investigation Report.* Washington DC: World Bank, June 2 2023: VIII.

PART 3

Operational Issues

Introduction to Part 3: Operational Issues

This part includes seven contributions, each focused on different operational issues that confront the IAMs today. The first three chapters (Chapters 10–12) explore the challenges facing IAMs in providing remedy from different perspectives.

In Chapter 10, Ricard Bissell describes the evolution of the IAMs' treatment of remedy for harm to affected communities, beginning with the experience of the Panel. The Panel's authorities were particularly limited with respect to remedy because it can only make factual findings relating to compliance, without the associated authority to make recommendations or monitor the institution's responses. Bissell, who was one of the first Panel members and the second chair of the Panel, recalls the "intractable" conflicts over not *whether,* but *when,* a remedy would be provided. In the early years of the Panel, Bank Management proposed a remedial management plan during the eligibility phase, as a way of avoiding an investigation. After the Board curbed that practice, debates over remedy shifted to the Panel's role in monitoring implementation of the management plan. Today, the debate over remedy is in the context of International Finance Corporation (IFC)/Multilateral Investment Guarantee Agency (MIGA) lending to the private sector, where the Bank has less leverage and the project proponents do not typically engage in the kind of development planning necessary to fashion a remedy.

The challenge of gaining a remedy in private sector lending noted by Bissell is highlighted in the case study of the cement company in Egypt's Wadi al-Qamar. Author Suzan Nada chronicles both the damage caused by the proposed expansion of cement production and the ultimately frustrating effort to gain a remedy through the Compliance Advisor Ombudsman (CAO) of the IFC. Many factors conspired against the complainants in their effort to curb the pollution and get compensation for the harm. In the end, the CAO process took too long, and meanwhile IFC exited the investment in part to avoid addressing the issues raised by the complaint. Although little help to these requesters, this case was one of several that pushed the IFC to adopt a "responsible exit" strategy.

Lori Udall focuses on the overall impact of the Inspection Panel on the practice of involuntary resettlement in Bank-financed projects. Since its inception, the Panel has investigated thirty-two cases alleging violations of the involuntary resettlement policy. Despite persistent evidence of resettlement failures from these cases and others through the years, the World Bank continues to repeat the same mistakes with respect to involuntary resettlement. The resettlement policy is unique among the safeguard policies in that it specifically includes a requirement to provide remedy, preferably in the form of comparable land or housing rather than money. Although Panel cases have frequently resulted in compensation for people improperly excluded from the resettlement plan, compensation (even including land) is frequently viewed as inadequate, leaving people in far worse condition than they were before the resettlement. Udall argues avoiding projects that cause involuntary resettlement in the first place is critical. To do this the Bank needs to move toward more bottom-up community-based development and away from top-down national development that too freely sacrifices local communities for the ostensible benefit of the greater public good.

The next two chapters (Chapters 13 and 14) address two legal-related aspects of IAM cases. First, Joe Athialy considers the implications for IFI accountability systems of the holding in the 2019 U.S. Supreme Court that IFIs do not have absolute immunity. The case, *Jam v. Int'l Finance Corp.*, was brought by artisanal fishermen in India whose traditional livelihoods were disrupted by an IFC-financed coal-fired power plant. The Court held that under US law, that there are narrow exceptions to the immunity from lawsuit afforded the Bank and other international organizations, including an exception for lawsuits relating to economic activity taking place in the United States. With at least some future lawsuits possible, Athialy contends that the IAMs gain renewed significance, because their investigative findings could reasonably be used in court proceedings. Athialy argues that potential legal repercussions for non-compliance could compel the World Bank, for example, to enhance transparency, engage communities, and fortify safeguards. Amid challenges and past lapses, a recalibrated Panel, empowered to prevent harm, could emerge as crucial for more just, transparent, and equitable global development.

In Chapter 14, Gregory Berry makes the case for stronger action by IFIs to prevent reprisals against requesters and other environmental and human rights defenders and to reduce the level of impunity for the perpetrators. Shrinking civil society space has led to more reprisals against defenders and more impunity for those that have committed the reprisals, posing a fundamental threat to the accessibility and credibility of the IAM system. Berry argues for several essential responses to reprisals. First, IAMs and other oversight mechanisms, such as for audit or ethics must be empowered to protect the safety of defenders by self-initiating investigations into credible concerns of reprisals. The IAMs should also accept anonymously submitted complaints that allege fear of reprisals. Zero tolerance policies are not enough; both the IAMs and the IFIs have to persistently and relentlessly enforce their policies prohibiting all retaliatory acts.

The final pair of chapters address the dispute resolution functions within IAMs. In Chapter 15, Scott Adams and Aparna Mukajee provide a general review of the elements necessary to increase the chances of a successful dispute resolution process. They address a series of questions regarding dispute resolution at the IAMs, including: how should parties decide whether to participate in dispute resolution?; what are the roles of advocates and advisors?; when can dispute resolution provide accountability and remedy?; and why is it important for dispute resolution to be independent rather than embedded in DFI management? The chapter encourages further reflection on these questions as a way to enhance dispute resolution's effectiveness in addressing all stakeholder interests in the dispute resolution processes.

In this Part's final chapter, Gina Barbieri explores the relationship between compliance review and dispute resolution at the IAMs, where the two functions are often combined, raising questions about how or even whether to sequence them. Barbieri sees the two functions as complementary and explores the concept of joint fact finding among the contesting parties as a way of recognizing and enhancing this complementarity. Joint fact-finding facilitates cooperation among the stakeholders to build a joint understanding of the factual basis of their conflict – both for the purpose of feeding into compliance review and as a starting point for dispute resolution. By introducing the possibility of a hybrid approach involving joint fact-finding, Barbieri challenges the bipolar views many in the accountability community have about the two functions. But with this increased complexity comes the promise of greater cooperation between the two functions, including the use of hybrid approaches, that could enhance the effectiveness of both.

CHAPTER 10

Three Decades of Seeking Elusive Remedies

*Richard E. Bissell**

1 Introduction

In the area of accountability, remedy is a topic to be approached with some trepidation. Throughout three decades of proliferating Independent Accountability Mechanisms (IAMs), remedy has been the issue least addressed by the leadership of the financial institutions. Most Management and Board members find any remedial action threatening, wherever it falls on the remedy spectrum, from apology-for-error to financial compensation. The pursuit of remedy builds on the demonstrated existence of harm, which is embarrassing at the least, and brings a focus on consequences and actionable steps for those people whose lives have been damaged, as well as for environmental violations. This short essay addresses the evolution of remedy, beginning with the experience of the first mechanism, the World Bank Inspection Panel (the Panel), which included only a compliance review function without associated authority to make recommendations or monitor the institution's responses. The essay considers these authorities and the addition of a dispute resolution function in other IAMs.

2 The Inspection Panel's Design Flaws Regarding Remedy

The logical framework for the Panel and subsequent compliance mechanisms was that a compliance investigation would examine whether damage has been caused by the international financial institution's (IFI) non-compliance, and, if so, the expectation was that the Bank Management would remedy the situation. In reality, those holding the levers of power in IFIs, whether Board members, Presidents, or senior Managers, found this framework hard to accept. For those who wish to systematize our understanding of remedy in IAMs, therefore, there is a paucity of logic, consistent practice, or theory to draw upon. We need to reconsider how we stumbled into this structural

* Richard E. Bissell is the Lead Compliance Officer for the Social and Environmental Compliance Unit at the United Nations Development Programme.

dilemma and tease out the case-based experience on which we can start to build a knowledge base. Much of what follows draws upon practical experience across a broad and representative sample of the IAM community, including the World Bank, Asian Development Bank (ADB), African Development Bank (AFDB), European Bank for Reconstruction and Development (EBRD), and United Nations Development Programme (UNDP).

It is important to begin with the thirty years of experience of the Panel on this topic because the World Bank's struggles provide an opportunity to see progress, or lack thereof, in the ability of the accountability community to deliver sufficient remedies to affected communities, populations, and environments. Some might be surprised by the potential impact of IAMs, given that the Panel only had a compliance review function, has never had the power to make recommendations, and was carefully mandated to be a fact-finding or independent investigative body, with any potential remedies left to management and the Board to sort out. For some of the designers of the Panel, the requesters' complaints of harm served only to launch the case, rather than to shape the ultimate impact of an investigation. For others, it was optimistically assumed that a responsible Bank Management would not only bring a project into compliance in response to a Panel report, but also provide remedy to those who had brought the allegations of harm to the attention of the Panel in the first place.

From the first days of the Panel, the issue of remedy and remedial actions stimulated intractable disputes both within and outside the Bank. As reflected in General Counsel Ibrahim Shihata's 1994 book on the Panel,[1] the provision of remedial action plans included in the original 1993 Resolution sparked controversy with civil society. It gave management an opportunity to provide the Panel with an action plan, within three weeks of the submission of a complaint, with "evidence that it has complied, or intends to comply with the Bank's relevant policies and procedures."[2] Note that the question of mitigating harm to the complainants was not mentioned. Shihata cites objections from Daniel Bradlow, Lori Udall, and David Hunter that such a provision would be abused to shut down a potential investigation before the complainant had a chance to engage fully with the Panel. Shihata thought the concerns were overblown. After all, "if the complainant remains dissatisfied in spite of the declared remedial actions by the Bank's Management, because of the inadequacy of such actions or because they have not been properly implemented, it can pursue its

1 IBRAHIM F.I. SHIHATA, THE WORLD BANK INSPECTION PANEL, 100–101 (1994).

2 SHIHATA, *supra* note 1, at 76–77 (discussing Paragraph 18 of the resolutions creating the Panel).

complaint before the Panel … "[3] If Shihata thought that giving a complainant a chance to file a second complaint would address their concerns, he misunderstood the limited capacity of community groups to engage in a protracted struggle to get justice from the World Bank.

By the time of Shihata's second volume on the Panel in 2000, Shihata had to devote copious space to the way in which the Panel and Management jousted over the place of remedy at that early stage in the process after a complaint was received.[4] Management quickly perceived that an over-the-top response to the complaint, addressed primarily to the Board, could persuade the Board to reject or reduce the proposal for an investigation at the eligibility phase. Faced with an elaborate plan from management to bring a project into compliance, the Panel members began to undertake field-based, mini-investigations called "preliminary assessments" after registration, to gather sufficient evidence to prove that the management response was inadequate. Board meetings over a recommendation from the Panel that a complaint was eligible for an investigation became battlegrounds.

The crucial issue was that Management and much of the Board wanted the Panel to focus only on management actions that might lead to non-compliance with Bank policies–but the trigger for registering a complaint was that harm had been done to communities and the environment. Bank Management professed that such harm was a failure of the borrowers as implementers, not of the Bank. The Panel circumvented this argument by using the policy on project supervision as a keystone of most subsequent inspections, with a focus on the failures of Bank staff to keep a project compliant with Bank policies to avoid and mitigate any harm to communities. An early case for the Panel, regarding the Jamuna Bridge investigation, brought this issue to light, where the Bank sought to blame the Bangladeshi government for failing to include 75,000 residents on the char islands in the resettlement plan. Because the issue of involuntary resettlement was the most visible of safeguard policies, Bank Management soon shifted direction, working closely with the government to include all the displaced people in the remedial plan with compensation.

The original Resolution gave the Panel no role in determining remedies and redress for harm after completing their investigation and reporting to the Board. Accordingly, the remedies debate focused on preliminary eligibility steps rather than the ability to ensure that there would be remedies for the hardship incurred and the associated tangible incentives for communities

3 *Id.* at 100.

4 Ibrahim F.I. Shihata, The World Bank Inspection Panel: In Practice, 219–226 (2000).

to make the effort to complain to the Panel. Intense debates centered on the Board in the late 1990s over this issue, and several others, such as how to clarify the Board's direction to the Panel about how to engage on redress and remedy. Formal "Clarifications" were negotiated in 1996 and 1999 to at minimum call a truce on this aspect of the Panel relationship with Management and the Board. Panel reports on eligibility were more routinely approved in the immediate aftermath of the 1999 Clarification. The Board largely took the issue of "harm" off the table as a criterion of eligibility, and the leadership asked the Board to approve eligibility reports on a no-objection basis.

Controversy over mitigation of harm shifted to the post-investigation phase, and what might be decided by Management and the Board as actions to address the non-compliance findings of the Panel reports. The record did not improve. In one survey of all Panel investigations up to 2004, it was reported that only ten out of twenty-eight complaints registered by the Panel resulted in any "project level impacts."[5] For the complainants, there was little or no mitigation of consequence resulting from the findings of non-compliance in a wide range of high-stakes cases, such as Yacyreta,[6] Itaparica,[7] Lesotho Highlands,[8] Lake Victoria,[9] and Chad-Cameroon pipeline.[10] Interestingly, one case that had unexpectedly positive results was the NTPC Singrauli case in India, where Management persuaded the borrower to create an Independent Monitoring Panel (IMP) to "systematically & regularly review and advise on implementation of the R&R [rehabilitation and resettlement] program for the [National Thermal Power Corporation] NTPC power generation project funded by the World Bank."[11] Many residents found the IMP to be very helpful and it can be seen as positive for some of those whose complaints were mitigated. As a model for other World Bank responses to Panel investigations, however, the IMP failed; it was a one-off. In no subsequent investigations did Management achieve any visible remedy through the rare instances of creating such mechanisms. The

5 Dana Clark et al, eds., Demanding Accountability: Civil-Society Claims and the World Bank Inspection Panel, 257–69 (2003).

6 World Bank Inspection Panel, *Argentina and Paraguay-Yacyreta Hydroelectric Project: Report and Recommendation of the Inspection Panel (English)* (Sept. 30, 1996).

7 World Bank Inspection Panel, *Brazil – Itaparica Resettlement and Irrigation Project: Management Response to the Request for Inspection (English)* (March 12, 1997).

8 World Bank Inspection Panel, *Lesotho – Lesotho Highlands Water Project: Notice of Registration (English)* (May 14, 1999).

9 World Bank Inspection Panel, *Kenya – Lake Victoria Environmental Management Project: Inspection Panel Report (English)* (Dec. 15, 2000).

10 World Bank Inspection Panel, *Chad – Petroleum Development and Pipeline Project: Report and Recommendation on Request for Inspection (English)* (July 23, 2002).

11 Clark, *supra* note 6, at 180–83.

closest was the experience with the Chad-Cameroon Pipeline project investigation, where the review bodies established had little to no impact, but it can be argued that it became a precedent for monitoring mandates to be embedded in the accountability mechanisms of other institutions.[12]

3 The Evolution of the IAMs and Remedy

3.1 *Dispute Resolution as a Direct Driver of Remedy*

As to the present, the world of accountability has moved on. When new accountability mechanisms were established over the last three decades, there were additional institutional models other than the Panel to draw on. For example, many development finance institutions created dispute resolution units to work in parallel with their compliance review units. Proponents of dispute resolution argued that specific concerns of harm could be rapidly addressed by a neutral party convening Management and the complainants to negotiate appropriate relief of harm. Policy compliance was not included in the purview of such units. The first attempt to create a multi-function office was the Compliance Advisory Ombudsman (CAO) at the International Finance Corporation, with each of its three functions in separate silos. According to one study, the CAO has achieved measurable mitigation of harm in ten of its problem-solving cases, and in none of its compliance reviews.[13] On the other hand, the Asian Development Bank created two very separate offices for the two functions, and there was no collaboration between them. There were demonstrated limitations for dispute resolution units to get results any more rapidly and effectively than the attempts of compliance review units to mitigate harm. In some institutions, too, there was a requirement that any complaints had to be considered first by dispute resolution, in a transparent attempt to reduce the number of compliance investigations. Indeed, in the most recent rewrite of the EBRD Independent Project Accountability Mechanism (IPAM) procedures, a new complaint is referred first to the problem-solving unit to determine the attractiveness of dispute resolution before considering compliance review. Despite their obvious faults, problem-solving mechanisms provided real-time

12 World Bank & International Finance Corporation, *Chad-Cameroon Petroleum Development Pipeline Project: Overview*, VII (Dec. 2006).

13 Meagan Pearson, *Data Doesn't Support IFC/MIGA's Remedy Proposal*, ACCOUNTABILITY COUNSEL BLOG, (Mar. 6, 2023).

experimental contexts for considering remedial approaches that might offer greater justice for damaged communities and environments.

3.2 *The Power to Make Recommendations*

Unlike the Panel, many compliance review mechanisms now have a mandate to make recommendations based on the findings of non-compliance in the investigation report. There is no single institutional model. For some, the focus is on the drafting and approval of the Management Action Plan (MAP) both to bring a project into compliance and to mitigate the harm done or that could be done by the project. This is true of the ADB, where the Compliance Review Panel (CRP) has the right to comment on a Management Action Plan before its submission to the Board, and the CRP's recommendations are formally submitted to the Board along with the draft MAP. In a somewhat different approach, at the EBRD the IPAM has the power to recommend changes to the project and actions to address the harm or potential harm. In addition, the IPAM is tasked with sharing the draft MAP with the original complainants in order to get their comments on the likely effectiveness of the proposed remedies. At the UNDP, the Social and Environmental Compliance Unit (SECU) is empowered to make recommendations in its compliance report about remedying non-compliance, as well as to mitigate damage that has not been otherwise addressed through dispute resolution at the Stakeholder Response Mechanism.

3.3 *Monitoring and Remedies*

An important role played by an increasing number of IAMs is to monitor the implementation of the approved MAP, and thus test whether management has sustainably mitigated the harm from the project. At the ADB, the CRP monitors management performance of the MAP for up to three years. At the AFDB, the Compliance Review and Mediation Unit (CRMU) monitors implementation for up to five years. Even at the World Bank's last review of the Panel, a limited mandate to monitor was established, to be triggered only at the invitation of the Board. The effectiveness of that provision will need to be tested over time to determine the support of the Board and senior management for involvement of the Panel. The monitoring mandate at the UNDP's SECU has no time limit, with such oversight to last until the Administrator's decision and the MAP are fully implemented. An important step forward for the EBRD, AFDB, ADB, and UNDP has been to establish that the accountability mechanisms can, in the course of monitoring, undertake field monitoring missions if they judge them to be needed for monitoring. Such missions not only fill in the factual weaknesses in reports submitted by Management, but they also bring the original complainant back into the process. Who would know better than the complainants if the MAP has been successful in mitigating harm?

It is evident that we are in a creative period. New approaches are being designed and tested in real time in the absence of a persuasive "best practice." Fortunately, the IAM community has a strong "learning by doing" attitude, and with periodic reviews of the mechanisms by institutional learning, course corrections can be expected. There is also a fertile debate underway on what constitutes appropriate remedies. The advantage of a dispute resolution process is that both parties are encouraged to put their proposed remedies on the table. The downside of that approach is that the community enters the process in a weak position relative to the financial institution, and little leverage is available to the mediator to change that imbalance.

Compliance review mechanisms attempting to give greater attention to harm and its mitigation have leverage in their ability to make recommendations in their reports and shape the MAP before adoption by the Board. In the drafting of the UNDP SECU charter, greater focus on harm was seen in the provision enumerating likely remedies to be invoked for particular circumstances. They range from symbolic measures, such as institutional apologies, to concrete changes in the management of the project, to compensation for specific damage. In the most recent reform of the AFDB CRMU, it was specified that an investigation report may not recommend compensation or any other benefits to the complainants.

Finally, one has to address the difficulties posed by having two functions within one accountability mechanism, regardless of whether the two parts are unified or separate, and by having requirements for sequencing the use of compliance review and problem-solving. The mistake of specifying a one-size-fits-all approach is that each complainant comes to the mechanism with a specific intent; for some it is to change institutional policies, while for others it may be to mitigate specific harm, and for others still it could be both. The emerging consensus is that sequencing should be flexible enough to enable the complainants to choose the clearest path forward. Their best estimate of which function will facilitate their goals should be allowed to determine the sequencing. Decades of experience among the IAMs has demonstrated that the preliminary discussion during registration about the complainants' choice is an invaluable opportunity for learning which potential outcomes will best meet community concerns. Accountability mechanisms are not intuitively obvious to much of the public, and it is important that the choice of venue gives effective agency to the complainant. In the UNDP mechanisms, comprising both the SECU and Security Risk Management (SRM), a complainant can pursue one or the other, or both simultaneously. The SECU does not have the power to dictate a solution, but it does have a role as an independent investigative body to present its best expert view on providing remedies in the public final report to the complainants and to the Administrator, as the final decision maker.

3.4 *Future of Remedy*

The future of remedy can only be imagined; the world of IAMs is awash with new and innovative approaches to the issue. There are generic shortcomings in all of the institutional approaches to development finance that undermine the ability of accountability mechanisms to mitigate harms that result from policy compliance failures. The External Review of IFC/MIGA conducted in 2020 provides a frank and thoughtful consideration of the consequences of findings on non-compliance from the CAO and how remedial actions may flow from a judgment of non-compliance.[14] It addresses the thorny issue of responsibility, which is divided in the IFC's case between the IFC and the client. A storm of criticism greeted the 2023 issuance of how the IFC proposes to implement the recommendations of the External Review.[15] The critics focused particularly on the clear unwillingness of IFC management to foresee taking responsibility for harm done to communities. Indeed, the IFC saw a role in remedial measures only "in exceptional circumstances" and that generally the obligation would fall on IFC clients or sovereign guarantors.[16] The commentaries expressed frustration that the IFC draft approach neither adopted the specific reforms on remedial measures proposed by the External Review nor reflected the spirit of the Review that the IFC could be a model leader on remedy among IFIs.[17]

Responsibility for remedy will not be a short debate, as indicated by the 2022 report from the UN High Commission on Human Rights, from their

14 Peter Woicke, et al., *External Review of IFC/MIGA E&S Accountability, including CAO's Role and Effectiveness Report and Recommendations* (June 2020), https://thedocs.worldbank.org/en/doc/578881597160949764-0330022020/original/ExternalReviewofIFCMIGAESAccountabilitydisclosure.pdf (last visited Jan. 17, 2025).

15 IFC, *External Review: IFC/MIGA Update of Non-policy Actions*, (https://www.ifc.org/content/dam/ifc/doc/2023/202104-ifc-miga-non-policy-actions-update.pdf (last visited Jan. 17, 2025).

16 U.N. Human Rights Office of the High Commissioner, *IFC/MIGA Draft Approach to Remedial Action Comments and Recommendations of the UN Human Rights Office*, 8 (Apr. 13, 2023).

17 *See id.*; *see also* Earth Rights International, *Submission of EarthRights International on the Draft IFC/MIGA Approach to Remedial Action* (Mar. 20, 2023).

Accountability and Remedy Project.[18] Its focus on non-state-based grievance mechanisms provides much to inspire those thinking about the future of remedy; to be specific, it has thirteen recommendations for action by key stakeholders. Their bottom line is that the accountability community is on an extended journey with the agenda of remedy, and its importance will only increase.

Conceptually, the major challenge remains that too many people in decision-making positions continue to believe the relationship between remedy and policy compliance is "either/or." The story of the Panel is instructive in this regard, where the Bank insists that Panel reports must focus on regaining compliance, not on remedying the harm that triggered the case in the first place. Instead, the relationship must become "and."

Some of the visionaries involved in designing the Panel thought remedy and compliance could be mutually reinforcing. Making that proposition a reality falls to an emerging generation, both at the World Bank and the larger world of development finance.

Bibliography

Clark, Dana, et al. *Demanding Accountability: Civil-Society Claims and the World Bank Inspection Panel.* Lanham: Rowland & Littlefield, 2003: 257–269.

EarthRights International. *Submission of EarthRights International on the Draft IFC/MIGA Approach to Remedial Action.* Washington DC: EarthRights International, March 20, 2023. https://earthrights.org/wp-content/uploads/2023/04/ERI-Submission-on-IFC-MIGA-Remedial-Approach-4.20.23.pdf.

Fairman, David, et al. *External Review of IFC/MIGA E&S Accountability, including CAO's Role and Effectiveness Report and Recommendations.* Washington DC: World Bank, June 2020. ExternalReviewofIFCMIGAESAccountabilitydisclosure.pdf (worldbank.org).

International Finance Corporation. *External Review: IFC/MIGA Update of Non-policy Actions.* Washington DC: IFC, July 26, 2023.

Pearson, Meagan. *Data Doesn't Support IFC/MIGA's Remedy Proposal.* San Francisco: Accountability Counsel, March 6, 2023. https://www.accountabilitycounsel.org/2023/03/data-doesnt-support-ifc-migas-remedy-proposal/.

Shihata, Ibrahim F. I. *The World Bank Inspection Panel.* Oxford: Oxford University Press, 1994: 100–101.

18 U.N. Human Rights Office of the High Commissioner, *Remedy in Development Finance: Guidance and Practice* (Feb. 23, 2022).

Shihata, Ibrahim F. I. *The World Bank Inspection Panel: In Practice.* Oxford: Oxford University Press, 2000: 219–226.

United Nations Human Rights Office of the High Commissioner. *Remedy in Development Finance: Guidance and Practice.* Geneva: United Nations, February 23, 2022.

United Nations Human Rights Office of the High Commissioner. *IFC/MIGA Draft Approach to Remedial Action Comments and Recommendations of the UN Human Rights Office.* Geneva: United Nations, April 13, 2023: 8.

World Bank Inspection Panel. *Argentina and Paraguay- Yacyreta Hydroelectric Project: Report and Recommendation of the Inspection Panel (English).* Accessed December 30, 2024. https://documents.worldbank.org/en/publication/documents-reports/documentdetail/832261468740399783/argentina-and-paraguay-yacyreta-hydroelectric-project-report-and-recommendation-of-the-inspection-panel.

World Bank Inspection Panel. *Brazil – Itaparica Resettlement and Irrigation Project : Management Response to the Request for Inspection (English).* Accessed December 30, 2024. https://documents.worldbank.org/en/publication/documents-reports/documentdetail/242831468744265638/brazil-itaparica-resettlement-and-irrigation-project-management-response-to-the-request-for-inspection.

World Bank Inspection Panel. *Chad – Petroleum Development and Pipeline Project : Report and Recommendation on Request for Inspection (English).* Accessed December 30, 2024. https://documents.worldbank.org/en/publication/documents-reports/documentdetail/740981468768846131/chad-petroleum-development-and-pipeline-project-report-and-recommendation-on-request-for-inspection.

World Bank Inspection Panel. *Kenya – Lake Victoria Environmental Management Project: Inspection Panel Report (English).* Accessed December 30, 2024. https://documents.worldbank.org/en/publication/documents-reports/documentdetail/755071468771310495/kenya-lake-victoria-environmental-management-project-inspection-panel-report.

World Bank Inspection Panel. *Lesotho – Lesotho Highlands Water Project : Notice of Registration (English).* Accessed December 30, 2024. https://documents.worldbank.org/en/publication/documents-reports/documentdetail/566201468772185775/lesotho-lesotho-highlands-water-project-notice-of-registration.

World Bank & International Finance Corporation. *Chad-Cameroon Petroleum Development Pipeline Project: Overview*, VII (Dec. 2006).

CHAPTER 11

Exiting the Disaster, Evading the Responsibility? Wadi al-Qamar – The Moon Valley

*Suzan Nada**

1 Introduction

Wadi al-Qamar in Alexandria, Egypt, is a residential area developed in the 1940s, according to the maps registered and issued by the Egyptian Survey Authority (ESA). It was designed to overlook the sea and is currently home to over 60,000 people. They say that it was named for the beautiful sight of the moonlight hitting the malt fields that used to cover the area.

In 1948, the Egyptian Government established the Alexandria Portland Cement Company. It was privatized in 2000 by Lafarge Egypt Company, which sold 50 percent of the stocks to TITAN Cement Egypt in 2002. The TITAN Group is a multinational company manufacturing cement and construction materials. Lafarge Egypt was responsible for the management of the Company until May 2008, when, with the support of the International Finance Corporation (IFC), TITAN Cement Egypt bought Lafarge's share to own the Company outright.

The factory is only sixty meters away from the Wadi al-Qamar residential area. Until 1996, the factory was operating four furnaces using wet processes to manufacture cement. In that year, the management requested the construction of a fifth furnace to operate on dry processing; the fifth furnace started operating in 2002.

As the impacts of these developments became apparent on the surrounding environment and local communities, some groups raised complaints about the project locally and some raised their complaints to the IFC's Compliance Advisor Ombudsman (CAO).

* Suzan Nada is a labor and legal activist, accountability and resolution expert, human rights lawyer, co-founder of the Bread and Freedom political party in Egypt, and Coordinator of the Coordinating Committee to Support Wadi al-Qamar.

2 The Complaining Parties

2.1 *Irregular or Temporary Workers*

The first group of complainants comprised irregular or temporary workers, who had worked for a long time at the factory. Some of them had regular contracts and tenure with medical insurance and pensions; however, the management reduced their numbers, making many of them irregular workers through a specialized recruiting company. Due to high rates of unemployment in Egypt, workers had to agree to sign fixed-term contracts, renewable annually. Because this step removed the rights of these workers to medical and social insurance and pensions, they attempted to resist this act of dispossession by organizing several peaceful strikes.

With the January 25 Revolution of 2011, workers came together in an independent union and joined the Egyptian Trade Union Federation (ETUF). This union was never officially recognized under the laws later introduced by the State. In 2012, workers organized a picket line, calling for their medical and social insurance to be reintroduced, and for pay and bonuses equal to regular workers. However, the police stormed the picket line inside the company's grounds using batons, weapons, and dangerous police dogs. Several workers were injured, and twenty-two workers were arrested because the company claimed that they detained the manager of the recruiting company TITAN that was under contract to recruit workers.

The twenty-two workers were detained for two months before being released. The lawsuit, which received international exposure, resulted in their acquittal, but the company laid them off anyway.

2.2 *Early Retirement Workers*

The second group comprised early retirement workers, who were employed when the Egyptian State owned the company – from its establishment in 1948 until its privatization in 2002. These workers were subject to the Egyptian Labor Law of the Public Sector, which requires the establishment of a pension fund for workers that pays workers their receivables when they retire. It also specifies that workers may – when the company is privatized – get a percentage of stocks at a price lower than the trading price that may be paid in installments and/or deducted from the worker's annual profits.

Many of these workers were retired early by the management in return for low bonuses that varied from one worker to another, with no standards. In addition, the company neither disbursed their sums from the pension fund nor compensated them for the stocks, the value of which had been deducted from their salaries throughout their time with the company. These workers filed a lawsuit before the Alexandria Administrative Judiciary Court of the State Council on January 3, 2016, hoping for a court order in their favor. The outcome of the 2016 suit is still pending. In the meantime, the Administrative Judiciary Court of the State Council issued a court order finding that the company had violated Article 45 of Law 203 of 1991 and that the plaintiff workers were eligible to resume working and receive their sums.

2.3 *Residents of Wadi al-Qamar*

The third group of stakeholders was the People's Movement to Support Residents of Wadi al-Qamar. Since its establishment, the cement factory has caused resentment in the residential area of Wadi al-Qamar for blocking the residents' access to the sea and polluting the area. The privatization of the factory in 2002 and the construction of the fifth furnace exacerbated the pollution because of the increased production, low chimneys, and proximity to the residents. Residents complained that both children and adults suffered from respiratory diseases and other ailments because of the smoke and dust.

Residents negotiated unsuccessfully with the management of the company and became convinced that the company was procrastinating. Accordingly, the residents established the Coordinating Committee to Support Wadi al-Qamar in 2014 during an unofficial meeting among representatives of the well-known families in the area. Under its Articles of Association, the Committee's mission is to communicate with the residents and advocate their cause. The Committee helped the residents file their complaint to the IFC Compliance Advisor Ombudsman (CAO).[1]

The cement factory harmed not only the complaining parties, but also Egyptian citizens in general and Alexandrian residents in particular. It led to environmental pollution in an area that once was truly the "Wadi al-Qamar," a hub for therapeutic tourism, transforming it into one of the world's most polluted areas. The factory also impacted the fish population, which is a source of income and food for the residents of the area. Furthermore, the enlarged factory caused greater pollution to the Middle East's top supplier of table salt, the El-Mex Salines Company, which was located close to TITAN's buildings and extensions.

In short, the cement factory impacted everyone in the region, and news of its environmental violations circulated widely among citizens, in newspapers, and in other mass media. The Egyptian Parliament held several hearings on the pollution from the factory. In the aftermath of the January 25 Revolution, efforts were consolidated to face this multi-pronged threat to health, the

1 *See* IFC's Compliance Advisor/Ombudsman, *Egypt: Alex Dev-01/ Wadi al-Qamar* https://docs.google.com/document/d/1YG0lNhrPPQ3m3T2XsZwbe7wFCaGiL3iI/edit (last visited Dec. 20, 2024).

environment, and livelihoods. The People's Movement to Support Residents of Wadi al-Qamar was established as an umbrella for several groupings and advocates, including:

- *The People's Movement to Support Residents of Wadi al-Qamar – Front of Defending Rights and Freedoms*: This body included several civil society organizations (CSOs): the Egyptian Center for Economic and Social Rights (ECESR), the Egyptian Initiative for Personal Rights (EIPR), the Egyptian Commission for Rights and Freedoms (ECRF), and several human rights lawyers.
- *The Permanent Conference for Workers of Alexandria*: This is an umbrella trade union representing a large number of independent trade unions and many working advocates.
- *The Independent Association of TITAN Cement Workers*: The Association is tasked with defending Wadi al-Qamar and confronting TITAN Cement Egypt Company.

Several public conferences were held, and various statements were issued and released on a wide scale. In addition, signatures were collected and submitted to state agencies, and legal bodies were formed to deal with lawsuits related to workers of TITAN Cement Egypt Company. A lawsuit claiming the invalidity of the company's contract was filed. In 2014, I was invited to speak at a symposium as part of the International Monetary Fund (IMF)/World Bank Spring Meetings in Washington DC. The symposium was supported by the Bank Information Center (BIC), a US CSO. Several other CSOs, World Bank officials, and officials of the Office of the CAO attended the meetings.

During the symposium, I highlighted the negative impacts and repercussions of TITAN's cement factory, including the environmental damage and abdication of the residents' right to a healthy life according to human and labor rights. It was during this visit that we became aware that we could file a complaint to the Office of the CAO. The complaint was formulated and submitted later in 2014.

3 Subject Matter of the Complaint

In 2010, the IFC had approved an €80 million capital investment in a subsidiary of TITAN Group. The investment was allocated to promote the expansion of the Egyptian commercial processes of TITAN and included Alexandria Development Ltd. IFC's investment was aimed at improving the environmental performance of TITAN's cement factory by raising the efficiency of the pollution rate and increasing energy efficiency.

The complaint made the case that IFC's decision to fund this project was entirely misguided. IFC's publications state that the corporation's framework revolves around sustainability and affirms a strategic commitment to sustainable development as part and parcel of IFC's approach to risk management. Such an approach highlights preventative policies and performance indicators related to the environment and social impacts. However, IFC complied with neither environmental nor workers' rights standards. The violations are detailed below.

3.1 *The Factory Operated Illegally with No License to Operate*

The factory did not receive the license to operate required by Egyptian Law, as stated in the State Commissioners Authority's report in Lawsuit No. 11632 of 1964 by the Alexandria Administrative Judiciary Court. The Blue Circle Company acquired a *temporary* six-month license to operate the fifth furnace on February 5, 2001 until it met certain legal requirements; the Company has never fulfilled these requirements. On February 28, 2004, the license was nonetheless renewed for 5 years to end on January 31, 2010. After Blue Circle was merged with Alexandria Portland Cement Company, they submitted a request to the El-Agamy District Office to renew the license and issue a new license under the name of the Alexandria Portland Cement Company. This license was issued on May 28, 2009, requiring that the factory commence operations only after acquiring the final license from the Industrial Development Authority (IDA). However, the factory continued to operate at full capacity, and the El-Agamy District Office renewed the temporary license in July 2011 for another five years.

In its report, the Egyptian State Lawsuits Authority mentioned that renewing a temporary license removes the quality of being temporary altogether and is an illicit attempt to make a temporary license permanent. Thus, the report recommended issuing a court order to shut the company down, as it was being operated without a license. The Company's behavior violates several Egyptian laws – such as Law No. 453 of 1954 and the Environment Law No. 4 of 1994 – which address dangerous and hazardous places and those harming health and the environment. The company's failure to acquire the license is related to a precondition that it receive approval by the Ministry of Environment. Egyptian law stipulates conducting a comprehensive study of the environmental impact by the relevant bodies; this requirement was not fulfilled. The failure to comply with the environmental assessment requirement is also a violation of IFC standards, notably ESS1 Assessment and Management of Environmental and Social Risks and Impacts.

3.2 *The Company Seized Public Lands by Force in Violation of the Law*

The company seized sixty meters of the public road in front of the factory by force and built an iron fence in front of the company's main gate on the public road. In response to the residents' complaint, an order was issued by the State Commissioners Authority to remove the fence. It had not been removed as of the date of this writing (November, 2023).

3.3 *The Local Community and Impacted Groups Objected to the Company*

The company did not involve stakeholders and those harmed by the project's environmental and social impacts, contradicting the IFC's Performance Standard 1 that stipulates the necessity of involving stakeholders impacted by the project. Residents of Wadi al-Qamar continue to object to the existence of the factory and its fifth furnace in their area, because it jeopardizes their health and safety and encroaches on their livelihoods by polluting seawater and harming fish stocks.

3.4 *Elected Parliamentary Bodies Objected to the Company's Behavior*

The first objection in Parliament was in 2007. The Chairman of the then-People's Assembly forwarded the matter to the Environmental Protection Committee of the Local Popular Council (LPC). A committee was formed, including health and environment experts and executive members, to study the issue. The committee issued its report in July 2008, describing the company's violations as "severe;" it also stated that the emissions resulting from the company caused grave harm to the population and neighboring companies and machinery, and a significant hazard to citizens' health. Despite these findings, the company did not implement any of the committee's recommendations or those of the LPC. For example, the company did not periodically change the filters or end the use of diesel fuel and mazut. It even started using coal. Nor did it relocate away from inhabited areas as the committee recommended in its report.

3.5 *Owners of Neighboring Factories Objected to and Were Impacted by the Company*

Objection to the pollution caused by the factory expanded to include other industrial facilities in the area established before TITAN's cement factory, notably the El-Mex Salines Company site. Established in 1805, El-Mex Salines is the Middle East's oldest and largest salt-producing company. The Company extracts salt from the sea using evaporation pans covering almost thirty-eight million square meters that could be exposed to emissions from the factory's main outdoor chimney, depositing cement dust on the salt. After El-Mex Salines filed a lawsuit against TITAN Cement, the court assigned an expert to discover the direct impact on the salt pans and warehouses. The expert's report confirmed that the salt in the pans and warehouses exposed to the chimney's gas is coated with an obvious grey cement layer.

3.6 *The Factory Causes Environmental Pollution*

Article 34 of Egypt's Environment Law stipulates that a project's site should be suitable to ensure that the limits of air pollutants in an area are not exceeded. The IFC's Performance Standard 3 for sustainability seeks to prevent or reduce negative impacts on human health and environmental safety, and Performance Standard 1 stipulates that businesses should respect human rights. The factory violates all of these standards. Moreover, public health continues to deteriorate, with residents – both children and adults – still suffering from respiratory and other illnesses.

3.6.1 Dust Emissions and Particulates

The report by the Ministry of Justice, filed in the context of Lawsuit No. 238 of 2010 (Urgent) Alexandria Court, indicated that the factory produces nearly 4,750 tons of cement per hour, with an average gas flow rate from the chimney of about 890,617 cubic meters. Since the average gas emissions were around 120 milligrams per cubic meter after filtration, experts estimated that the average amount of dust coming out of the chimney was equal to about forty kilograms per hour, 1,700 kilograms per day, or 570 tons per year. Residents of the area breathe the dust, and it accumulates in their food, houses, and bedrooms.

The IFC's Performance Standard 1 says that in case of a variation between local standards and those accredited by financial institutions, the stricter of the two standards should be applied. In this instance, there was a failure to apply even the less-strict standards.

3.6.2 The Use of Coal

According to Article 42 Clause 2, Egyptian law prohibits the use of coal in urban areas and near residential areas. Furthermore, Performance Standard 3 is aimed at limiting greenhouse gas emissions; in its strategy for achieving sustainable development and combating climate change, the World Bank had previously announced new restrictions on projects using coal as an energy source in order to limit greenhouse gas emissions.

Nonetheless, TITAN Cement Egypt Company began using coal as a fuel to operate the factory in 2015, increasing particulate emissions, adding carbon pollution to nitrogen and sulfur, and generating emissions of heavy metals such as mercury, lead, dioxin, and furan.

Interestingly, some workers mentioned that the management threatened to fire them if they disclosed the use of coal. This statement was recorded and documented during an interview with one of the workers while filming a movie on the use of coal directed by Shereen Talaat and titled *Van Gogh: An Incomplete Portrait*.

3.6.3 Sound Pollution and Noise

Only a few meters separate the factory and the residential area. Thus, sounds resulting from operating machinery, vehicles, and mills cause severe noise pollution and discomfort to the residents due to the factory being too close.

3.6.4 Impact on the Safety and Security of Residents

Residents affirm that the oscillations resulting from operating machinery, equipment, and mills were so severe that they caused cracks in some neighboring buildings and led to some of their external parts falling repeatedly. These incidents are major threats to safety, security, and real estate.

3.7 *The Management of the Company Called for Displacing Local Residents (Performance Standard 5)*

Performance Standard 5 is related to land acquisition and involuntary resettlement. In an interview published in *Al-Ahram Weekly* on November 5, 2011, the Deputy CEO of TITAN Cement Egypt Company – who is also the Head of the Cement Division of the Construction Materials Chamber at the Federation of Egyptian Industries (FEI) – called for forcibly displacing the residents and attacked calls for environmental protection and sustainability as "destructive." He also mentioned that the cement industry faced violent attacks, such as the one calling for relocating the factory to the desert side under – he said – the pretext of polluting the environment. These calls, he claimed, threaten and hinder the industry.

4 Progress and Outcome of the Investigations

The Coordinating Committee lodged its complaint with the CAO in April 2015. The CAO issued its report on July 22, 2021, six years and three months after the complaint had been filed.

According to the report, the CAO's investigation team – including officials from the Office and two external consultants (one an expert in labor and the other in air quality) – reviewed the files of IFC's projects and conducted interviews with the financing officials with direct knowledge of the matter. In January 2017, the team made a field visit to Cairo and Alexandria to meet with representatives of the complaining parties, residents of Wadi al-Qamar, current and ex-workers of the Alexandria Portland Cement Company (TITAN), management officials at the company, and other stakeholders and relevant parties.

The report noted that after the field visit, representatives of the company – with the assistance of some policemen – threatened the stakeholders and representatives of CSOs who attended the interview. The report confirmed many of the complainant's allegations. To quote the executive summary of the report:

> In this report, CAO identifies instances of IFC's non-compliance with the E&S [Environmental & Social] policies and procedures during the period of IFC's review and supervision of the project. CAO also makes findings in relation to adverse environmental and/or social outcomes, including the extent to which these are verifiable.
>
> At the pre-investment review stage, CAO finds that IFC did not meet the required standard of review. Specifically, the CAO finds that IFC's review was not appropriate given the nature and scale of the project or commensurate with the level of E&S risks and impacts, as required by the Sustainability Policy.
>
> IFC's pre-investment review noted that the plant's airborne emissions were higher than WBG [World Bank Group] standards and that the plant was located in close proximity to communities in a mixed use industrial-residential area. However, IFC's E&S review did not adequately assess or address the impacts of air pollution or noise from the plant on local residents and did not analyze potential cumulative impacts in the project area, particularly in relation to air quality, noise and human health.
>
> Key E&S assessment documents were not disclosed to the affected community, and IFC did not adequately assess the client's community disclosure and engagement practices in accordance with relevant requirements.
>
> Further, CAO finds that IFC erred in its decision that the project did not trigger the requirement for "broad community support". Given the proximity to residential areas and the impacts of pollution on community health, these impacts should have been considered "significant" and IFC should have ensured that the company carried out a process of free, prior and informed consultation before making the investment.
>
> IFC's appraisal did not adequately assess risks and impacts to the client's workers. IFC did not identify legacy issues relating to post-privatization early retirement programs carried out at APCC [Alexandria Portland Cement Company] under the joint venture in 2002 and 2003 as required

> by the Sustainability Policy. Although PS2 [Project Standard 2] requires that core labor protections relating to working conditions, freedom of association and health and safety be extended to indirectly employed workers, IFC did not assess the client's approach to the engagement of contract workers against requirements of PS2 or national law. This was a significant oversight in context where the client employed over 700 contract workers.[2]

5 A Questionable Transaction

While the report found in favor of the complaining parties, it was a merely theoretical document. As noted above, it was issued six years and three months after the complaint had been filed. And before it was issued, IFC had sold its stocks in the project back to the parent company.

Apparently, IFC was aware – before the report was issued – of the mistakes, violations, and harms the project and its extensions caused. In 2019, before publication of the CAO's report, the IFC sold its interest in the project to TITAN Cement Egypt Company.[3] The sales agreement included the financial liabilities, policies, and reports until the price is fully paid. However, it did not tackle broader environmental and social standards and IFC's own standards. As a result of this sale, TITAN Cement Egypt Company's commitment to IFC was terminated, and with it the company's obligation to comply with the IFC's Performance Standards.

IFC had the right to sell its stocks, and the parent company had the right to purchase them. But the transaction raises several questions. For example, does the sale necessarily mean surrendering the rights of all workers, residents, neighboring companies and factories, and the local and global environment?

IFC helped enlarge and expand a project whose harm and violations to its own standards were proven. Is it acceptable for IFC to exit when a legitimate, valid complaint is pending? Does IFC's exit and sale of its stake in the project exempt it from the liability of harming others? Further, IFC sold the stocks to the party that has a record of ignoring both complaints and standards and calling in police and other forces to respond to peaceful protests.

---

2 *See* CAO, *Compliance Investigation Report CAO Investigation of IFC's Environmental and Social Performance in Relation to its Investment in Alexandria Development Limited, Egypt* (March 2023); Bank Information Center, *Titan Cement- Alexandria* https://bankinformationcenter.org/en-us/project/ifc/ (last visited Dec. 20, 2023).

3 *See* CAO, *supra* note 2, at 6.

Given the way the sale was made, it appears likely that IFC will keep ignoring environmental and social standards. It appears to have been a deliberate strategy for IFC to avoid all commitments and liabilities by exiting the project, before it was implicated by the findings in the report.

While the sale agreement included the financial liabilities, policies, and reports until the price was fully paid, it did not include commitments relating to meeting IFC or national environmental and social standards. As a result of this sale, TITAN Cement's commitment to IFC was terminated, with little point left in discussing compliance with IFC's Performance Standards.

6 Hope Persists

The delay in the CAO's release of its investigation's findings undermined the ability to provide any effective redress to the complainants, despite the broad validation of their concerns. For the system to provide hope in this case and cases like it, we call for institutions and IAMs to:

- Review the standards that were ignored or bent in this project – as clarified by the report – to avoid such damage in the future;
- Determine realistic, suitable, and binding dates for the investigation of complaints, and the presentation of the final reports;
- Allow investigative bodies to issue urgent reports on violations before the completion of the final report and to call for interim measures, to prevent the recurrence of similar cases where companies or institutions evade responsibility; and
- Adopt clear standards for IFIs to responsibly exit projects and ensure that they comply with these standards. If necessary, standards should be applied retrospectively to remedy the damage to which non-compliance may have contributed.

[Editor's Note: In part because of concerns raised in the context of this and other cases, IFC published a "responsible exit strategy" in October of 2024. Under this strategy, the IFC will use five key principles to determine whether and how to exit from a project with considerations of its environmental and social impacts:

- Evaluate the achievement and sustainability of the targeted development impact;
- Address E&S issues;
- Use leverage pre-exit;
- Consider institutional constraints and precedential implications; and
- Consider impact on mobilization.

The IFC will also weigh factors such as, "its leverage, reputational risk, legal liability, and external partners," when determining how to act. While the efficacy of this approach remains to be seen, it illustrates an acknowledgement within the IFC "that the projects it has financed do not leave people who are meant to benefit in worse condition." *See* International Finance Corporation, IFC's Approach to Responsible Exit (Oct. 4 2024).]

Bibliography

Bank Information Center, *Titan Cement-Alexandria*, BIC https://bankinformationcenter.org/en-us/project/ifc/ (last visited Dec. 20, 2023).

International Finance Corporation's [IFC] Compliance Advisor/Ombudsman [CAO], *Compliance Investigation Report CAO Investigation of IFC's Environmental and Social Performance in Relation to its Investment in Alexandria Development Limited, Egypt*, CAO (March 2023).

CAO, *Egypt: Alex Dev-01/ Wadi al-Qamar* https://docs.google.com/document/d/1YG0lNhrPPQ3m3T2XsZwbe7wFCaGiL3iI/edit (last visited Dec. 20, 2024).

Carla García Zendejas, *Responsible Exit: A Critical Step for Accountability, But Real Test Lies Ahead.* CIEL (Oct. 7, 2024).

CHAPTER 12

World Bank Forcible Resettlement: the Need for More Inspection Panel Scrutiny

*Lori Udall**

1 Introduction

Since the Inspection Panel's inception in 1993, more than half of all of its requests (89 out of 173) have involved the involuntary resettlement of people in World Bank Projects. Even though the Panel has investigated only thirty-two of those cases, some facts are indisputable: involuntary resettlement almost exclusively results from top-down decisions that adversely impact marginalized sections of local communities such as Indigenous Peoples, minorities, fisher folk, poor farmers, and those without land tenure. The Bank and host country typically try to justify involuntary resettlement as a necessary cost of larger development projects, where people living in the project area need to be moved to accomplish the project's goals.

The World Bank's disastrous record in involuntary resettlement dates back far beyond the Inspection Panel's creation. In fact, a particular project, the Sardar Sarovar dam on the Narmada River in India, and the historic grassroots resistance to it, became the impetus for the Bank's Board to create the Panel. The building and implementation of the Sardar Sarovar dam and the accompanying forced relocation was so egregious that in 1992 a review team (the Morse Commission) wrote an entire book covering all the violations of Bank safeguard policies. The involuntary resettlement of Adivasi tribal people in the project area was often accompanied by police force and violence, to the extent that the Morse Commission said that continued resettlement would be completed only through "unacceptable means."[1] The Morse Commission documented the failure to accurately count the numbers of those to

* Lori Udall has over 30 years of experience in the review, design, and operations of independent accountability mechanisms.

1 Bradford Morse & Thomas Berger, Sardar Sarovar: The Report of the Independent Review, xi–xx, 349–58 (1992) ("The opposition especially in the submergence area has ripened into hostility. So long as the hostility endures progress will be impossible except as a result of unacceptable meanness.").

be resettled, a lack of land for resettlement, the moving of people by police force, and other human rights abuses; it was a case study in how not to conduct resettlement. One of the chronic failures in those years was the inability to calculate the actual number of those being displaced. In Sardar Sarovar, years after the appraisal it became clear the Bank had underestimated the number of people displaced by at least 250,000.

This was in 1992; in that era, projects like the Sardar Sarovar dam, the Singrauli Coal project also in India, Transmigration in Indonesia, Polonoroeste in Brazil, and Nam Thun II in Thailand were protested by grassroots and international activists alike.[2] The creation of the Inspection Panel in 1993 established a channel for people who had been harmed by Bank projects to appeal to an independent body for an investigation and assessment of potential violations of World Bank policies. Many of those activists fighting against resettlement impacts believed that if the Bank would simply implement and enforce its own safeguard policies, it would provide some remedy to the communities. The Board of Executive Directors was willing to create this mechanism if its mission was narrowly defined, and the Panel reported directly to them.

The fundamental elements of the World Bank's Operational Policy and Bank Practice (OP/BP 4.12) are that resettlement should be avoided or minimized wherever feasible, resettlement activities should be conceived as sustainable development projects where displaced people share in project benefits, and affected and displaced people should be assisted to improve their livelihoods or at least to restore their previous standard of living.[3]

Fast forward to 2016 when the Inspection Panel issued their first *Emerging Lessons Series: Involuntary Settlement*.[4] This Report drew on the Panel's Experiences and lessons from its twenty-two year caseload. By 2016, the Panel had received 105 requests for inspection. Out of the thirty-two cases that were investigated, twenty-one involved forcible resettlement. Several of the cases were problematic projects where the Bank had grossly underestimated the number of people to be displaced, such as the Ghana Second Urban Environment Sanitation Project (USEP), and The Albania Integrated Coastal Zone Management and Clean-Up Project. The Democratic Republic of Congo (DRC) Forest-Related Operations, although not a resettlement project, was another

2 For a discussion of the Bank's impact in these and other projects, see BRUCE RICH, MORTGAGING THE EARTH: THE WORLD BANK, ENVIRONMENTAL IMPOVERISHMENT AND THE CRISIS OF DEVELOPMENT (1994).

3 World Bank, *Operation Manual- OP 4.12- Involuntary Resettlement* (Dec. 2001).

4 World Bank Inspection Panel, *Emerging Lessons Series No 1: Involuntary Resettlement* (Apr. 2016).

case in which Pygmy people who were impacted by the project were not identified or counted adequately.[5] The main conclusions from the Report were that the Bank's policy goal of implementing resettlement as sustainable development projects had not been achieved in most cases because they had failed to analyze the full costs and impacts of resettlement.[6] The Panel also concluded that the Bank should implement better analysis of the full economics of resettlement and include a thorough examination of what it takes to restore and improve the incomes and livelihoods of those who are resettled.[7]

The Panel drew seven lessons from its review of projects from 1994–2014:[8]

- The risks of involuntary resettlement should be assessed comprehensively before a project begins:
  - In the Uganda Private Power Generation Project (Bujagali), the Panel found that when the previous project was stopped, the resettlement of a portion of the 8,700 people had already started.[9] When the project commenced, the Panel found that the resettlement plan did not effectively assess the impacts of the previous resettlement, and affected people were left out of the new resettlement plan.
  - In the Kenya Natural Resources Management Project, the implementing agency had no mandate or experience in resettlement or with community access to forest resources.[10]
- Meaningful consultation and participation should be an essential part of involuntary resettlement programs.
  - In the Mumbai Urban Transport Project, the Bank's largest urban resettlement project at the time, the Panel found that the meeting with

5 World Bank Inspection Panel, *The Inspection Panel at Fifteen*, 67 (Jan. 2009) (wherein the Panel noted shortcomings in the delineation of project-affected areas that did not include all people who would be affected and that somehow "these people have fallen off the radar screen") https://documents.worldbank.org/en/publication/documents-reports/documentdetail/997441468157510017/the-inspection-panel-at-fifteen-years (last visited Jan. 26, 2025).

6 The World Bank Inspection Panel, *Emerging Lessons Series No 1: Involuntary Resettlement*, IV (Apr. 8, 2016).

7 *Id.*

8 *Id.*, Appendix B, List of Panel cases analyzed.

9 *See* Inspection Panel, *Report and Recommendation on a Request for Inspection–Republic of Uganda Private Power Generaltion (Bujagali) Project (P089659); Water management and Development Project (P123204); and Energy for Rural Transformation Phase III Project (P133312)* (Sept. 2018) https://www.inspectionpanel.org/sites/default/files/ip/PanelCases/110-113-Inspection%20Panel%20Report%20and%20Recommendation-16Dec2016.pdf (last visited Jan. 24, 2025).

10 Inspection Panel, *supra* note 6, at 5–6.

affected people consisted of informing them of what was going to occur rather than soliciting participation.[11]
  - In the Nepal Power Project, the affected people had little knowledge of their resettlement because the documents were only in English, and only made available and translated seven years later.[12]
- If the Bank's resettlement policy is utilized, then there should be preparation of a resettlement policy framework or a resettlement action plan.
  - The choice of the appropriate resettlement instrument is the cornerstone of effective resettlement. In the Ghana UESP II Case, the project continued without a resettlement plan or policy framework. The lack of preparation adversely impacted the identification of project risks and proper consultation.[13]
- There should be active supervision of resettlement projects to properly identify and resolve issues.
  - In the Cambodia Land Management and Administration Project, attention to the social impacts of land titling, including possible evictions, was not systematic and there was a lack of expertise on social safeguards.[14]
- Compensation to project-affected people should be timely and needs to have a sound method of valuing the amount of compensation.
  - The Nepal Power Development Project, for example, failed to complete compensation payments because there was confusion about when payment should be released, and this resulted in economic strain on communities.[15]
- A local grievance redress mechanism needs to be available and accessible to the affected people.
  - In the Nepal Power Development Project, the affected people were unaware of their right to engage with a redress mechanism. The Panel found there was not an accessible mechanism available.[16]

---

11 World Bank Inspection Panel, *Investigation Report- India: Mumbai Urban Transport Project* (*IBRD Loan No. 4665–IN; IDA Credit No. 3662–IN*) (Dec. 21, 2005) https://documents1.worldbank.org/curated/en/645491468283447968/pdf/34725.pdf (last visited Jan. 26, 2025).

12 Inspection Panel, *supra* note 6, at 8–9.

13 *Id.* at 9–10.

14 World Bank Inspection Panel, *Investigation Report- Cambodia: Land Management and Administration Project* (*Credit No. 3650–KH*) (Nov. 23, 2010) https://documents1.worldbank.org/curated/en/183101468229739528/pdf/580160INVR0INS1se0only1910BOX353791.pdf (last visited Jan. 26, 2025).

15 World Bank Inspection Panel, *Nepal: Power Development Project* (*P043311*) (Feb. 12, 2015) https://www.inspectionpanel.org/sites/default/files/ip/PanelCases/87-Investigation%20Report-Nepal%20Power%20Development%20Project.pdf (last visisted Jan. 24, 2025).

16 Inspection Panel, *supra* note 6, at 13.

- The goal of livelihood restoration is most effective when there is transitional support, development assistance and alternatives to resettlement are provided.[17]
  - In the Kenya Electricity Project, the Panel thought that "land for land" was a positive development, but the Panel found that the resettlement site has poor pastoral land for cattle, which provided subsistence security and cash income for the affected people. The affected Maasai people were left without their cultural center, which provided tourism income.[18]

Following the publication of *Emerging Lessons on Involuntary Resettlement,* World Bank President Jim Yong Kim stated that he knew resettlement was an area the Bank needed to improve, and he added "I am confident that the lessons identified by the Panel in this report will help greatly in that effort."[19]

The Inspection Panel *Emerging Lessons Report* followed on the heels of the 2012 and 2014 internal World Bank reports on involuntary resettlement that were not released until March 2015, after the Bank weakened its ten safeguard policies through an extensive revision and reinvention of its policies.[20] Most significantly, the Environmental and Social Framework disposes of Bank staff responsibility for policy enforcement, and puts the onus on the Bank's borrower, the majority of which do not have resettlement or Indigenous People's policies. The new framework came into effect in 2018, but the Panel has not yet handled a case filed under the newer policy.

After the internal Bank Reports were made public, President Kim also expressed concern:

> We found major problems. One is that we haven't done a good job in overseeing projects involving resettlement; two we haven't implemented those plans well enough, and three, we haven't put in place strong tracking systems to make sure that our policies were being followed. We must and will do better."[21]

17 *Id.* at 4–16. The Panel is restricted to drawing from Panel cases and cannot comment more broadly on Bank performance in projects involving resettlement.

18 *Id.* at 16.

19 *Id.* at 32.

20 World Bank, *Social Development Department Inventory Resettlement Review, Phase 1: Inventory of Bank financed projects that triggered the Involuntary Resettlement Policy (1990–2010)*, Draft World Bank Social Development Projects (2012).

21 World Bank, *Press Release* (Mar. 4, 2015). After a Panel presentation, the Bank's Chief Counsel Alberto Ninio responded that there was no disagreement on the conclusions reached in the Inspection Panel Report, and that the Bank had been working to improve resettlement outcomes, adding "This is the most difficult issue when it comes to development."

Kim announced an action plan and stated, "[o]ur policy is that if we resettle someone from their home, we will assist efforts to *improve or at least restore their incomes and living standards* (emphasis added)".[22]

Kim's statement reflected the fact that the policy goals enshrined in Bank policies from the beginning have rarely, if ever, been accomplished. Despite President Kim's concern, seven years later many of these lessons and recommendations have not been considered or implemented by Bank operations.

The three reports that documented serious failures apparently did not discourage the Bank from pursuing forcible resettlement on a large scale in development projects going forward. The weakened policy framework may make matters worse, as there is less commitment to restoring the quality of life of those resettled. Most activists, anthropologists, and academics that study or work on resettlement have rejected the Bank's Environmental and Social Framework and the Environmental and Social Standards as unacceptable because the Bank has squandered responsibility.

The Bank's experience with resettlement is tragically not unique. In 2018, the celebrated anthropologist Michael M. Cernea and lawyer Julie K. Maldonado produced a book revealing the disastrous state of development caused by forced relocation of marginalized people across the globe.[23] While of course not all the highlighted projects were funded by the World Bank, the Bank does not emerge from analysis as a social safeguard leader in the field, but rather as a contributor to the disaster.

In the opening chapter, Cernea and Maldonado propound that "forced displacements are expanding, compounding harmful economic pauperization and cultural impacts."[24] The authors also note that the magnitude of the researched evidence points to major failures in reconstructing livelihoods. The frameworks are failing, they argue, because most borrowing countries do not have proper legislation or policy dealing with resettlement, and there is lack of funding and poor implementation.[25]

The levels of resettlement are staggering:

> The World Bank estimated in 1994 that 10 million people per year were displaced in developing countries by activity in only three economic sectors (hydropower, urban, and transport) producing 100 million people

22 *Id.* at 2.

23 MICHAEL CERNEA & JULIE K. MOLDONADO (EDS.), CHALLENGING THE PREVAILING OF DISPLACEMENT AND RESETTLEMENT 2 (2023).

24 *Id.*

25 *Id.*

> displaced per decade. For the following decade (2001–2021), they estimate along similar criteria but also included additional economic sectors [indicating] that the number displaced would be about 15 million per year, resulting in 150 million displaced people for the first decade of the 21st Century. For the decade 2011–2020 and as the pace of infrastructure building accelerates, the estimated magnitude of forcible displacement is likely on conservative estimates to exceed 20 million people per year which means 200 million or even more for a decade.[26]

Cernea and Maldonado also emphasized data from the 2012 and 2014 internal World Bank reports noting that:

> Even the minimal level of restoring pre-displacement level was achieved in less than one-third of the Bank's many hundreds of projects. The other two-thirds of the projects are listed as either having *failed* to achieve the minimal policy goal of income restoration or as projects [where] the Bank *didn't know* what happened to the livelihoods of the populations displaced. This low percentage is the sad recognition that two out of every three projects have failed to deliver to the displaced people what the World Bank and their countries' governments had committed to deliver. *This is a remarkable admission of failure and of ignorance about displacements' outcome* (emphasis added).[27]

One of the chapters, *Boomtown Risks and Community Harm in an Infrastructure Project*, discusses a Bank resettlement project in Uganda where there was lack of consultation and failure to monitor, supervise, or identify actual numbers of people to be displaced, or the government's lack of capacity to implement resettlement projects.[28] The Inspection Panel wrote that, "[t]he particulars in the Project demonstrate how a combination of poor planning, weak risk analysis, and accompanying mitigation measures, coupled with the lack of understanding of community dynamics led to serious harm."[29]

In November 2023, the Inspection Panel issued a new Advisory Report on Livelihoods that again reflects poorly on World Bank involuntary resettlement

26 *Id*, at 4.

27 *Id.* at 16.

28 Elana Berger & Moses Ntenga, *Boomtown Risks and Community Harm in an Infrastructure Project, in* Michael Cernea & Julie K. Moldonado, eds., Challenging the Prevailing of Displacement and Resettlement 95 (2023).

29 *Id.*

activities. Thirty-nine cases were considered in the report, and of these twenty-three were registered. The Panel recommended an investigation in nine of the cases. Six of the cases involved involuntary resettlement.[30] The Report details that in most cases, communities that were forcibly displaced did not have their livelihoods restored. The advisory details several recurring issues in World Bank projects, including lack of consultation and lack of understanding of local conditions; failure to accurately determine numbers of people to be displaced; and extensive problems in affected people recovering their livelihoods. In Brazil's Teresina Resettlement, the training programs used for restoration were pre-existing national programs that impacted people did not know how to approach.[31] Additionally, these impacted people had to compete with 100,000 residents from other areas. The Panel suggested that the Bank determine whether the programs were accessible to the affected people.

The India Amaravati project was a land pooling scheme where landowners gave up their farmland in exchange for smaller plots with public services. The Panel wrote that "affected persons participating in this scheme needed to transition from rural farm-based livelihoods to urban non-farming livelihoods. This was a drastic social change that inherently involved high risks of impoverishment. Furthermore, many of the [project-affected people] lacked formal education and had low literacy, and many had farmed their whole lives."[32] The Report further stated that "[p]roperty value does not automatically translate to a production system or employment that can sustain a family into the future and improve their standard of living."[33]

In another India case, R Water Supply and Sanitation Project for Low Income States, the Requesters complained that a water treatment plant impacted their goat pastures, the collection of medicinal herbs, and their access to red mud used for painting houses. The construction of the plant also made it more difficult to collect wood for fires and to fence home gardens. The Panel findings stated that the social assessment and tribal development plan did not adequately assess customary land, cultural, and religious uses and practices.[34]

In the Panel Report's conclusions, they state: "The Panel cases show that at times, the more vulnerable and marginal people are more likely to be

30 World Bank Inspection Panel, *Ensuring Development While Securing Livelihoods* 6 (2023).

31 World Bank Inspection Panel, *Brazil Teresina Enhancing Municipal Governance and Quality of Life Project Additional Financing (P14870)* (July 22, 2020), https://www.inspectionpanel.org/sites/www.inspectionpanel.org/files/cases/documents/140-Investigation%20Report-22%20July%202020.pdf (last visited Jan. 26, 2025).

32 *Id.* at 22–23.

33 *Id.* at 23.

34 *Id.* at 18.

overlooked in census surveys, data and assessments. As a result, they are not adequately consulted or included in livelihood restoration and improvement strategies, leading to further marginalization and impoverishment."[35] The Report also indicates that close monitoring and supervision has not occurred in many cases.

In 2023, Requesters filed a complaint on the Tanzania Resilient Natural Resource Management for Tourism and Growth and cited threats of eviction, violence, theft of cattle, and lack of prior consultation with indigenous communities. The Request filed by the Oakland Institute on behalf of local communities also alleged that park rangers in Ruaha National Park were responsible for extrajudicial killings, human rights abuses, and disappearances of affected community members.

Initially, the Panel reported that the harm related to the Bank's indigenous policy was not plausibly linked to the project, and that no resettlement was taking place. However, later the World Bank suspended project disbursement on April 18, 2024 due to noncompliance with "safeguard requirements including resettlement procedures and compensation, grievance monitoring and reporting."[36] On January 22, 2025, the World Bank cancelled the project due to ongoing violations. The Oakland Institute issued a message from the affected people: "The impacted communities call on the World Bank to fully assume its responsibility and urgently take action to answer our plea for justice. Our lives are on hold as the threat of eviction looms over us every single day."

Can it be true that so little has changed in the implementation of involuntary resettlement in Bank projects since the early 1990's? The same mistakes and miscalculations are clearly still being made in Bank operations. With this poor record of resettlement, the only possible conclusion is that no more World Bank funding should be spent on forcible resettlement; given that few borrower governments have adequate resettlement policies in place, continued support of forced resettlement only invites more failure and resulting destitution for communities. The bottom line seems to be that involuntary resettlement of communities to make way for top-down development is difficult, and that it is probably impossible to restore all impacted people's livelihoods.

The Bank has also announced it will once again provide funding for large hydro projects, which will inevitably involve resettlement. If the World Bank moved towards bottom-up community-based development that responds to climate change events and community goals, it could avoid forced resettlement in many cases. Whether related to climate change or not, the Bank should

35 *Id.* at 30.

36 Inspection Panel, *Second Request for Inspection, Tanzania: Resilient Natural Resources for Tourism and Growth* 2 (May 17, 2024).

reject projects involving the forcible resettlement of large numbers of people, especially where there is no clear land base to move people. The Bank should also be held accountable for violations of policy by Bank shareholders, Executive Directors, parliaments, and taxpayers.

With the evidence compiled over thirty years, it is obvious that the Inspection Panel today needs more authority. The upcoming review of the Bank's Accountability Mechanism does not include a review of the Panel's mandate and authority, which is unfortunate because the Panel's powers desperately need to be expanded so that problems can be corrected early and often. In particular, the Board should empower the Inspection Panel in the following ways:

1. The Panel needs teeth. It should have the same monitoring and reporting authority enshrined in other compliance mechanism policies. Monitoring should be continued for five years after the publication of Panel Investigation Reports, and the monitoring reports should be sent directly to the Board with findings and recommendations.
2. The Panel should be empowered to conduct spot checks through site visits to any World Bank project involving involuntary resettlement that has become problematic.
3. During eligibility or investigation or at any time during the Panel process, the Panel should be empowered to recommend suspension of a project to the Board.
4. The Panel should be able to return to legacy Bank resettlement projects that were previously investigated and still have outstanding issues, and make recommendations to the Board and management on remedy.

Going forward, if the World Bank cannot enforce its own policies, it should avoid funding projects that involve forcible resettlement and only fund resettlement that is based on bottom-up community consent. This is particularly important if the Bank expects to be a leader in climate change finance. Climate change will put pressure on many communities, requiring difficult decisions about whether to resettle whole neighborhoods, regions, and even countries. Perhaps lessons learned over the past decades in misapplying its resettlement policies in the context of development-induced displacements may be easier to apply in the climate context where the Bank is not directly responsible for financing the displacement.

Bibliography

Berger, Elana, and Moses Ntenga. "Boomtown Risks and Community Harm in an Infrastructure Project," in *Challenging the Prevailing of Displacement and Resettlement*, edited by Michael Cerna and Julie K. Moldonado, 95. New York: Routledge, 2023.

Berger, Thomas, and Hugh Brody. *Sardar Sarovar, Report of the Independent Review, Bradford Morse.* Ottawa: Resources Futures International, 1992: 356.

Cernea, Michael, and Julie K. Moldonado. *Challenging the Prevailing of Displacement and Resettlement.* New York: Routledge, 2023: 2.

World Bank. *Operation Manual- OP 4.12- Involuntary Resettlement.* Washington DC: World Bank, December 2001. https://thedocs.worldbank.org/en/doc/b192cc75476bc0d5a54a1e4ceba50776-0290012023/original/OP-4-12-Involuntary-Resettlement.pdf/

World Bank. *Social Development Department Inventory Resettlement Review, Phase 1: Inventory of Bank financed projects that triggered the Involuntary Resettlement Policy (1990–2010).* Washington DC: Draft World Bank Social Development Projects, 2012.

World Bank Inspection Panel. *Investigation Report- India: Mumbai Urban Transport Project (IBRD Loan No. 4665–IN; IDA Credit No. 3662–IN).* Washington DC: World Bank, December 21, 2005. https://documents1.worldbank.org/curated/en/645491468283447968/pdf/34725.pdf.

World Bank Inspection Panel. *The Inspection Panel at Fifteen.* Washington DC: The World Bank, 2009: 67. https://documents.worldbank.org/en/publication/documents-reports/documentdetail/997441468157510017/the-inspection-panel-at-fifteen-years.

World Bank Inspection Panel. *Investigation Report- Cambodia: Land Management and Administration Project (Credit No. 3650–KH),* THE INSPECTION PANEL Nov. 23, 2010) https://documents1.worldbank.org/curated/en/183101468229739528/pdf/580160INVR0INS1se00nly1910BOX353791.pdf.

World Bank Inspection Panel. *Emerging Lessons Series No 1: Involuntary Resettlement.* Washington DC: World Bank, April 2016.

World Bank Inspection Panel. *Report and Recommendation on a Request for Inspection- Republic of Uganda Private Power Generaltion (Bujali) Project (P089659); Water manamgenet and Development Project (P123204); and Energy for Rural Transpformation Phase III Project (P133312).* Washington DC: World Bank, September 2018. https://www.inspectionpanel.org/sites/default/files/ip/PanelCases/110-113-Inspection%20Panel%20Report%20and%20Recommendation-16Dec2016.pdf.

World Bank Inspection Panel. *Brazil Teresina Enhancing Municipal Governance and Quality of Life Project Additional Financing (P14870).* Washington DC: World Bank, July 22, 2020. https://www.inspectionpanel.org/sites/www.inspectionpanel.org/files/cases/documents/140-Investigation%20Report-22%20July%202020.pdf.

World Bank Inspection Panel. *Ensuring Development While Securing Livelihoods.* Washington DC: World Bank, 2023: 6.

CHAPTER 13

The World Bank, the Inspection Panel and Immunity

*Joe Athialy**

1 Introduction

The establishment of the World Bank Inspection Panel (the Panel) marked a significant development, driven by the struggles and campaigns of people's movements and civil society organizations (CSOs), during a period when the World Bank Group operated under the shield of absolute immunity. A bold experiment in bolstering transparency and accountability within the Bank, the Panel's three-decade journey has been characterized by different highs and lows. The Bank, buoyed by its perceived insulation from legal consequences, indulged in weakening the mandate of the Panel time and again, armed with the confidence that, except for some irritation in the NGO-community, it didn't have anything else to lose.

The landscape shifted, however, with the 2019 judgement by the US Supreme Court in *International Finance Corporation v Jam*, which declared that international organizations, including the World Bank, do not enjoy absolute immunity.[1] This judicial ruling has the potential to be a transformative factor for both the Bank and the Panel. Its ramifications compel a re-evaluation of power dynamics, governance structures, and accountability mechanisms.

For the Bank, navigating the new pathways necessitates a recalibration of its practices and approach. The once-steadfast shield, now punctured by legal vulnerabilities, demands a more transparent engagement with affected communities, robust project assessments, and diligent adherence to safeguards. The loss of absolute immunity presents the Bank with an opportunity, perhaps even an imperative, to strengthen its mechanisms for addressing grievances, ensuring its independence and responsiveness regarding Panel findings.

* Joe Athialy heads the Centre for Financial Accountability, India.

1 *See Jam v. International Finance Corp.*, 586 U.S. ___, 139 S. Ct. 759 (2019).

DOI:10.1163/9789004729735_018

In a post-immunity world, the significance of the Panel's role to scrutinize, recommend, and demand corrective actions assumes renewed gravity. The Panel's findings and recommendations relating to policy non-compliance may now be subjected to subsequent legal actions brought by affected communities, potentially ushering in new consequences for lapses in adherence to policies and standards. Knowing that the Panel findings could lead to litigation, Bank staff could take their role of assessing the environmental and social risks, as well as closely monitoring impacts, more seriously. The Bank may not so easily ignore the Panel's findings, which could be a beacon to take quick and adequate actions to address community concerns.

The US Supreme Court's landmark decision has the potential to redefine not only the contours of accountability within the Bank but also the landscape of global development finance. As the Bank adjusts to the ramifications of this ruling, the Panel stands poised as a dynamic agent of change, assuming a pivotal position in a more transparent, accountable, and equitable future for international development initiatives.

2 Origins of the Panel

India played a significant role in the creation of the Panel. Its genesis can be traced back to the Sardar Sarovar Narmada Dam project, which was financed by the World Bank in the 1980s. The Narmada Dam project faced widespread opposition from affected communities and civil society groups, who raised concerns about its negative social and environmental impacts.

The issues raised by the grassroots movement, the Narmada Bachao Andolan (Save Narmada Movement – NBA) resonated globally, putting an international spotlight on the negative impacts of the Narmada Dam, which had been approved by the Bank two years before the Indian Environment Ministry cleared the project.

The growing concerns over the negative impacts of the Narmada Dam project forced the World Bank into yielding to the demand for an Independent Review Commission (the so-called "Morse Commission") in 1991 – then an unprecedented step, marking the first instance of the Bank subjecting a project financed by it to review. The Morse Commission's findings raised serious questions about the efficacy of the Bank's safeguard policies, accentuating the need for an autonomous framework of accountability.[2]

2 Bradford Morse & Thomas Berger, Sardar Sarovar: The Report of the Independent Review, xi–xx, 349–58 (1992).

While the Bank tried to downplay the findings of the report, CSOs around the world called for greater transparency and accountability, and the creation of a body that could investigate complaints from affected communities and ensure compliance with safeguard policies. The organized campaign and advocacy efforts by the CSOs resulted in the establishment of the Inspection Panel in 1993 – the first of its kind in any multilateral financial institution. Looking back at the Panel, while the Bank feels that it "has shown that it's possible to democratize the oversight and accountability process, and hold ourselves accountable to the people we serve,"[3] it needs to recognize that the Panel, as in the case of most of the progressive policies of the Bank, emerged from grounded, local resistances.

It's another matter that three decades after the Independent Review found serious violations in the Narmada Dam project, and despite the withdrawal of Bank support, the project continued pulling in public resources for its completion. It was inaugurated by the Prime Minister in 2017 as a 'birthday gift' to himself, with 200,000 people forced to sacrifice their houses and fields for the dam. Thomas Berger, Deputy Chairman of the Independent Review had said then, referring to the dam, "unless a project can be carried out in accordance with existing norms of human rights and environmental protection, norms espoused and endorsed by both the World Bank and many borrower countries, the project ought not to proceed."[4]

The Panel did indeed represent a breakthrough in international law, serving as the prototype for international financial organizations, and as a tool in the hands of the communities to hold investors accountable and to protect peoples' rights. Today, nearly twenty other similar mechanisms exist – including at most major development banks – all modelled in some way on the World Bank's pioneering effort.[5]

2.1 *Challenges to the Panel's Effectiveness*

Despite its well-intentioned inception, the Panel has itself been entangled in procedural issues as well as challenges arising from its limited mandate and outreach in the past three decades. These issues are further demonstrated by the fact that in the past three decades it has received only 165 complaints out of 13,300 projects–just 1.2% of all projects, many of which the Bank itself

3 The World Bank Inspection Panel, *Inspection Panel Marks its 25th Anniversary* (Nov. 16, 2018).

4 Thomas R. Berger, *The World Bank's Independent Review of Sardar Sarovar Projects,* 9 AM. U. INT'L L. REV. 33 (1993).

5 *See* Gonzalo Castro de la Mata, et al., *Opinion: Inspection Panel Marks 25 Years of Accountability at the World Bank,* DEVEX (Dec. 16, 2018).

categorizes as having high or substantial negative environmental and social impacts.

Institutionally, the Panel has faced challenges. Time and again, Bank Management has tried to clip the Panel's wings, weakening and limiting its mandate. This started within the first few years of its inception. Since the initial cases that the Panel received in its first three years were controversial, the actions taken by the Panel did not resonate with the interests of the Management or some of the Bank's borrowers, resulting in growing opposition to the Panel process in the Board of Executive Directors.[6] Attempts to weaken the Panel were evident in multiple review processes thereafter. As recently as 2021, when a committee of the Bank's Board attempted to make significant changes to the Panel's mandate without transparent public consultation, experts and activists had warned that "without input from the very people the panel was designed to serve – communities impacted by the Bank – the Board risks making decisions in the dark that could lead to a weakened mechanism because it lacks the knowledge and insight gained by people who stand to both gain and lose the most from the reforms."[7]

The onus of knowing about the Bank's involvement in projects largely falls on the affected communities, who often are less literate, unfamiliar with the internet and unlikely to navigate through the Bank's website, at the receiving end of a farcical public consultation hearing, and unaware about the Bank's safeguard policies. At best, their grasp of these policies remains sketchy, further compounded by a tenuous understanding of the established complaint mechanisms. Moreover, impact assessment studies and the monitoring of safeguard policy implementation are carried out by the client and their consultants. The Panel lacks an independent mechanism to verify the authenticity of these assessments or monitoring reports.

The political context in which these communities raise complaints is also often overlooked. Many countries where these complaints originated face shrinking democratic spaces, and widespread intimidation and reprisals against people who dared to challenge the government or a corporation is common. With the media heavily controlled and constitutional bodies compromised, avenues for justice or remedies for communities become increasingly limited.

6 Daniel D, Bradlow, *Lessons From The NGO Campaign Against The Second Review Of The World Bank Inspection Panel: A Participant's Perspective*, 7 ILSA J. INT'L & COMP. L. 247 (2001).

7 Natalie Bridgman Fields, et al., *Opinion: The Case for Public Reforms to the World Bank's Inspection Panel*, DEVEX (Dec. 13, 2019).

When communities finally file complaints despite all these obstacles, and in cases where the Panel or other Independent Accountability Mechanisms (IAMs) found serious violations of policies, the IAMs lacked the power to make recommendations or hold staff accountable for erroneous risk assessments. A case in point is the Tata Mundra project in India.

3 The Tata Mundra Case

Launched in 2007, this $4 billion, 4000 MW coal-fired thermal power project on the western coast of India was partly financed by the International Finance Corporation (IFC), the private sector arm of the World Bank Group (WBG). This venture, heralded as India's pioneering ultra-mega power project to meet the nation's growing energy demands, assumed an air of invincibility, even in the face of documented violations.

Ironically, the involvement of international lending entities like the IFC inadvertently prolonged these violations. The IFC's reluctance to wield its influence as a financier and failure to drive course correction in project trajectories, allowed violations to persist. Even when its own policy standards were openly flouted, it often turned a blind eye, resulting in irreversible damages to people's livelihood and environment.

In 2011, people affected by precisely these issues filed a complaint about the project to IFC's IAM, the Compliance Advisor Ombudsman (CAO). After an exhaustive investigation, the CAO's report in 2013 laid bare the flagrant breaches of the IFC's Performance Standards, exposing a glaring chasm between proclaimed intention and actual execution. The CAO report found that:

- Environmental and social risks and impacts of the project were not considered and addressed;
- There was no social baseline data;
- IFC's policies for land acquisition were not applied, despite physical and economic displacement;
- Inadequate attention was paid to the requirement of biodiversity conservation;
- The IFC failed in its review and supervision of the impacts on the airshed and marine environment;
- The IFC failed to examine the cumulative impact of projects around Tata Mundra; and
- The fishworkers and farmers who were the most severely affected by this project were not even considered "project-affected."

The CAO concluded that "… the above weaknesses in IFC's E&S review of CGPL [Coastal Gujarat Power Limited] did not support the formation of a robust view as to whether the project could be expected to meet the requirements of the Performance Standards over a reasonable period of time, the threshold question in terms of IFC's decision to invest."[8]

However, the IFC preferred not to act on the CAO's report. Not only did this make a mockery of the findings of the IFC's own accountability mechanism, it also undermined the mandate of the CAO by ignoring its findings and not taking the appropriate recourse actions. The CAO's subsequent monitoring reports revealed that the issues remain unaddressed.

The failure of institutional processes forced the community to knock on the doors of the judicial system of the United States, where the IFC is registered, for remedy. Hiding behind the immunity clause, the IFC tried to evade taking responsibility for the damages their lending caused. After a process of dismissals and appeals, the matter reached the US Supreme Court, where it was heard and a final judgement delivered.

3.1 *World Bank Immunity on Trial*

In 2015, after exhausting every available recourse, the fishing communities and farmers filed a suit in the U.S. District Court of Washington, DC, against the IFC over the destruction of their livelihoods and property and health hazards caused by the Tata Mundra power plant.[9] The plaintiffs, represented by EarthRights International (ERI), included fisherfolk adversely affected by the project, farmers affected by increasing groundwater salinity and contamination of their farmland by ash and dust, the Machimar Adhikar Sangharsh Sangathan (Association for the Struggle for Fisherworkers' Rights) and the Navinal Panchayat (village), a local government entity.

The District Court initially found that the IFC was immune from suit, which the plaintiffs appealed at the D.C. Circuit Court of Appeals. On Appeal, the three-judge panel recognized the "dismal" situation, noting that the IFC did not deny that the plant had caused substantial damage and yet found the IFC could not be sued based on the Circuit's previous decisions.[10] In her dissenting opinion, however, Judge Nina Pillard highlighted that the Court was bound by earlier precedents, which she described as "wrongly decided" and suggested they should be reconsidered. She essentially gave a roadmap for the

8 *See* Office of the Compliance Advisor Ombudsman, *CAO Audit of IFC Investment in Coastal Gujarat Power Limited, India*, Audit Report (Aug. 22, 2013).

9 *Jam v. International Finance Corp.*, 172 F. Supp 3d 104, 108–109 (D.D.C. 2016).

10 *Jam v. International Finance Corp.*, 860 F. 3d 703 (D.C. Cir. 2017).

appeal to the Supreme Court when she suggested the D.C. Circuit had taken "a wrong turn" when it "grant[ed] international organizations a static, absolute immunity".[11]

In its historic decision on February 27, 2019 the U.S. Supreme Court decided that international organizations like the World Bank Group do not enjoy absolute immunity. The court's majority decision overturned a 74-year-old presumption that international financial institutions could not be sued when their development projects hurt local communities.[12] Simply put, with this judgement, the World Bank and other international financial institutions can be sued anywhere for the damages they are causing to people and the environment. For years, the World Bank has operated as if it were above the law, at times pursuing reckless lending projects that inflicted serious human rights abuses, and then leaving the communities to fend for themselves.[13]

3.2 *Implications for the Bank and* IAMs

The establishment of the Panel (and similar other IAMs) occurred during a period when the Bank enjoyed absolute immunity from legal repercussions. This immunity provided the Bank with a sense of impunity that in turn enabled the institution to tinker at its discretion with the mandate and powers of the Panel, which by then had emerged as a final recourse for communities aggrieved by projects funded by the Bank. These communities found themselves compelled to accept the Panel decisions, regardless of whether their complaints were rejected on technical grounds, met with wishy-washy reports or reports devoid of proactive actions from Management, or responded to other pressures.

However, the lifting of immunity has significantly shifted the ground. For communities whose grievances were insufficiently addressed by the Panel or instances in which the Bank chose to disregard findings and abstain from corrective measures, legal remedies now present a viable course of action. The Bank has a choice to make: to pursue its old ways of functioning or recognise the changing times and take steps to prevent a deluge of legal cases. Since the Supreme Court verdict, the reporting lines of the CAO were redirected from the World Bank President to the Board, showing a positive response from the Bank.

11 *Id.* at 708.

12 Sasha Chavkin, *No Longer Above The Law, The World Bank Faces Fight of Its Life,* INTERNATIONAL CONSORTIUM OF INVESTIGATIVE JOURNALISTS (Mar. 13, 2019).

13 For more on the case, see EarthRights International, *Budha Ismail Jam, et al v.* IFC, https://earthrights.org/case/budha-ismail-jam-et-al-v-ifc/ (last visited Oct. 16, 2023).

An empowered Panel, with more powers and authority to deal with and satisfactorily settle the grievances of people and communities, will go a long way in gaining the confidence of communities as a genuine destination for addressing grievances. This includes not only the power to investigate but also the capacity to issue time-bound recommendations for rectifying violations. The pivotal alteration in this regard is the provision of *suo moto* powers of the Panel. This alteration would enable the Panel to initiate investigations into projects that are in high-risk categories, and to take proactive measures to prevent irreparable harm. This departure from the status quo, where communities (in almost all cases) approach the Panel after harm has been incurred, aligns with a preventive approach, an essential alteration to mitigate potential legal consequences.

Moreover, to ensure equitable decision-making and robust project oversight, the active engagement of affected communities across all tiers of decision-making and project monitoring is imperative. By affording these communities a voice, their concerns can be duly acknowledged and their interests safeguarded. This not only promotes inclusivity but also contributes to better project outcomes.

4 The Bank's Opportunity

Nothing can restore faith in the Bank and its IAMs as much as taking proactive action in addressing the harm caused by Bank-financed projects. Nowhere during the litigation against the IFC in the case of Tata Mundra (*Jam vs IFC*) did it deny the social and environmental damages caused due to its lending. However, when the case resumed in the District Court, it escaped from paying the liabilities for the damages on a narrow interpretation of law.

Legally speaking, the Bank is not liable to pay anything to the badly impacted fisher-people and farmers. But morally, it is. Without its lending, the project would not have occurred. By ignoring the findings of its own accountability mechanism, it not only undermined its mandate but also lost a chance to undo some of the damages done to people and the environment by its own failure to apply environmental protections.

It could still try to do that. It could reach out to people and help them restore their livelihoods and the damaged coastline and farmlands. Such a gesture would convey that the Bank is serious in addressing the violations of its own policies as recorded by its accountability mechanisms. This could prevent future complainants from seeking legal remedy as their first option.

5 Conclusion

The erosion of the Bank's immunity status has ushered in a new era, necessitating a reconsideration of the dynamics between the Bank, its mechanisms like the Panel, and the communities they impact. The potential for legal recourse now underscores the significance of granting the Panel greater authority, including the ability to proactively investigate high-risk projects and make binding recommendations. Concurrently, involving affected communities in decision-making processes remains a cornerstone of ensuring accountability and equitable development outcomes.

Bibliography

Berger, Thomas R. "The World Bank's Independent Review of Sardar Sarovar Projects," American University International Law Review, 9, no. 1 (1993): 33.

Bradlow, Daniel D. "Lessons From The NGO Campaign Against The Second Review Of The World Bank Inspection Panel: A Participant's Perspective." *ILSA Journal of International and Comparative Law*, 7, no. 247 (2001): 247.

Chavkin, Sasha. "No Longer Above The Law, The World Bank Faces Fight of Its Life." International Consortium of Investigative Journalists, March 13, 2019.

Compliance Advisor Ombudsman. *CAO Audit of IFC Investment in Coastal Gujarat Power Limited, India*, Audit Report. Washington DC: CAO, August 22, 2013.

de la Mata, Gonzalo Castro, et al. "Opinion: Inspection Panel Marks 25 Years Of Accountability at the World Bank." DEVEX, December 16, 2018.

EarthRights International. "Budha Ismail Jam, et al v. IFC." EarthRights International. Accessed December 16, 2023.

Fields, Natalie Bridgman, et al. "Opinion: The Case for Public Reforms to the World Bank's Inspection Panel." DEVEX, December 13, 2019.

https://www.devex.com/news/opinion-the-case-for-public-reforms-to-the-world-bank-s-inspection-panel-96223.

Morse, Bradford, and Thomas R. Berger. *Sardar Sarovar-The Report of the Independent Review*. Ottawa: Resources Future International, 1992.

World Bank Inspection Panel. *Inspection Panel Marks its 25th Anniversary*. Washington DC: World Bank, November 16, 2018.

CHAPTER 14

Ending Violence in Development Finance: Actions to Affirmatively Prevent and Stop Reprisals against Rights Defenders

*Greg Berry**

1 Introduction

In January 2016, the United Nations Sustainable Development Goals (SDGs) officially came into force, commencing a global push to end poverty, respond to climate change, and meet a range of environmental and social targets to secure a sustainable future.[1] Rooted in the imperative to "foster equitable social development and inclusion,"[2] the sixteenth SDG is a covenant to significantly reduce all forms of violence; promote the rule of law; and ensure responsive, inclusive, participatory, and representative decision making at all levels.[3] Multilateral Development Banks (MDBs) expressed full support of the SDGs as they sought trillions in capital increases to implement the agenda.[4]

---

* Gregory Berry is a policy associate at Accountability Counsel. Prior to this, he served two years as a staff attorney for the New York State Supreme Court, Appellate Division.

1 United Nations General Assembly, *G.A. Res 70/1, Transforming our world: the 2030 Agenda for Sustainable Development* (Oct. 21, 2015).

2 United Nations General Assembly, *G.A. Res 66/288, The Future We Want*, para. 4, (July 27, 2012) (*The Future We Want* is the outcome document of the June 2012 UN Conference on Sustainable Development [Rio+20], and a foundational document for the 2030 SDGs).

3 UN Department of Economic and Social Affairs, *Sustainable Development Goal 16*, https://sdgs.un.org/goals/goal16 (last visited Jan. 24, 2025) ("Promote peaceful and inclusive societies for sustainable development, provide access to justice for all and build effective, accountable, and inclusive institutions at all levels.").

4 *See* World Bank, et al., *From Billions to Trillions – Transforming Development Finance Post-2015 Financing for Development: Multilateral Development Finance* (Apr. 16, 2015), https://thedocs.worldbank.org/en/doc/622841485963735448-0270022017/original/DC20150002EFinancingforDevelopment.pdf (last visited Jan. 24, 2025).

2 "She Multiplied"

Three months after the launch of the SDGs, Berta Cáceres, a prominent Lenca indigenous and environmental rights campaigner, was assassinated in her home in La Esperanza, Honduras.[5] The Inter-American Commission on Human Rights (IACHR) strongly condemned the killing, noting a documented history of harassment and death threats against her for organizing efforts to protect the Gualcarque River in Honduras from the internationally financed Agua Zarca hydroelectric dam project.[6] In 2021, both the ex-CEO and the Director of Environmental and Social Development from the dam construction firm were found guilty of helping to coordinate her murder.[7]

Just weeks after the assassination, Berta's daughter, Laura Zúñiga Cáceres, spoke of the inspiration of her mother's legacy at a U.S. Congressional briefing.[8] I attended the briefing as a law student just beginning a career as a global justice advocate. As I listened through a translation headset, I heard a clear mandate for all who pursue just, inclusive, and rights-based approaches to development:

> Berta Cáceres, my mother, is not dead. She multiplied. So it is our job, everyone whose lives she touched in some way, to continue multiplying her.[9]

Berta Cáceres fought for indigenous peoples to be included in development decisions. Her activism was the epitome of SDG 16, but the global commitment

---

5 The Goldman Environmental Prize, *2015 Goldman Prize Winner, Berta Cáceres* (2015), http://www.goldmanprize.org/recipient/berta-caceres/ (last visited Dec. 16, 2024).

6 Inter-American Commission on Human Rights, *IACHR Condemns the Killing of Berta Cáceres in Honduras* (Mar. 4, 2016), https://www.oas.org/en/iachr/media_center/preleases/2016/024.asp (last visited Jan. 24, 2025).

7 Reuters, *Honduras Court Convicts Ex-Dam Executive in Murder of Celebrated Environmentalist*, THE N. Y. TIMES (Jul. 5, 2021); Elisabeth Malkin, *Seven Convicted in Killing of Prominent Honduran Environmentalist*, THE N. Y. TIMES (Nov. 29, 2018).

8 Center for Economic and Policy Research, *U.S. Congressional Briefing: The Assassination of Berta Cáceres and Ongoing Killings and Attacks Targeting Social Activists in Honduras*, YouTube (Mar. 23, 2016), https://www.youtube.com/watch?v=dt17ZbujkoU (last visited Jan. 24, 2025).

9 Rebecca Watts, *Congressional Briefing: The Assassination of Berta Cáceres and Ongoing Killings and Attacks Targeting Social Activists in Honduras*, Center for Economic and Policy Research (Mar. 30, 2016), https://cepr.net/congressional-briefing-the-assassination-of-berta-caceres-and-ongoing-killings-and-attacks-targeting-social-activists-in-honduras/ (last visited Jan. 24, 2025).

alone did not protect her rights or life. Even now, the words of SDG 16 cannot protect the safety of Berta's family and associates.[10] Many MDBs and other development finance institutions (DFIs) have since published statements and policies asserting zero tolerance for reprisals against whistleblowers and rights defenders, but again the words on paper have not ended violence against people who have demanded accountability for internationally financed projects.[11]

Not enforcing a zero-tolerance policy demonstrates tolerance. If DFIs take the hopeful vision of a just and inclusive transition to a sustainable future seriously, they must act affirmatively to cut at the roots of reprisals. Two essential changes are needed. First, Independent Accountability and Audit Mechanisms must be empowered to protect the safety of defenders by self-initiating investigations where there are credible concerns of reprisals, and by accepting anonymously submitted complaints. Second, DFIs must evolve to grow teeth for enforcing measures against retaliatory acts. Perhaps this year, the 25th anniversary of the UN Declaration on human rights defenders,[12] will be the year that the legacy of Berta Cáceres and countless other rights defenders are honored and multiplied by true *anti*-reprisal efforts.

3 The State of "Zero-tolerance" Policies

Reprisals, which encompass threats, killings, and other forms of violence against rights defenders, are becoming increasingly widespread in development finance contexts,[13] and evidence indicates that serious instances are

10 Inter-American Commission on Human Rights [IACHR], *Precautionary Measures No. 405–09 and 112–16, Berta Isabel Cáceres, her nuclear family, members of COPINH, et al. regarding Honduras*, IACHR Res. 88/2021 (Nov. 15, 2021), https://www.oas.org/en/iachr/decisions/mc/2021/res_88-21_mc_405-09_112-16_hn_en.pdf (last visited Jan. 24, 2025) (finding serious and urgent risks of irreparable retaliatory harm to members of Berta's family and the organization she co-founded, five years after Berta's passing).

11 *See, e.g.*, Dalile Antúnez, *Wearing Blinders: How Development Banks are Ignoring Reprisal Risks*, Coalition for Human Rights and Development (June 2022); *see also* Eva Hershaw, et al., *Uncovering the Hidden Iceberg*, Allied Data Working Group (Apr. 22, 2022) (finding alarming patterns of non-lethal attacks, including threats, harassment, smear campaigns, and stigmatization against indigenous peoples and land and environmental defenders).

12 United Nations General Assembly, *G.A. Res 70/161, Human rights defenders in the context of the Declaration on the Right and Responsibility of Individuals, Groups and Organs of Society to Promote and Protect Universally Recognized Human Rights and Fundamental Freedoms* (Feb. 10, 2016), https://www.refworld.org/docid/56dd31954.html (last visited Jan. 24, 2025).

13 *See* Global Witness, *Standing Firm: The Land and Environmental Defenders on the Frontline of the Environmental Crisis* (Sept. 2023); Office of the United Nations High Commissioner

most likely underreported due to a lack of systematic monitoring and fear of further reprisals.[14] The upward trend is evident despite several DFI zero-tolerance commitments.[15] The independent accountability mechanisms (IAMs) of many DFIs have developed policy guidance to implement zero-tolerance commitments, but they consistently assert a lack of influence and resources to enforce against reprisals.[16] A toolkit endorsed by a network of

---

for Human Rights [OHCHR], *Remedy in Development Finance: Guidance and Practice*, 30 (2022); World Bank Inspection Panel, *Right to Be Heard: Intimidation and Reprisals in World Bank Inspection Panel Cases* (Dec. 2021) (documenting increased reprisal allegations raised in complaints); *Defending Tomorrow: The climate crisis and threats against land and environmental defender*, Global Witness (July 2020); Coalition for Human Rights in Development, *Uncalculated Risks: Threats and attacks against human rights defenders and the role of development financiers* (May 2019).

14 *See* Alliance for Land, Indigenous and Environmental Defenders [ALLIED], *A Crucial Gap: The Limits to Official Data on Attacks Against Defenders and Why It's Concerning*, International Land Coalition (July 12, 2021).

15 *See, e.g.*, International Finance Corporation [IFC], *Position Statement on Retaliation Against Civil Society and Project Stakeholders* (Oct. 2018); European Bank for Reconstruction and Development [EBRD], *Statement on Retaliation Against Civil Society and Project Stakeholders* (Jan. 2019), https://www.ebrd.com/documents/strategy-and-policy-coordination/ebrd-statement-on-retaliation.pdf (last visited Jan. 24, 2025); World Bank, *World Bank Commitments Against Reprisals* (Mar. 2020); Inter-American Development Bank Group [IDB], *Environmental and Social Policy Framework*, para. 7.2 (Sept. 2020).

16 *See, e.g.*, World Bank Inspection Panel, *Guidelines to Reduce Retaliation Risks and Respond to Retaliation During the Panel Process* (Mar. 2016) ("The Panel [responds to retaliation] in close coordination with the Bank's Senior Management, recognizing that in most cases it will be necessary for Bank Management to lead the efforts"); Compliance Advisor Ombudsman of the International Finance Corporation and Multilateral Investment Guarantee Agency [CAO], *Approach to Responding to Concerns of Threats and Incidents of Reprisals in CAO Operations* (Apr. 2018) ("CAO is not an enforcement mechanism, and does not have any direct ability to physically protect complainants or safeguard people from the possible consequences of engaging in a CAO process or cooperating with CAO"); Independent Redress Mechanism of the Green Climate Fund [GCF IRM], *Supporting Operating Procedures of the Independent Redress Mechanism on Retaliation*, 15 (Jan. 2021) ("While the IRM is committed to minimising the risks of retaliation in relation to its processes, it also recognises the limitations it faces in its ability to mitigate risks and protect those involved"); Independent Complaints Mechanism [ICM] of FMO, PROPARCO, and the Deutsche Investitions- und Entwicklungsgesellschaft [DEG], *Position Statement on Addressing Risk of Reprisals related to ICM Operations* (Feb. 2021), https://www.proparco.fr/en/ressources/non-retaliation-statement-independent-complaints-mechanism-position-statement-addressing (last visited Jan. 24, 2025) ("The ICM is not an enforcement mechanism, it cannot physically protect complainants"); Asian Infrastructure Investment Bank [AIIB], *The Project-affected People's Mechanism: Rules of Procedure of the Project Affected Peoples Mechanism*, 9.2.2, https://www.aiib.org/en/about-aiib/who-we-are/project-affected-peoples-mechanism/how-we-assist-you/rules/index-part9.html (last visited Jan. 24, 2025) ("Neither AIIB nor the PPM is an enforcement mechanism.

IAMs serving major DFIs emphasizes this dilemma, and urges the Executive Boards of financial institutions to address the accountability gap by, among other things, (a) developing institutional policies to guide reprisal risk assessments; (b) systematically reporting on reprisals to deter future instances of retaliation; (c) appointing focal points accountable for institutional responses; and (d) including enforceable anti-reprisal clauses in loan agreements.[17] Nevertheless, a majority of DFI's have yet to match their zero-tolerance commitments with anti-reprisal actions to ensure the safe use of IAMs.

Zero-tolerance policies at DFIs largely did not exist when the organization that Berta Cáceres co-founded, Consejo Cívico de Organizaciones Populares e Indígenas de Honduras (COPINH)[18] began seeking accountability from actors supporting the Agua Zarca dam project. A complaint filed by COPINH to the Compliance Advisor Ombudsman (CAO) of the International Finance Corporation (IFC) alleged serious acts of violence, including murder, against Lenca environmental defenders,[19] but the CAO ultimately determined that it "[did] not have the mandate to further assess or handle the case" after ascertaining that the project was no longer being considered by an IFC-supported mezzanine fund.[20] As part of its assessment of the complaint, the CAO held telephonic meetings with the IFC and the mezzanine fund to understand how they understood the situation.[21] Although there was opportunity to do so, it is unclear whether the IFC or CAO warned other implicated DFIs of the actual and potential harm to encourage a response to the violence prior to Berta's assassination.[22]

Consequently, the PPM is unable to physically protect or safeguard people from possible consequences of engaging in a PPM process or cooperating with PPM personnel.").

17 Inter-American Development Bank [IADB], *Guide for Independent Accountability Mechanisms on Measures to Address the Risk of Reprisals in Complaint Management: A Practical Toolkit*, 63–73 (2019).

18 *See* Consejo Cívico de Organizaciones Populares e Indígenas de Honduras(English translation: "National Council of Popular and Indigenous Organizations of Honduras.") [COPINH], http://copinh.org/ (last visited Jan. 24, 2025).

19 General Coordinator, COPINH, *Letter of Complaint from COPINH to the Compliance Advisor Ombudsman* (Oct. 9, 2013), https://www.cao-ombudsman.org/sites/default/files/downloads/Reclamo_CAO_October92013.pdf (last visited Jan. 24, 2025).

20 Compliance Advsor/Ombudsman, *CAO Assessment Report: Regarding community concerns in relation to IFC's CAMIF project* (#26590), 5 (Jan. 2014).

21 *Id.*, at 4–5.

22 The author was unable to find public information on these potential conversations. The CAO's Operational Guidelines in effect at the time permitted the CAO to collaborate with the IAMs of other organizations when it was "engaged in complaints" that overlapped with their jurisdictions. The Guidelines state that information sharing must be in accordance with IFC and MIGA disclosure policies "that require the confidentiality of certain business information to be respected" and the standing Staff Rules of the World Bank

Following Berta's murder, COPINH implored the remaining backers of the project, including the Dutch development bank, Netherlands Development Finance Company (FMO), the impact investor/development financier Finnfund, and the Central American Bank for Economic Integration (CABEI), to responsibly withdraw from the project.[23] It was not until one year after the UN Special Rapporteur on the Rights of Indigenous People highlighted the situation in a report that recommended revocation of the Agua Zarca project,[24] that FMO and Finnfund officially announced their exit.[25] CABEI ended its involvement nearly three years later, having paused disbursement of funds to the project in 2016.[26] Despite reflecting on the importance of consultation and building positive relationships with community stakeholders in an official statement announcing its withdrawal, CABEI has since been implicated in promoting at least one other project that has neglected the rights of indigenous peoples and failed to fully assess the risks of retaliation against defenders.[27]

Group. *See* Compliance Advsior/Ombudsman, *CAO Operational Guidelines*, para. 1.1, 1.4 (2013), https://www.accountabilitycounsel.org/wp-content/uploads/2017/07/CAOOperationalGuidelines2013_ENGLISH.pdf (last visited Jan. 24, 2025). The Staff Rules of the World Bank Group prohibit disclosure of non-public information "to any third party for any reason." Non-public information is defined as "information generated by the Bank Group that has not been approved for release outside the Bank Group in accordance with the Bank Group's rules." *See* World Bank, *The World Bank/IFC/MIGA Staff Rules*, at 3.01, 5.01 (Dec. 2004), https://thedocs.worldbank.org/en/doc/827331374675391404-0220012004/render/03.01STANDARDSOFPROFESSIONALCONDUCTDecember12004.pdf (last visited Jan. 24, 2025).

23 *See* COPINH, *COPINH demands the definitive withdrawal of the Banks that finance the Agua Zarca Project* (Apr. 21, 2016), https://copinh.org/2016/04/el-copinh-exige-el-retiro-definitivo-de-los-bancos-que-financian-el-proyecto-agua-zarca/ (last visited Jan. 24, 2025); *see also* COPINH, *The FMO and its lying report* (Sep. 30, 2016), https://copinh.org/2016/09/el-fmo-y-su-informe-mentiroso/ (last visited Jan. 24, 2025).

24 Human Rights Council, *Report of the Special Rapporteur on the Rights of indigenous peoples on her visit to Honduras*, A/HRC/33/42/Add.2 (Jul. 21, 2016), https://digitallibrary.un.org/record/847080?ln=en (last visisted Jan. 24, 2025).

25 COPINH, *COPINH communicates that FMO and FinnFund have confirmed their official exit from the murderous Agua Zarca project* (Jul. 6 2017), http://copinhenglish.blogspot.com/2017/07/copinh-communicates-that-fmo-and-finn.html?m=1 (last visisted Jan. 24, 2025).

26 *See* Central American Bank for Economic Integration [CABEI], *CABEI formalizes its definitive dissociation from the Agua Zarca Project* (Apr. 17, 2020), https://www.bcie.org/en/news-and-media/news/article/cabei-formalizes-its-definitive-dissociation-from-the-agua-zarca-project (last visited Jan. 24, 2025).

27 *See, e.g.*, Independent Redress Mechanism, *Compliance Review Report Case C-0006-Nicaragua (FP146: Bio-CLIMA: Integrated climate action to reduce deforestation and strengthen resilience in BOSAWÁS and Rio San Juan Biospheres)* (Aug. 31, 2022), https://irm.greenclimate.fund/sites/default/files/case/en-irm-case-c0006-final-compliance-review-report.pdf (last visited Jan. 24, 2025).

The failure to prevent further serious acts of retaliation is not a problem limited to a handful of institutions, but is rather a status quo that demands reform.[28]

4 The Change Needed

The global consensus on the SDGs demands an affirmative shift toward respecting the rights of communities and supporting their safety when they peacefully assert their rights.[29] Doing so requires courageous reform, in which DFIs must be willing to place the priorities of project-affected communities at the same level or even above current and future business relationships and competition for clients.[30] DFIs must strengthen support for local communities to help them understand and defend their rights using community-centered and rights-forward development models that mitigate risks of reprisals by preventing conflicts at the outset.

Reprisal risks are only growing as civic space continues to shrink.[31] DFIs must therefore act now to improve institutional rigor and accountability for

28 *See* Rabi Thapa, *Realizing zero tolerance against reprisals: Safeguarding communities' right to be heard without fear of retaliation*, Accountability Matters Quarterly Newsletter, The World Bank (Jan. 19 2023), https://www.worldbank.org/en/programs/accountability/brief/realizing-zero-tolerance-against-reprisals.

29 *See* UN General Assembly, *Addis Ababa Action Agenda of the Third International Conference on Financing for Development,* A/RES/69/313, 18 (July 27, 2015) (Addis Ababa Action Agenda) ("We underline the need to promote peaceful and inclusive societies for achieving sustainable development and to build effective, accountable and inclusive institutions at all levels. Good governance, the rule of law, human rights, fundamental freedoms, equal access to fair justice systems and measures to combat corruption and curb illicit financial flows will be integral to our efforts.").

30 *See* Pascal Djohossou, et al., *The Community-led Worldview of Systems Change: A Framework Centering Local Knowledge and Aspirations in Pursuit of Transformational Sustainability and Resilience (Part 1)*, 17 KNOWLEDGE MANAGEMENT FOR DEV. J.: UNCOMFORTABLE TRUTHS IN INTERNATIONAL DEVELOPMENT: APPROACHES TO THE DECOLONIZATION OF KNOWLEDGE FROM DEVELOPMENT PRACTICE, POLICY AND RESEARCH (2023); *see also* Anne-Birgette Albrectson, *Why collaboration will be key to achieving the Sustainable Development Goals,* World Economic Forum, FUTURE OF WORK (Jan. 31 2017); Joyeeta Gupta & Courtney Vegelin, *Sustainable development goals and inclusive development,* 16 INTERNATIONAL ENVIRONMENTAL AGREEMENTS: POLITICS, LAW, AND ECONOMICS, THEMATIC ISSUE: MAKING THE SDGS SUCCEED 433 (Jun. 2016).

31 *See* UN Human Rights Council, *Cooperation with the United Nations, its representatives and mechanisms in the field of human rights – Report of the Secretary-General,* A/HRC/54/61(Aug. 21, 2023), https://www.ohchr.org/en/documents/reports/ahrc5461-cooperation-united-nations-its-representatives-and-mechanisms-field (last visited Jan. 24, 2025).

context-based reprisal risk prevention and meaningful response when risks manifest into harm.[32]

5 Empowering IAMs to Curb Reprisals

Maximizing IAM safety and accessibility is critical to protecting rights defenders who rely on IAMs as a last resort for justice in contexts of shrinking or repressed civic space, or in other oppressive situations.[33] Insofar as risks of retaliation can deter project-affected people from filing complaints in these situations, IAMs must be allowed to accept and investigate complaints submitted anonymously because of grounded concerns about actual or potential retaliation. However, promises of confidentiality alone are not enough, especially considering the risks of unauthorized or accidental data breaches prevalent in the use of technology for complaints handling. Acknowledging these risks, the Social and Environmental Compliance Unit (SECU) of the United Nations Development Programme (UNDP) has offered a compelling model. SECU's "Guidelines to Managing and Responding to Risks of Intimidation and Reprisals in the Context of SECU Activity" pioneers a distinct process that promotes proactive investigation of reprisals when complaints would otherwise be considered ineligible, for example, in the case of complaints submitted anonymously.[34]

Further, more IAMs should be empowered to self-initiate investigations and otherwise follow up on reprisal concerns raised in otherwise ineligible complaints. A few IAMs already have or are in the process of introducing these processes,[35] and DFIs must embrace the trend. The best way to ensure that

32 *See* Coalition for Human Rights and Development, *Misplaced Trust: Why Development Banks Should Not Rely on Their Clients to Address Reprisal Risks* (July 2023).

33 *See, e.g.*, Accountability Counsel and Arab Watch Coalition, *Our Last and Only Resort: What Happens When Development Goes Wrong in the Middle East and North Africa?* (Sept. 2022), https://accountabilityconsole.com/stories/our-last-and-only-resort/.

34 United Nations Development Programme [UNDP], Office of Audit and Investigations [OAI], *Guideline to Managing and Responding to Risks of Intimidation and Reprisals in the Context of SECU Activity*, Annex to the UNDP, OAI, Investigation Guidelines: SECU (Draft), 25–29 (2010), https://www.accountabilitycounsel.org/wp-content/uploads/draft-secu-investigation-guidelines-english.pdf#page=25 (last visited Jan. 24, 2025).

35 *See, e.g.*, Independent Recourse Mechanism of the African Development Bank [AfDB IRM], *Operating Rules and Procedures*, 75 (iv) (Jul. 2021), https://www.afdb.org/en/documents/independent-recourse-mechanism-operating-rules-and-procedures-january-2015-updated-july-2021 (last visited Jan. 24, 2025); Green Climate Fund [GCF], *Decision of the Board on updated Terms of Reference of the Independent Redress Mechanism (Revised)*, 12 (2017),https://irm.greenclimate.fund/sites/default/files/document/bbm-2017-10-decision

reprisals do not get swept under the rug is to honor independence and to trust the discernment of IAMs in their decisions to investigate. In principle, instances of reprisals threaten the integrity of reporting under the environmental and social standards that underpin development finance. IAMs should therefore be able to follow up on allegations of reprisals as a stand-alone eligibility claim, to assure accurate reporting in the service of accountability. Accordingly, where investigations confirm attempts to suppress the voices of project-affected people, IAMs must be able to recommend immediate actions, including halting loan disbursals and redesigning projects alongside community stakeholders, to stop threats, harassment, or violence.

6 Growing Teeth

For any zero-tolerance policy to work, it must be enforced and not merely encouraged. Chronologies of IAM cases reveal that DFIs continue to support clients with documented histories of suppressing rights defenders with intimidation and violence.[36] Failing to enforce zero-tolerance policies enables more violence, and it exposes DFIs to a host of reputational, financial, political, and potentially legal risks.[37]

A few DFIs expressly consider instances of retaliation to be sanctionable, including through the termination of present and future contracts.[38] This concept must be proliferated. Some DFIs have developed practical guidance

-board-updated-terms-reference-independent-redress-mechanism-revised.pdf (last visited Jan. 24, 2025); UNDP & OAI, *Investigation Guidelines: Social and Environmental Compliance Unit (Draft)*, 24, 27, 37 (Nov. 11, 2022), https://www.accountabilitycounsel.org/wp-content/uploads/draft-secu-investigation-guidelines-english.pdf (last visited Jan. 24, 2025); International Climate Initiative [IKI], *Independent Complaint Mechanism Policy*, §§ 2.7(b), 5 (Feb. 1, 2022), https://www.international-climate-initiative.com/fileadmin/iki/Dokumente/Beschwerdemechanismus/IKI_ICM_policy_EN_202202.pdf (last visited Jan. 24, 2025).

36 Sara Jaramillo, *Why Do Multilateral Development Banks Finance Repeat Offenders?*, Accountability Console (Apr. 3, 2023).

37 UN Human Rights Council, *Report of the Special Representative of the Secretary-General on the Issue of Human Rights and Transnational Corporations and Other Business Enterprises, John Ruggie*, A/HRC/17/31 (Mar. 21, 2011), https://documents-dds-ny.un.org/doc/UNDOC/GEN/G11/121/90/PDF/G1112190.pdf?OpenElement (last visited Jan. 24, 2025).

38 *See* EBRD, *Retaliation Against Civil Society and Project Stakeholders* (Jan. 2019) (defining threats of retaliation as a prohibited coercive practice under the EBRD's Enforcement Policy and Procedures); AfDB, *Sanctions Procedures of the African Development Bank Group*, 4.2(d) (Nov. 18, 2014), https://www.afdb.org/sites/default/files/2019/05/10/afdb_sanctions_procedures_-_november_2014.pdf (last visited Jan. 24, 2025) (defining efforts

to promote context-specific screening and effective responses to resolve and prevent retaliation.[39] The next step must be to apply that guidance to their own operations. DFIs must stop offloading and start enforcing responsibility for reprisals.[40]

To apply sanctions responsibly, DFIs must not default to quietly withdrawing from projects tarnished by reprisals – the Agua Zarca dam project as a prime example. Although not publishing reasons for exit may sometimes be the best approach to protect the safety of individuals, often quietly exiting without condemning abuse or supporting the rights of defenders can worsen violence if defenders are blamed for deals gone bad.[41] Further, DFIs should not use the excuse of exit to deny investigation of their own actions in enabling or overlooking threats against defenders, or systemic issues that exacerbate the root causes of conflict and reprisals.[42] Accordingly, IAMs should have a role in ensuring that zero tolerance policies are honored, and the most sensible way is by allowing them to investigate whether responses to reprisals are pursued sufficiently, responsibly, and in good faith. In this way, the responsiveness of DFI staff to safety concerns associated with projects under their supervision can be evaluated to improve performance and implementation of zero tolerance policies.[43]

Coordination between DFIs is also critical in ensuring that reprisals do not continue when bad actors seek alternative financing in the face of sanctions. In this regard, IAMs must coordinate efforts to amplify instances of reprisals to their respective institutions to motivate unified responses to violence. Most IAM policies require general coordination with peer mechanisms, and some have developed policies to coordinate around reprisals.[44]

---

to impair, harm, or threaten any party or the property of the party to improperly influence the actions of a party as sanctionable coercive practices).

39 *See* IFC & Inter-American Investment Corporation, *Good Practice Note for the Private Sector: Addressing the Risks of Retaliation Against Project Stakeholders* (2021), https://www.ifc.org/content/dam/ifc/doc/mgrt/idb-invest-and-ifc-reprisals-gpn.pdf (last visited Jan. 24, 2025).

40 Coalition for Human Rights and Development, *supra* note 32.

41 *Id.*

42 *See* Coalition for Human Rights in Development, *Uncalculated Risks: Threats and Attacks Against Human Rights Defenders and the Role of Development Financiers*, 35 (May 2019).

43 *See, e.g.*, United Nations Development Programme, *Policies and Procedures of Annual Performance Reviews*, https://popp.undp.org/procedure/annual-performance-review (last visited Dec. 16, 2023) ("Step 3: Request additional feedback from others").

44 *See* Independent Consultation and Investigation Mechanism of the Inter-American Development Bank Group, *Guidelines for Addressing Risk of Reprisals in Complaint* Management, 4.6 (2019), https://www.iadb.org/document.cfm?id=EZSHARE-525549286-337

7 Conclusion

Sustainable development cannot be achieved where the repression of civic space is condoned.[45] Reform and coordination is needed to fulfill the central promise of the SDGs to leave no one behind.[46] To achieve this, DFIs must ensure safe avenues to provide redress, both for unintended environmental and social harm and intentional abuses against rights defenders. It is the duty of all of us in the accountability community to multiply the important work of indigenous, environmental, and human rights defenders acting to inspire adherence to the SDGs.

Bibliography

Accountability Counsel and Arab Watch Coalition. *Our Last and Only Resort: What Happens When Development Goes Wrong in the Middle East and North Africa?* San Francisco: Accountability Counsel, September 2022. https://accountabilityconsole.com/stories/our-last-and-only-resort/.

AfDB. *Sanctions Procedures of the African Development Bank Group.* Côte d'Ivoire: African Development Bank, November 18, 2014: 4.2(d). https://www.afdb.org/sites/default/files/2019/05/10/afdb_sanctions_procedures_-_november_2014.pdf.

AfDB, et al. *From Billions to Trillions – Transforming Development Finance Post-2015 Financing for Development: Multilateral Development Finance.* Washington DC: World Bank, April 16, 2015. https://www.iadb.org/en/news/announcements/2015-04-16/joint-statement-by-mdbs-on-financing-for-development%2C11140.html.

Albrectson, Anne-Birgette. "Why collaboration will be key to achieving the Sustainable Development Goals," World Economic Forum, January 31, 2017.

https://www.weforum.org/agenda/2017/01/realising-the-potential-of-cross-sector-partnerships/.

(last visited Jan. 24, 2025); UNDP & OAI, *Guideline to Managing and Responding to Risks of Intimidation and Reprisals in the Context of SECU Activity*, Annex to the UNDP, OAI, Investigation Guidelines: SECU (Draft), 12 (2010), https://www.accountabilitycounsel.org/wp-content/uploads/draft-secu-investigation-guidelines-english.pdf#page=25 (last visited Jan. 24, 2025).

45 *See, e.g.*, United Nations Sustainable Development Group, *Operationalizing Leaving No One Behind: Good Practice Note for UN Country Teams*, 55 (Mar. 2022).

46 UN Sustainable Development Group, *Universal Values: Principle Two: Leave No One Behind* (2023).

Alliance for Land, Indigenous and Environmental Defenders [ALLIED]. *A Crucial Gap: The Limits to Official Data on Attacks Against Defenders and Why It's Concerning*. Rome: International Land Coalition, July 12, 2021. https://www.landcoalition.org/en/resources/a-crucial-gap-the-limits-of-official-data-on-attacks-against-defenders-and-why-its-concerning/.

Antúnez, Dalile. *Wearing Blinders: How Development Banks are Ignoring Reprisal Risks*. Washington DC: Coalition for Human Rights and Development, June 2022. https://rightsindevelopment.org/wearing-blinders/.

Asian Infrastructure Investment Bank [AIIB]. *The Project-affected People's Mechanism: Rules of Procedure of the Project Affected Peoples Mechanism*. Accessed December 17, 2024: 9.2.2, https://www.aiib.org/en/about-aiib/who-we-are/project-affected-peoples-mechanism/how-we-assist-you/rules/index-part9.html.

Compliance Advisor Ombudsman of the International Finance Corporation and Multilateral Investment Guarantee Agency [CAO]. *CAO Operational Guidelines*. Washington DC: CAO, 2013: para 1.1, 1.4. https://www.accountabilitycounsel.org/wp-content/uploads/2017/07/CAOOperationalGuidelines2013_ENGLISH.pdf.

CAO. *Approach to Responding to Concerns of Threats and Incidents of Reprisals in CAO Operations*. Washington DC: CAO, April 2018. https://www.cao-ombudsman.org/about-us/approach-reprisals.

Central American Bank for Economic Integration [CABEI]. *CABEI formalizes its definitive dissociation from the Agua Zarca Project*. Honduras: CABEI, April 17, 2020. https://www.bcie.org/en/news-and-media/news/article/cabei-formalizes-its-definitive-dissociation-from-the-agua-zarca-project.

Center for Economic and Policy Research. "U.S. Congressional Briefing: The Assassination of Berta Cáceres and Ongoing Killings and Attacks Targeting Social Activists in Honduras." March 23, 2016. https://www.youtube.com/watch?v=dt17ZbujkoU.

Coalition for Human Rights in Development. *Uncalculated Risks: Threats and attacks against human rights defenders and the role of development financiers*. Washington DC: Coalition for Human Rights in Development, May 2019. https://rightsindevelopment.org/uncalculatedrisks/.

Coalition for Human Rights and Development. *Misplaced Trust: Why Development Banks Should Not Rely on Their Clients to Address Reprisal Risks*. Washington DC: Coalition for Human Rights and Development, July 2023. https://149805364.v2.pressablecdn.com/wp-content/uploads/2023/07/Misplaced-Trust-ENG.pdf.

"Consejo Cívico de Organizaciones Populares e Indígenas de Honduras ("National Council of Popular and Indigenous Organizations of Honduras.") [COPINH]." Accessed December 16, 2024. http://copinh.org/.

COPINH. *The FMO and its lying report*. Honduras: COPINH, September 30, 2016. https://copinh.org/2016/09/el-fmo-y-su-informe-mentiroso/.

COPINH. *COPINH communicates that FMO and FinnFund have confirmed their official exit from the murderous Agua Zarca project.* Honduras: COPINH, July 6, 2017. http://copinhenglish.blogspot.com/2017/07/copinh-communicates-that-fmo-and-finn.html?m=1.

COPINH, *COPINH demands the definitive withdrawal of the Banks that finance the Agua Zarca Project.* Honduras: COPINH, April 21, 2016. https://copinh.org/2016/04/el-copinh-exige-el-retiro-definitivo-de-los-bancos-que-financian-el-proyecto-agua-zarca/.

Djohossou, Pascal, et al. "The Community-led Worldview of Systems Change: A Framework Centering Local Knowledge and Aspirations in Pursuit of Transformational Sustainability and Resilience (Part 1)." *Knowledge Management for Development Journal: Uncomfortable Truths in International Development: Approaches to the Decolonization of Knowledge from Development Practice, Policy and Research.* (2023): 17.

European Bank for Reconstruction and Development [EBRD]. *Retaliation Against Civil Society and Project Stakeholders.* London: EBRD, January 2019. https://www.ebrd.com/documents/strategy-and-policy-coordination/ebrd-statement-on-retaliation.pdf

EBRD. *Statement on Retaliation Against Civil Society and Project Stakeholders.* London: EBRD, January 2019. https://www.ebrd.com/documents/strategy-and-policy-coordination/ebrd-statement-on-retaliation.pdf

General Coordinator, COPINH. *Letter of Complaint from COPINH to the Compliance Advisor Ombudsman.* Washington DC: CAO, October 9, 2013. https://www.cao-ombudsman.org/sites/default/files/downloads/Reclamo_CAO_October92013.pdf.

Global Witness. *Defending Tomorrow: The climate crisis and threats against land and environmental defender.* London: Global Witness, July 2020. https://www.globalwitness.org/en/campaigns/environmental-activists/defending-tomorrow/.

Global Witness. *Standing Firm: The Land and Environmental Defenders on the Frontline of the Environmental Crisis.* London: Global Witness, September 2023. https://www.globalwitness.org/en/campaigns/environmental-activists/standing-firm.

Green Climate Fund. *Decision of the Board on updated Terms of Reference of the Independent Redress Mechanism (Revised).* Incheon City: Green Climate Fund, 2017: 12. https://irm.greenclimate.fund/sites/default/files/document/bbm-2017-10-decision-board-updated-terms-reference-independent-redress-mechanism-revised.pdf

Goldman Environmental Prize. "2015 Goldman Prize Winner, Berta Cáceres." Accessed December 16, 2024. http://www.goldmanprize.org/recipient/berta-caceres/.

Gupta, Joyeeta, and Courtney Vegelin. "Sustainable development goals and inclusive development." *International Environmental Agreements: Politics, Law, and Economics, Thematic Issue: Making the SDGs Succeed,* 16 (June 2016).

Hershaw, Eva, et al. *Uncovering the Hidden Iceberg*. Rome: International Land Coalition, April 22, 2022. https://www.landcoalition.org/en/resources/uncovering-the-hidden-iceberg/.

International Climate Initiative (IKI). *Independent Complaint Mechanism Policy*. Berlin: IKI, February 1, 2022: sect. 2.7(b), 5. https://www.international-climate-initiative.com/fileadmin/iki/Dokumente/Beschwerdemechanismus/IKI_ICM_policy_EN_202202.pdf.

Independent Complaints Mechanism [ICM] of FMO, PROPARCO, and the Deutsche Investitions- und Entwicklungsgesellschaft [DEG]. *Position Statement on Addressing Risk of Reprisals related to ICM Operations*. PROPARCO, February 2021. https://www.proparco.fr/en/ressources/non-retaliation-statement-independent-complaints-mechanism-position-statement-addressing

Independent Consultation and Investigation Mechanism of the Inter-American Development Bank Group [IADB]. *Guidelines for Addressing Risk of Reprisals in Complaint* Management. Washington DC: IADB, 2019: 4.6. https://www.iadb.org/document.cfm?id=EZSHARE-525549286-337

Independent Redress Mechanism of the Green Climate Fund [GCF IRM]. *Supporting Operating Procedures of the Independent Redress Mechanism on Retaliation*. Incheon City: Green Climate Fund, January 2021: 5. https://irm.greenclimate.fund/document/supporting-operating-procedures-irm-retaliation.

Independent Recourse Mechanism of the African Development Bank [AfDB IRM]. *Operating Rules and Procedures*. Côte d'Ivoire: African Dvelopment Bank, July 2021: 75(IV). https://www.afdb.org/en/documents/independent-recourse-mechanism-operating-rules-and-procedures-january-2015-updated-july-2021.

Inter-American Commission on Human Rights [IACHR]. *IACHR Condemns the Killing of Berta Cáceres in Honduras*. Washington DC: Organization of American States, March 4, 2016. https://www.oas.org/en/iachr/media_center/preleases/2016/024.asp.

IADB. *Guide for Independent Accountability Mechanisms on Measures to Address the Risk of Reprisals in Complaint Management: A Practical Toolkit*. Washington DC: IADB, 2019: 63–73. https://lnadbg5.adb.org/ocrp002p.nsf.

IADB. *Environmental and Social Policy Framework*. Washington DC: IADB, September 2020: para. 7.2. https://www.iadb.org/en/mpas.

International Finance Corporation [IFC]. *Position Statement on Retaliation Against Civil Society and Project Stakeholders*. Washington DC: IFC, October 2018. https://www.accountabilitycounsel.org/wp-content/uploads/10518-ifc-position-statement-on-retaliation-and-threats-of-reprisals.pdf.

IFC & Inter-American Investment Corporation. *Good Practice Note for the Private Sector: Addressing the Risks of Retaliation Against Project Stakeholders*. Washington DC:

IFC, 2021. https://www.ifc.org/content/dam/ifc/doc/mgrt/idb-invest-and-ifc-reprisals-gpn.pdf.

Jaramillo, Sara. "Why Do Multilateral Development Banks Finance Repeat Offenders?" San Francisco: Accountability Console, April 3, 2023. https://accountabilityconsole.com/newsletter/articles/why-do-multilateral-development-banks-finance-repeat-offenders/.

Malkin, Elisabeth. "Seven Convicted in Killing of Prominent Honduran Environmentalist." *The New York Times*, November 29, 2018. https://www.nytimes.com/2018/11/29/world/americas/honduras-bertha-caceres.html.

Reuters. "Honduras Court Convicts Ex-Dam Executive in Murder of Celebrated Environmentalist." *The New York Times*, July 5, 2021. https://www.nytimes.com/2021/07/05/world/americas/honduras-Berta-Caceres-murder.html.

Thapa, Rabi. "Realizing zero tolerance against reprisals: Safeguarding communities' right to be heard without fear of retaliation." *Accountability Matters Quarterly Newsletter*. January 19, 2023. https://www.worldbank.org/en/programs/accountability/brief/realizing-zero-tolerance-against-reprisals.

United Nations Development Programme [UNDP], Office of Audit and Investigations [OAI]. *Guideline to Managing and Responding to Risks of Intimidation and Reprisals in the Context of SECU Activity*. Geneva: United Nations, 2010: Annex to the *UNDP, OAI, Investigation Guidelines: SECU (Draft)*, 25–29. https://www.accountabilitycounsel.org/wp-content/uploads/draft-secu-investigation-guidelines-english.pdf#page=25.

UNDP, OAI. *Investigation Guidelines: Social and Environmental Compliance Unit (Draft)*. Geneva: United Nations, November 11, 2022: 24, 27, 31. https://www.accountabilitycounsel.org/wp-content/uploads/draft-secu-investigation-guidelines-english.pdf.

UNDP. Policies and Procedures of Annual Performance Reviews, "Step 3: Request additional feedback from others," in *Policies and Procedures of Annual Performance Reviews*. Washington DC: Geneva. Accessed December 16, 2024.

United Nations General Assembly. *G.A. Res 66/288, The Future We Want*. Geneva: United Nations, July 27, 2012: para. 4. https://sustainabledevelopment.un.org/futurewewant.html.

United Nations General Assembly. *G.A. Res 70/1, Transforming our world: the 2030 Agenda for Sustainable Development*. Geneva: United Nations, October 21, 2015. https://www.un.org/en/development/desa/population/migration/generalassembly/docs/globalcompact/A_RES_70_1_E.pdf.

United Nations General Assembly. *A/RES/69/313 Addis Ababa Action Agenda of the Third International Conference on Financing for Development* (Addis Ababa Action Agenda). Geneva: United Nations, July 27, 2015. https://www.refworld.org/docid/56dd31954.html.

United Nations General Assembly. *G.A. Res 70/161, Human rights defenders in the context of the Declaration on the Right and Responsibility of Individuals, Groups and Organs of Society to Promote and Protect Universally Recognized Human Rights and Fundamental Freedoms.* Geneva: United Nations, February 10, 2016. https://www.refworld.org/docid/56dd31954.html.

United Nations Human Rights Council. *Report of the Special Representative of the Secretary-General on the Issue of Human Rights and Transnational Corporations and Other Business Enterprises, John Ruggie, A/HRC/17/31.* Geneva: Washington DC, March 21, 2011. https://documents-dds-ny.un.org/doc/UNDOC/GEN/G11/121/90/PDF/G1112190.pdf?OpenElement.

United Nations Human Rights Council. *Report of the Special Rapporteur on the Rights of indigenous peoples on her visit to Honduras, A/HRC/33/42/Add.2.* Geneva: United Nations, July 21, 2016. https://digitallibrary.un.org/record/847080?ln=en.

United Nations Human Rights Council. *Cooperation with the United Nations, its representatives and mechanisms in the field of human rights – Report of the Secretary-General, A/HRC/54/61.* Geneva: United Nations, August 21, 2023. https://www.ohchr.org/en/documents/reports/ahrc5461-cooperation-united-nations-its-representatives-and-mechanisms-field.

United Nations Office of the High Commissioner for Human Rights Office of the United Nations High Commissioner for Human Rights [OHCHR]. *Remedy in Development Finance: Guidance and Practice.* Geneva: United Nations, 2022: 30. https://www.ohchr.org/sites/default/files/2022-03/Remedy-in-Development.pdf.

United Nations Sustainable Development Group. *Operationalizing Leaving No One Behind: Good Practice Note for UN Country Teams.* Geneva: United Nations, 2022: 55. https://unsdg.un.org/sites/default/files/2022-04/Operationalizing%20LNOB%20-%20final%20with%20Annexes%20090422.pdf#page=56.

United Nations Sustainable Development Group. *Universal Values- Principle Two: Leave No One Behind.* Geneva: United Nations, 2023. https://unsdg.un.org/2030-agenda/universal-values/leave-no-one-behind.

Watts, Rebecca. *Congressional Briefing: The Assassination of Berta Cáceres and Ongoing Killings and Attacks Targeting Social Activists in Honduras.* Washington DC: Center for Economic and Policy Research, March 30, 2016. https://cepr.net/congressional-briefing-the-assassination-of-berta-caceres-and-ongoing-killings-and-attacks-targeting-social-activists-in-honduras/.

World Bank. *The World Bank/IFC/MIGA Staff Rules.* Washington DC: World Bank, December 2004: 3.01, 5.01. https://thedocs.worldbank.org/en/doc/827331374675391404-0220012004/render/03.01STANDARDSOFPROFESSIONALCONDUCTDecember12004.pdf).

World Bank. *World Bank Commitments Against Reprisals*. Washington DC: World Bank, March 2020. https://www.worldbank.org/en/projects-operations/environmental-and-social-framework/brief/world-bank-commitments-against-reprisals.

World Bank Inspection Panel. *Guidelines to Reduce Retaliation Risks and Respond to Retaliation During the Panel Process*. Washington DC: World Bank, March 2016. https://www.inspectionpanel.org/news/inspection-panel-releases-guidelines-address-retaliation.

World Bank Inspection Panel. *Right to Be Heard: Intimidation and Reprisals in World Bank Inspection Panel Cases*. Washington DC: World Bank, December 2021. https://www.inspectionpanel.org/sites/default/files/publications/Emerging-Lessons-Series-07-Intimidation-and-reprisals-in-IPN-Cases-Dec2021_0.pdf.

CHAPTER 15

Collaborative Dispute Resolution: Five Essential Questions

Scott Adams and Aparna Mukerjee***

Introduction

We congratulate the World Bank Inspection Panel (the Panel) on its 30th anniversary. The Panel was the first independent accountability mechanism (IAM) at a development finance institution (DFI). We would like to acknowledge and thank all the current and previous Panel members and staff for their dedication and hard work diligently serving affected communities and the World Bank mission with independence and professionalism for the last three decades.

In August 2017, the World Bank Board of Executive Directors (the Board) initiated a review of the Inspection Panel toolkit to examine whether the Panel required any updates to continue to operate effectively under the new Environmental and Social Framework (the 2017 Review). The Board-approved Terms of Reference for the 2017 Review included an "assessment of, and findings related to, the benefits and disadvantages; financial and operational costs; and risks to the World Bank, as well as potential impacts on project-affected communities," of including dispute resolution in the Panel's toolkit.[1] The 2017 Review included an analysis of various dispute resolution options and noted that all the other IAMs, except the Panel, offer requesters the opportunity to ask for dispute resolution (also referred to as "problem-solving" by some IAMs).[2] An analysis of DFIs' rationale for including dispute resolution (DR) in their respective IAMs is beyond the scope of this essay, but reasons likely include offering additional choices and options for addressing grievances from locally impacted communities, ensuring accountability, preventing conflict escalation, supporting empowerment and participation of local communities,

* Scott Adams is Senior Dispute Resolution Officer at the World Bank Accountability Mechanism Dispute Resolution Service.

** Aparna Mukerjee is a lawyer and internationally accredited mediator based in Chennai, India whose experience includes mediating cases for several IAMs.

1 Daniel Bradlow, *External Review of the Inspection Panel's Toolkit*, The World Bank, 11 (May 14, 2018).

2 *Id.* at 11.

© SCOTT ADAMS AND APARNA MUKERJEE, 2026 | DOI:10.1163/9789004729735_020

mitigating reputational risk for DFIs, enhancing institutional learning, and improving project implementation and outcomes. In September 2020, as a result of the 2017 Review, the Board approved a Resolution establishing the World Bank Accountability Mechanism (AM), which houses both the Inspection Panel and a newly created Dispute Resolution Service (DRS).

The Panel's 30th anniversary milestone provides an important opportunity for reflection on the general development and practice of IAMs over the last three decades. This essay focuses on five questions related to the practice of DR at the IAMs, including reflections on current practice and potential new uses and applications of DR in the future. The purpose is to provide interested stakeholders with practical information they can use in their interactions with IAM DR functions – such as local communities, civil society organizations (CSOs), public- and private-sector clients of DFIs, or mediators/facilitators in their DR practice.

We have identified five key questions regarding the dispute resolution process and explored the answers to these in this essay. The five questions are:

1. How Should Parties Decide Whether to Participate in DR?
2. What are the Roles of Advocates and Advisors?
3. Does DR Provide Accountability and Remedy?
4. How Can DR Foster Institutional Learning for DFIs?
5. Why Is it Important for DR to be Independent rather Than Embedded in DFI Management?

1 How Should Parties Decide Whether to Participate in DR?

A common misunderstanding among stakeholders is that the DR process will be an adversarial and adjudicative process like court or arbitration, where each side will present their respective "case" and positions and the IAM will decide who is right and who is wrong and then make binding decisions on how the issues should be resolved. In fact, this is not the typical approach among IAMs. Most, if not all, IAM-DR functions employ a collaborative approach in which project-affected communities, sometimes supported by CSO advisers and/or lawyers, and DFI clients try to resolve their differences and address issues of mutual concern with the assistance of professional neutrals (mediators or facilitators).

Most IAMs work to help all concerned parties understand the DR process and make an informed decision about whether to participate. This is critical because DR processes may end up being time and resource-intensive commitments that may not be appropriate for every community, company, or government. Common factors for parties to consider include:

- *Potential Outcome*
  - What are their goals and desired outcomes? How do they define success and is a collaborative approach the best way to achieve it?
  - Are the issues of sufficient importance to warrant the effort required for DR?
- *Assessment of Options*
  - What are the alternatives?
  - What is the cost/risk of not reaching an agreement?
  - Are there legislative, legal, and/or policy determinations needed for a successful resolution that are outside the authority of the concerned parties?
  - How will participating in collaborative DR impact their legal rights?
  - Is sufficient time available to address the key issues?
  - Will participating in a DR process like this advance or impede other strategies they are pursuing?
  - How much will the process cost in time and money? Does their constituency have sufficient resources to participate or is there a way to access the needed resources? Are there other options that will be quicker and more cost-effective?
  - Does DR offer an opportunity to preserve or improve essential relationships with other parties? For project proponents, will participating in DR enhance their social license to operate?
  - Will participation help to unite and organize their constituency, or increase internal conflicts and organizational challenges?
- *Good Faith Participation*
  - Are all key parties willing to participate in good faith? Is there sufficient incentive and leverage to ensure the good faith of participants?
  - Are the parties reasonably likely to implement any agreements reached?
  - Are they willing to be open, collaborate, and listen to other parties to understand their needs and interests? Are they ready to explain their concerns to help others understand their perspectives?
  - Do they trust the IAM to conduct a fair and effective process? Is it credible and able to provide the necessary neutrality, resources, and support for a collaborative DR process?
- *Power Dynamics and Safety*
  - Can power imbalances be sufficiently addressed to allow for meaningful participation?
  - Does participation in the DR process increase any potential risks for harm to the individual, party, or others?

2 What Are the Roles of Advocates and Advisors?

Local communities are often supported by CSOs and/or lawyers when they bring their case to an IAM.[3] In many instances, the affected community learns about the existence of the IAM from advisors. Advisors can provide information and perspective to help communities decide whether they should engage in a DR process.

While it is most common for affected communities to be accompanied by advisors, the roles and principles described in this part could potentially apply to advisors of any party, including advisors to private companies and public-sector agencies.

Because the collaborative DR processes of IAMs differ from more adversarial approaches to resolution, the role of advisors may also differ. In both adjudication and arbitration, for example, advocates prepare their cases and make oral and written submissions on behalf of parties. The process pits parties against each other; both sides know that, in the end, they can only be winners or losers. Parties take a back seat, leaving written and verbal communication with the judge or arbitrator to their lawyers. Collaborative DR processes, on the other hand, encourage parties to speak directly to the facilitator or mediator and each other. These processes are designed to help each party better understand each other's positions and interests. Parties are encouraged to listen, ask questions, and understand each other before exploring possible options for mutually agreeable solutions. A party's advisors will still advocate for the party and contribute to finding comprehensive and sustainable solutions to project-related social and environmental challenges, while simultaneously promoting dialogue and understanding and helping the parties reach a mutually acceptable resolution in a cooperative and constructive manner. The wide range of roles that can be taken on by advisors participating in DR are included in Annex 1.

3 Does Dispute Resolution Provide Accountability and Remedy?

Among IAMs, there is not yet a consensus on a definition of "accountability." In the context of IAMs, "accountability" is focused on the relevant DFI that is the subject of the complaint. Professor Jonathan Fox, Director of the Accountability Research Center at American University, highlights the "profound

3 For the purposes of this essay, we will use the general term "advisors" to include the various kinds of external groups and individuals that may be supporting and advising a community.

fuzziness" around what counts as "accountability." As he states in Chapter 1 of this book, "in the accountability field, definitions vary but they tend to involve some combination of answerability, consequences or sanctions, and redress."[4] Jason A. Springs, Professor of Religion, Ethics, and Peace Studies at the University of Notre Dame's Kroc Institute for International Peace Studies, refers to the substance of accountability as "bringing truth to light, recognizing and accepting responsibility, [and] responding to those who have been harmed."[5] Mark Bovens, Professor of Public Administration at the Utrecht University School of Governance, offers a concise description of accountability as "the obligation to explain and justify conduct."[6] As DFIs by definition work internationally, local practices and definitions of accountability may vary, and also need to be taken into consideration. Margaux Day, Executive Director of Accountability Counsel, explains, "the question of what accountability means has a multi-faceted answer, and it must be answered by those who are most impacted."[7]

While we will not attempt here to provide an authoritative definition of accountability, we do agree with Professor Springs that "impunity emerges when accountability is abandoned."[8] In our dispute resolution practice, we therefore attempt to facilitate discussions among parties about "accountability," defined in a holistic and relational manner, to include:

- Meeting needs of the parties and attending to the safety and well-being of all participants in the process;
- Fulfilling responsibilities in the context of interdependent and complex relationships between those experiencing harm or the threat of harm, those contributing to harm, and other stakeholders who are involved or affected;
- Considering histories, contexts, and causes of harm and its impact;
- Understanding interconnections and promoting just relations between individuals, groups, and communities; and
- Using data and knowledge to help parties make informed decisions.

DR processes aspire to do all of this in a way that is collaborative, non-adversarial, proactive, preventive, future focused, and educative, rather than punitive. Furthermore, in DR processes, the discussion often focuses on accountability of

4 Jonathan Fox, *supra* Chapter 1.

5 JASON A. SPRINGS, *Doing Justice Differently: From Revolution to Transformation in Restorative Justice and Political Reconciliation*, *in* DANIEL PHILPOTT & JENNIFER LLEWLLYN, EDS., RESTORATIVE JUSTICE, RECONCILIATION, AND PEACEBUILDING 253 (2014).

6 Mark Bovens, *Analysing and Assessing Accountability: A Conceptual Framework*, 13(4) EUROPEAN L. J. 450 (2007).

7 Interview with Margaux Day in *Accountability Matters* (April 2024).

8 Bovens, *supra* note 6.

the relevant development project as a whole, including multiple actors, and not limited to the individual DFI financier. When DFI management is participating in a DR process, complainants may be able to engage directly with them and their client/borrower to develop a common understanding of the depth, causes, context, and conditions of any harm (or potential harm) and how to create conditions where the harm is stopped or prevented. This can include acknowledging the impacts of a project and the needs of the complainants, jointly making plans for a better way forward, and agreeing on specific responsibilities for carrying out the plan.

Even with the best of intentions and rigorous due diligence and project supervision, DFI projects may still lead to harm to people in the community and other stakeholders. While non-compliance with a DFI's policies and standards may lead to harm, harm may occur even when there is full project compliance. It is important to note that harms may also occur simultaneously in the context of many positive project benefits and outcomes, such as job creation, vital infrastructure development, an improved standard of living, access to education and healthcare, lower greenhouse gas emissions, and so on. One frequent challenge is that there can be "winners and losers." That is, some benefit while others bear the costs, and project impacts that negatively and disproportionately affect the most vulnerable, marginalized, and poor can be contrary to a DFI's core mission and purpose.

Regarding remedy, the Compliance Advisor Ombudsman (CAO), the independent accountability mechanism for the International Finance Corporation (IFC) and Multilateral Investment Guarantee Agency (MIGA), defines "providing remedy as the act of effectively remediating adverse project impacts."[9] CAO further defines effective remedy as involving a number of components:

- It seeks to redress situations that expose people and the environment to potential or actual harm.
- It seeks to 'make whole' project-affected people and the environment.
- It helps to prevent future harm.
- It is not only an outcome, but also a process that places agency in the harmed person and acts toward restoring the dignity that was lost in the harm.[10]

Dispute resolution in the IAM context is voluntary, and therefore remedy cannot be guaranteed. Moreover, even when parties voluntarily reach agreements, differences may remain as to whether such agreements constitute "remedy."

9 CAO, *Insights on Remedy: The Role of Dispute Resolution in Remedy* (Feb. 6, 2023).

10 *Id.*

So, in response to the question of whether dispute resolution provides remedy, the best answer is "sometimes."

4 How Can Dispute Resolution Foster Institutional Learning for DFIs?

Some IAMs have specific advisory service mandates in their governing policies. This work typically involves gathering insights and analysing trends from both dispute resolution and compliance review cases to catalyze learning and help enhance DFI performance on key environmental and social issues. As independent neutrals, dispute resolution professionals can play a unique role in facilitating and fostering learning and knowledge sharing for host DFIs, as well as for other key stakeholders such as public- and private-sector clients, civil society actors and advocates, and project-affected communities. For example, IAM dispute resolution staff can convene information-sharing and learning events during a case, helping specific parties find mutually beneficial solutions to their issues, or provide inspiration and useful models for other development projects in the sector, country or region. DR case reports and public disclosures can document lessons and good practices. DR staff can also produce their own publications beyond individual cases, such as CAO's DR "Reflections from Practice" series[11] and its "Guidance Note on Gender-Inclusive Dispute Resolution."[12]

IAM dispute resolution functions can convene thematic and/or regional learning events and policy dialogues, using their facilitation skills to help find common ground and generate workable solutions among diverse stakeholders with differing views. They can find ways to respond to DFI requests for practical advice on approaches to better predict and resolve citizen grievances, including using borrower systems and project mechanisms. For example, the IAM for the Asian Development Bank (ADB) has provided training on grievance redress mechanisms for ADB staff and government agencies executing and implementing ADB-financed projects. IAM dispute resolution experts can serve as a knowledge platform and support host DFIs to improve the capacity of management, operations, and project teams to better respond to citizen feedback and complaints, and to predict and prevent conflict.

11 Compliance Advisor/Ombudsman, *Reflections from Practice*, https://cao-ombudsman.org/dr-practice/ (last visited Dec. 4, 2024).

12 Compliance Advisor/Ombudsman, *Guidance Note on Gender-Inclusion Dispute Resolution* (Jan. 1, 2019).

5 Why Is It Important for Dispute Resolution to be Independent Rather Than Embedded in DFI Management?

A key ethical requirement for professional mediators and neutrals is to be impartial and free from favoritism, bias, or prejudice.[13] Given that most IAM dispute resolution processes are voluntary, the IAM's influence and effectiveness in the dispute resolution context is dependent upon the parties' trust in the IAM (including any contracted mediators, facilitators, and consultants) as neutral and impartial. It is therefore essential that all dispute resolution processes (including mediations) are conducted in an impartial manner and avoid conflicts of interest, appearance of conflict of interest, and conduct that gives the appearance of partiality. Organizational independence from host institution management is critical for mechanisms to remain impartial, in fact and in appearance. Moreover, in some IAMs, DFI management can participate in DR as an observer, or even as a direct party, and it is important to differentiate their role as a participant with institutional interests and a stake in the outcome from the role of the impartial IAM. DFIs can potentially bring a lot of valuable experience and knowledge to a DR process for the benefit of all parties, but they are not neutral brokers vis-a-vis community interests due to their role as project proponents and their financial relationship with the borrower/client. Internal firewalls and confidentiality protections are also needed within IAMs to clearly separate dispute resolution and compliance review functions and roles, and to protect confidentiality of the dispute resolution process. Like compliance functions, IAM DR staff need authority to make decisions and recommendations without undue influence from management or other stakeholders.

6 The Future

IAMs need to be constantly learning and seeking ways to improve the delivery of their services. Feedback from direct parties and other stakeholders who engage with DR functions, robust monitoring, and evaluation are important to inform and improve their work, as well as to hold them accountable to their own policies and principles. The network of IAMs provides a forum for engaging with fellow IAMs and other stakeholders to brainstorm, share lessons and

13 *See, e.g,* American Bar Association & Association For Conflict Resolution, *Model Standards of Conduct For Mediators jointly adopted by the American Arbitration Association* (Sept. 2005); International Ombuds Association, *Code of Ethics* (Mar. 27, 2022).

experiences, and innovate. Fellow *Perspectives* author Gina Barbieri explores the idea of whether independent fact-finding could be conducted in some cases through cooperation between DR and compliance functions in consultation with the parties, rather than forcing a binary choice between the two options.[14] Civil society organizations have recommended that "complainants should be allowed to choose dispute resolution, compliance review, or both and their sequence."[15] In another *Perspectives* essay, Natalie Bugalski and David Pred of Inclusive Development International describe how binding arbitration could complement the work of IAMs in some cases.[16] We are also excited by the possibility of IAMs assisting local communities and CSOs to share their respective experiences and lessons with one another.

We would like to close with an expression of gratitude: to the IAMs; to the affected communities who have the courage to make their voices heard and who place their trust in us; to the civil society actors who provide feedback and insight and continue to hold IAMs, as well as their host institutions, accountable; to all the DFI development professionals who work hard and tirelessly to improve the lives of the world's poorest and most vulnerable; to the private and public sector DFI clients who are willing to engage collaboratively and in good faith with affected communities to find mutually beneficial solutions; and to the DFI Boards that support the IAMs and defend their independence.

Annex: Potential Roles of Advisors to the Community in the IAM-DR Process

Informing and Advising the Community about the IAM Process. Sharing views and relevant experience regarding the credibility and effectiveness of the IAM and the role of neutral mediators. Presenting the potential risks and challenges with the IAM process. Assisting parties in understanding the IAM policy and procedure, whether they have grounds for a complaint, and helping them formulate and submit their complaint.

Preparation. Helping affected communities in understanding the DR/mediation process and in setting realistic goals and preparing them for the

14 Barbieri, *infra* Chapter 16.

15 Multiple Authors, *Good Policy Paper: Guiding Practice from the Policies of Independent Accountability Mechanisms*, Center for International Law and Policy (Dec. 2021).

16 Natalie Bugalski & David Pred, *Can Mediation Provide Remedy for Human Rights Violations? A Quest for Justice Using a Development Bank Accountability Mechanism* (2023), available at https://digitalcommons.wcl.american.edu/accountability-perspectives/ (last visited Feb. 14, 2025).

discussions ahead. Assisting complainants in preparing and presenting any documentation they need for the process and in preparing for individual meetings and sessions.

Agreement to Mediate / Dispute Resolution Framework. Helping complainants understand and negotiate ground rules that will govern the process, covering such issues as handling the media, disclosure of information, and confidentiality. Such ground rules as well as the agreed objectives, scope, participants, methods, stages, and timelines of the dispute resolution process are often documented in an agreement to mediate or Dispute Resolution Framework.

Research and Data Sharing. Providing relevant and reliable data on the issues, helping to inform the collaborative DR process with accurate information.

Effective Representation and Stakeholder Engagement. Helping bring together diverse community members, sometimes with competing priorities or differing opinions, to foster meaningful dialogue and representation and ensure that the broader affected community is consulted throughout a DR process.

Strengthening Capacity. Helping train and building the capacity of community representatives in a variety of areas, such as public speaking, community organizing, understanding relevant technical reports and data, and understanding their rights (both legally and regarding IFI safeguards and policies).

Balance of Power. Where power imbalances exist between the parties, helping those who are at a disadvantage by providing support, information, and sometimes access to the media or influential allies.

Communication. Acting as advocates for communities while also facilitating open communication between the parties to foster a better understanding of each other's perspectives. Advisors help complainants to organize their thoughts and materials and effectively communicate during sessions and debriefing afterward. They may also advise parties on questions that it may be helpful for them to ask other parties or the mediator/facilitator to gain more information about the substance of the case or procedure involved.

Building Consensus. Working towards building consensus among stakeholders by highlighting shared interests and identifying potentially mutually beneficial solutions.

Exploration of Options. Helping to generate and explore various settlement options that meet the communities' needs, encouraging creative problem-solving.

Reality Check. Providing a realistic assessment of the strengths and weaknesses of the complainants' position, helping them make informed decisions during negotiations and realistically evaluate other available options.

Managing Emotions. Assisting in keeping discussions focused and constructive during DR processes, which can be emotionally charged.

Setting a Constructive Tone. Setting the tone for constructive engagement by maintaining professionalism and promoting productive dialogue.

Advocacy for Access to Information. Ensuring that all relevant information is accessible to stakeholders in the DR process and assisting complainants in gaining information from outside stakeholders.

Public Awareness and Education. Engaging the public and raising awareness about the collaborative efforts, when appropriate and in line with any confidentiality agreements between the parties; fostering support for social and environmental initiatives.

Long-Term Sustainability. Emphasizing the importance of considering long-term sustainability and ecological impacts in any proposed solutions.

Legal and Policy Expertise. Advisors with legal expertise can provide guidance on relevant regulations, laws, and IFI policies, ensuring that any agreements comply. Helping complainants gain a thorough understanding of legal rights and options available so that parties make an informed choice about whether to engage in the process and understand what other options are available to them if the process does not work out. If additional processes are ongoing, such as in national courts or elsewhere, advisors can help the party map and understand how these processes work.

Documentation. Assisting in documenting meetings and the terms of any agreements reached to ensure clarity and ease of implementation.

Monitoring and Accountability. After agreements are reached, supporting complainants in monitoring progress and helping ensure that commitments are upheld. This may complement, but is not to be confused with, the impartial role of the IAM in monitoring DR agreements.

Bibliography

American Bar Association & Association For Conflict Resolution. *Model Standards of Conduct For Mediators jointly adopted by the American Arbitration Association.* Los Angeles: American Arbitration Association, September 2005.

Barbieri, Gina. "The Promise of Collaborative Problem Solving in Enhancing IAM Effectiveness," *infra* Chapter 16.

Bovens, Mark. "Analysing and Assessing Accountability: A Conceptual Framework." *European Law Journal,* 13, no. 4. July 2007: 450.

Bradlow, Daniel. *External Review of the Inspection Panel's Toolkit.* Washington DC: World Bank, May 14, 2018: 11.

Bugalski, Natalie, Mark Grimsditch, and David Pred. "A Relevant Case of the World Bank Exercising its Political Will," in *Challenging the Prevailing Paradigm of Displacement and Resettlement. Risks, Impoverishment, Legacies, Solutions*, edited by Michael Cernea and Julie Maldonado, 180–200. New York: Routledge, 2018.

International Finance Corporation [IFC] Compliance Advisor/Ombudsman [CAO]. *Guidance Note on Gender-Inclusion Dispute Resolution*. Washington DC: IFC, January 1, 2019.

CAO. *Reflections from Practice*. Accessed December 4, 2024. https://cao-ombudsman.org/dr-practice/.

International Ombuds Association. *Code of Ethics*. Seattle: International Ombuds Association, March 27, 2022.

Day, Margaux. Interview in *Accountability Matters*. (April 2024).

Fox, Jonathan. "What Counts as Accountability," *supra* Chapter 1.

Multiple Authors. *Good Policy Paper: Guiding Practice from the Policies of Independent Accountability Mechanisms*. Washington DC: Center for International Environmental Law, December 2021.

Philpott, Daniel, and Jennifer Llewellyn. "Doing Justice Differently: From Revolution to Transformation in Restorative Justice and Political Reconciliation" in *Restorative Justice, Reconciliation, and Peacebuilding*. New York: Oxford Academic, 2014: 253.

CHAPTER 16

The Promise of Joint Fact Finding in Enhancing IAM Effectiveness

*Gina Barbieri**

1 Introduction

As a junior human rights lawyer in the mid-1990s in South Africa, I represented a client who had been shot by his employer. We sued the employer for damages, won the case, and my client received compensation. After the trial, he asked me whether I knew why he had been shot, what drove the employer to do what he had done. He wanted to reconcile himself with the outcome and needed this explanation to do so. He also wanted an apology. You don't sue for an explanation or an apology. Recognizing that judicial mechanisms may not always meet all our clients' interests, my mentor at the time recommended that I develop my knowledge of alternative dispute resolution and, in particular, mediation or "collaborative problem solving." This would have required that I spend more time understanding the harmed employee's expectations and, while not being able to adjudicate the criminal act, may have been able to address his needs for deeper understanding, and perhaps even reconciliation. And so began my passion for, and practice of, collaborative problem solving with a focus on mediation.

2 The Promise of Collaborative Problem Solving

Most accountability mechanisms offer two alternatives to addressing complaints: dispute resolution or problem solving (which I will refer to as "collaborative problem solving"), and compliance (which I view as being akin to independent fact finding and will use these terms interchangeably). The former typically engages the use of mediation as a process structure to address the complaint. Mediation may be defined as "the intervention in a negotiation

* Gina Barbieri is a South African human rights lawyer and expert in environmental and social accountability systems design and practice.

DOI:10.1163/9789004729735_021

or a conflict of an acceptable third party who has limited or no authoritative decision-making power, who assists the involved parties to voluntarily reach a mutually acceptable settlement of the issues in dispute." Further, "(i)n addition to addressing the substantive issues, mediation may also establish or strengthen relationships of trust and respect between the parties or terminate relationships in a manner that minimizes emotional costs and psychological harm."[1]

While there are many different definitions of collaborative problem-solving processes, I am going to focus on the use of mediation, primarily because mediation is the process typically used by IAMs to carry out their dispute resolution or problem-solving mandates. According to Menkel-Meadow et al., "[t]heorists and practitioners of mediation claim a central core of functions for mediation:

- that it is a consensual process, both in participation and in agreements reached;
- that it is, at its core, voluntarily engaged in;
- that it is participatory by the principles engaged in whatever problem or issue is presented at the mediation (who may have representatives who appear as well);
- that it is 'facilitated' by a third party 'outside' the immediate dispute or conflict (the 'neutrality' principle reframed to reflect some of the recent developments in use of expert facilitators);
- that it seeks to develop solutions to problems or resolutions of conflicts or disputes on terms of mutual agreement and fairness to the parties;
- that it seeks to facilitate mutual understanding and apprehension of the other parties' needs, interests and situations."[2]

Many also argue that confidentiality is a key function or principle underpinning the mediation process. While views differ in this regard, offering confidentiality can undoubtedly be very helpful in creating the safe space necessary to bring parties together to discuss complex disputes. Western models of mediation practice describe confidentiality as being

> [on] two levels: the entire mediation is in confidence. It is held in private. What is discussed remains private and the outcome is only publicized if the parties agree. The private meetings between the mediator and parties

---

1 Christopher W. Moore, The Mediation Process: Practical Strategies for Resolving Conflict (3rd ed. 2003).

2 Carrie Menkel-Meadow, et al., Mediation: Practice, Policy, And Ethics (2006).

work at a deeper level of confidentiality. No private information shared with the mediator in a private meeting with one party can be passed to the other party without express permission.[3]

The definition of these functions or principles certainly influences many IAMs in how their mediation processes are conducted. They exert a heavy influence on the way in which ground rules are both negotiated between the parties and ultimately form part of the process design. These principles should not be considered exhaustive and, even if they were, it is doubtful that they alone are sufficient to ensure fair and equitable outcomes result from the kinds of development disputes being mediated by IAMs.

During a collaborative problem-solving process, relationships and power dynamics can shift, often in a direction that provides communities who have been harmed with a clear and direct channel toward having a voice in the manner in which harms will be addressed, and through a process that builds the capacity of community representatives, fostering closer working relationships between the parties to enable a more obvious landscape for those parties to use in future disputes. The process lends itself to the creation of trust and a deeper understanding between the parties of what their interests are beyond stated positions and demands. And importantly, it enables development of a full suite of outcomes that can address those interests, rather than just stated positions, hopefully rendering more sustainable and effective outcomes.

But the benefits of this approach are hard to come by in situations where the scale of the power imbalance between the community that has been harmed and the private sector actor is far greater than in many other situations in which problem solving is being used as a response to a defined dispute. I would argue that the basic principles of the Western mediation model outlined earlier are insufficient for the kinds of development disputes IAMs are engaging in, and that we are obliged to consider ways to scaffold the process further if we are to achieve fair and equitable outcomes. The effectiveness criteria for non-judicial grievance mechanisms[4] (effectiveness criteria) are useful and relevant in this regard, and arguably should also form part of any mediator's framework.

3 The Center for Effective Dispute Resolution, CEDR Mediator Handbook (Oct. 2004).

4 United Nations Human Rights Office of the High Commissioner, *Guiding Principles on Business and Human Rights* (2011).

3 Effectiveness Criteria for Non-Judicial Grievance Mechanisms and More

The effectiveness criteria require the process utilized by non-judicial recourse mechanisms to be:

- Legitimate: enabling trust from the stakeholder groups for whose use they are intended, and being accountable for the fair conduct of the grievance process;
- Accessible: being known to all stakeholder groups for whose use they are intended, and providing adequate assistance for those who may face particular barriers to access;
- Predictable: providing a clear and known procedure with an indicative time frame for each stage, and clarity on the types of process and outcome available and means of monitoring implementation;
- Equitable: seeking to ensure that aggrieved parties have reasonable access to sources of information, advice, and expertise necessary to engage in a grievance process on fair, informed, and respectful terms (this includes the capacity building);
- Transparent: keeping parties to a grievance informed about its progress, and providing sufficient information about the mechanism's performance to build confidence in its effectiveness and to meet a public interest at stake;
- Rights compatible: ensuring that outcomes and remedies accord with internationally recognized human rights;
- A source of continuous learning: drawing on relevant measures to identify lessons for improving the mechanism and prevent future grievances and harm.

Application of the principles of mediation, along with the effectiveness criteria, will go a long way to building rights-compatible processes that lead to fair and equitable outcomes. But many challenges still remain, given the complexity of the disputes IAMs are being required to address and the grave inequity that exists between the parties.

I therefore advocate for additional building blocks in the collaborative problem-solving process which include:

- an analysis of the power imbalance and assessment of what each party may be required to do to attempt to level the playing field as much as possible, considering whether this can be done transparently and in discussion with both parties – for instance, whether complainants will need to continue an advocacy campaign during a mediation process; capacity building requirement of all parties; assessment of which other actors should be invited to participate;

- encouraging thorough storytelling by the parties as part of an initial assessment of the complaint by the IAM;
- the crafting of ground rules akin to pre-mediation agreements that take into account any power imbalance and try as far as possible to ensure adherence to the effectiveness criteria outlined above;[5]
- establishing community feedback loops for ongoing communication through the process; and
- establishing a monitoring mechanism to ensure proper implementation of any agreements reached.

The early "story-telling" phase of mediations in the development context often reveals disputes of fact that lie at the core of the problem. Communities impacted by project operations and the private sector operators are often at odds about the nature of the harm, whether there has been any policy non-compliance, and who is responsible for the harm. With limited baseline data to make a determination, and where third-party actors may not be bound by agreements obligating participation in the complaints handling process, these disputes of fact can present obstacles to finding solutions. They also contribute toward power imbalances, with the party that has access to more resources being able to procure "expert" opinion to support their position. To further complicate matters, determination of disputes of fact is not an automatic process point for mediation. It is important to consider what collaborative problem solving tools can be deployed in these circumstances, and whether these same tools, used to resolve disputes of fact, could apply more broadly to independent fact-finding processes.

4 Joint Fact-Finding: a Silver Bullet?

Where disputes of fact become an insurmountable obstacle preventing parties from moving forward with the mediation process, collaborative problem solving can be used to embark upon a joint fact-finding exercise. This is where I believe the promise of mediation can really come to life for accountability mechanisms, not only in resolving disputes of fact for the purposes of moving a mediation process forward, but also to help imagine a new tool for mechanisms to consider.

---

5 For another perspective that includes additional building blocks, see Compliance Advisor/Ombudsman [CAO], *Reflections from Practice: Getting Started with Dispute Resolution* (2021), available at https://www.cao-ombudsman.org/sites/default/files/2021-05/CAO_1_Getting Started.pdf (last visited Dec. 5, 2024).

So what is joint fact-finding? The IFC's IAM, the Compliance Advisor Ombudsman (CAO) provides the following description:

> Joint Fact-Finding (JFF) is a collaborative process in which parties in conflict work together with experts to address disputes of fact, differing expert opinions, or disputable scientific information. Typically, the parties jointly identify the issues, define the scope of the engagement, select the experts, provide inputs to the design of the process, and participate in fact-finding activities.[6]

Applications of this approach across different sectors abound, particularly where the analysis of scientific or technical data requires consensus as part of negotiations concerning a wider basket of issues:

> [JFF] brings experts, policymakers and stakeholders together to analyze scientific or technical data and try to draw conclusions. Instead of each party or participant generating evidence or arguments to support their prior assumptions (and political interests), the stakeholders jointly select one or more qualified advisors to help them sort through various sources of evidence … JFF requires face-to-face dialogue and movement toward consensus by continually narrowing areas of scientific disagreement. It usually precedes or is part of a larger collaborative decision-making process in which the results are agreements in the form of recommendations to elected or appointed decision-makers.[7]

Joint fact-finding draws on many of the principles of collaborative problem-solving practice to answer questions that require the determination of a set of facts. This process can be used to overcome negotiation obstacles as part of a problem-solving intervention, or mediation. It can also be used as a stand-alone intervention. Susskind et al. writes that:

> Experience around the world demonstrates that effective JFF efforts can: i) increase participation in, understanding of, and support for … decision making by stakeholders; ii) reduce or manage conflict that is inevitable

6 CAO, *Reflections from Practice: Joint Fact Finding* (Jan. 1, 2018), https://www.cao-ombudsman.org/resources/reflections-practice-series-3-joint-fact-finding (last visited Jan. 26, 2025).

7 Shafiqul Islam & Lawrence Susskind, *Using Complexity Science and Negotiation Theory to Resolve Boundary-Crossing Water Issue*, JOURNAL OF HYDROLOGY 589 (2018).

> in the face of conflicting interests; iii) possibly prevent litigation; iv) integrate the insights from multiple scientific disciplines; v) incorporate local or "non-traditional" knowledge into public decision making; and vi) lead to the creation of ongoing adaptive management efforts that help decision makers deal with uncertainties and unavoidable knowledge gaps.[8]

There are some examples of IAMs using JFF in their dispute resolution processes. A case in point is a complaint brought to the CAO, regarding the Oyu Tolgoi project in Mongolia.[9] Here, Khanbogd soum herders and the company engaged in a joint fact-finding process to conduct an assessment of, *inter alia,* the impacts on livelihoods of a copper and gold mine operated by Rio Tinto Plc. The aim of the JFF was to generate independent information regarding the impacts of company's operations on herders' livelihoods and the adequacy of the company's compensation processes. These recommendations were then the subject of a mediated negotiation in terms of which the parties agreed to jointly develop an implementation plan. JFF in a case like this will help to level the playing field and go some way toward ensuring a fair and equitable process. Rather than leaving the parties to carry the burden of establishing as fact their bargaining platforms, the JFF in this context would remove that burden, create equal access to information, and allow determination of fact to facilitate negotiation on how to address the finding.

Many key collaborative problem-solving principles are in play where a JFF process is utilized – for example, capacity building for the parties, development of trust and relationship building, and discussion of the interests in the complaint beyond articulated positions so that the JFF terms of reference can be appropriately defined. Additionally, community agency becomes a driving force in the conduct of the process. The ultimate result of a JFF process is that independent fact finding is taking place, but through the use of collaborative problem-solving principles. No longer is independent fact finding a process that happens to the parties. It is a process driven by the parties.

---

8 Lawrence Susskind, et al., *Towards a More Humble Enquiry: The Practice of Joint Fact-Finding, in* MASAHIRO MATSUURA & TODD SCHENK, EDS., JOINT FACT-FINDING IN URBAN PLANNING AND ENVIRONMENTAL DISPUTES (2017).

9 Compliance Advisor/Ombudsman, *Mongolia: Oyu Tolgoi-01/ Khanbogd,* https://www.cao-ombudsman.org/cases/mongolia-oyu-tolgoi-01khanbogd (last visited Dec. 5, 2024).

5 Collaborative Problem Solving in Compliance Investigations

The question arises whether it is possible for an IAM to use a process such as JFF to address questions of compliance. Generally speaking, compliance investigations are akin to an independent fact-finding process. The IAM is considered an independent entity tasked with making determinations of fact, reviewing institutional compliance with relevant environmental and social policies, assessing harm, and recommending remedial actions where appropriate. While IAMs themselves are structured and staffed differently, at the core of their compliance or independent fact-finding mandate is the ability to consider disputes of fact and, through various means, answer those disputes of fact on behalf of the parties. The IAMs will typically engage with the complainants, Bank staff, and other relevant stakeholders to gather information regarding the complaint. Experts may be appointed by the IAMs to assist in analyzing data and developing findings on behalf of the IAM. There are also examples of where the IAMs may enable complainants and the institution to comment on draft findings and participate in the development of institutional action plans that respond to the findings.

It is time to consider whether the independent fact-finding mandates of the IAMs can be carried out through the use of collaborative problem-solving principles, thereby capitalizing on the strengths of both tools rather than remaining a binary choice that requires parties to elect one or the other.

I have mentioned the obvious benefits of using the collaborative problem-solving process in this context, but there are a few less obvious ones:

- using collaboration to develop the terms of reference and appointment of experts may result in less institutional reluctance to embrace findings and recommendations;
- helping to provide a counterbalance to the ever-present, and one could argue inevitable, tension that exists between an IAM and its institutional home by moving away from a "battle of the experts" to a joint process of determining a set of facts;
- avoiding a situation where Boards of Directors are asked to "arbitrate" disputes between an IAM and management regarding determination of noncompliance and resultant remedial actions;
- avoiding the "battle of the experts" scenario, where management hires its own experts to dispute the findings of an IAM;
- providing a clear pathway for complainant and management engagement in determining action plans to ensure compliance with recommendations; and
- placing community agency at the heart of the process.

While use of JFF in a compliance context may sound resource-intensive, the actual costs may not be much greater than the resources already deployed to conduct typical independent fact-finding processes. And even if they do, the other benefits mentioned earlier may make it worthwhile.

This approach will also pose process and outcomes risks. For example, where there is an imbalance of power, sufficient resources would need to be allocated to the process to ensure parties can participate on an equal footing. This may mean appointing legal advisors, hiring highly skilled process facilitators with relevant expertise, and establishing extensive capacity building for the parties prior to commencement of the process. Guardrails may need to be established and agreed to upfront to ensure there is no "watering down" of the compliance function. For example:

- acceptance by all parties of the binding nature of the findings that result from the JFF process;
- a clear determination regarding the terms of reference for the JFF process, including whether recommendations will be made to the institution to remedy any non-compliance;
- whether a mediated approach will be used to negotiate implementation of any resultant recommendations; or
- whether the IAM should be vested with the discretion to decide which approach to use, or whether an opt out model should be encouraged.

It may also be necessary to determine an "exclusions list" for those types of complaints that would not or could not be addressed through processes such as this. For example, where complainants raise issues of ongoing physical harm, criminal acts of violence, or gender-based violence. The risks certainly require more analysis and consideration than I am providing in this perspective.

6 Innovation to Enhance Effectiveness – but No Silver Bullet

The use of JFF has another advantage as it could add another option to the frequent discussions among IAMs regarding the appropriate sequencing of dispute resolution and compliance processes. Some mechanisms enable a parallel process, granting the complainants full discretion regarding which process to use as a starting point. Others have flexibility to catalyze one or the other at any time. And there are also those mechanisms that have a stricter process flow, typically requiring parties to choose one or the other. While the discussion of which tool to use, and when to use it is important, it is equally important to start considering whether a more hybrid approach to addressing complaints would be valuable in strengthening IAM effectiveness in a context where this is becoming more and more difficult to secure. And so, just like that young human rights lawyer seeking alternative ways to address as many of my clients' needs and interests as possible, my hope is that IAMs continue to consider the tools they are using to achieve maximum effectiveness for communities who have been harmed, and the institutions they seek to hold accountable.

Bibliography

International Finance Corporation [IFC] Compliance Advisor/Ombudsman [CAO]. *Mongolia: Oyu Tolgoi-01/ Khanbogd.* Accessed December 5, 2024. https://www.cao-ombudsman.org/cases/mongolia-oyu-tolgoi-01khanbogd.

Center for Effective Dispute Resolution. *CEDR Mediator Handbook*, 4th ed. London: CEDR Publishing, October 2004.

Compliance Advisor/Ombudsman. *Reflections from Practice: Getting Started with Dispute Resolution.* Accessed December 5, 2024. https://www.cao-ombudsman.org/sites/default/files/2021-05/CAO_1_GettingStarted.pdf.

Menkel-Meadow, Carrie, et al. *Mediation: Practice, Policy and Ethics.* Boston: Aspen Publishers, 2006.

Moore, Christopher. *The Mediation Process: Practical Strategies for Resolving Conflict*, 3d ed. San Francisco: Jossey-Bass, 2003.

United Nations Human Rights Office of the High Commissioner. *Guiding Principles on Business and Human Rights.* Geneva: United Nations, 2011. https://www.ohchr.org/sites/default/files/Documents/Publications/GuidingPrinciplesBusinessHR_EN.pdf.

PART 4

Critiques of IAMs

Introduction to Part 4: Critiques of IAMs

The four pieces in this Part are all premised on the assumption that the Panel is failing in some way to be an effective accountability mechanism that delivers satisfactory relief to complainants and leads to significant improvements in World Bank policies and operations.

The first article, by Juan Pablo Bohoslavsky and C.P. Chandresekar, argues that the Bank has human rights responsibilities that it has consistently failed to fulfill. They note that this failure is particularly evident in the case of the Panel and the obligation to provide a remedy. Panel cases, perhaps inevitably, raise human rights issues, but the Panel has failed to address the human rights issues specifically raised in the cases cited and the Bank's human rights responsibilities more generally.

The article by Natalie Bridgeman Fields provides the perspective of an advocate who has helped many complainants bring cases to the Panel. She argues that the Panel has not been effective in providing appropriate relief to her clients, some of whom feel that they took a big risk in bringing a complaint to the Panel and that they did not get sufficient relief to justify the risk. Given the very real risk of reprisals against complainants, this is an important point. However, Bridgeman Fields also recognizes that the Panel and similar accountability mechanisms do offer an important means of holding the multilateral development banks accountable when they fail to comply with their own policies. These compliance findings may help improve the Banks' future performance but they do not necessarily help protect complainants from the consequences of non-compliance.

The third contribution, by Dustin Schäfer, argues that the existence of the Panel is based on the mainstream view, that is the Bank's view, of development. Schafer argues that this view is flawed and needs to be challenged and ultimately replaced by a more inclusive and sustainable view of development. He concludes that this means that the Panel cannot really resolve the development problems with Bank-funded projects or provide adequate redress for complainants. He calls for communities and their civil society allies to challenge the Bank's and the Panel's view of development and to advocate for a new approach to development.

In the final chapter, Lalanath Da Silva and Giarda Giancarla focus on the Panel's inability to make binding decisions. They argue that this should change and the Panel should be given the power to make binding decisions. They argue that there are precedents of the Bank accepting independent entities having binding decision-making authority – such as the administrative tribunal and the Bank's acceptance of binding arbitration in its contractual arrangements with suppliers. They also challenge the notion that the Panel is unusual because it is dealing with complainants who do not have a contractual relationship with the Bank since they come from communities that are third party beneficiaries of Bank project loans.

CHAPTER 17

The World Bank's Roadmap and Human Rights Responsibilities

Juan Pablo Bohoslavsky and C.P. Chandrasekhar***

1 The World Bank and Human Rights

The World Bank has been under pressure to devise a process for "evolving" its mission, operations, and resources, acknowledging that decades of engagement with low- and middle-income countries has resulted, paradoxically and contrary to its official mission, in a "crisis of development." The Bank bluntly notes in the opening to its December 2022 *Evolution Roadmap* that, "after decades of progress, growth and poverty reduction have stalled."[1] Indeed, this "crisis of development" threatens to unleash political instability around the world.

Pressure to reform the institution is coming not only from civil society organizations but also from member governments of the Bank, particularly from countries in the Global South where leaders face political backlash for the devastating effects of neoliberal reforms. As the Roadmap notes, "urgent action is needed to address the growing crisis of poverty and economic distress, and global challenges, including climate change, pandemic risks, and rising fragility and conflict."[2] Indeed, economic and environmental crises are triggering civil strife, eroding social cohesion, and encouraging far-right, religious fundamentalist, and authoritarian tendencies that severely erode human rights.

* Juan Pablo Bohoslavsky is a Researcher at Argentina's National Scientific and Technical Research Council (CONICET), Universidad Nacional de Río Negro (CIEDIS).

** C.P. Chandrasekhar is a Senior Research Fellow at the Political Economy Research Institute, University of Massachusetts.

1 World Bank, *Evolving the World Bank Group's Mission, Operations, and Resources: A Roadmap*, 1 (Dec. 18, 2022).

2 *Id.*

 | DOI:10.1163/9789004729735_023

Given this context, it is worth recalling that the Bank is bound by international human rights law[3] and that – with questionable success –[4] it has been trying to integrate these legal norms into its own policies and practices.[5] It is also timely to recall that the 2016 WB "Vision Statement"[6] noted that "the World Bank's activities support the realization of human rights expressed in the Universal Declaration of Human Rights." The World Bank Inspection Panel (the Panel) is – at least on paper – a key institutional player that should strengthen and bolster the Bank's accountability in respecting and meeting the standards of international human rights law.[7]

2 The Evolution Roadmap: A Shift in Focus with Very Modest Ambitions

Compared to those voices advocating for systemic changes,[8] the World Bank's *Evolution Roadmap* has very modest ambitions, broadly sticking to versions of the usual Gross Domestic Product (GDP)-linked development indicators. It seeks to expand the Bank's vision and mission by broadening its limited "twin goals" of "ending extreme poverty and boosting shared prosperity" by 2030, to emphasize sustainability, resilience, and the creation of global public goods as a way of addressing challenges such as climate change and pandemic preparedness, prevention, and response. The *Roadmap* redefines inclusiveness to pay more attention to middle-income countries that also face challenges to their sustainable development. But it leaves unaddressed the issue of whether

3 Daniel Bradlow, *The World Bank, the IMF, and Human Rights*, 6 TRANSNATIONAL LAW & CONTEMPORARY PROBLEMS 47–90 (1996).

4 UN Special Rapporteur on Extreme Poverty and Human Rights, *The World Bank is a Human Rights-Free Zone*, Press Release (Sept. 29, 2015), https://www.ohchr.org/en/press-releases/2015/09/world-bank-human-rights-free-zone-un-expert-extreme-poverty-expresses-deep (last visited Jan. 24, 2025).

5 Siobhán McInerney-Lankford, *International human rights law, politics and international financial institutions: the case of the World Bank*, in B. ANDREASSEN, ED., RESEARCH HANDBOOK ON THE POLITICS OF HUMAN RIGHTS LAW (2023).

6 World Bank, *A Vision for Sustainable Development, Environmental and Social Framework* (Aug. 4, 2016).

7 Viorica Vita, et al., *The World Bank Inspection Panel and International Human Rights Law* (NYU Law Clinic on International Organizations), 2007, https://www.iilj.org/publications/world-bank-inspection-panel-international-human-rights-law-%EF%BB%BF/ (last visited Jan. 24, 2025).

8 *UDHR and IPN anniversaries underscore urgent need for Human Rights policy at all IFIs* (Bretton Woods Project), July 2023.

this extension will be in addition to an increased engagement with low-income countries (LICs). The *Roadmap* is largely a promise to review the World Bank's operating model, and perhaps more importantly for the institution, to find ways of increasing resources and enhancing its "financial model,"[9] to achieve these loosely defined objectives.

Rather than breaking away from the reliance on traditional indicators and the tethering of multilateral public finance to private finance and instead incentivizing private finance to wade into areas with low profit probabilities but high social returns, the *Roadmap* seems to be strengthening the Bank's outdated tendencies. The Bank could feasibly address some of these issues by importing a select set of outcome indicators that more generally reflect advances and regressions on human rights into the development-indicators framework. The Organization for Economic Co-operation and Development (OECD), for example, declared as long ago as 2006 that human rights should be integrated into development.

3 Incorporating Human Rights into World Bank Indicators

Even the World Bank acknowledges in its *Evolution Roadmap* the need to explore new indicators for measures of prosperity. While any single indicator is inadequate in terms of coverage and reliability, a combination of indicators that go beyond just GDP, for example, do help assess progress on the sustainable development front and rank countries in terms of relative achievement.

The World Bank's *Roadmap* notes that, "[t]he evolution exercise will review the current approach and explore the possibility of using new indicators for measuring prosperity."[10] In that spirit and given that the World Bank is technically part of the U.N. system – which codifies human rights in its Charter – the case can be made for a richer set of indicators that acknowledge human rights. As explained, the World Bank Group is bound by international human rights law, which includes civil, political, economic, social, and cultural rights. Yet the notion of development that it follows does not include the full realization of all human rights. It is urgent to design and effectively implement development indicators with a strong human rights focus that accurately measure outcomes. Furthermore, it is technically possible to do this and should in fact be mandatory.

9 Andrea Molinari & Leticia Patrucchi, *World Bank Group Evolution: Technical fixes or urgently needed reform?*, BRETTON WOODS PROJECT AT ISSUE (July 2023).

10 World Bank, *supra* note 1, at 6.

The framing of these indicators must be guided by the obligation to contribute to the advancement and full realization of all human rights. At the minimum this should include:

(i) The right to food, in the form of universal access, for free or at heavily subsidized prices for those who require it, to a minimum quantity, comprising staples and other elements that meet basic caloric and nutritional requirements;

(ii) The right to education, with free and compulsory access to school up to the higher secondary level for all children in the relevant age group;

(iii) The right to health, with universal access to free primary and secondary health care;

(iv) The right to employment, with a guarantee to provide, on demand, a certain number of days of employment in a year at the national minimum wage, failing which the beneficiary would be eligible for an equivalent unemployment allowance to cover the shortfall.

Needless to say, realizing these targets would require the allocation of adequate resources from state budgets relative to GDP. Development policy recommendations from the World Bank should advocate for the necessary fiscal space to provide that allocation.

United Nations Trade and Development (UNCTAD) recently developed a Sustainable Development Finance Assessment (SDFA) Framework[11] for policymakers of developing countries to assess the development finance that each of them may need to achieve structural transformation, and to realize the most significant Sustainable Development Goals (SDGs), while at the same time ensuring the sustainability of their external and public sector financial positions. While SDFA seeks broadly to facilitate the achievement of SDGs, it is perfectly compatible with a more specific and concrete human rights approach.

4 A Role for Hybrid Indicators

Incorporating human rights elements into the set of indicators can be facilitated by the use of hybrid indicators that link financial trends and movements

11 UN Centre on Trade and Development, *UNCTAD Sustainable Development Finance Assessment (SDFA) Framework: linking debt sustainability to the achievement of the 2030 Agenda* (DA Covid-19 Project Paper 16/22), Nov. 29, 2022, https://mobilizingdevfinance.org/research-material/unctad-sustainable-development-finance-assessment-sdfa-framework-linking-debt (last visited Jan. 24, 2025).

in crucial outcome indicators. "Hybrids" involve the simultaneous use of more than one indicator when attempting to assess determinants of or influences on progress or absence thereof in crucial human development areas. As an example, one indicator for which information is already available to the World Bank is the value of the public-health-sector budget in relation to annual external debt payments. This ratio would give a general idea of the priority given to realizing the population's right to health. To assess the fallout of different levels of diversion of budgetary resources away from public health to servicing of external debt, parallel trends in indicators such as neonatal, infant, and maternal mortality rates can be examined. Debt-sustainability analyses can then concretely integrate the debt-driven consequences of limited public health spending. This would reveal the amount of additional resources needed in this area based on the specific overall health situation and challenges a country faces. The development indicator here connects external financial sustainability, public-sector financial sustainability, and the realization of specific human rights.

Focusing on specific features of the right to health does not mean that issues such as underspending and overspending in general are not relevant to assessing the impact of public finance on human rights. Rather, other perspectives need to be added and integrated into the universe of development indicators in order to understand and show more holistically the causes and effects of the main global social, economic, and environmental challenges that countries confront. Promoting good governance and protecting minimum fiscal capacity for rights-sensitive budget items are mutually reinforcing goals.

Similar indicators can also link the level of a population's access to clean water and sanitation with the country's spending to service external debt. More specifically, changes in indicators such as water system functionality, safe management of sewage, water quality, sustainability, sanitary risk, and the enabling environment, can be measured and assessed relative to debt repayments.

Measures of gender equality offer an example of how human rights-centered development indicators can be elaborated in a detailed and sophisticated way. A measure, for example, of the asymmetry in the distribution of heath care work among men and women in a given country could also be related to sums directly devoted in the public budget to the care economy and to the level of external debt-service payments.

Such conjoined indicators could help the World Bank, its shareholders, and constituents better understand the extent to which a given debt burden is sustainable from a human rights perspective. As mentioned earlier, this information can – and should – inform the due diligence that creditors perform when assessing the credit risk of a given borrowing state and, ultimately, help determine whether and under which conditions debt relief should be granted or agreed.

Movement toward these outcomes entails greater reliance on a framework that emphasizes development policy lending (which supports the overall development effort), as opposed to investment or project lending (or financing focused on individual projects). The difficulty is that the Bank links development policy financing to "assessment of performance against a set of indicators in the form of institutional or policy reform measures that reflect progress in implementing a country-owned reform programme."[12] But the agenda for reform and the indicators linked to it privilege private initiatives over proactive state intervention. Combined with associated privatization, this approach prioritizes fiscal consolidation of a kind that limits state capacity and embraces markets that function within power structures.

5 The Role of the Inspection Panel

The current World Bank framework, as signaled in the *Roadmap*, must change its lending practices to advance human rights, especially social and economic rights. As all human rights are interdependent – something seen particularly dramatically during the pandemic – the attainment of social and economic human rights can, in turn, advance the right to health and even the right to life. Furthermore, the Bank, as any other multilateral financial institution, should not be deterred from adopting a human rights approach in its decisions and daily practices by allegations – or fears of allegations – that it is meddling in countries' internal politics or that it is increasing bureaucracy and transactional costs.

Human rights recognized in international conventions are not about politics, but about universally agreed upon moral and legal values. Anticipating the effect of loans and policy recommendations on human rights and development does not create inefficiency; rather, inefficiency derives from the failure to meet basic institutional objectives by repeatedly prescribing the same policy recipes that harm instead of benefit the people of developing countries.

The establishment of the Inspection Panel in 1993 as an independent accountability mechanism was a significant step toward getting the World

12 Juan Bohoslavsky & C.P. Chandrasekhar, *World Bank Group's Roadmap and Human Rights: Sidestepping What Really Matters* (Bretton Woods Project), Apr. 11, 2023, at 11 (quoting World Bank Group).

Bank to recognize and guard against or redress potential human rights violations in the projects it finances. The Inspection Panel provides a forum for individuals to report violations in Bank-funded projects and obtain redress for harms they have faced from projects financed by the World Bank. Private individuals or communities can submit petitions to the Inspection Panel, claiming that "their rights or interests have been or are likely to be directly affected by an action or omission of the World Bank as a result of a failure of the Bank to follow its operational policies and procedures with respect to the design, appraisal, and/or implementation of a project financed by the Bank."[13] Such acts or omissions include situations where "the Bank is alleged to have failed in its follow-up of the borrower's obligations under loan agreements with respect to such policies and procedures."[14]

In practice, while the Panel has made some difference, its interventions have fallen short of requirements. It does not manage to ensure that the voices of those likely to be affected by projects financed by the World Bank are heard adequately at the planning stage. It often acknowledges violations when much damage has already been done. Many projects with damaging consequences have gone to completion even since the launch of the Panel. Even when it investigates, identifies violations, and assesses the extent of damage caused, it does not have the power or the resources to ensure that the victims are adequately compensated.

Moreover, being focused on assessing the impact of projects financed by the World Bank, the Panel does not recognize the damage done by conditioning Bank financing on the adoption or implementation of macroeconomic or financial policies that influence the pace and pattern of development. Whatever the Bank's reading of a situation, the policies at the back of the books providing these analyses adhere to the same neoliberal prescriptions that exacerbate the inequities embedded in markets with participants who are asset-rich and exert differential power.

In this respect, the Inspection Panel should not wear blinders when assessing the cause of the actual or potential adverse effects on people's human rights; otherwise, its ultimate objective would be to work as an ambulance treating symptoms instead of improving World Bank's policies and preventing damage. As explained by a number of scholars from different regions in a recent open letter addressed to the Bank and the UN, "SDG 10 is not a separate,

13 *See* International Bank for Reconstruction, World Bank Inspection Panel, *Resolution No. IBRD 93–10*, para. 12 (Sept. 22, 1993); International Dev. Association World Bank Inspection Panel, *Resolution No. IDA 93–6*, para. 12 (Sept. 22, 1993).

14 *Id.*

stand-alone goal: all economic, financial, and social policies should be assessed in terms of their likely impact on this goal. This would clearly signal our collective ambition to forge a more equal world."[15]

If the World Bank does not develop and adopt a robust legal approach that includes human rights indicators to measure, assess, and, if necessary, recalibrate its own policies, how is the Inspection Panel supposed to effectively carry out its responsibilities? The Inspection Panel, which claims to be an independent body, must examine the implications of the World Bank's policy framework and on its own initiative (*juria curia novit*) apply the applicable human rights standards to assess and decide on the impact of cases referred to it.

Bibliography

Bohoslavsky, Juan and C.P. Chandrasekhar. *World Bank Group's Roadmap and Human Rights: Sidestepping What Really Matters*. London: Bretton Woods Project, April 11, 2023: 11.

Bradlow, Daniel. "The World Bank, the IMF, and Human Rights." *Transnational Law & Contemporary Problems*, 6. (1996): 47–90.

Bretton Woods Project. "UDHR and IPN anniversaries underscore urgent need for Human Rights policy at all IFIs." *Bretton Woods Observer*. (Summer 2023).

McInerey-Lankford, Siohán. "International human rights law, politics and international financial institutions: the case of the World Bank," in *Research Handbook on the Politics of Human Rights Law*, edited by Bard Andreassen, ch. 15. Cheltenham: Edward Elgar Publishing, 2023.

Molinari, Andrea, and Leticia Patrucchi. "World Bank Group Evolution: Technical fixes or urgently needed reform?" *Bretton Woods Project At Issue*. (July 2023).

Oxfam. *Open Letter to the United Nations Secretary-General and President of the World Bank-Setting Serious Goals to Combat Inequality*. London: Oxfam, July 17, 2023.

United Nations Conference on Trade and Development. "UNCTAD Sustainable Development Finance Assessment (SDFA) Framework: linking debt sustainability to the achievement of the 2030 Agenda." DA Covid-19 Project Paper 16/22. Geneva: United Nations, November 29, 2022.

15 Oxfam, *Open Letter to the United Nations Secretary-General and President of the World Bank-Setting Serious Goals to Combat Inequality* (July 17, 2023), https://www.oxfamfrance.org/communiques-de-presse/setting-serious-goals-to-combat-inequality-open-letter-to-the-united-nations-secretary-general-and-president-of-the-world-bank/ (last visited Jan. 24, 2025).

United Nations Special Rapporteur on Extreme Poverty and Human Rights. "The World Bank is a Human Rights-Free Zone." news release, September 29, 2015.

Vita, Viorica, Rachel Tan, and Nealofar Panjshiri. "The World Bank Inspection Panel and International Human Rights Law."*International Organizations (IO) Clinic at NYU School of Law* (2007).

World Bank. *1999 Clarification of the Board's Second Review of the Inspection Panel.* Washington DC: World Bank, 1999.

World Bank. *A Vision for Sustainable Development, Environmental and Social Framework.* Washington DC: World Bank, August 4, 2016.

World Bank. *Evolving the World Bank Group's Mission, Operations, and Resources: A Roadmap.* Washington DC: World Bank, December 18, 2022: 1.

World Bank Inspection Panel. *The World Bank Inspection Panel.* Washington DC: World Bank, September 22, 1993: para. 12.

CHAPTER 18

"Use and Improve" Is My Accountability Mantra, despite Thirty Years of Eye-Opening Disappointments

*Natalie Bridgeman Fields**

1 Introduction

Standing on the banks of the Biobío River high in the Andes one morning in the late 1990s, I stood five feet away as Chilean military police aggressively tear gassed and arrested Indigenous Mapuche women who were blocking bulldozers from driving up the road to destroy their ancestral homes. They were being forced off their land for a dam project supported by the International Finance Corporation (IFC). That day changed my life when one of the protesters called to me, as the only foreigner there, saying "It's your government funding this project!" It was a literal call to action, not to act as a white savior, but to take responsibility for a mess I had a part in creating as a US citizen, with my government's outsized vote at the IFC's World Bank Group. Only a year before, accountability for harm caused by international development finance had already absorbed my intellectual world. I had discovered that a burgeoning system had the potential to enable aggrieved people to be heard in their demands for accountability.

This case in Chile that inspired my career led to the establishment of the IFC's accountability office, the Compliance Advisor Ombudsman (CAO), one of the first of a handful of mechanisms that existed after the very first, the World Bank Inspection Panel (the Panel) was established in 1993. These mechanisms were not created because the World Bank Group was in a reflective moment; they were forced on the Bank because the US Congress, in response to a series of well publicized disasters funded by the Bank, threatened to withhold funding for the Bank until they created the Panel. The CAO was created to avoid that threat of withheld funding from happening again. Whereas the Panel was Board-reporting, IFC management designed the CAO to report to the Bank President, forestalling the more independent option of reporting to the Board.

* Natalie Bridgeman Fields founded the non-profit, legal organization Accountability Counsel, which she led for fourteen years.

© NATALIE BRIDGEMAN FIELDS, 2026 | DOI:10.1163/9789004729735_024

It has been a rocky thirty years; several dozen independent accountability mechanisms (IAMs)[1] are now up and running, but they have delivered communities more disappointments than accountability.[2] But it is worth understanding the context of why, despite beginnings that foreshadowed the institutional failures we see now, these outcomes still do not deter me and a growing group of colleagues from promoting the use and improvement of accountability mechanisms. As the multilateral financial institutions now seek to control an increasing amount of climate-related finance, the accountability mechanisms have never been more important.

2 Racism, Privilege, and Access at Development Banks Shape Accountability

Since the creation of the multilateral development banks (MDBs) after WWII, projects like the one on the Biobío in Chile were, and still are, outrageously commonplace in terms of the type of harm they produce. Those who are most vulnerable – the poor, Indigenous People, women, girls, and LGBTQIA+ people – are the first to suffer in the name of 'progress' from which they rarely benefit. The banks are able to act with impunity because those harmed have the least power, and their interests are only nominally represented by their governments. Many countries have a poor track record of advocating for the voices of their own marginalized populations. Further, borrowing countries at development banks are themselves marginalized by design. Rich countries dominate a vote allocated according to shares owned in the bank, leaving the poor countries with a muted voice.

People harmed often cannot ask local or national governments for help, as they are the project proponents. Speaking out can put people at risk of retaliation. They cannot realistically sue implementing companies, agencies, or their own governments for abuses due to legal restrictions, nor can they easily sue the development banks that invoke arguments that they are immune from suit. Media exposure that shames the banks, political action to influence the banks' boards of directors, and community-organized civil disobedience are often the strongest tools available to harmed communities. Time after time

1 *See* Accountability Console, *Independent Accountability Mechanisms*, https://accountabilityconsole.com/iams/ (last visited Dec. 15, 2024).

2 *See* Accountability Console, *Complaints,* https://accountabilityconsole.com/complaints/visualize/ (last visited Dec. 15, 2024) (for complaint outcome data).

during the World Bank Group's first fifty years, however, those tools were *not* enough to prevent repeated cases of harm and abuse.

At the same time, up through the 1990s, startlingly few people had the privilege,[3] desire, and access to influence the harmful behavior of the banks from the outside. Two of those people working to bring the voices of those harmed to the attention of the World Bank's board were my mentors: Dana Clark and David Hunter at the Center for International Environmental Law. I worked for them in 1998 as they were supporting communities to use the new accountability mechanism at the World Bank, the Inspection Panel, that they and others, like Lori Udall from the Environmental Defense Fund, had urged the Bank to create. They supported complaints that allowed people harmed in Paraguay, for example, to engage directly, in a new way, that bridged the yawning divide between Bank decision-makers and those impacted by their decisions. While this was a novel development in international law, I saw a pattern where the Bank silenced and ignored Black and Brown people in Bank-impacted communities, while allowing white, educated, American and European professional activists in donor countries to push open the doors of the Bank and jolt the institution to respond.

This dynamic was a predictable consequence of racism and institutional biases that made my own audience with the powerful possible. As Americans, we could draw on our government's voting power at the Bank as a tool of influence.[4] I began my professional life's work by seeing how outrageously unfair this system was, but seeing my own access, I became part of it.

Privileged by my race, nationality, and education level, I learned albeit uncomfortably to exploit my privileges in a very Washington DC way: for the purpose of opening doors for my colleagues around the world who deserved their own direct access. In the 1990s, I jumped in with two feet as I saw how urgent it was to bolster community tools for accountability at each of the world's dozen or so finance and development institutions – no matter how weak or completely absent they were at that time. The promise was too great when just one project could displace and harm the lives of millions of

3 By privilege, I acknowledge that multilateral institutions are rife with racism, class bias, national origin bias, language and literacy bias, educational bias, gender bias, and a host of other intensified reflections of the world in which we live. As a white, educated, American citizen, my access is a reflection of the intentionally racist power dynamics of these institutions. Those with the most at stake, the most to lose when international finance and development goes wrong, are officially (through voting power) and implicitly (through bias), denied a powerful role in their own destiny.

4 *See* World Bank, *Voting Power*, https://www.worldbank.org/en/about/leadership/votingpowers (last visited Dec. 15, 2024).

people for generations to come. There was so much work to do – not just to get accountability mechanisms to hear the grievances of those harmed, but to get them to listen *directly* to affected people and prompt them to respond with appropriate remedy.

All these years later, the racist and biased systems of access to powerful institutions persist. While I've worked for decades to deeply listen to communities and bring their own voices to the accountability mechanisms, instead of speaking for those communities, the racism and other biases of these institutions still limit what the banks hear and how they respond.

3 The Limits of Power and Independence at Accountability Mechanisms

In the year 2000, I worked as a consultant to the Panel when the field was just starting to expand, and a dispute resolution feature was being added to newer mechanisms, including the CAO and the InterAmerican Development Bank's (IDB's) mechanism. Unlike other IAMs, the Panel remained a compliance-only mechanism at that time, and for many years to come.[5]

One summer day in a windowless room, I sifted through rows and rows of document boxes taller than I was, reading every word and developing a shortlist of investigation questions for an Inspection Panel member's interview of the Bank official responsible for decisions that violated Bank policy in a project site I had just visited in South America. But during the interview, I sat next to the Panel Member as they skipped the most crucial questions. While the Panel Member may have believed that accountability mechanisms should have enough independence to make unpopular decisions that uphold bank policy, they believed *even more* that the mechanism should not exercise so much independence that they alienate the institution's Board of Directors and staff.

Here was the quandary of the Panel's original compromise at its creation; despite their clear conflicts of interest, both the Bank's Board and its management are perversely required to *voluntarily* cooperate for success at the final stages of the otherwise-independent Panel process. While the United States and some Europeans extracted as much independence as they could from the Bank's board to lessen its impunity back in 1993, the Panel represents the *least* that the Board was willing to give up in order to keep the donor money flowing through replenishment processes. The result was a quasi-independent process

5 *See* Dilek Barlas, *supra* Chapter 6.

where the Panel was independent in developing their findings, until it mattered, when a political body (the Board) took control and decided what to do with the Panel's findings and management's proposed response. At the time, the Panel was revolutionary. But thirty years later, the initial obvious flaws born of this anachronistic compromise have become untenable.

3.1 *When the IAM Process Works, but Insufficient Power Robs Communities of Outcomes*

While US power was influential in brokering this deal, major borrowing country clients of the MDBs (*e.g.* China and India) have, since the beginning, demanded impunity for their abuses of their own people at project sites supported by the banks. Time and again in my own direct work with communities, I have experienced borrowing countries simply refusing to pay attention to those harmed after the Inspection Panel or similar compliance mechanisms had done a fair and impartial review. Quasi-independence is not enough when independence is needed. And powerlessness is not enough when confronted with absolute power.

There are examples throughout IAM history of powerful borrower countries simply ignoring accountability mechanisms – to the borrowing country's perceived ultimate advantage, and to the detriment of local people who suffer. This is, of course, a foreseeable response to IAMs that lack power to implement their findings independently.

In India, for example, the World Bank Group has a long history of lending to projects and companies that harm people and the environment (*e.g.,* the Narmada Dam (World Bank), Jharkhand Water Project (World Bank), Assam Tea (IFC), and Tata Mundra Coal Power Plant (IFC)).[6] There is an equally long history of public verification of that harm by official Bank inquiries and compliance reviews at accountability mechanisms.[7] The Indian Government's

6 *See* Joe Athialy, *supra* Chapter 13.

7 For Narmada Dam, see World Bank Group, *India – Narmada river development – Gujarat: Sardar Sarovar Dam and Power Project (English)*, http://documents.worldbank.org/curated/en/918961468044374790/Sardar-Sarovar-Dam-and-Power-Project) (last visited Dec. 15, 2024). For Jharkhand Water Project, see World Bank Group, *India: Rural Water Supply and Sanitation Project for Low Income States (P132173)-First Request*, Case 128, Request 18/06, https://www.inspectionpanel.org/panel-cases/rural-water-supply-and-sanitation-project-low-income-states-p132173-first-request (last visited Dec. 15, 2024). For Assam Tea Project, see World Bank Group, *India: Tata Tea-02/Assam*, Case No. Tata Tea 25074, https://www.cao-ombudsman.org/cases/india-tata-tea-02assam (last visited Dec. 15, 2024). For Tata Mundra Coal Power Plant, see World Bank Group, *India: Tata Ultra Mega-01/Mundra and Anjar*, Case No. Tata Ultra Mega 25797, https://www.cao-ombudsman.org/cases/india-tata-ultra-mega-01mundra-and-anjar (last visited Dec. 15, 2024).

response to criticism of projects of national importance, or the IFC's response in concert with its corporate clients, is to stonewall, delay, or simply ignore the violations of social and environmental policy, and international law.

A case to the World Bank Inspection Panel from Tibet in the year 2000 is an extreme example of a compliance investigation that found non-compliance with multiple social and environmental policies and implicated, indirectly, Chinese abuses, but the Chinese evaded accountability. As a consultant to the Panel at the time, I witnessed the Chinese government simply withdraw the controversial project from World Bank support just hours before the Board would have canceled the China Western Poverty Reduction project due to the non-compliance, thus removing the Bank's power over the borrower. China decided to go it alone and implement the project of forced relocation of ethnic Han into Tibet without Bank support, without standards or accountability, and to the great detriment of the Tibetan people.[8] "You have to crack a few eggs to make an omelet," the Chinese office at the World Bank was accustomed to saying in the 1990s.

After my time at the Inspection Panel, I spent a decade as a corporate, human rights, and environmental litigator in the United States. I then returned to accountability mechanism work with a deeper understanding of what suing perpetrators of abuses in courts requires of those harmed. Remedy is extraordinarily rare. I took a consulting job at the European Bank for Reconstruction and Development (EBRD), redesigning their accountability mechanism based on consultations with the public, complainants, civil society, bank staff, and the Bank's board. This deep dive into the EBRD's workings taught me how intentionally constructed some of the barriers for communities seeking access to accountability mechanisms. Accountability mechanisms are viewed as an annoyance to many MDB staff and managers, and the barriers to entry for communities are in many cases *decisions*, not mistakes. The same Bank Management who made these accessibility decisions had a role in approving responses to the EBRD accountability mechanism's compliance findings.

Almost twenty years after the Tibetan people lost their struggle with forced relocation, World Bank President Jim Kim pointed his finger at me on stage at a public conference in Oxford and said that the forcibly displaced communities in Nepal that I was trying to discuss with him were just like people in the United States subject to eminent domain (*i.e.*, they were just cracked eggs).[9] Never mind the evidence my team had provided the Bank for years about the

8 *See* Jarrett Murphy, *World Bank Project Drops Plans for Tibet*, CBSNEWS (July 5, 2000).

9 *See* Marc Gunther, *Natalie Bridgeman Fields; Holding the powerful accountable*, NONPROFIT CHRONICLES (MAY 2, 2017).

lack of compensation, threats, detention, and beatings these communities were enduring as part of violations of the Bank's own policies. Impunity is not just a borrowing country value.

The European Investment Bank (EIB) had a similar failure in a Nepali transmission line case, where instead of adhering to the EIB Ombudsman's set of recommendations to address non-compliance, the Nepalese government simply refused to cooperate and evaded accountability, without EIB using its leverage as it could have.[10] The EIB's response was too little, too late, to matter to the Nepalese communities who filed the complaint.

These are examples of IAMs *doing their jobs as designed,*[11] but failing to result in accountability. Even in these cases of "successful outcomes" of the IAM processes, accountability is not the result if the banks then fail to respond with remedy because of limited leverage over the borrower, failure to use that leverage, or failure to change their own practice.

3.2 *When IAMs Independence Is Undermined, the Pendulum Begins to Swing*

For the past 14 years, up until 2023, I ran Accountability Counsel, an organization I founded to support communities in understanding and effectively using accountability mechanisms as a tool for justice. By the time I started the organization, the field of IAM practice was growing and had expanded to include dispute resolution at most IAMs, but there were still just a handful of advocates helping communities to use the mechanisms.

By 2009, the pendulum that swings through the accountability mechanism world was obvious. In the 1990s, the Panel had to fight tooth and nail to even exist and for even a semblance of quasi-independence.[12] Civil society pushed hard on that pendulum from the outside to defend the founding Panel members and secretariat's early work to hold up the Panel's limited powers. But then the Panel started issuing strong compliance reports that validated community experiences of forced displacement and other harms. Even though, as discussed above, so many of these reports were ignored, the bad publicity from the Bank's own accountability mechanism was too much, and the Bank's embarrassment led to backlash.

---

10 *See* Accountability Counsel, *Nepal: 220 kV Marsyangdi Corridor Transmission Line*, https://www.accountabilitycounsel.org/client-case/nepal-220-kv-marsyangdi-corridor-transmission-line/#overview (last visited Dec. 15, 2024).

11 *See* Violet Benneker, et al., *Glass Half Full? The State of Accountability in Development Finance* (Center for International Environmental Law, et al.), at 34 (2016).

12 *See* Eduardo Abbott, *supra* Chapter 5.

Subsequent Panel members and staff responded to the backlash by beginning a dispute resolution "pilot" program without transparent procedures that ended up preventing public compliance findings in some circumstances, including cases I worked on firsthand.[13] At the same time, the Bank started "Panel-proofing" conflicts by referring them not to the independent Inspection Panel, but to a new Management-run Grievance Redress Service (GRS),[14] an entity without a clear mission (I saw three different and conflicting descriptions of its goals at one point within a one-month period). Through my work at Accountability Counsel, we worked with communities frustrated by the GRS as well. While the Panel did need dispute resolution tools, instead of asking the Board to create them with transparency of procedure and operations, the Bank buried a dispute resolution function deep within a conflicted arm of Bank management. The pendulum was coming back fast.

Knowing from the start how much pressure is coming down on accountability systems, the second pillar of Accountability Counsel's work is to conduct advocacy to push on that pendulum and urge IAM improvements, to call out biases and failures, and lift up good practice and policy. The third element is action-oriented research to show what is happening in the system and allow advocacy for use of that data to improve it and to chart the pendulum's swing.

At the beginning, I performed all three of the program roles. I worked as a lawyer and partner with communities for cases in Papúa New Guinea (World Bank),[15] Peru (IFC),[16] Mexico (Overseas Private Investment Corporation (OPIC)),[17] and as a supporting advocate on dozens of other cases. I worked on

13 *See* Natalie Bridgeman Fields & Kindra Mohr, *The World Bank's failed accountability experiment: Why the Inspection Panel's'Pilot' should dead end* (The Bretton Woods Project), Aug. 4, 2016, https://www.brettonwoodsproject.org/2016/08/world-banks-failed-accountability-experiment-inspection-panels-pilot-dead-end/#:~:text=The%20Panel%20is%20right%20to,be%20put%20to%20an%20end (last visited Jan. 26, 2025).

14 *See, e.g.*, Chair Summary, *Report and Recommendations to the Board on the Review of Inspection Panel's Toolkit* (Oct. 31, 2018), https://documents1.worldbank.org/curated/en/768191541646040975/pdf/10-31-18-IPN-toolkit-FINAL-with-change-requested-from-US-11022018-636772248345759387.pdf (last visited Jan. 26, 2025).

15 For Complaint details, see The World Bank Inspection Panel, *Papua New Guinea: Smallholder Agricultural Development Project*, Case No. 62, Request No. 9/10, https://www.inspectionpanel.org/panel-cases/smallholder-agriculture-development-project (last visited Dec. 15, 2024).

16 For Complaint details, see Compliance Advisor/Ombudsman, *Peru: Maple Energy-01/Nuevo Sucre and Canaan*, Complaint No. Maple Energy 26110, https://www.cao-ombudsman.org/cases/peru-maple-energy-01nuevo-sucre-and-canaan (last visited Dec. 15, 2024).

17 For Complaint details, see U.S. International Finance Development Corporation, *Mexico Cerro de Oro Hydroelectric*, https://www.dfc.gov/who-we-are-office-accountability-public-registry-cases/mexico-cerro-de-oro-hydroelectric (last visited Dec. 15, 2024).

policy at every accountability mechanism, advocated that new ones be created, and initiated work on the Accountability Console – a database to track and visualize complaint and institution data and to compare mechanisms. A few years in, I began to hire what is now an exceptional team of diverse, talented people who are changing the field in positive ways.

All these years later, the organization has delivered a host of policy improvements at every IAM, has worked with communities on a group of rare cases where communities have directly benefited from remedial action (mostly from dispute resolution), and has delivered research laying the system and its impacts bare. I also worked for decades with colleagues around the world to create a team of advocates, who in turn support a brave group of local and regional organizations to do this work in borrowing countries, upending the makeup of who has access to the banks. I'm so proud of the field-building we have done that has created a robust civil society community. But even with Accountability Counsel's efforts that continue today, there remains so much work to do for the next generation taking on these issues.

At the World Bank Group, the pendulum has been swinging faster lately and is taking aim at what little independence the accountability mechanisms have. The need for accountability mechanisms to have the independent power to direct outcomes that benefit communities could not have been made more clear than in 2023, looking at the IFC's recent collusion with its client, Bridge International Academies (*aka* NewGlobe), to cover up cases of child sexual abuse and labor rights violations at private, for-profit schools in Kenya.[18] The IFC staff went so far as to negotiate a non-disclosure agreement with its client Bridge to prevent harmful information from reaching the market – even by the CAO – as the company sought an additional round of financing. The World Bank President further undermined the CAO's independence and accountability efforts by swapping out the leader of the CAO for one who would improperly place the lead CAO compliance investigator of Bridge on leave before the investigation report into Bridge could come out. The CAO's investigator remains on administrative leave today.[19]

4 What Political Bodies Can Do to Modernize Accountability

In all of these years of working on nearly every aspect of accountability mechanism policy and practice, I've observed that without appropriate bank staff

18 *See* Sophie Edwards, *IFC Slammed by its Own Watchdog for Ignoring Child Sex Abuse Allegations*, DEVEX (Oct. 26, 2023).

19 *Id.*

incentive structures and remedy frameworks that actually deliver remedy to communities, the whole field is navel-gazing and often causing more harm in the process. These learnings sketch out a roadmap of reforms needed in international finance and development. As climate finance increasingly uses public institutions as a tool, the reforms need to account for the next fifty years of impacts.

4.1 *Poor Incentive Structures Can Prevent Good Community Outcomes*

While compliance and dispute resolution functions have wide differences in mandate and operation, they are both influenced in significant ways by the personalities of the people in the relevant accountability mechanisms, government units, companies, and Bank offices involved in the case, and by the strength of their commitment – or lack thereof – to seeing that communities are treated fairly.

Locating where a mechanism has to depend most on relationships for progress is a good guide to finding where the policy framework governing the mechanism is weakest. For IAMs, it's at the very last stage, where implementation depends on good will instead of sound policy. Personalities and relationships can determine whether or not remedy follows when accountability mechanisms find noncompliance or whether broker agreements occur through dispute resolution. Former Dutch World Bank Board Member, Koen Davidse, comes to mind as a long-standing accountability champion protecting the Panel process and working to deliver outcomes for communities.

When there are relationships of respect between accountability office staff and those among bank staff and board who are committed to accountability and treating communities with dignity, the mechanisms can be at their most effective. Strong community advocates and international allies are almost always *additionally* required for accountability mechanisms to function in a way that benefits communities and holds institutions to account.

Sometimes, however, despite good intentions and the potential for good institutional and community outcomes, personal circumstances can get in the way. The MDB staff are from all over the world, and they work in places like Washington DC, London, Manila, Abidjan, Seoul – places often far from their homes and countries of origin, where they require visas from the banks if they and their families want to stay. Jobs at these banks are often lucrative, and golden handcuffs can bind the decisions of bank employees who are loyal to their employer more than to their employer's ultimate mission.

I have seen this play out even at the Panel and other IAMs, where staff of the mechanism have come from the Bank's internal units and seek to stay at the Bank after their tenure at the mechanism ends, resulting in conflicts of interest that have harmed communities as they placate Bank Management and powerful Board members. Pre- and post-employment bans that prevent a revolving door (as is required for the Panel Members) can go a long way to addressing this problem.

Finally, staff incentive structures at development banks are a problem that leads to repeated harm from the same types of projects, over and over again. Where career advancement depends in part on quickly completing projects and disbursing money,[20] these incentives can be at odds with careful consideration and prevention of project impacts and close consultation with affected communities; essentially, these incentives conflict with good safeguard compliance.

Bank staff should be rewarded not on loan volume, but based on the impacts that the projects have on local affected communities (not just intended project beneficiaries) and their constructive responses to grievances.[21] Project-affected people, and the ecosystems they depend on, must be seen as rights holders with commensurate Bank duties to those rights holders that are reflected in loan agreements.

I have heard from Bank staff and board members over and over that "we won't be competitive if our projects are too slow out the door," meaning if we take too long on safeguards – but that is the point and value-add of public development banks. Safeguards and capacity building around them are what differentiates development from commercial banks. They *can* support projects that do not cause conflict and harm and that *benefit* the poorest of the poor at project sites. They can incentivize safeguard compliance and harm prevention at every stage of the project cycle.

4.2 *Without Better Harm Prevention and Remedy Frameworks That Deliver, We Are Navel-Gazing and Causing Harm*

Over the past thirty years, even in the cases where IAM compliance findings demonstrated that Bank policy non-compliance harmed a community, remedy at the community level has been rare. And then, it is usually only after communities and their allies have mounted political campaigns at the banks' Boards to get action that a small number of these cases have resulted in positive changes at the project level. Thus began the last decade of civil society campaigning for development banks to establish remedy frameworks so that communities are

---

20 *See* Bretton Woods Project, *World Bank Staff Incentive*, 85 BRETTON WOODS UPDATE (Apr. 8, 2013) (re "volume targets").

21 This is not to say they should be rewarded if there are no complaints, but rather, they should be rewarded for working through a grievance process in a constructive, compliant way.

not just holding meaningless paper after years of effort, or having to struggle upstream to get results. The remedy campaign continues today, with a focus on IFC after extensive documentation of its failure to respond appropriately to findings of noncompliance.[22] We are on a new framework, as IFC's initial approach was criticized as largely supporting current practice and refusing to evolve from the system that is failing communities.[23]

Without robust remedy frameworks, accountability mechanisms can and do cause harm. They act as an accountability fig leaf, shielding the MDBs from more robust legal liability.

Further, it is not a neutral act to find non-compliance and then have the Bank fail to act on remedying that non-compliance. In the case of the Nepali transmission line project mentioned above, villagers spent countless hours in meetings (under threat and surveillance), first understanding the accountability mechanism process, then gathering their experience into written format to submit a complaint, then spending time meeting around all the required follow-up to ensure the complaint was eligible, all while resisting major Nepalese military police retaliation in the form of arrests and illegal detention.[24] These villagers are farmers, parents, shopkeepers; they are people whose livelihoods depend on the time they spend tending to their duties. Some live a several days' walk from the meeting places. This level of community time and investment is similar for complainants across all accountability offices. They are not paid to spend time on an accountability process, and their livelihoods can and do suffer as a result. When all of their investment leads to nothing from the mechanism's process, and they have lost income and have been hurt in retaliation, as happened in Nepal, the process causes harm. Even a policy

22 *See Insights on Remedy; The Remedy Gap: Lessons from CAO, Compliance and Beyond* (The Office of the Compliance Advisor/Ombudsman [CAO]), Apr. 2023, https://www.cao-ombudsman.org/sites/default/files/2023-04/CAO%20Advisory%20Note_Remedy%20Gap_April%2013%202023_updated.pdf (last visited Jan. 26, 2025); *see also* Accountability Console, *Complaints*, https://accountabilityconsole.com/complaints/visualize/? (last visited Dec. 15, 2024).

23 *See* Accountability Counsel, et al., *Joint CSO Statement Calls on IFC and MIGA to Strengthen its New Approach to Remedial Action Policy* (Feb. 22, 2023). For IFC/MIGA's remedy framework proposal, see The Office of the U.N. High Commissioner on Human Rights, *IFC/MIGA Draft Approach to Remedial Action: Comments and Recommendations of the UN Human Rights Office* (Apr. 13, 2023), https://www.ohchr.org/sites/default/files/documents/issues/development/dfi/OHCHR-comments-IFC-MIGA-Approach-to-Remedial-Actions_13-April-2023.pdf (last visited Jan. 26, 2025).

24 *See* Accountability Console, *Power Development Project*, https://accountabilityconsole.com/complaints/power-development-project/ (last visited Dec. 15, 2024).

'win' out of a complaint process, such as a change in policy that will purportedly avoid the same harm in the future, is not a community-facing remedy.

Without robust remedy frameworks, it is becoming irresponsible to promote the use of certain IAMs when a community seeks guidance. The need for reform is urgent. Even with poor odds of getting meaningful remedy, impacted communities will still make the hard choice to use IAMs, and we owe it to them to improve their odds of remedy.

The MDB shareholders should require the banks to withhold final payments until borrowers cooperate with IAM outcomes (either through working with the bank to implement management action plans or upholding negotiated agreements). Initial remedy funds should be set aside at the start of both public and private projects so that the accountability mechanisms can direct remedial funds straight to communities who need them. Reforms must include blacklisting companies or governments that fail to uphold their end of accountability process outcomes; a similar measure is already taken in response to corruption investigations.

5 Exceptions Are Worth It and Can Be Spectacular

I started this work in the early days of the now well-established IAM field. But I have *continued* in this field, as a consultant to accountability mechanisms, as a lawyer advocating alongside communities, as a policy advocate and consultant working to design and revise accountability policies, because *these mechanisms and the institutions that house them can be improved, and communities can and do benefit.* Indeed, communities come to accountability mechanisms when they have been seriously wronged and have *no better options*. I've been alongside communities many times as they have made the hard decision to commit to an accountability mechanism process despite bad odds, because their odds without an IAM process are even worse.

Despite the gloomy assessment that dominates this chapter, I and other CSO colleagues remain deeply committed to the success of corporate and institutional accountability mechanisms. While policy wins that promote transparency and accountability are worth celebrating, communities who achieve fair treatment and remedy for harm (or harm prevention) are the real point. I have been part of enough community victories to see the deep value of this admittedly flawed system.

In Oaxaca, Mexico, I had the privilege of standing alongside Indigenous Chinanteco communities demanding a halt to the construction of a hydroelectric facility that would remove their access to clean water at a culturally important spring.[25] They succeeded in using OPIC's dispute resolution process (now part of the US Development Finance Corporation) to reach an agreement with the project sponsor to halt the project. Now, over a decade later, the spring is still a community focal point and critical water resource – and a celebrated source of community pride. The organizing done as part of that complaint process brought the communities surrounding the spring closer together, benefitting their civic institutions in the long run. This victory was worth the years I spent on advocating for reforms at the OPIC Office of Accountability, which then supported the platform for this win. This victory was worth years of effort that community members put into the complaint process. The accountability mechanism process – although even in this case not without major flaws – ultimately worked.

Similarly, in Haiti, I was present at the signing of an agreement between Haitian farmers and their families, representing years of work by the communities; local advocates; Accountability Counsel advocates Lani Inverarity, Megumi Tsutsui, and Samer Araabi; as well as IDB accountability office staff and IDB project teams. The agreement pledged to remedy some of the unimaginable harm that the IDB's financing of a sweatshop on their farmland caused when it was suddenly taken without consultation or proper compensation. Today, a large part of that agreement has been implemented; some farmers have new land, some have agricultural inputs to improve their ability to farm, and some have microfinance for new small businesses. Here too, it was worth years of my prior effort alongside many advocates to reform the IDB's accountability office to see this victory made possible. In this single case achievement, my life's commitment to accountability mechanisms feels vindicated, because for many in the Haitian communities, this victory has been a lifeline.[26] These results matter so much to so many.

6 Conclusion: the Work to Use and Improve IAMs Is Still Critically Important

So yes, I am an accountability mechanism cynic, but also a leading champion of the existence, use, and improvement of these mechanisms. As climate finance

25 *See* Accountability Console, *Mexico Cerro de Oro Hydroelectric*, https://accountabilityconsole.com/complaints/mexico-cerro-de-oro-hydroelectric/ (last visited Dec. 15, 2024).

26 *See* Inter-American Development Group, MICI, *Productive Infrastructure Program – Request II*, Project No. HA-L1055, (Jan. 12, 2017), https://www.iadb.org/en/mici/complaint-detail?ID=MICI-BID-HA-2017-0114&nid=21822 (last visisted Jan. 26, 2025).

leans on public development and multilateral institutions to use their infrastructure to address climate action, mitigation, and loss and damage funds, accountability for these uses must improve.

One of the advances I have seen in this field over the past thirty years is the sheer number of people, now hundreds, who are now aware of accountability offices as a tool and are capable of supporting communities through the complaint process. These advocates' time and effort alongside communities in the complaint process must, however, be well balanced with their investments in the advocacy required to improve mechanisms and the institutions that house them in all of the ways I have described, including through working to build political power for accountability at the level of the boards of directors. I believe the pendulum will swing toward withholding funding for the development banks to ensure better functioning on accountability issues before the decade is out.

I remain hopeful because there is no other choice. I have the privilege and responsibility to keep working toward a more just system of development finance because millions of people harmed each year still need a working system to support their demands for respect.

Bibliography

Abott, Eduardo. "The Inspection Panel Early Years (An Inside Story) in *Perspectives on Accountability at International Financial Institutions: Thirty Years after Creation of the World Bank Inspection Panel*, edited by Daniel Bradlow, et al. Leiden: Forthcoming Brill, 2025. https://digitalcommons.wcl.american.edu/accountability-perspectives/12/.

Accountability Console. *Complaints*. Accessed December 15, 2024. https://accountabilityconsole.com/complaints/visualize/.

Accountability Console. *Independent Accountability Mechanisms*. Accessed December 15, 2024. https://accountabilityconsole.com/iams/.

Accountability Console. *Mexico Cerro de Oro Hydroelectric*. Accessed December 15, 2024. https://accountabilityconsole.com/complaints/mexico-cerro-de-oro-hydroelectric/.

Accountability Console. *Power Development Project*. Accessed December 15, 2024. https://accountabilityconsole.com/complaints/power-development-project/.

Accountability Counsel et al. *Joint CSO Statement Calls on IFC and MIGA to Strengthen its New Approach to Remedial Action Policy*. February 22, 2023.

Accountability Counsel. *Nepal: 220 kV Marsyangdi Corridor Transmission Line*. Accessed December 15, 2024. https://www.accountabilitycounsel.org/client-case/nepal-220-kv-marsyangdi-corridor-transmission-line/#overview.

Athialy, Joe."The World Bank, the Inspection Panel and Immunity", in *Perspectives on Accountability at International Financial Institutions: Thirty Years after Creation of the World Bank Inspection Panel*, edited by Daniel Bradlow, et al. Leiden: Forthcoming Brill, 2025. https://digitalcommons.wcl.american.edu/accountability-perspectives/13/.

Barlas, Dilek. "Thirty Years of Community-Centered Accountability in International Development Key Developments at the World Bank Inspection Panel," in *Perspectives on Accountability at International Financial Institutions: Thirty Years after Creation of the World Bank Inspection Panel*, edited by Daniel Bradlow, et al., Leiden: Forthcoming Brill, 2025, https://digitalcommons.wcl.american.edu/accountability-perspectives/6/.

Benneker, Violet, et al. *Glass Half Full? The State of Accountability in Development Finance*, edited by Caitilin Daniel, et al, 34. Amsterdam: SOMO, 2016.

Bretton Woods Project. "World Bank Staff Incentive." *The Bretton Woods Updates*, 85, (April 8, 2023).

International Finance Corporation (IFC) Compliance Advisor/Omnibus (CAO). *Peru: Maple Energy-01/Nuevo Sucre and Canaan,* Complaint No. Maple Energy 26110. Filed April 6, 2010, Accessed December 15, 2024. https://www.cao-ombudsman.org/cases/peru-maple-energy-01nuevo-sucre-and-canaan.

Chair Summary. *Report and Recommendations to the Board on the Review of Inspection Panel's Toolkit*. Washington DC: World Bank, October 31, 2018.

Inter-American Development Group, MICI. *Productive Infrastructure Program – Request II,* Project No. HA-L1055. Washington DC: Inter-American Development Bank, January 12, 2017.

Edwards, Sophie. *IFC slammed by its own watchdog for ignoring child sex abuse allegations*. Washington DC: Devex, October 26, 2023.

Fields, Natalie Bridgeman, Kindra Mohr. *The World Bank's failed accountability experiment: Why the Inspection Panel's'Pilot' should dead end.* London: Bretton Woods Project, August 4, 2016.

Gunter, Marc. "Natalie Bridgeman Fields; Holding the powerful accountable. *Nonprofit Chronicles*. (May 2, 2017).

Murphy, Jarrett. "World Bank Project Drops Plans for Tibet." *CBS News*. July 5, 2020.

The Office of the Compliance Advisor Ombudsman [CAO]. *Insights on Remedy; The Remedy Gap: Lessons from CAO, Compliance and Beyond.* Washington DC: CAO, April 2023.

United Nations High Commissioner on Human Rights. *IFC/MIGA Draft Approach to Remedial Action: Comments and Recommendations of the UN Human Rights Office.* Geneva: United Nations, April 13, 2023.

United States International Finance Development Corporation, *Mexico Cerro de Oro Hydroelectric.* Washington DC: U.S. International Finance Development Corporation, November 30, 2010.

World Bank. *Voting Power.* Accessed December 15, 2024. https://www.worldbank.org/en/about/leadership/votingpowers.

World Bank Group. *India – Narmada river development – Gujarat : Sardar Sarovar Dam and Power Project.* Washington DC: World Bank, March 6, 1985.

World Bank Group. *India: Tata Ultra Mega-01/Mundra and Anjar,* Case No. Tata Ultra Mega 25797. Washington DC: World Bank, June 14, 2011.

World Bank Group. *India: Tata Tea-02/Assam,* Case No. Tata Tea 25074. Washington DC: World Bank, February 2, 2013.

World Bank Group. *India: Rural Water Supply and Sanitation Project for Low Income States (P132173)-First Request,* Case 128, Request 18/06. Washington DC: World Bank, September 21, 2018.

World Bank Inspection Panel. *Papua New Guinea: Smallholder Agricultural Development Project,* Case No. 62, Request No. 9/10. Washington DC: World Bank, December 8, 2009.

CHAPTER 19

Between Disruption and Legitimation of Development

A Critical Perspective on the Inspection Panel and a Call for More Radical Thinking within the Accountability Community

*Dustin Schäfer**

1 Accountability in a Politically Inhibited Environment

In this essay, a power-sensitive bureaucratic approach is applied to analyze the Panel's impact and its institutional environment. Using factors that influence *learning* within international organizations reveals that the conditions to trigger institutional *learning* in the World Bank (the Bank) can be described as politically inhibited.[1] Moreover, institutional responses to the Panel are not considered voluntary *learning*. Despite this, complainants successfully used the process to temporarily overcome power imbalances, and the Panel repeatedly triggered far-reaching institutional responses.[2]

* Dustin Schäfer is the Head of the International Finance Institution team at Urgewald, Germany.

1 Thorsten Benner, et al., *Internationale Bürokratien und Organisationslernen: Konturen einer Forschungsagenda* ['International Bureaucracies and Organizational Learning: Outline of a Research Agenda'], 16(2) Zeitschrift für Internationale Beziehungen 219 (2009).

2 *See, e.g.*, World Bank Inspection Panel, *Argentina, Paraguay: Yacyretá Hydroelectric Project*, https://www.inspectionpanel.org/panel-cases/yacyreta-hydroelectric-project (last visited Jan. 24, 2025); World Bank Inspection Panel, *India: Mumbai Urban Transport Project (First Request)*, https://www.inspectionpanel.org/panel-cases/mumbai-urban-transport-project-first-request (last visited Jan. 24, 2025); World Bank Inspection Panel, *India: Mumbai Urban Transport Project (Second Request)*, https://www.inspectionpanel.org/panel-cases/mumbai-urban-transport-project-second-request (last visited Jan. 24, 2025); World Bank Inspection Panel, *India: Mumbai Urban Transport Project (Third Request)*, https://www.inspectionpanel.org/panel-cases/mumbai-urban-transport-project-third-request (last visited Jan. 24, 2025); World Bank Inspection Panel, *Albania: Integrated Coastal Zone Management and Clean-Up Project (First Request)*, https://www.inspectionpanel.org/panel-cases/integrated-coastal-zone-management-and-clean-project-first-request (last visited Jan. 24, 2025); World Bank Inspection Panel, *Albania: Integrated Coastal Zone Management and Clean-Up Project (Second Request)*, https://www.inspectionpanel.org/panel-cases/integrated-coastal-zone-management-and-clean-project-second-request (last visited Jan. 24, 2025); World Bank Inspection Panel, *Cambodia: Land Management and Administration Project*,

The influencing factors are divided into an infrastructure bundle and a politics bundle. The infrastructure bundle contains those characteristics of an institution that are static at a given point in time of observation. These factors can also change, but with a certain path dependency.[3] The politics bundle contains dynamic factors that map the agency of involved internal or external stakeholders and thus capture policy dynamics that influence *learning* processes.[4] I will share some research findings on the Panel using the described approach.

The Panel is "politically inhibited" in contributing to institutional *learning* and represents a highly contested political space in which it operates as a mostly independent body. The independence of the Panel from Management depends, among other factors, on its leadership. By this, I mean the ability of the Panel chair to establish a working relationship with Management that allows the mandate to be fulfilled while keeping processes free from Management interference.

Bureaucratic fights around the mandate and procedures of the Panel are focused on the early stages of the processes, not infrequently to avoid the registration of a complaint. This is of high relevance for the political oversight of the quality of World Bank operations, since the early phase of World Bank project cycles represents a blind spot in the accountability framework. The Independent Evaluation Group (IEG) stated that "there is no independent mechanism or data on operational quality."[5] Accordingly, not only is the quality of operations structurally neglected at the beginning of the projects, but the Panel is limited in its ability to point out problems at an early stage.

---

https://www.inspectionpanel.org/panel-cases/land-management-and-administration-project (last visited Jan. 24, 2025); World Bank Inspection Panel, *Uganda: Transport Sector Development Project- Additional Financing*, https://www.inspectionpanel.org/panel-cases/transport-sector-development-project-additional-financing (last visited Jan. 24, 2025); World Bank Inspection Panel, *Congo, Democratic Republic of: High Priority Roads Reopening and Maintenance (2nd Additional Financing) (P153836)*, https://www.inspectionpanel.org/panel-cases/high-priority-roads-reopening-and-maintenance-2nd-additional-financing-p153836 (last visited Jan. 24, 2025); World Bank Inspection Panel, *Haiti: Mining Dialogue Technical Assistance*, https://www.inspectionpanel.org/panel-cases/mining-dialogue-technical-assistance (last visited Jan. 24, 2025).

3 Benner et al., *supra* note 1, at 222–24 (discussing formal structure, resources, standard operating procedures, incentive systems, and organizational culture).

4 *Id.* (discussing policy dynamic factors including leadership, external political pressure and bureaucratic politics).

5 World Bank, *Knowledge Flow and Collaboration under the World Bank's New Operating Model*, Independent Evaluation Group 24 (2019) [hereinafter 2019 IEG Report].

The Board is responsible for ensuring sufficient resources within the lending function; its oversight function is neither effective nor consistent. Project teams are less willing to cooperate and learn due to the existing incentive systems. Where the Panel repeatedly reveals that lack of resources causes negative impacts, the Board has a contradictory role. On the one hand, Management is requested to address non-compliance found by the Panel. On the other hand, it is the Board as representatives of World Bank shareholders that prioritizes low borrowing costs and thus structurally prevents proper due diligence, high quality at entry, and effective accountability processes. Moreover, the factual arguments produced by the Panel are not the most significant factor in the Board's decision-making that is largely influenced by (geo)politics. The political bargaining power of major borrowers is reinforced by the mere possibility that they may forego World Bank loans in the future. Greater opposition accompanies the handling of a Panel complaint, and the Panel is ultimately less effective in the major borrowers' states.

Incentives, criticized for decades, continue to perpetuate an organizational culture that obstructs citizen-driven accountability. The phase of "hostile managers"[6] continues to characterize the organizational culture in the Panel's institutional environment. Any effort to promote institutional *learning* is affected by the incentive system with the result that "lending pressure crowds out learning."[7] The pursuit of increased lending constrains the potential for stronger accountability structures. However, the Panel has the potential to change its own conditions temporarily from a state of "politically-inhibited" to a state of "politics-driven."

One project in which all these factors came into play is the Uganda Transport Sector Development Project (TSDP) and the related ninety-eight complaints filed with the Panel. The TSDP was financed through two loans from the International Development Association; the complaints related to the additional $75 million, provided in 2011, that was aimed at upgrading and rehabilitating a sixty-six kilometer road between Kamwenge and Fort Portal in western Uganda. The complaints received political attention because of the extent and severity of negative impacts caused by gender-based violence. Moreover, the complaint process represents both an example of the structural weaknesses

6 Benjamin Sovacool, *Monitoring the Moneylenders: Institutional Accountability And Environmental Governance at The World Bank's Inspection Panel*, 4(4) EXTRACTIVE INDUSTRIES AND SOCIETY 902 (2017).

7 World Bank, *Learning and Results in World Bank Operation: How the Bank Learns*, Investigation Report 18 (2014).

in the World Bank's accountability system and, at the same time, serves as an example of how a complaint process can act as a starting point for remedy.

The Panel was "politically-inhibited" until the registration of the complaint could no longer be averted. The facts on the ground were clear, and the potential for political scandal was known. Only with registration, and thus the fact that local impacts would be made public through a Panel investigation report, did the reputational risk to the Bank become clear. The Bank took the allegations seriously, which led to an increase in the importance of the leadership. Through its reporting, the Panel brought the focus of media, political, and institutional attention on Management. The IEG confirms that high visibility of Management associated with crises or shocks is one reason the Bank responds more quickly and effectively in a situation of crisis.[8] Crises of varying scope can arise due to the transparency and visibility that the Panel process creates. These crises can overcome political limitations. With the registration of the case, the state changed to "infrastructure-driven." From this point on, the increasing influence of infrastructural factors favored the role of the Panel over bureaucratic resistance. The institutional reactions on the part of the World Bank can be interpreted as an attempt to limit reputational damage. The Panel investigation report helped to maintain the state and take extra measures beyond the project level. We can rate the explanatory power of external political pressure as high, which is consistent with the finding that decision-making by the Board is not solely fact-based but also motivated by political considerations.

In the interplay between external political pressure, leadership, and bureaucratic politics, the existing potential of the complaint procedure can temporarily overcome institutional and bureaucratic resistance, as well as obstructive incentives. If this succeeds, a politics-driven state temporarily fosters institutional responses. As political pressure for legitimacy increases, the Panel's procedures become more important and put it in a stronger position. The legitimizing function that the Panel performs to deal with complaints brings us to the role of the *development* discourse.

2 Limited Accountability Risks Depoliticizing and Legitimizing Harmful Practices

On the discursive level, Ferguson points out that the two meanings of *development* are often confused. On the one hand, *development* is understood as a

8 2019 IEG Report, *supra* note 5, at XVI.

"process of transition or transformation toward a modern, capitalist, industrial economy" and, on the other hand, as the "reduction or amelioration of poverty and material want."[9] This double meaning makes it possible to legitimize failure to achieve one of the two objectives by referring to the other meaning. Ferguson argues that the integration and structuring of critique are integral to *development* discourse, legitimizing the continuation of *development* interventions despite their repeated failures:

> In 'development,' ... 'problems' and 'calls for reform' are necessary to the functioning of the machine. Pointing out errors and suggesting improvements is an integral part of the process of justifying and legitimating 'development' interventions. Such an activity may indeed have some beneficial or mitigating effects, but it does not change the fundamental character of those interventions.[10]

The Panel process, with its extensive reports, contributes to and is interwoven with the *development* discourse. By allowing complainants to participate in the reporting process, albeit to a very limited extent, the Panel helps to legitimize both the data collected and the overall process. The unequal involvement between complainants and Management inherent in the Panel process gives Management a recurring opportunity to render the identified problems as technical, and keeps the World Bank in control of outcomes. Due to the technicalization[11] of the problems and the role of Management In solving the identified problems, it does not seem surprising that the only proposals formulated are those that fall under the control, or within the business, of the Bank. Management is repeatedly legitimized as a problem solver through the production of the management action plans. Despite the potential for politicizing practices, the Panel process as currently designed thus facilitates the legitimization of harmful *development* practices. The Panel process serves the characteristic argumentative structure of *development* discourse: "We've recognized the problem (1) and we know the solution (2) and we're working on it (3) and we're making progress (4)."[12]

The TSDP can serve as an example again: the TSDP aimed to build the capacity to implement the project in the relevant implementing agency. The lack of

9 James Ferguson, The Anti-Politics Machine: Development, Depoliticization, and Bureaucratic Power in Lesotho 15 (1994).

10 *Id.* at 285.

11 Marieke Louis, & Lucile Maertens, Why International Organizations Hate Politics 142, 147 (2021).

12 Aram Ziai, Development Discourse and Global History. From Colonialism to the Sustainable Development Goals 199–200 (2016).

capacity, in turn, was identified by the Panel investigation as a cause of negative impacts. Management responded by proposing the creation of more capacity. Accordingly, lack of capacity acts as a justification for poor implementation by the borrower, and as a legitimization for additional lending for the lending institution. Despite the fact that the Panel identified that the project was not ready for implementation, the investigation served as the starting point for a discussion on additional loans.[13] It seems to be the case that "the only 'advice' that is in question here is advice about how to 'do development' better. There is a ready ear for criticisms of 'bad development projects,' so long as these are followed up with calls for more 'good development projects'"[14]

The legitimizing effect of the *development* discourse, which is interwoven with the accountability discourse, can also be demonstrated by the example of the *greater common good*.[15] Management has frequently criticized the Panel for causing risk aversion in the Bank's operations. Risk aversion in this context means that certain project types were temporarily or permanently avoided because they appeared too risky. The risk described here is the World Bank's reputation in case of failure and public outcry resulting from a Panel investigation, not necessarily aversion to the risk faced by affected communities or the environment. Management thus considers risk aversion as a negative consequence of the Panel's work. However, risk aversion can only be viewed as primarily negative if one either attributes a positive effect to the affected projects that are avoided or if one contrasts the negative consequences with positive effects and assumes their sacrifice is for the *greater common good*. Robert Wade's analysis of the World Bank during the implementation of the Sardar Sarovar Dam in India entails vivid examples of these legitimation strategies. Then Vice President David Hopper considered impacts of displacement peripheral to the project, repeatedly saying, "[y]ou can't make omelets without breaking eggs."[16] Addressing the negative impact of lack of water supply to those living downstream from the Sardar Sarovar Dam, one project staff member responded, "[w]e are bringing drinking water to x hundred villages in Gujarat that have never had reliable supplies

---

13 World Bank Inspection Panel, *Transport Sector Development Project – Additional Financing (P121097)*, Investigation Report 98 (2016).

14 James Ferguson, *supra* note 9, at 284–85.

15 Arundhati Roy, *The Greater Common Good*, 16 Frontline 11 (June 4, 1999); Tania Murray Li, The Will to Improve: Governmentality, Development, and the Practice of Politics (2007); Aram Ziai, *supra* note 12.

16 Robert Hunter Wade, *Muddy Waters: Inside the World Bank as it Struggled with the Narmada Project*, 46 Economic and Political Weekly, 40, 48 (2011).

before."[17] The negative impacts of downstream people are thus legitimized by the promised access to water "to x hundred villages in Gujarat." In preparation for *development* interventions, the need to transform and modernize a particular sector in order to achieve certain economic metrics is cited as the basis for achieving poverty reduction, which legitimizes the impoverishment of others. This results in a circular discursive argument:

> It allows countless interventions with often highly dubious aims and effects to be launched in the name of the common good while being supported or even conducted by people who would otherwise not subscribe to these aims and effects. And it allows institutions like the World Bank to co-opt critical approaches and initiatives by claiming that they are pursuing the same goal as the institution itself – development.[18]

Development as a goal, with all its different meanings and contradictions, seems to represent a discursive intersection. Institutional risk aversion makes it hard to find "bankable" projects for task team leaders.

This could explain why those who are in the business of identifying projects consider risk aversion as something bad. Based on the countless cases of harmful projects, and the fact that neither practices nor power imbalances have changed much, activists and post-development thinkers have criticized development practices and the concept for decades[19] and suggested the concept as such be abandoned.[20]

Panel members seem to be positioned in between these two groups. On the one hand, they are not directly exposed to institutional incentives as task team leaders are. Moreover, Panel members themselves repeatedly reveal the structural problems of current development practices. On the other hand, they still consider the very same lending practices as a legitimate intervention, and consequently, restrictions on lending, such as risk aversion, as an obstacle to achieving *development*. This is where the development discourse harmonizes contradictions in development practices and objectives, removes politics from political causes, and thus legitimizes its continuation.

---

17 *Id.*, at 46–47.

18 ZIAI, *supra* note 12, at 66 (emphasis in original).

19 Esteva Gustavo, *Development: Metaphor, Myth, Threat*, 3 DEVELOPMENT: SEEDS OF CHANGE 78–79 (1985); MAJID RAHNEMA & VICTORIA BAWTREA EDS., THE POST-DEVELOPMENT READER (1997); Roy, *supra* note 15; Ferguson, *supra* note 9; Li, *supra* note 15.

20 ZIAI, *supra* note 12, at 59–69.

Because of its limited mandate, the Panel's proposed solutions remain entangled in development discourse. For the most part, the Panel can only argue technically and on a case-by-case basis, calling on Management to seek more expertise in the future, to better anticipate problems, and to better oversee projects. It is not uncommon for the Panel's identification of a lack of capacity to serve as legitimation for the World Bank to plan new interventions. In this skeptical reading, we can conceptualize the Panel complaint process as an institutionalized form of depoliticization in which the *development* discourse provides the logic to legitimize the continuation of *development* practices even if they have failed.

3 Critical Examination of the Interweaving of Development and Accountability

The pervasive and widespread *belief in development* not only functions as a discursive intersection between all groups of actors but also harmonizes existing conflicting goals by increasing the willingness to compromise, thus contributing to the continuation of existing practices. This raises a specific responsibility for all those who ascribe to themselves the objective of strengthening citizen-driven accountability. Strengthening citizen-driven accountability from within the institutions requires power-sensitive thinking that reflects on dominant practices, structures, methods, concepts, and discourses. Beyond that, accountability experts must have the will and ability to address power imbalances.

Accountability experts should consider and be vocal about the fact that neither *development* policy nor *accountability* practices are apolitical. Overcoming inequalities, poverty, or oppression requires more than just technical solutions. Every intervention operates in a local context, with a history riddled with different and conflicting actor interests and power constellations. Consequently, all interventions enter, intentionally or not, into existing political dynamics.[21] Recognizing this can also mean deciding to not intervene, because "it is not correct usage to apply the term 'development' to the process of knocking down one thing and building something else in its place. Calling such initiatives 'development' conceals the fact that they are human choices, that is, activities that human beings are *free not to do*."[22]

In their reporting, accountability experts also need to question the claim to the universality of *development*. Political problems need political solutions.

21 *See generally* FERGUSON, *supra* note 9.

22 C. DOUGLAS LUMMIS, RADICAL DEMOCRACY 63 (1996) (emphasis in original).

In this process, accountability experts should consciously disrupt dominant discourses that structure or channelize demands for reform. This will open up space for more emancipative approaches to deal with system-immanent conflicts of goals. The political will to take the risks involved can be the starting point to take political responsibility for accountability policy practices and their (un)intended effects.

Development as a concept and discourse has played a decisive role in harmonizing different approaches and goals by experts in the field. Accountability as a concept and practice has been fought and undermined from the very beginning, all the way through to today. This tension lies in the very nature of accountability mechanisms, and it is hard to imagine how it could be different. Management, the President, legal counsel, and the Board have a conflict of interest, and their perspectives are affected by strong incentive systems that prioritize lending over anything else. Thus, we also need to be honest about the fact that accountability processes and their institutional embedding are not designed to provide a fair process.

Accountability experts must stop reproducing the myth that *development* will help as soon as planning is applied accordingly. It seems to be more realistic and worthwhile to campaign for truly independent accountability systems that can work in hostile environments and interrupt harmful practices instead of assuming that one day, the political environment will change and accountability and *learning* will be part of the organizational culture. Therefore, bureaucratic fights must be acknowledged and considered in the design of accountability mechanisms. As argued above, we must not ignore the legitimizing logic of the *development* discourse. Everyone supporting citizen-driven accountability must counteract the power-stabilizing effects of their practices. Concrete starting points for reflecting on our day-to-day practices include acknowledging depoliticizing logic, recognizing harmful practices, questioning expertise, and addressing conflicts of interest, injustices, and power imbalances. The emancipatory potential of the Panel is both a curse and a blessing. The complaint processes go against the claim of international financial institutions of being non-political by revealing political responsibilities. Complaints processes thus inevitably generate resistance, as they highlight the structural contradictions of current development policy. If the resistance to this disappears completely one day, we should be worried.

4 Conclusion

This essay argues that institutional and political factors limit the Panel's work. This condition is a path dependency that has existed in varying degrees since the Panel's inception. The Panel thus represents an institutionally and politically contested space in which its mandate and the processes must be repeatedly re-established. The limitations of accountability practice at the Panel and other IAMs serve to maintain current power relations and legitimize harmful practices. Dismantling the *development* discourse and its effects could help the field overcome constraints in the future.

The Panel has undoubtedly elicited far-reaching institutional responses, but we can and must do better to prevent *development*-induced and legitimized violence. The crises of our time are moving too fast for us to continue to be satisfied with tiny policy steps that are often followed by pushbacks. It is important to remember the idea, promise, and ambition of citizen-driven accountability, and to prevent its practices from becoming mere Management tools. Accountability experts work in a field that has emerged in response to arguably one of the most influential protest movements within the global political economy – the Narmada Bachao Andolan. We still owe it to this movement. As accountability experts, it is our responsibility to push the boundaries of what we can demand and what we can do in the spirit of citizen-driven accountability.

Bibliography

Benner, Thorsten, et al. "Internationale Bürokratien und Organisationslernen: Konturen einer Forschungsagenda" ['International Bureaucracies and Organizational Learning: Outline of a Research Agenda']. *Zeitschrift für Internationale Beziehungen*, 16, no. 2 (2009): 219.

Ferguson, James. *The Anti-Politics Machine: Development, Depoliticization, and Bureaucratic Power in Lesotho*. Minneapolis: University of Minnesota Press, 1994: 15.

Gustavo, Esteva. "Development: Metaphor, Myth, Threat." *Development: Seeds of Change*, 3 (1985): 78–79.

Li, Tania Murray. *The Will to Improve: Governmentality, Development, and the Practice of Politics*. Durham: Duke University Press, 2007.

Louis, Marieke, and Lucile Maertens. *Why International Organizations Hate Politics*. New York: Routledge, 2021: 142, 147.

Lummis, C. Douglas. *Radical Democracy*. Ithaca: Cornell University Press, 1996.

Rahnema, Majid, and Victoria Bawtree. *The Post-Development Reader*. London: Zed Books, 1997.

Roy, Arundhati. "The Greater Common Good." *Frontline*, 16, no. 11 (June 4, 1999). https://web.cecs.pdx.edu/~sheard/course/Design&Society/Readings/Narmada/greatercommongood.pdf.

Sovacool, Benjamin. "Monitoring The Moneylenders: Institutional Accountability And Environmental Governance at The World Bank's Inspection Panel." *Extractive Industries and Society*, 4, no. 4. (2017): 902.

Wade, Robert Hunter. "Muddy Waters: Inside the World Bank as it Struggled with the Narmada Project." *Economic and Political Weekly*, 46, no. 40. (2011): 48.

World Bank Inspection Panel. *Transport Sector Development Project – Additional Financing* (P121097). Investigation Report. Washington DC: World Bank, 2016: 98.

World Bank. *Learning and Results in World Bank Operation: How the Bank Learns*. Independent Evaluation Group. Washington, DC: World Bank, 2014: 18.

World Bank. *Knowledge Flow and Collaboration under the World Bank's New Operating Model*. Independent Evaluation Group. Washington DC: World Bank, 2019: 24.

Ziai, Aram. *Development Discourse and Global History. From Colonialism to the Sustainable Development Goals*. New York: Routledge, 2016: 199–200.

CHAPTER 20

Should Decisions of Independent Accountability Mechanisms be Binding?

Lalanath de Silva and Giada Giacomini***

1 Introduction

Independent Accountability Mechanisms (IAMs) are essential entities tasked with delivering justice and redress with fairness to project-affected peoples, ensuring that impacted communities' voices are heard and their rights are upheld in the context of projects financed by International Financial Institutions (IFIs). However, a significant limitation of IAMs is their lack of binding decision-making power, which raises serious concerns regarding their effectiveness in addressing grievances and providing meaningful remedies. After processing a complaint, IAMs make recommendations based on their findings of non-compliance to the parent institution's Board of Directors or to the head of the parent institution to make decisions on the outcome of the complaint. The absence of binding authority poses a fundamental problem, as it undermines the potential for IAMs to hold IFIs accountable for the harm caused by their projects.

In this chapter, we argue that IAMs should be empowered with binding decision-making authority to enhance their effectiveness and ensure that justice is served and remedies are delivered. We support this argument by analyzing the right of access to justice. We also examine existing mechanisms with binding decision-making power that have already been created or acknowledged by IFIs; these mechanisms include IFI administrative tribunals for employees, arbitration processes for commercial disputes, integrity related sanctions regimes, and the appeal bodies that hear access to information decisions. The IFIs' embrace of binding decisions in these contexts demonstrates that nothing prevents IFIs from taking a binding approach if they decide to do so.

* Lalanath de Silva, PhD, LL.M, is the Managing Director of Transparentem (an NGO) and the Panel Member for compliance review at the Independent Complaints Mechanism of the International Climate Initiative of the German Government.

** Giada Giacomini, PhD, is a postdoctoral researcher at the International Law Department, Geneva Graduate Institute of International and Development Studies (Switzerland).

DOI:10.1163/9789004729735_026

To strengthen our case for granting IAMs binding decision-making power, we will adopt a five-pronged approach. First, we will demonstrate that the establishment of administrative tribunals is not merely a byproduct of contractual agreements but rather the result of bargaining power dynamics of stakeholders connected to IFIs. Second, we will explore the notion of a contractual relationship between project-affected peoples and IFIs, contending that this relationship argues for accountability and binding resolutions. Third, we will address how the growing dissatisfaction among project-affected people concerning IFI dispute resolution and delivery of redress, highlights the pressing need for remediation of harms identified by IAMs, emphasizing that the financial responsibility for such remediation should fall on the IFI itself rather than the borrower or contracting party. Fourth, we will examine the growing number of binding access-to-information appeals bodies that provide a model and a precedent for granting project-affected people a forum to seek binding decisions. Finally, we will argue that IAMs with binding decision-making power will constitute a far more effective alternate justice system than the current IAMs. In turn, IAMs with binding decision-making power will significantly increase the likelihood of judiciaries recognizing and deferring to them, rather than seeking to undermine the traditional privileges and immunities that have until recently protected IFIs from liability for harm caused by their projects. Taken together, these arguments make a compelling case for the necessity of binding decisions within IAMs to provide a more just and equitable framework for addressing the concerns of those most affected by IFI-funded projects.

2 Accountability: the Limits of the IAMs

While the broader implications of the judgment that appeared to limit the IFC's absolute immunity from legal action have been extensively discussed,[1] our analysis focuses specifically on the role of the CAO and its inability to ensure that the IFC provided adequate and appropriate redress to affected parties. Within the context of the United Nations, provisions that guarantee jurisdictional immunity also impose the obligation to create adequate effective

1 *See* F. Rossi, *The International Law Significance of Jam v. IFC: Some Implications for the Immunity of International Organizations*, 13(2) DIRITTI UMANI E DIRITTO INTERNAZIONALE 305–318 (2019); *see also* Peter Boldt & Bethany Pereira, *Jam v. IFC – What does it mean for accountability?* (Green Climate Fund), Mar. 29, 2019; Independent Reporting Mechanism & Accountability Counsel, *World Bank Group Absolute Immunity Ends in Landmark U.S. Supreme Court Decision* (Feb. 27, 2019).

alternative mechanisms to resolve disputes with third parties. Article 105 of the United Nations Charter, which seems to suggest a functional nature of immunity, does not address this aspect, and the 1946 Convention on the Privileges and Immunities of the United Nations recognizes an almost absolute jurisdictional immunity. However, it includes a clause, in Section 29 of Article VIII, which requires the establishment of alternative solutions.[2] In the contemporary context of international law, there is heightened focus on preserving the individual right to an adequate remedy, which indicates that the existence of effective internal recourse mechanisms is inherent in the recognition of organizational immunity. In the absence of such mechanisms, one may encounter a denial of justice, contravening conventional provisions for the protection of human rights, and a substantive denial of the rule of law. Irrespective of the correlation between the recognition of immunity and the availability of alternative justice mechanisms, the obligation for organizations to establish such remedies is clear, as stipulated in Section 29 of the Convention on the Privileges and Immunities.[3] Finally, as already recognized by the International Court of Justice in its advisory opinion on the *Effect of Awards* case, the need to provide means for resolving disputes with private parties may also stem from concerns related to respect for human rights.[4]

While the specific functions of IAMs exhibit slight variations, typically encompassing compliance, dispute resolution, and advisory with associated outreach, their overarching purpose and mandate are predominantly framed as "accountability" and "redress" functions. This is evident in the CAO's Operational Guidelines,[5] in the Project Accountability Policy of the European Bank

2 United Nations General Assembly, *Convention on the Privileges and Immunities of the United Nations*, United Nations-Treaty Series: 1946–1947, 30, Art. VIII, Sect. 29 (Feb. 13, 1946) ("United Nations shall make provisions for appropriate modes of settlement of: (a) Disputes arising out of contracts or other disputes of a private law character to which the United Nations is a party; (b) Disputes involving any official of the United Nations who by reason of his official position enjoys immunity, if immunity has not been waived by the Secretary-General.") [hereinafter Privileges & Immunities Convention].

3 *Id.*

4 International Court of Justice, *Effect of Awards of Compensation Made by the United Nations Administrative Tribunal, Advisory Opinion*, I.C.J. Reports (1954); *see also* European Court of Human Rights, *Waite and Kennedy vs Germany*, Application no. 26083/94 (Feb. 18, 1999) [Waite and Kennedy v. Germany].

5 Compliance Advisor/Ombudsman, *CAO's Operational Guidelines*, The World Bank (Oct. 13, 2016) https://documents1.worldbank.org/curated/pt/137211476348756904/pdf/108859-WP-ENGLISH-CAO-Operational-Guidelines-2013-PUBLIC.pdf (last visited Jan. 25, 2025).

for Reconstruction and Development,[6] in the establishment of the Independent Redress Mechanism (IRM) as an accountability and redress mechanism in the Governing Instrument of the Green Climate Fund (GCF),[7] and most notably in the customarily acknowledged designation of the group itself – "Independent Accountability Mechanisms" (IAMs).

Accountability is a concept typically defined in broad terms as "an obligation or willingness to accept responsibility or to account for one's actions."[8] However, various scholars have deconstructed the concept into slightly different elements. Accountability for international organizations (IOs) is a complex and multifaceted concept that encompasses legal, political, financial, and social dimensions. The legal aspect of accountability involves binding IOs to international law and national regulations, although the extent of this obligation remains uncertain.[9] For instance, Woods identifies the core components of accountability as transparency, compliance and enforcement.[10] Stiglitz also identifies three components, albeit with a slightly different framework.[11] He posits that accountability necessitates certain clearly defined objectives, a reliable method of evaluating whether those objectives have been met, and consequences for both the achievement and non-achievement of objectives.

The concept of social accountability has emerged to bridge the gap between IOs and affected citizens, with civil society actors playing a crucial role in enhancing transparency and accountability.[12] This approach is exemplified by mechanisms like the World Bank Inspection Panel, which seeks to bridge the gap between civil society demands and accountability procedures for the operations of the World Bank. However, the accountability of IOs for human rights violations remains a challenging issue, particularly due to limited remedies and broad immunities, even in a post-conflict context where international organizations might bear responsibilities for violations of customary human

---

6 European Bank for Reconstruction and Development, *Project Accountability Policy* (April 2019).

7 Green Climate Fund, *Governing Instruments of the Green Climate Fund* (Apr. 16, 2018).

8 Merriam-Webster, *accountability*, https://www.merriam-webster.com/dictionary/accountability#dictionary-entry-1 (last visited Dec. 6, 2024).

9 *See generally* JAN KLABBERS, AN INTRODUCTION TO INTERNATIONAL ORGANIZATIONS LAW (2022); August Reinisch, *Accountability of International Organizations According to National Law*, 36(01) NETHERLANDS YEARBOOK OF INT'L L. 119 (2005).

10 NGAIRE WOODS, ACCOUNTABILITY, GOVERNANCE, AND REFORM IN THE INTERNATIONAL FINANCIAL INSTITUTIONS (2001).

11 Joseph Stiglitz, *Democratizing the International Monetary Fund and the World Bank: Governance and Accountability*, 16(1) GOVERNANCE 111–139 (2003).

12 Alexsandro E. Pereira, et al., *Accountability in International Organizations: the case of World Bank Inspection Panel (1993–2015)*, 11(1) BRAZIL POLITICAL SCIENCE REV. (2017).

rights norms.[13] The conclusion drawn from these definitions is that the final, and indeed essential, element of accountability should be enforcement of a legal basis for remedy, and consequences established in a binding way for the entity that has violated their legal obligations towards individuals and communities. The ancient Roman Law maxim *Ubi Jus, Ibi Remedium* ("where there is right, there is remedy") expresses a fundamental aspect of accountability, rule of law, and access to justice.[14]

These two elements of enforcement and consequences translate into what might be classified as corrective, preventive, and punitive accountability. Corrective accountability leads to redress for mistakes and harms committed because of non-compliance or failure of responsibility.[15] Preventive accountability should lead to improved procedures and systems that ensure the same mistake or harm does not recur in the future.[16] Punitive accountability leads to the sanctioning (often through dismissal) of the individual official whose dereliction of responsibility or non-compliance caused the mistake or harm. It refers to a form of accountability that emphasizes punishment and retribution as a means of ensuring compliance and addressing wrongdoing. This concept is evident in various contexts, including penal systems, governance, and social policies. As a matter of fact, IAMs only deal with corrective and preventive accountability and do not deal with punitive accountability, as the latter

13 Matteo Tondini, *Putting an End to Human Rights Violations by Proxy: Accountability of International Organizations and Member States in the Framework of Jus Post Bellum*, TMC ASSER PRESS 187 – 212 (2008).

14 *See, e.g.*, Kristin Boon, *The United Nations as Good Samaritan: Immunity and Responsibility*, 16(2) CHICAGO J. INT'L L. (arguing that the *tour court* assertion of absolute U.N. immunity would not pass an assessment of accountability, distributive justice, or economics).

15 Corrective accountability is a concept that emphasizes the need for organizations and individuals to take responsibility for their actions and make necessary improvements based on performance evaluations and feedback. This approach aims to enhance overall performance and address any shortcomings identified through various accountability mechanisms. *See* Peter Otegbeye, *Accountability: A Corrective Mechanism in Resolving Organizational Challenges* (2016), https://papers.ssrn.com/sol3/papers.cfm?abstract_id=2738419 (last visited Dec. 6, 2024).

16 Preventive accountability in public administration refers to mechanisms and practices aimed at ensuring responsible governance before potential issues arise. This approach focuses on proactive measures to maintain integrity, transparency, and efficiency in public sector operations. One key aspect of preventive accountability is the establishment of clear laws, regulations, and performance management systems. These provide a framework for public officials to operate within, reducing the likelihood of misconduct or inefficiency. *See also* Jen Steffek, *Public Accountability and the Public Sphere of International Governance*, 24(1) ETHICS & INTERNATIONAL AFFAIRS 45–67 (2010).

usually falls to the human resources departments of IFIs and is covered by the staff rules of conduct.

Despite IAMs addressing corrective and preventive accountability, IAMs, by virtue of their recommendatory nature, possess limited to no capacity independently to enforce compliance and ensure consequences for actions or inactions of the management of their parent institutions that have resulted in harm. While certain IAMs, such as the IRM or the Asian Development Bank's Compliance Review Panel (CRP), have been mandated with additional powers to influence and contribute to the determination of remedial action plans, as well as monitor their implementation, none possess the authority to ensure the adoption of their findings or to enforce remedial action plans to guarantee that remedy is ultimately provided to those affected. The power of enforcement and ensuring compliance ultimately resides with the final decision-maker, generally the President or Board of the institution in conjunction with the management of the institution.

Hitherto, IAMs have predominantly relied on the goodwill or commitment of management within the parent institution from its Board or President. IFI's have been driven by pressure from civil society and the reputational risks faced by their institutions when harms are not redressed and become widely known, to ensure minimal remediation. While this approach has (arguably) been effective in prompting IFIs to update their policies and safeguards (preventive accountability), it has been significantly less successful in producing tangible and identifiable remedies for affected individuals. This phenomenon has been consistently reported by complainants and civil society organizations,[17] as well as Accountability and Remedy Project of the Office of the High Commissioner for Human Rights (OHCHR),[18] with *Jam v. IFC* serving as the most prominent example.

Recent data disclosed in the External Review of the 2000 External Review of the CAO, indicate that 68% of complaints filed since 2013 resulted in compliance review investigations rather than alternative dispute resolution.[19] Of the remaining 32% of cases that proceeded to alternative dispute resolution, 75% were resolved satisfactorily, suggesting that harm was likely remediated. However, based on data available for sixteen cases since 2008, the

17 *See* Center for International Environmental Law, *Glass Half Full: The State of Accountability in Development Finance* (Jan. 2016).

18 *See* United Nations High Commissioner for Human Rights, *Improving accountability and access to remedy for victims of business-related human rights abuse through non-State-based grievance mechanisms*, A/HRC/44/32, 46 (May 19, 2020).

19 World Bank, *External Review of IFC/MIGA E&S Accountability, including CAO's Role and Effectiveness Report and Recommendations* (2020).

External Review asserts that "most CAO non-compliance findings do not lead to effective remedy."[20] An analysis of the 16 cases shows that in 50% of cases, remedies were unsatisfactory, while in 37% they were partially satisfactory, and in 13% satisfactory.[21] These statistics raise concerns regarding the efficacy of delivering remedies through the current accountability mechanisms at the IFC and are broadly applicable to other IFIs and DFIs.

As noted above, the IAMs, rather than being vested with binding decision-making authority, primarily serve the function of receiving complaints, addressing them through a fair process, and issuing findings and recommendations. The actual authority to make binding decisions rests with the governing body – typically the Board of the institution in question, including in the case of the CAO. Additionally, the responsibility for developing and implementing remedies, if applicable, is usually delegated to the management of the parent institution, subject to the Board's overriding authority.

As set forth in this chapter, this operational structure, deeply entrenched in the governance frameworks and cultures of IAMs worldwide, merits reconsideration and reform. Specifically, the IAMs' lack of binding decision-making authority undermines their ability to deliver remedy and contravenes the project-affected people's right of access to remedy, a critical element of accountability. A binding mechanism would not be new to the IFIs, because, as explored below, other accountability and/or redress mechanisms established or recognized by IFIs are endowed with binding decision-making authority.

3 The IAMs' Failure to Satisfy the Right to an Effective Remedy

The right to an effective remedy is a fundamental principle in international law, recognized by various human rights instruments and tribunals.[22] In particular,

20 *Id.* at 71.

21 *Id.* at 31.

22 The right to remedy is found in the following instruments: International Covenant on Civilian and Political Rights (adopted December 16, 1966, in force March 23, 1976); American Convention on Human Rights (adopted November 22, 1969, entered into force July 18, 1978); European Convention on Human Rights (adopted Nov. 4, 1950, entered into force, Sept. 3, 1953); Arab Charter on Human Rights (2019); ASEAN Human Rights Declaration of 2012, as well as in regional instruments emanating from Principle 10 of the Rio Declaration concerning the right of access to information such as the Aarhus Convention (Convention on Access to Information, Public Participation in Decision-making, and

the Aarhus Convention and the more recent Escazu Agreement both affirm the right of access to justice in environmental matters.[23] The Inter-American Court of Human Rights has acknowledged this right as encompassing both the right to an effective remedy and the guarantees of due process.[24] Similarly, the European Court of Human Rights has worked to overcome challenges in exercising this right, highlighting the growing concern among international human rights tribunals to safeguard access to justice at national and international levels.[25]

The right to remedy has not yet reached the status of general international law applicable to IOs and IFIs. As a result, it is currently regarded as a *lex ferenda* standard, representing an aspirational legal norm.[26] The normative framework of this right involves two core obligations. First, it demands that individuals who present credible claims of human rights violations have adequate access to accountability mechanisms, a concept often referred to as access to justice. Second, these mechanisms must be capable of delivering meaningful and substantive redress to those who have experienced human rights violations. A core component of the right to an effective remedy is the provision of adequate reparation for the harm suffered. Reparation can take various forms, including restitution (restoring the victim to the situation they were in before the violation occurred); compensation (monetary redress for harm suffered, including physical, emotional, or material damage); rehabilitation (medical, psychological, or social services provided to victims to support their recovery); satisfaction (measures that acknowledge wrongdoing, such as public apologies or commemorative acts); and guarantees of non-repetition

---

Access to Justice in Environmental Matters, 2001) and the Escazu Agreement (Regional Agreement on Access to Information, Public Participation and Justice in Environmental Matters in Latin America and the Caribbean, 2021).

23 *Id.*

24 *See* Inter-American Court of Human Rights, *State Obligations in Relation to the Environment in the Context of the Protection and Guarantee of the Rights to Life and to Personal Integrity: Interpretation and Scope of Articles 4(1) and 5(1) in Relation to Articles 1(1) and 2 of the American Convention on Human Rights*, OC-23/17, Inter-American Court of Human Rights (Nov. 15, 2017), https://www.corteidh.or.cr/docs/opiniones/seriea_23_ing.pdf (last visited Jan. 25, 2025).

25 Antônio Augusto Cançado Trinadade, *The Interrelation between the Access to Justice (Right to an Effective Remedy) and the Guarantees of the Due Process of Law*, The Access of Individuals to International Justice, Collected Courses of the Academy of European Law, Oxford (2011).

26 STIAN JOHANSEN, THE HUMAN RIGHTS ACCOUNTABILITY MECHANISMS OF INTERNATIONAL ORGANIZATIONS 11 (2020).

(structural reforms or changes to policies that prevent similar violations from occurring in the future).

In the IAMs' current governance structure, decisions regarding complaints submitted by affected communities are ultimately made by the IFIs' Board of Directors or President. IFI Boards of Directors and Presidents are political in nature, their constituents often representing the interests of State parties. Vesting decisions in political bodies that are not independent violates the fundamental principle of access to justice discussed above. While IAMs do not purport to function as judicial bodies akin to national or international courts or tribunals, they share the goal of providing a fair resolution of claims brought against the IFI, and they operate under procedural rules that incorporate many of the core principles of natural justice and due process, giving them a decidedly "quasi-judicial" character.[27] These due process rules often include protections for the independence of the decision-makers in the accountability mechanisms, arrangements for impartial investigation, the right to be heard, and transparency in decision-making processes, all of which contribute to the credibility and legitimacy of IAMs in fulfilling their mandate.[28] Despite this problematic structural issue, IFIs rely on their IAMs as a defense to claims that their immunity protects them from accountability for harms done to project affected people. Yet, the non-binding nature of the IAMs decision-making coupled with entrusting the decision-making on the outcome of complaints to a political body, undermines the IFI's ability to rely on its IAM as a remedy delivering mechanism.

Despite these procedural safeguards, the IAMs' lack of authority to render binding decisions raises critical concerns regarding their effectiveness in delivering justice and undermines the IFIs' reliance on IAMs to fulfill their obligation to provide access to remedy. The ultimate decision-making power resides with actors who may be far removed from the realities faced by the communities who file complaints, which can dilute the right of access to remedy. This disjunction between process and outcome underscores the need to

---

27 *See generally* OWEN MCINTRYE & SURESH NANWANI, EDS., THE PRACTICE OF INDEPENDENT ACCOUNTABILITY MECHANISMS (IAMS) TOWARDS GOOD GOVERNANCE IN DEVELOPMENT FINANCE (2023); *see generally* JOHANSEN, *supra* note 26; PIERRE SCHMITT, ACCESS TO JUSTICE AND INTERNATIONAL ORGANIZATIONS: THE CASE OF INDIVIDUAL VICTIMS OF HUMAN RIGHTS VIOLATIONS (2017).

28 The UN Guiding Principles on Business and Human Rights provides the most widely recognized criteria for IAMs and include legitimacy, transparency, predictability, accessibility, equitability, rights-compatibility, and being a source of learning. Many of these are compatible with and/or form part of due process. The United Nations Office of Human Rights, *Guiding Principles on Business and Human Rights* (2011).

re-examine the operational frameworks of IAMs, particularly in terms of how their quasi-judicial functions align – or fail to align – with the broader goals of accountability and redress.

Justice and access to remedy are best served when decisions are made by neutral, impartial, and independent bodies. While not wholly independent from their parent institutions, IAMs have been expressly designed to maximize independence, precisely due to their recognition of independence as an important principle that inspires credibility and trust in the IAM. Currently, however, it is not the IAM that decides on the outcome of a complaint but rather the Board or President of the parent institution. Boards and Presidents are, by their very nature, political bodies made up of members with varying social, economic, and political interests that they are legitimately expected to openly pursue in performing their functions. This has meant that in practice, political and other extraneous considerations have often played a key role in decisions taken by Boards and Presidents on IAM recommendations. It has been observed by civil society organizations in numerous cases, for example IFC's Tata Mundra case in India,[29] Asian Development Bank's (ADB) Customary Land case in Samoa,[30] and the ADB's Railway Rehabilitation case in Cambodia,[31] where the President or Board members decided or voted contrary to the IAMs recommendations or were not unanimous in their decisions, even though there were harms that were identified by the IAM.

In the Tata Mundra case, the CAO of the IFC received two complaints.[32] In 2011, local fisherfolk from a coastal community in Gujarat, India, raised concerns about a 5000-Megawatt coal-fired power plant, among others, by complaining to the CAO. The CAO determined that the IFC had contravened its own environmental and social safeguard policies. The IFC's management responded with a remedial action plan. However, the CAO deemed the proposed measures inadequate for fully addressing the concerns raised. In 2016, the community decided to pursue legal action and filed a lawsuit against the IFC in the U.S. District Court. The *Jam v. IFC*[33] case has been cited, discussed, analyzed, and debated to such an extent that it has become nearly

29 EarthRights International, *Bedha Ismail Jam, et al., v. Int'l Finance Corp.*, https://earthrights.org/case/budha-ismail-jam-et-al-v-ifc/#:~:text=From%20the%20beginning%2C%20the%20IFC,if%20sufficient%20steps%20were%20not (last visited Dec. 6, 2024).

30 Inclusive Development International, *Official Investigation Finds ADB Failed to Consult Samoan People Before Pushing Harmful Land Reforms* (Sept. 13, 2016).

31 Equitable Cambodia, *The Railway Case* (Aug. 18, 2016).

32 CAO, *India: Tata Ultra Mega-01/Mundra and Anjar*, https://www.cao-ombudsman.org/cases/india-tata-ultra-mega-01mundra-and-anjar (last visted Dec. 7, 2024).

33 *Jam et al vs International Finance Corporation,* 481 F. Supp. 3d 1, 4, 13–14 (D.D.C. 2020).

legendary in legal discourse.[34] It was at this juncture that the IFC's immunity from litigation in US courts was challenged and subsequently adjudicated on appeal by the U.S. Supreme Court.

In Samoa's Customary Land case, the Asian Development Bank's Compliance Review Panel (CRP) received a complaint alleging that a Bank-funded technical assistance project had failed to meet environmental and social safeguards.[35] After review, the CRP found the case eligible for processing and recommended a compliance investigation. The issue then went to the Bank's Board Compliance Review Committee (BCRC), composed of six Board members, including one representing Samoa. However, the BCRC decided against recommending a compliance review, noting that on the question of harm, it had received "detailed but conflicting opinions" from the CRP and the Office of the General Counsel (OGC), leaving the Committee unable to reach a consensus. The ADB's Board later adopted this recommendation, and the case was not investigated. Two matters are worth noting. First, the Executive Director for Samoa[36] participated and voted on the BCRC on this decision not to proceed with an investigation regarding a complaint about a project that provided technical assistance to the government of Samoa. Second, the BCRC allowed the General Counsel to opine on the question of harm when that was a task entrusted to the CRP by the Accountability Policy of the Bank adopted by the Board. The CRP had consulted both the complainants and the management of the ADB in presenting its report to the BCRC.[37] However, the

---

34 Wenjun Yan & Lin Shang, *Forget International Law Not: IFC Loses Absolute Immunity in Jam v. International Finance Corporation,* 13(03) BEIJING L. REV. 662–672 (Sept. 2022); Nicholas Johnson, *Jam v. IFC: One Step Forward, Two Steps Back?,* 19(2) SUSTAINABLE DEV. L. AND POLICY 16 (2018) ; Yohei Okada, *The Immunity of International Organizations Before And After Jam V IFC: Is The Functional Necessity Rationale Still Relevant?,* 72 QUESTIONS OF INT'L L. 29 (2020); Dhruv Sharma, The *Immunities of International Organisations: Jam v. IFC and the Need for External Review Mechanisms,* 2 NAT'L L. UNIV., DELHI J. LEG. STUDS. 41 (2020); Wenjun Yan, & Lin Shang, *Forget International Law Not: IFC Loses Absolute Immunity in Jam v. International Finance Corporation,* 13 BEIJING L. REV. 662 (Sep. 2022).

35 Asian Development Bank Compliance Review Panel, *Samoa: Promoting Economic Use of Customary Land and Samoa AgriBusiness Support Project,* https://lnadbg4.adb.org/dir0035p.nsf/alldocs/JABM-A983HD?OpenDocument (last visited Dec. 7, 2024).

36 Asian Development Bank, *Annual Report 2016: Members, Capital Stock, and Voting Power (as of 31 December 2016)* (Apr. 21, 2017).

37 Asian Development Bank Board of Directors, *Chair's Summary of the Board Compliance Review Committee and Compliance Review Panel's Report on Eligibility of the Compliance Review Request for TA 4712, 7387, and 8481: Promoting Economic Use of Customary Land and Grant 0392: Samoa Agribusiness Support Project* (Samoa), Asian Development Bank (July

management essentially had a "second shot" in the absence of the complainants to address the issue of harm with the BCRC via the General Counsel. This appears to be contrary to the general rules of due process and manifests the political nature of Board deliberations on complaints.

Finally, in Cambodia, a complaint was filed alleging that a 600-kilometer railway rehabilitation project had caused serious harm to thousands of affected people. The ADB's CRP found numerous instances of non-compliance with the Bank's environmental and social safeguards and recommended comprehensive remedies for those affected.[38] The ADB's Board, however, adopted a modified version of these recommendations following deliberations among Board members from both developed and developing Asian countries.[39]

This case illustrates how a bank's Board of Directors can revise recommendations from an IAM, even though the Board itself did not participate in the initial complaint review or investigation. While this action is within the ADB Board's authority, the ability to alter recommendations from a quasi-judicial body – one that has followed due process and based its findings on evidence – raises concerns about the effectiveness of such a mechanism as an alternative system of remedy or justice. Each of the above three cases brought to an IAM illustrate an example of where the Board/President of the IFI concerned took a political decision, sometimes ignoring the factual findings of the IAM or changing the recommended remedy.

Each of these three cases illustrate how the Board or the President of an organization can make a political decision that sometimes ignores the factual findings of the IAM.[40] As the next part will demonstrate, other internal justice mechanisms, such as administrative tribunals for employer-employee disputes, operate with a significant distinction: while they, like IAMs, report to

---

20, 2016) https://lnadbg4.adb.org/dir0035p.nsf/attachments/SAM-EligibilityReport-18Aug_Web.pdf/$FILE/SAM-EligibilityReport-18Aug_Web.pdf (last visited Jan. 25, 2025).

38 Asian Development Bank Compliance Review Panel, *Greater Mekong Subregion: Rehabilitation of the Railway in Cambodia Project*, https://lnadbg4.adb.org/dir0035p.nsf/alldocs/RDIA-8XT5DA?OpenDocument (last visited Dec. 7, 2024).

39 Asian Development Bank Board of Directors, *Decision of the Board of Directors of the Asian Development Bank*, (Jan. 31, 2014).

40 Another interesting case not discussed here, for reasons of space, concerns a complaint filed by an Indigenous People from Nicaragua before the Green Climate Fund IRM. Notwithstanding that the Board adopted procedures and guidelines that defined how a report from the IRM ought to be dealt with by the GCF Board, several procedural deviations were made by the Board in arriving at its final decision. *See* Toby McIntosh, *Green Climate Fund Giving Unequal Access to Report on Controversial Project*, Eye on Global Transparency (May 11, 2023; Toby McIntosh, *GCF Board Excludes Internal Body From More Oversight of Controversial Project*, Eye on Global Conspiracy (July 2023).

the Board, their decisions are binding on the IFI and are neither questioned nor altered by the Board's highest political authority.[41]

4 Justice and Accountability through Mechanisms with Binding Power

Although the IFIs have been resistant to granting the IAMs' binding decision-making authority, it is not because they cannot do it or do not know how to do it. This part describes four examples where IFIs have accepted binding decision-making powers for independent bodies: administrative tribunals for employee relations, arbitration mechanisms for commercial context, integrity-related sanction regimes, and appellate bodies for reviewing access to information decisions. At the very least, these examples demonstrate that the IFIs could submit themselves to a binding process if they wanted to. The examples also give us insight into how the IAMs could operationalize binding decision making.

4.1 *Administrative Tribunals*

Most IFIs have established administrative tribunals for handling complaints brought by their employees that serve as an internal mechanism for employees to hold the organizations accountable. This internal human resources-related accountability system is sometimes delineated in the constitutive charters of these organizations and at other times negotiated by staff collectives and established by the governing bodies of the IFIs. These structures have been established as mechanisms of last resort for staff members alleging non-observance of their contracts of employment or terms of appointment or other human resource-related rules and norms. These tribunals are generally composed of several judges, appointed by, yet independent of, the institution. In contrast to IAMs, the decisions rendered by these tribunals are final and binding on both the institution and the aggrieved employee.[42]

41 *See infra* text accompanying notes 42–47 (discussing administrative tribunals).

42 *See, e.g., World Bank Administrative Tribunal, Administrative Tribunal Statute*, Sect. XI (Apr. 30, 1980) https://tribunal.worldbank.org/statute (stating that its decisions are final and conferring to this body a proper judicial status); *see also* Asian Development Bank Administrative Tribunal, *Statute of the Administrative Tribunal of the Asian Development Bank*, Art. IX (Feb. 21, 2021) (stating that its decisions are "final and binding"); *see also* International Labor Organization, *Statute of the Administrative Tribunal of the International Labour Organization*, Art. VI (Jul. 7, 2014) https://www.ilo.org/resource/statute-administrative-tribunal-international-labour-organization (last visited Jan. 25, 2024) (stating that the tribunal's decisions are "final and without appeal").

Administrative tribunals provide an interesting precedent for IAMs because the tribunals' jurisdiction is frequently regarded as "complementary" to and required by the IFI's immunity from suit in national courts.[43] The recognition that labor disputes require alternative forms of remedy has been predominantly derived from human rights law. The European Court of Human Rights even stipulated, in the case of *Waite and Kennedy v. Germany*, that "a material factor in determining whether granting … immunity from … jurisdiction is permissible is whether the applicants had available to them reasonable alternative means to protect effectively their rights under the Convention."[44] In essence, the existence of an effective alternative remedy allows courts to conclude that further judicial remedies may not be required through domestic litigation. In many common law jurisdictions, the availability of such alternative remedies has been established as a basis for denying judicial review of executive or administrative decisions. This principle underscores the potential importance of independent, effective, and binding IAMs as alternative avenues for securing remedies. By providing a robust means of redress, IAMs may further reduce the likelihood of litigation, despite the immunity from domestic court proceedings, as illustrated *in Waite and Kennedy v. Germany*.

The argument for independent access to justice with binding decision-making authority has been cogently presented in the context of employer-employee disputes. This has resulted in the proliferation of administrative tribunals and the utilization of tribunals within collective bodies such as those of the International Labour Organisation.[45] However, this argument has not yet been extended to disputes arising with third parties, such as project-affected individuals and communities, despite the evident relevance of human rights concerns that they frequently raise. At the remedy level, a critical issue is that neither employees of international organizations nor communities harmed by their actions have access to legal remedies at the national level because IFIs are clothed with immunity from liability. This gap underscores the necessity for international organizations to provide an equally effective alternative mechanism for redress in both cases. However, there remains a significant disparity between the administrative tribunals of IFIs addressing employer-employee disputes that have binding decision-making authority and IAMs addressing grievances of project affected people that have only

43 August Reinisch, *The Immunity of International Organizations and the Jurisdiction of their Administrative Tribunals*,7(2) CHINESE J. INT'L L. 285–306 (May 22, 2008).

44 European Court of Human Rights, *Waite and Kennedy vs Germany*, Application no. 26083/94, §68 (Feb. 18, 1999).

45 International Labor Organization, *The Tribunal*, https://www.ilo.org/ilo-administrative-tribunal/tribunal (last visited Dec. 7, 2024).

recommendatory functions, with binding decision-making power being vested in a political body.

While the initial ruling in *Jam v. IFC* provided some prospects for recourse through a national court system, the subsequent judgments of the US District Court in 2020 have reinforced the immunity of the IFC and precluded any access to justice for the affected parties. A more positive example is the recent settlement in a class action suit brought against IFC by project-affected people from Honduras alleging IFC's complicity in violent land-grabbing conducted by a palm oil company that was being financed by IFC. The case was settled and IFC agreed to "contribute funds to community support interventions, identified and selected by plaintiffs and class members ... for the benefit of the class members and others similarly affected in or from the region."[46] This settlement augurs well for IFIs taking more responsibility for remediation, even without admitting liability for the harms or surrendering their privileges and immunities. Given that IFI immunity is still virtually impenetrable, it is imperative that affected parties have alternative means of justice through efficacious and binding mechanisms.

In sum, IFI employees have access to tribunals with the authority to issue binding findings of non-compliance with the core labor provisions. In contrast, innocent beneficiaries and third parties whose rights – including labor rights and rights to livelihood – are infringed upon in connection with projects funded by these institutions often find their claims adjudicated by a political body: the Board of Directors of the IFI. This occurs even when their claims have been substantiated, and remedial actions recommended by an IAM, raising concerns about the consistency and impartiality of the adjudicatory process for non-employee stakeholders.

4.2 *Arbitration*

The second pertinent example in this context is that of arbitration – a form of alternative dispute resolution, wherein disputes are adjudicated outside the judicial system by independent third parties known as arbitrators. Typically, arbitration is employed in commercial contractual disputes, and, in this instance, the arbitrator's decision is legally binding on both parties. Arbitration clauses of this nature are commonplace in goods and service contracts entered into by IFIs and other international organizations.

---

46 EarthRights International, *Historic Settlement in Case Alleging International Finace Corporation Abetted Murder in Honduras* (Oct. 3, 2024) https://earthrights.org/media_release/historic-settlement-in-case-alleging-international-finance-corporation-abetted-murder-in-honduras/ (last visited Jan. 25, 2025).

Arbitration serves a particularly significant function for international organizations, where it is advantageous to circumvent local court systems that may harbor potential biases and whose decisions have limited applicability beyond national boundaries.[47] Given that most countries are signatories to the New York Convention, which ensures that arbitration decisions are legally enforceable globally, this mechanism provides a more expeditious, equitable, and efficient route than litigation, especially considering the immunity of most international organizations.[48]

These rationales can be similarly applied to disputes at the IAM level. Like arbitration, IAMs provide a more equitable platform for both aggrieved parties and IFIs; they offer an alternative dispute resolution mechanism when domestic judicial systems are either unavailable or unsuitable; and they possess the ability to facilitate more cost-effective and expedient resolution of disputes for all parties involved.

In arbitration, the IFI and the contracting third party agree to submit the dispute to a neutral third party – arbitrator(s) – and to be bound by the arbitrator's decision. If an institution can enter into such binding agreements for contractual disputes, it logically follows that there should be no obstacle to making the decisions of its own IAM binding, particularly in cases where the mechanism has found harm caused by non-compliance with the institution's policies and regulations. Later in this article, we examine why third-party beneficiaries of IFI projects and programs have a social license or social contract that justifies such beneficiaries being treated more or less as contracting parties.[49]

4.3 *Sanctions Appeals Tribunals*

When a borrower or client of an IFI is found to have engaged in fraud, corruption, collusion, or any other similar prohibited practice, IFIs reserve the right to impose sanctions on these organizations. Sanctions can also be applied to a company that may not be in a contractual relationship with an IFI or one of its projects if it engaged in fraudulent activities relating to a project or to the funds of the IFI. These sanctions range from a reprimand to debarment (including

47 For further discussion on the importance of arbitration for international organizations see Nobert Horn, *The Development of Arbitration in International Financial Transactions*, 16(3) ARBITRATION INTERNATIONAL 279–296 (Sep. 1, 2000).

48 United Nations Commission on International Trade Law, *Convention on the Recognition and Enforcement of Foreign Arbitral Awards*, The United Nations (1958).

49 We will explore the nature of the contractual relationship between IOs and the beneficiaries of the social and environmental safeguards in part 5.2 *Rationale for Binding Decision Power of IAMs*, below.

exclusion from future contracting with the IFI). In instances of debarment, sanctions imposed by one IFI may also be adopted and applied by other IFIs through their subscription to mutual sanctions lists (cross-debarment). Borrowers, clients, or those subject to debarment may subsequently appeal this decision to a higher independent body (generally called Sanctions Appeal Tribunals or Panels), typically comprising several judges and established by the IFI. Decisions rendered by this body are non-appealable and binding on both the IFI and the appealing commercial entity.[50]

Sanctions appeal bodies provide an avenue for IFI contractors, clients, companies, and borrowers to challenge debarment or sanctions for corruption or fraud before an independent and impartial entity. These bodies operate without interference from the political considerations of the IFI's Board or President. In such cases, the IFI positions itself as the "victim" of misconduct, as its funds have been misused. However, this type of victimhood is fundamentally different from that experienced by project-affected communities.

When imposing sanctions, the process reflects a form of "victim's justice," tainted with bias and prejudice that necessitates counterbalancing with impartiality and fairness. To ensure this, sanctions appeal boards are established with independence and binding decision-making authority. In contrast, when an IFI's actions harm a community, the final decision-making power remains with the Board, raising concerns about fairness and impartiality. Justice cannot be left in the hands of the entity that is causing or facilitating harm. Project-affected people deserve the protection of an independent and impartial body with binding decision-making power to counterbalance the bias and prejudice (or appearance thereof) that would be inherent in a political Board or President.

What rationale justifies denying this same right to project-affected communities while extending it to other stakeholders such as contractors and borrowers? The inconsistency is indefensible and demands urgent redress.

4.4 *Access to Information Appeal Bodies*

Many IFIs have adopted policies to increase transparency and access to information, recognizing openness as a principle of good governance.[51] These institutions implemented new policies during the 1990s to enhance the accessibility of information about their policies and projects. Anyone, whether

50 For a detailed example of how this process works at an IFI, see World Bank, *Sanctions Systems*, https://www.worldbank.org/en/about/unit/sanctions-system (last visited Dec. 8, 2024).

51 Paul Nelson, *Multilateral development banks, transparency and corporate clients: public–private partnerships and public access to information,* 23(3) PUBLIC ADMINISTRATION AND DEVELOPMENT 249–257 (Aug. 2003).

related to an IFI or not, may request information from the organization. Information requests are then evaluated, and a decision is made to provide or deny access. Denials of access must be for one or more of the reasons set out in the IFI access to information policy. Any dissatisfied requester can appeal the decision. Many IFIs have a two-stage appeal process where first an internal body (often called an Access to Information Committee) consisting of senior staff decides the appeal. If the Access to Information Committee denies the request for appeal, a second appeal can be made to an independent appeals body or panel. The vast majority of these appeal bodies within IFIs have a "final" decision-making power in relation to the disclosure of information.[52] The World Bank's Access to Information Appeals Board, for example, "has the authority to uphold or reverse the relevant decisions of the Access to Information Committee, and the Appeals Board's decisions in such instances are final."[53] Similarly, at the Asian Development Bank, if the Access to Information Committee upholds the initial rejection of an information request, the requester can appeal to the Independent Appeals Panel (IAP), which has the final decision on the release of the information. Similar appeals mechanisms exist at the African Development Bank,[54] the European Bank for Reconstruction and Development,[55] the European Investment Bank,[56] and the United Nations Development Programme.[57]

52 There are exceptions to this. In fact, some institutions fail to establish robust access to information obligations or confer binding decision-making authority to their appeals bodies. For instance, the Green Climate Fund's Information Appeals Panel (IAP) merely provides a recommendation to the Board, the Ethics and Audit Committee, or the Executive Director, who then makes the final decision. This system essentially entrusts the same individuals responsible for initially denying the information request with the authority to rule on the appeal, a process that is both deeply flawed and ineffective. Such an approach is inconsistent with established international best practices. *See* Green Climate Fund, *Information Disclosure Policy for the Green Climate Fund* 9, Sect. XI, 33–35 (July 28, 2019).

53 World Bank, *The World Bank Policy on Access to Information* para. 8(b)(ii), para. 38 (June 3, 2016).

54 African Development Bank, *Disclosure and Access to Information,* para. 4.5.4 (Jan. 11, 2013) ("The decisions of the Appeals Panel will not be re-considered by any other Appeals Committee, authority or jurisdiction of the Bank Group.").

55 European Bank for Reconstruction and Development, *Access to Information Policy,* Sect. 3, para. 5.2(III) (Oct. 2024) ("Except as set out in Part 3, paragraph 5.3 below, the decision of the Information Appeals Panel shall be final.").

56 European Investment Bank, *EIB Group Transparency Policy* (Nov. 18, 2021) (stating that the policy gives access to the binding EIB complaints mechanism, the European Ombudsmen, and the European Court of Justice for access to info violations).

57 United Nations Development Programme, *UNDP Information Disclosure Policy,* para. 21, https://www.undp.org/accountability/transparency/information-disclosure-policy (last visited Dec. 8, 2024) ("The Panel will have the authority to make the final decision ...").

These information appeal bodies share some common features with the IAMs. Neither the Access to Information Appeals Boards nor the IAMs require a pre-existing contract or relationship with the IFI, as is the case with administrative tribunals or arbitrators. Access to information is granted to any individual by IFIs, as they consider transparency a social obligation owed to the public. Similarly, IAMs entertain complaints from any party affected by IFI projects, and in this regard, the complainant has a more direct relationship with the IFI than an information requester. A key difference is that access-to-information panels typically provide remedies in the form of releasing documentation that may or may not have financial implications for the IFI. In contrast, IAMs' decisions may involve remedies with direct monetary consequences, giving rise to concerns for leaving decision-making in the hands of an IAM, an issue that is addressed below. At the very least, the fact that the decisions of an information appeal panel can bind the IFIs as a consequence of a request filed by project-affected people demonstrates that there are no structural barriers impeding the IAMs from granting similar authority to the decisions of an IAM. As discussed below, the reason IAMs do not have such authority must lie elsewhere – most likely in the scale and size of remedies that IAMs could impose.

5 The Non-Binding Nature of IAMs

5.1 *The Lack of a Contractual Relationship*

One of the key distinctions between the examples analyzed in the previous part and the functioning of IAMs lies in the nature of the relationships between the disputing parties and the institution involved. In the case of administrative tribunals and arbitrators discussed earlier (as opposed to Sanctions Appeals Boards or Information Appeal Panels), the disputes typically arise out of contractual relationships, where legal agreements explicitly govern the obligations, rights, and remedies of the parties. Contracts provide a clear legal framework that defines the nature of the dispute and the mechanisms for its resolution.

By contrast, in the case of communities or individuals affected by projects funded by IFIs, no such contractual relationship exists between the complainants and the institution. These communities have standing at the IAMs because they are negatively impacted by the project; they may or may not be among the intended beneficiaries of the project and they are almost never formal parties to a legal agreement with the IFI or the project sponsor. As a result, rather than relying on commitments in a legally enforceable contract, complainants to IAMs refer to the institution's policies, particularly its social, environmental, and human rights safeguards. The basis for the complaint must be rooted in claims of non-compliance with these internal policies and resulting harm, rather than a breach of contract.

In this context, IAMs play a critical role as the sole recourse for communities or individuals seeking redress for harm resulting from IFI-funded projects. However, the lack of a direct contractual relationship also means that IAMs operate in a fundamentally different legal space – one where the ability to impose binding decisions or remedies is limited, relying instead on the institution's voluntary adherence to its own accountability processes and commitments. This distinction underscores the unique challenges faced by complainants in such cases, as they must navigate institutional frameworks without the legal certainty provided by contractual agreements.

One counterargument is that the ability of the administrative tribunals and arbitrators discussed above to render binding decisions stems from the fact that the disputes they address are based on legally binding agreements.[58] In contrast, a common argument against making IAM decisions binding is the nature of the claims they address, which are often tortious or delictual in nature. Unlike contractual disputes, where obligations are explicitly outlined in legal agreements, tortious claims involve civil wrongs, such as harm caused by negligence, nuisance, trespass, or deliberate acts or omissions. The harms IAMs handle typically arise from non-compliance with environmental, social, or human rights standards or safeguards of the IFI rather than breaches of contractual obligations. As such, these claims more closely resemble issues addressed in civil tort/delictual litigation rather than contractual disputes, leading some to argue that IAMs lack the legal grounding necessary to impose binding decisions, particularly where the relationship between the complainants and the institution is not contractual.

5.2 *Rationale for Binding Decision Power of IAMs*

While it is true that two of the examples previously discussed (tribunals and arbitrators) are grounded in contractual agreements, this contractual basis alone does not automatically justify the establishment of independent bodies by IFIs, vested with binding decision-making powers. In each of these cases, alternative structures could have been implemented. For instance, rather than creating binding tribunals or arbitral mechanisms, IFIs could have opted for models similar to IAMs – independent bodies tasked only with

58 *See generally* Daniel Bradlow, *Private Complaints and International Organizations: A Comparative Study of the Independent Accountability Mechanisms in International Financial Institutions*, GEORGETOWN J. INT'L L (2014); AUGUST REINSCH, INTERNATIONAL ORGANIZATIONS BEFORE NATIONAL COURTS (2000).

investigating complaints and issuing recommendations to the Boards of IFIs, leaving the final decision to institutional discretion. Another possibility would have been for the contracts to simply defer disputes to litigation in national courts, sidestepping the need for quasi-judicial bodies altogether.

However, the key difference lies in the practical realities of market power. The private sector, particularly commercial entities engaged in high-stakes contracts with IFIs, is unlikely to accept agreements with institutions that enjoy broad legal immunity without securing access to an independent dispute resolution mechanism with binding authority. This is because private corporations, contractors, and financial entities rely on the enforceability of their contracts, and without such guarantees, the risk of engaging with legally immune IFIs may outweigh the potential benefits. In this context, it is likely that IFIs had to offer binding arbitration or tribunal processes akin to judicial bodies to attract private sector cooperation and to reassure commercial actors that their disputes would be resolved in a fair, impartial, and binding manner.

Employees of IFIs have secured binding decision-making authority for their disputes largely due to the strength of their collective bargaining power. Additionally, the long-standing precedent set by the ILO Administrative Tribunal made the establishment of similar mechanisms within IFIs more readily accepted and justified. Labor unions and employee associations within these institutions have historically negotiated for access to independent and binding tribunals to resolve employment disputes. Without such mechanisms, employees would have no recourse against institutions shielded by immunity from national jurisdictions, which could have led to significant dissatisfaction and unrest within IFIs' workforces.

The establishment of binding tribunals, arbitral mechanisms, and sanction appeal panels are not merely a byproduct of contractual agreements. Instead, they reflect the outcome of bargaining processes in which IFIs, despite their legal immunities, had to negotiate with powerful market forces – namely, the private sector and labor unions. Both commercial entities and employees demanded access to remedies through binding, independent, quasi-judicial bodies, as they were otherwise excluded from conventional legal recourse due to the immunity protections afforded to IFIs. In this sense, the immunity of the IFIs weakened their bargaining position. To offset this challenge, IFIs were compelled to establish dispute resolution mechanisms that closely resembled courts in their authority and enforceability, ensuring that they could continue to attract private sector contracts and maintain harmonious labor relations.

Conversely, project-affected individuals possess minimal negotiating leverage with IFIs, IFI clients, or, in numerous instances, with their borrowing governments. Predominantly, project-affected individuals comprise Indigenous

People, impoverished agriculturalists, vulnerable fisherfolks, or urban slum inhabitants.[59] These project-affected individuals are geographically dispersed, and even when they coalesce to form associations seeking redress for harm, they remain less effectively organized and financially supported than IFI labor unions, staff associations, or chambers of commerce and trade associations. They are unable to initiate legal proceedings against IFIs because of immunity protection; lack collective bargaining power akin to employees; and have limited commercial authority, market influence, or adequate funding to pay for legal services. This observation does not negate the significance of grassroots movements and civil society that have been mobilized over the past three decades, particularly considering their fundamental role in advocating for the establishment of IAMs and more progressive environmental and social policies within IFIs.[60] Rather, it demonstrates that it is not the existence of a contract or other legal relationship that matters, but bargaining power that supports the establishment of independent, binding decision-making bodies for dispute resolution with an IFI. In the case of project-affected individuals, their bargaining power has been limited or insufficient to win these benefits and will likely remain so in the future. There remains a crying need for justice, and remedy for harm caused to vulnerable project-affected people due to non-compliance with environmental and social safeguards remains unfulfilled.

The second argument for treating IAMs as binding is based on recognizing the contract-like relationship between project-affected people and IFIs. This can be explained in three ways. First, project-affected people (even when they are not direct project beneficiaries) could be considered third-party beneficiaries of the environmental and social safeguard policies and the associated commitments in environmental and social management plans. In most countries, *ius quaesitum tertio* provides the ability for a third party to sue based on a contract if the third party is an intended, rather than just incidental, beneficiary. Given that the entire rationale for environmental and social safeguard policies and associated environmental management plans is to protect communities from environmental and social harm, project-affected people should be allowed to enforce those provisions of the loan agreement. Compliance with the environmental and social safeguard policies is a common provision in project loan agreements – and they, the community, are the "intended beneficiaries." The second way to understand the quasi-contractual relationship

59 *See* Accountability Console, *Complaints*, https://accountabilityconsole.com/complaints/map/ (last visited Dec. 8, 2024).

60 Dana Clark, et al., Demanding Accountability: Civil Society Claims and the World Bank Inspection Panel (2003).

projects have with affected communities is through the concept of a "social license." It is on the basis of promises IFIs make to promote development generally and to address the specific environmental and social risks (through, for example, environmental and social management plans) that an IFI-financed project is afforded a social license to operate. The social license runs from the community and is separate from any formal licenses issued by the national government – but it nonetheless provides a conceptual framework for treating at least the environmental and social commitments of a project as intended for, and enforceable by, the community.

The third and final argument is that developing country governments and commercial entities are increasingly dissatisfied with IFI management's insistence that funds for remediating harm identified by an IAM should be borne by the borrower or contracting party rather than the IFI. A curious yet serious anomaly and irrationality are embedded in the accountability concept of most IAMs. IAMs are mandated to examine the due diligence performed by their own parent IFI and the staff of that IFI, and not that of the borrower or client commercial entity. Having done so, the IAM finds that harm has been caused to complainants because of the IFI or its staff not complying with the IFI's own policies or procedures. The IAM then (sometimes) recommends action to remedy the harm. The logical consequence of this recommendation, if adopted by the Board or President of the IFI, is that the IFI opens its purse and pays for the remedy, as the fault was on its side. However, this is not necessarily (or even typically) the case. Often, IFI Boards, Presidents, and management then turn to the borrower or commercial client and ask them to pay for remediation. The Cambodia case cited above is an example of where the CRPs' findings found fault with the ADB and its staff, but the ADB Board decided that Cambodia should pay for the remedies.[61]

Sanctions Appeals Boards and Access to Information Panels are strong examples of quasi-judicial bodies established by IFIs outside of contractual frameworks. As illustrated above, these mechanisms allow complaints from virtually anyone, whether they are whistleblowing on fraud or corruption or challenging a denial of information. Both bodies hold binding decision-making authority within the IFIs' publicly accessible justice systems. IAMs also fall into this category and, similarly, share many procedural and investigatory methods with these bodies.

61 *See supra* note 38 and accompanying text.

Access to information is an internationally recognized right, as exemplified by instruments such as the Aarhus Convention[62] and the Escazu Agreement,[63] which enshrines the public's right to access environmental information, participate in decision-making processes, access justice, and receive protection from the state for environmental and human rights defenders. This right, along with other fundamental human rights – including access to remedy; Free, Prior, and Informed Consent (FPIC); and broader human rights obligations – are increasingly accepted as critical to ensuring transparency, accountability, and justice. In practice, administrative tribunals regularly uphold these rights, further embedding them into international and domestic legal frameworks. Many of these rights, such as access to remedy and FPIC, also intersect with principles of *jus cogens*, the highest norms of international law. Given this established international recognition, it is perplexing that IAMs, which are meant to serve as safeguards within international organizations, do not have binding decision-making power when adjudicating on such fundamental rights. The lack of binding authority undermines their effectiveness and calls into question the genuine commitment of international organizations to uphold these critical human rights.

This anomalous result has been disturbing to many governments, commercial companies, and civil society organizations dealing with IFIs in developing countries. In the long term, it is therefore of interest to these governments and commercial entities to bargain with IFIs to establish independent IAMs with binding decision-making power to decide fairly on complaints from project-affected people and to allow an IAM to determine who should pay for the remedies – the IFI, the borrower, or the commercial entity. In some cases, IAMs may find that the costs of remedies should be shared by the IFI and the borrower or commercial entity, while in others, they may find that the just the IFI ought to pay. Unless the harm is exclusively caused by the borrower or commercial entity alone, an IAM is unlikely to decide that the cost should be borne by them. Borrowers and commercial entities have far more bargaining power than project-affected individuals. However, at least in this area, they arguably have a common interest in seeking independent IAMs with binding decision-making power established by IFIs. A possible solution to

62 United Nations Economic Commission for Europe, *Convention on Access to Information, Public Participation in Decision-making and Access to Justice in Environmental Matters* (Aarhus Convention) (June 25, 1998).

63 United Nations, *Regional Agreement on Access to Information, Public Participation and Justice in Environmental Matters in Latin America and the Caribbean* (Escazu Agreement) (Mar. 4, 2018).

this predicament could be the institution of a ring-fenced remediation fund or purchasing liability insurance to rely upon when a monetary remedy is due to project-affected people. How to pay for the costs of potential harm caused by a project (such as in the construction or manufacturing industry) is a problem that has long been solved in the commercial world. Ring-fenced funds, liability insurance, and guarantees are just some solutions that are regularly used in projects that have potential for causing harm. IFIs can look at these methods and adopt solutions to internalize the costs of remedy when harm is caused by projects and programs funded by them.

As highlighted in the previous part, concerns about the scope and scale of potential liabilities if IAMs were empowered to issue binding remedies for affected communities should not deter appropriate IAM reforms. Arguably, the four examples of binding decision-making established by IFIs, to some extent, illustrate ring-fenced remedies. In the case of access to information the remedy is limited to the release of information. In the case of the sanctions appeals, the remedy is limited to removing sanctions. In the case of the administrative tribunals, the remedy may be undefined but is still limited to employee remedies (like salaries, reinstatement, or compensation for unfair dismissal) that are arguably not enormous. In the case of commercial arbitration, the parties are able to define the risk they are willing to take through contract, so that the remedy may lend itself to quantification for breaches. In contrast, some may argue that environmental and social harm addressed by IAMs is undefined and therefore the remedy would be potentially unbounded.

There are several ways in which to mitigate this concern while advancing the provision of adequate remedy. Ring-fencing or limiting the remedies that an IAM can grant through binding-decisions is one way to overcome this concern. Another pragmatic starting point would be to make IAM findings of fact and harm binding, while allowing the Board to retain discretion over the specific remedies. Remedies could also be capped at a predetermined amount or funded through a dedicated remediation fund. Crucially, the findings of an IAM investigation regarding policy violations and harm to project-affected people should not be subject to revision or reinterpretation by the Board. Reforms do not need to be seismic but can and should at least be incremental in allowing for independence, binding decisions, and the provision of adequate remedy.

This initial reform would strike a balance by introducing binding authority for IAMs' findings while preserving some discretion for the Board over remedies. It would mark a significant step toward the legalization and depoliticization of IAM processes, ultimately enhancing their credibility and fairness.[64]

64 In some IFIs (such as the ADB), the findings of the IAM are binding and not open to revision by the Board or the management. *See, e.g.*, Asian Development Bank, *Accountability*

6 Conclusion

Recent rulings, particularly the *Jam v. IFC* case, have introduced significant uncertainty into the landscape of IFIs, casting doubt on their liability, accountability, and immunity. In this context, proactive measures to enhance their accountability mechanisms can demonstrate IFIs' commitment to addressing these pressing concerns.

The argument for granting IAMs the authority to issue binding decisions has been articulated from both conceptual and precedent-based perspectives. While we firmly believe this argument is robust and, in many respects, inevitable, it is essential to recognize that such reforms will not come easily, but that they can at least be incremental. Implementing binding decision-making requires a fundamental restructuring of IAMs and a reevaluation of how IFIs and their borrowers engage with project-affected individuals and communities.

However, this necessity for reform should not be viewed as a barrier; rather, it should be embraced as an urgent imperative. By taking decisive action now, IFIs can mitigate the growing risk of protracted and costly litigation and the potential erosion of their immunity while reinforcing their role as environmentally and socially responsible actors in the development arena. The time to do this is now.

Acknowledgement

The authors thank Katrina Lehmann Grube for her contribution to the initial research for this paper during her tenure as an intern at the IRM of the GCF 2020/2021.

Bibliography

Accountability Counsel. *World Bank Group Absolute Immunity Ends in Landmark U.S. Supreme Court Decision*, San Francisco: Accountability Counsel, February 27, 2019.

Accountability Console. *Complaints*. Accessed December 8, 2024. https://accountabilityconsole.com/complaints/map/.

Mechanism Policy 36, para. 190 (Mar. 22, 2012). ("If the CRP [IAM] concludes that ADB's noncompliance caused direct and material harm, Management will propose remedial actions to bring the project into compliance with ADB policies and address related findings of harm.") Making the findings of fact and findings of harm binding would be a good start to the reforms suggested in this Chapter.

African Development Bank [AfDB]. *Bank Group Policy on Disclosure and Access to Information.* Côte d'Ivoire: AfDB, January 11, 2013: para 4.5.4.

Asian Development Bank [ADB]. *Accountability Mechanism Policy.* Washington DC: Asian Development Bank, March 22, 2012: para. 190.

ADB. *Annual Report 2016: Members, Capital Stock, and Voting Power (as of 31 December 2016).* Washington DC: ADB, April 11, 2017.

ADB Administrative Tribunal. *Statute of the Administrative Tribunal of the Asian Development Bank.* Washington DC: ADB, February 21, 2021: Art. IX.

ADB Board of Directors. *Decision of the Board of Directors of the Asian Development Bank.* Washington DC: Asian Development Bank, January 31, 2014.

ADB Board of Directors. *Chair's Summary of the Board Compliance Review Committee and Compliance Review Panel's Report on Eligibility of the Compliance Review Request for TA 4712, 7387, and 8481: Promoting Economic Use of Customary Land and Grant 0392: Samoa Agribusiness Support Project (Samoa).* Washington DC: Asian Development Bank, July 20, 2016.

ADB Compliance Review Panel. *Samoa: Promoting Economic Use of Customary Land and Samoa AgriBusiness Support Project.* Accessed December 7, 2024. https://lnadbg4.adb.org/dir0035p.nsf/alldocs/JABM-A983HD?OpenDocument.

Boldt, Peter, and Bethany Pereira. *Jam v. IFC – What does it mean for accountability?* Incheon: Green Climate, March 29, 2019.

Book, Kristin E. "The United Nations as Good Samaritan: Immunity and Responsibility." *Chicago Journal of International Law*, 16, no. 2 (2016).

Bradlow, Daniel. "Private Complaints and International Organizations: A Comparative Study of the Independent Accountability Mechanisms in International Financial Institutions." *Georgetown Journal of International Law* (2014).

Center for International Environmental Law. *Glass Half Full: The State of Accountability in Development Finance.* Amsterdam: SOMO, January 2016.

Clark, Dana, et al. *Demanding accountability: Civil society claims and the World Bank inspection panel.* Laham: Rowman & Littlefield, 2003.

Earth Rights International. *Historic Settlement in Case Alleging International Finace Corporation Abetted Murder in Honduras.* Washington DC: EarthRights International, October 3, 2024.

EarthRights International. *Bedha Ismail Jam, Et Al V. IFC.* Accessed December 6, 2024. https://earthrights.org/case/budha-ismail-jam-et-al-v-ifc/#:~:text=From%20the%20beginning%2C%20the%20IFC,if%20sufficient%20steps%20were%20not.

European Bank for Reconstruction and Development [EBRD]. *Project Accountability Policy.* London: EBRD, April 2019.

EBRD. *Access to Information Policy.* London: EBRD, October 2024: sect. 3, para 5.2(III).

European Investment Bank, The *EIB Group Transparency Policy*, European Investment Bank (Nov. 18, 2021).

Equitable Cambodia. *The Railway Case*. Phnom Penh: Equitable Cambodia, August 18, 2016.

Green Climate Fund. *Governing Instruments of the Green Climate Fund*. Incheon: Green Climate Fund, April 16, 2018.

Green Climate Fund, *Information Disclosure Policy for the Green Climate Fund*. Incheon:The Green Climate Fund, July 28, 2019: 9, Sect. XI, 33–35.

Horn, Nobert. "The Development of Arbitration in International Financial Transactions." *Arbitration International*, 16, no. 3 (September 1, 2000): 279–296.

Inclusive Development International. *Official Investigation Finds ADB Failed to Consult Samoan People Before Pushing Harmful Land Reforms*. Asheville: Inclusive Development International, September 13, 2016.

Inter-American Court of Human Rights [IACHR]. *State Obligations in Relation to the Environment in the Context of the Protection and Guarantee of the Rights to Life and to Personal Integrity: Interpretation and Scope of Articles 4(1) and 5(1) in Relation to Articles 1(1) and 2 of the American Convention on Human Rights, OC-23/17*. San José: Inter-American Court of Human Rights, November 15, 2017.

International Court of Justice. *Effect of Awards of Compensation Made by the United Nations Administrative Tribunal, Advisory Opinion*, I.C.J. Reports. The Hague: International Court of Justice, 1954.

International Labor Organization. *Statute of the Administrative Tribunal of the International Labour Organization*. Geneva: International Labor Organization, July 7, 2014: Art. VI.

International Labor Organization. *The Tribunal*. Accessed December 7, 2024. https://www.ilo.org/ilo-administrative-tribunal/tribunal.

International Finance Corporation's Office of the Compliance Advisor/ Ombudsman [CAO]. *CAO's Operational Guidelines*. Washington DC: The World Bank, October 13, 2016.

Johansen, Stian. Ø. "The Human Rights Accountability Mechanisms of International Organizations." *Cambridge University Press*. (2020): 11.

Johnson, Nicholas. "JAM v. IFC: One Step Forward, Two Steps Back?" *Sustainable Development Law & Policy*, 19, no. 2 (2018): 16.

Klabbers, Jan. *An Introduction to International Organizations Law*. Cambridge: Cambridge University Press, 2022.

McIntosh, Toby. *Green Climate Fund Giving Unequal Access to Report on Controversial Project*. Eye on Global Transparency, May 11, 2023.

McIntosh, Toby. *GCF Board Excludes Internal Body From More Oversight of Controversial Project*. Eye on Global Conspiracy, July 2023.

McIntyre, Owen, and Suresh. Nanwani. *The Practice of Independent Accountability Mechanisms (IAMs) Towards Good Governance in Development Finance*. Leiden: Brill Nijhoff, 2020.

Nelson, Paul. (2003). "Multilateral development banks, transparency and corporate clients: 'public–private partnerships and public access to information." *Public Administration and Development*, 23, no. 3 (August 2003): 249–257.

Okada, Yohei. "The Immunity of International Organizations Before And After Jam V IFC: Is The Functional Necessity Rationale Still Relevant?" *Questions of International Law*, 72. (2020): 29.

Otegbeye, Peter. "Accountability: A Corrective Mechanism in Resolving Organizational Challenges." Independent, PAPERS.SSRN.COM (2016).

Pereira, Alexsandro. E., R. R. Horochovski, M. M. A. Cruz, and N. Rodrigues. "Accountability in International Organizations: the case of World Bank Inspection Panel (1993–2015)." *Brazilian Political Science Review*, 11, no. 1 (2017).

Reinisch, August. *International Organizations Before National Courts*. Cambridge: University Press, 2000.

Reinisch, August. "Accountability of international organizations according to national law." *Netherlands Yearbook of International Law*, 36, no. 1 (2005):119.

Reinisch, August. "The immunity of international organizations and the jurisdiction of their Administrative Tribunals." *Chinese Journal of International Law*, 7, no. 2 (May 22, 2008): 285–306.

Rossi, Pierfrancesco. "The International Law Significance of Jam v. IFC: Some Implications for the Immunity of International Organizations." *Diritti Umani e Diritto Internazionale*, 13, no. 2. (2019):305–318.

Schmitt, Pierre. *Access to Justice and International Organizations: The Case of Individual Victims of Human Rights Violations*. London: Edward Elgar Publishing, 2017.

Sharma, Dhruv. "The Immunities of International Organisations: Jam v. IFC and the Need for External Review Mechanisms."*National Law University Delhi Journal of Legal Studies*, 2 (2020): 41.

Steffeck, Jen Steffek. "Public Accountability and the Public Sphere of International Governance." *Ethics & International Affairs*, 24, no. 1 (2010): 45–67.

Stiglitz, Joseph E. "Democratizing the International Monetary Fund and the World Bank: governance and accountability."*Governance*, 16, no. 1 (2003): 111–139.

Tondini, Matteo. *Putting an End to Human Rights Violations by Proxy: Accountability of International Organizations and Member States in the Framework of Jus Post Bellum*. The Hague: TMC Asser Press, 2008: 187–212.

Trinadade, Antônio Augusto Cançado. "The Interrelation between the Access to Justice (Right to an Effective Remedy) and the Guarantees of the Due Process of Law", in *The Access of Individuals to International Justice, Collected Courses of the Academy of European Law*. Oxford: Oxford University Press, 2011.

United Nations. *Regional Agreement on Access to Information, Public Participation and Justice in Environmental Matters in Latin America and the Caribbean* (Escazu Agreement). Geneva: United Nations, March 4, 2018.

United Nations Development Programme [UNDP]. *UNDP Information Disclosure Policy*. Accessed December 8, 2024: para. 21.

United Nations General Assembly. *Convention on the Privileges and Immunities of the United Nations*, United Nations-Treaty Series: 1946–1947. Geneva: United Nations, February 13, 1946: 30, Art. VIII, Sect. 29.

United Nations High Commissioner for Human Rights. *Improving accountability and access to remedy for victims of business-related human rights abuse through non-State-based grievance mechanisms, A/HRC/44/32*. Geneva: The United Nations, May 19, 2020: 46.

United Nations Economic Commission for Europe. *Convention on Access to Information, Public Participation in Decision-making and Access to Justice in Environmental Matters* (Aarhus Convention). Geneva: United Nations, June 25, 1998.

United Nations Office of Human Rights. *Guiding Principles on Business and Human Rights*. Geneva: United Nations, 2011.

United Nations Commission on International Trade Law. *Convention on the Recognition and Enforcement of Foreign Arbitral Awards.* Geneva: United Nations, 1958.

Woods, Ngaire. *Accountability, governance, and reform in the International Financial Institutions*. OxfordL University of Oxford, 2001.

World Bank. *The World Bank Policy on Access to Information*. Washington DC: The World Bank, June 3, 2016: para. 8(b)(II).

World Bank. *External Review of IFC/MIGA E&S Accountability, including CAO's Role and Effectiveness Report and Recommendations*. Washington DC: World Bank, 2020.

World Bank. *Sanctions Systems*. Accessed December 8, 2024. https://www.worldbank.org/en/about/unit/sanctions-system.

World Bank Administrative Tribunal. *Administrative Tribunal Statute*. Washington DC: World Bank, April 30, 1980: Sect. XI. https://tribunal.worldbank.org/statute.

Yan, Wenjun, and Lin Shang. "Forget International Law Not: IFC Loses Absolute Immunity in Jam v International Finance Corporation." *Beijing Law Review*, 13 no.3 (September 2022): 662–672.

PART 5

Next Steps on Accountability

Introduction to Part 5: Next Steps on Accountability

The six articles in this part are forward looking, focused on trying to identify the "next steps in accountability." The first author, Chris Stephens, is currently the General Counsel of the World Bank Group, and he brings this experience to discuss the future of the Inspection Panel and accountability systems at the World Bank Group in light of ongoing pressures that the Bank faces toward meeting increasingly complex demands under pressure to be more efficient. Two other articles are also from experienced "insiders" who bring their perspectives based experience working inside a multilateral development bank. Hamid Sharif was a lawyer at the Asian Development Bank (ADB) and later the first head of the compliance and integrity unit at the Asian Infrastructure Investment Bank. Suresh Nanwani, was a lawyer in the legal department at the ADB and later worked for the independent accountability mechanism at the ADB. Therefore, whether or not one agrees with their perspective or conclusions on next steps, their perspectives provide important and well-informed insights into the likely evolution of these mechanisms.

The two articles, by Aldo Caliari and Luiz Viera, discuss the need for an accountability mechanism for the IMF. Caliari discusses this issue in terms of the IMF's human rights responsibilities. Viera focuses more on the IMF's need to accept that the evolution in its functions makes the need for it to have its own independent accountability mechanism more evident and urgent.

The final article in this part, by Professor Danny Bradlow, argues that as the multilateral development banks become increasingly coordinated and function more as a unitary system, it is not efficient or effective for them each to have their own independent accountability mechanism. He argues that it would be more effective for them to create one independent accountability mechanism for all the banks. This would also enhance the independence of the mechanism.

 | DOI:10.1163/9789004729735_027

CHAPTER 21

Strengthening Accountability in Challenging Times: Insights from the General Counsel of the World Bank Group

*Christopher H. Stephens**

1 Introduction

Thirty years ago, the World Bank (the Bank) Board of Executive Directors (the Board) adopted a Resolution[1] to establish the World Bank Inspection Panel (the Panel) – the first independent accountability mechanism (IAM) of its kind among Multilateral Development Banks (MDBs). The Panel receives complaints from communities and individuals alleging harm arising from a failure by the Bank to comply with its own policies and procedures. James Wolfensohn, the Bank's President at the time, said the Panel was a "bold experiment in transparency and accountability that has worked to the benefit of all concerned."[2]

But it was more than bold. It was also a significant risk: by establishing an IAM, the World Bank was creating an independent unit, outside the influence of the Bank's operations functions, that could review its work, assess compliance, and publish reports that would be critical of the Bank's work. But – at the same time – the Panel was a concept that was vitally necessary and one whose time had come. Many international financial institutions (IFIs) like the Bank are immune from lawsuits arising from their operations, meaning that affected people do not have recourse to their national courts to resolve their grievances against them. But, if at the same time, these communities have no recourse to the courts or any alternative forum, they are without recourse, entirely – a result that is both manifestly unfair and also damaging to the reputation of the IFIs whose stated purpose is to deliver benefits to the same

* Senior Vice President and General Counsel of the World Bank Group.

1 The World Bank Inspection Panel, *Resolution No. IBRD 93–10* and *Resolution No. IDA 93–6* (Sep. 22, 1993) reinstated, amended and consolidated through The World Bank Inspection Panel, *Resolution No. IBRD 2020–0004* and *Resolution No. IDA 2020–0003* (Sep. 8, 2020) [hereinafter "2020 Panel Resolution"].

2 Alvaro Umaña, ed., *The World Bank Inspection Panel: The First Four Years (1994–1998)*, The World Bank, 3 (1998).

communities. As independent, neutral, and objective forums, the IAMs provide that recourse, hold institutions accountable, and better enable them to learn valuable lessons from their successes and shortcomings so that future projects achieve better outcomes while avoiding harm to people and communities. An effective IAM – actively overseen by the institution's board of directors – instills confidence in communities, civil society, subscribers to capital, and development partners. It is a win-win-win outcome that strengthens the institution and its ability to advance its strategic priorities and achieve its mission.

Over the next thirty years, the world's leading MDBs and IFIs followed the Bank's lead, setting up independent accountability mechanisms for communities and individuals affected by the projects financed by these institutions in order to provide a neutral forum to independently and objectively consider their concerns and facilitate redress as appropriate. Over time, the compliance functions performed by these mechanisms have been augmented by dispute resolution mechanisms (sometimes called problem-solving functions) that offer affected parties an option to have their concerns addressed and resolved by discussion and mediation, such as the Bank's Dispute Resolution Service (DRS).[3] These accountability functions typically operate alongside the oversight and dispute resolution mechanisms established by the Management of MDBs and IFIs to strengthen accountability, such as the Bank's Grievance Redress Service (GRS), which handles more than 150 cases a year.[4] With these initiatives, the Bank and other IFIs have expanded the toolbox, providing affected people with alternatives to address their concerns.

Many changes over time have expanded and adapted to a rapidly changing international development landscape. While global accountability has gained acceptance, strength, and effectiveness over the last thirty years, the world faces a period of great upheaval and uncertainty, with multiple crises – or *polycrises* – ranging from wars, civil unrest, food and water insecurity, climate change, biodiversity loss, gaps in infrastructure, and energy shortages and their spillover effects, including inflation, spiraling debt burdens, supply chain disruptions, currency exchange fluctuations, and fragility, conflict, and violence (FCV) situations among others. These circumstances have challenged

3 On September 8, 2020, the World Bank's Board adopted a Resolution establishing the World Bank's Accountability Mechanism, of which the Panel is now a part, and creating the Dispute Resolution Service (DRS). *See* World Bank Inspection Panel, *Resolution No. IBRD 2020–0005* and *Resolution No. IDA 2020–0004: The World Bank Accountability Mechanism* (Sep. 8, 2020) [hereinafter "2020 AM Resolution"].

4 The World Bank Group, *Grievance Redress Service*, https://www.worldbank.org/en/projects-operations/products-and-services/grievance-redress-service (last visited Dec. 14, 2024).

the Bank and other IFIs to reinvent their strategy, priorities, and operations to find more effective and efficient ways to deliver on their missions and achieve better results more urgently, while doing so without compromising the rigorous application of standards and safeguards consistent with sustainable and inclusive development, social inclusion, and greater transparency and accountability.

This essay offers some of my views regarding the Panel's role, and some of the key challenges facing the World Bank's Accountability Mechanism (which houses the Panel and the DRS) and similar independent accountability mechanisms established by other MDBs and IFIs. In particular, the essay focuses on the importance of the independence, integrity, and objectivity of accountability mechanisms; the need to enable greater access for communities and individuals to these mechanisms, while safeguarding the confidentiality of complainants in an environment of growing technological disruption; opportunities to explore common approaches[5] amongst multilateral development institutions and their accountability mechanisms; cooperation amongst accountability mechanisms to avoid the duplication of efforts, investment disincentives, and inconsistent outcomes; how to best integrate or coordinate all possible tools of accountability, including dispute resolution and compliance functions; and consideration of the impact of technological innovations and artificial intelligence on fact-finding, evidence gathering, and the advancement of accountability as a whole.

Ultimately, I argue that IAMs remain an indispensable feature for effective, transparent, and responsible sustainable development, but one that should continue to evolve to adapt to the needs of the times and to enable learning from past experiences, in an ongoing effort to deliver development assistance fairly and effectively.

2 The Mandate, Objectives, and Evolution of the Panel

2.1 *The Mandate of the Panel*

The Panel is mandated by the Board to independently review Bank management's compliance with applicable Bank policies and procedures in the context of the projects financed by the Bank.[6] In this sense, the creation of the

5 See *infra* notes 29 – 30 and accompanying text.

6 Notably, the Panel does not investigate or assess compliance by the Bank's borrowers (*i.e.*, the country or relevant implementing agency), but focuses on the Bank's compliance with its policies and procedures.

Panel was a departure from the past, where allegations of non-compliance were addressed only by Bank management through internal and administrative systems. This does not mean that the Bank's internal systems were replaced by the Panel, but rather that the Bank augmented its internal systems for monitoring compliance of its policies with an additional forum available at the option of affected people. The point is not to replace one process with another, but to provide alternative options to affected people so they can utilize the system best-suited to their circumstances.

As Ibrahim Shihata, General Counsel of the World Bank (1983–1998), argued:

> The creation of the Inspection Panel … complemented this internal system of accountability by giving a direct access to affected parties before the Panel (which is a facility of the Bank) and by requiring Management to present to the Board recommendations for corrective action in case the Panel finds a serious violation of Bank policies and procedures resulting in harm to such affected parties in the situations described above. The Board's decision on the actions to be taken by the Bank demonstrates the Bank's accountability for its actions or omissions.[7]

The Panel's powers to hold the Bank accountable are prescribed in the Inspection Panel Resolution.

2.2 *The Objectives of the Panel*

The Panel is available to communities and individuals who believe that they have been, or are likely to be, harmed by a Bank-funded project as a result of a failure of the Bank to comply with its own operational policies.[8] As of December 5, 2024, the Panel had received 173 requests for inspection and registered 125 requests concerning more than 25 policy issues.[9] The achievements of the Panel, in this context, have increasingly reflected the Bank's continued commitment and efforts to ensure accountability and transparency through compliance with its policies and standards.[10] This commitment

7 Ibrahim Shihata, *Issues Related to the Inspection Panel*, THE WORLD BANK LEGAL PAPERS 611 (2001).

8 2020 Panel Resolution, *supra* note 1, at para 13.

9 *See* World Bank Inspection Panel, *Panel Cases Data*, https://www.inspectionpanel.org/panel-cases/data (last visited Dec. 14, 2024).

10 World Bank Group, *Report and Recommendations on the Inspection Panel's Toolkit Review* (March 5, 2020), https://documents.worldbank.org/en/publication/documents-reports/documentdetail/972351583772786218/report-and-recommendations-on-the-inspection-panel-s-toolkit-review (last visited on Dec.14, 2024).

is demonstrated in the Bank's comprehensive and specific responses to the Panel's investigation reports. Beyond the Bank, the success of the Panel has also inspired multiple MDBs and IFIs to establish and strengthen their independent accountability mechanisms.

2.3 *Evolution of the Panel*

As external demands for accountability in international development finance and the Bank's internal policies and procedures have evolved, so have the mechanisms put in place to monitor the Bank's compliance. Most recently, in August 2017, the Board commissioned an External Review of the Panel's Toolkit to determine the improvements, reforms, and measures needed for the Panel to continue to operate effectively in the face of new Bank policies, such as the Bank's Environmental and Social Framework (ESF).[11] This was followed by the establishment of a Working Group of the Board of Executive Directors' Committee on Development Effectiveness (CODE) in July 2018. CODE was mandated to consider the findings of the 2017 review of the Panel's Toolkit, and, based on the lessons and experiences of the Panel, develop proposals for enhancing its effectiveness and value to the World Bank.[12]

In October 2018, the Board approved measures to formally recognize the Panel's advisory role, and the need for coordination between the Panel and accountability mechanisms of other MDBs and IFIs to more efficiently and effectively resolve complaints relating to projects financed by more than one IFI.[13] To further increase transparency in accountability processes, the Board approved an update to procedures for sharing the Panel's Investigation Report with requesters ahead of consideration by the Board. The Board also considered the importance of increasing accountability through dispute resolution, including by maintaining and strengthening the Bank's GRS and creating an independent dispute resolution process that is available at the option of the parties, not in place of the Panel's compliance function, but as an additional option. This disputes resolution function would supplement the Panel's work by offering an alternative that would help minimize costs and likely resolve grievances faster without the need for a full-fledged, costly and time-consuming investigation process.

Following the culmination of the review of the Panel's Toolkit, the Board adopted the revised Panel Resolution[14] and the World Bank Accountability

11 *Id.*
12 *Id.*
13 *Id.* at para. 5.
14 2020 Panel Resolution, *supra* note 1.

Mechanism Resolution[15] in September 2020. The revised Panel Resolution reaffirms the importance of the Panel's compliance function, as well as its independence and integrity. The Resolution further restates and consolidates the 1993 Panel Resolution, the 1996 Review of the Resolution,[16] and the 1999 Clarification,[17] and amends the 1993 Panel Resolution to reflect the subsequent decisions of the Board.

Through the Accountability Mechanism Resolution, the Board created the DRS, which now together with the Panel constitutes the World Bank Accountability Mechanism (AM).[18] The AM is headed by an independent Accountability Mechanism Secretary (the AM Secretary) who is supported by the Accountability Mechanism Secretariat. While the Panel now forms part of the AM, the Panel is not subject to the supervision of the AM Secretary and, most importantly, remains entirely independent of the operations units whose work it reviews and assesses. The Panel continues to report directly to the Board on its compliance review functions.

3 Key Challenges and Opportunities Going Forward

3.1 *The Independence, Integrity, and Objectivity of the Accountability Function*

Independence, objectivity, integrity, transparency, and competence are the fundamental pillars underpinning the credibility of accountability mechanisms and the confidence of all stakeholders in both the accountability system and in the institution generally. From the negotiations of the Resolution establishing the Panel, Board discussions focused particularly on questions of the independence, objectivity, and integrity of the Panel. Ultimately, the Board mandated the Panel to remain fully independent from Bank staff and management; this was reflected in the original 1993 Panel Resolution and is maintained in the 2020 Resolution. The most important objective was to ensure that the Panel is entirely separate from Bank Management and operations staff and the decision-making process regarding Bank operations that are subject to the

15 2020 AM Resolution, *supra* note 3.

16 World Bank Inspection Panel, *Review of the Resolution Establishing the Inspection Panel: 1996 Clarification of Certain Aspects of the Resolution*, (May 9, 1996).

17 World Bank Inspection Panel, *The 1999 Clarification of the Board's Second Review of the Inspection Panel* (Oct. 17, 1999).

18 2020 AM Resolution, *supra* note 3, at para. 2.

review by the Panel. As noted below, that separation – together with freedom from undue influence – is the fundamental precondition of objectivity.

The concept of "independence" is widely misunderstood or not fully understood. By definition, "independence" is a relative term: something is independent only in relation to something else. MDBs have several important functions that undertake audit, investigative, and/or analytic activities that review the functions or decisions of other units of the institution and are thus structured to be independent of those functions that they review. These independent units include – in addition to the compliance function of their IAMs – internal audit, ethics and anti-corruption, and independent evaluations units. Each of these is independent of the other units of the institutions that they review.

Each of these units is independent, not as an end in itself, but as a means of safeguarding its objectivity and shielding it from any undue influence or interference that could affect its impartiality.

For these reasons, the Panel is structured to be separated from the management and the staff whose work and decisions are the subject of the Panel's compliance reviews. Components of that independence are reporting lines, budget processes, staffing, and workforce planning, all of which are entirely separate from the management and staff whose work is reviewed.

Like all units in the Bank, however, the Panel is not independent from – and must remain accountable to – the Board of Executive Directors, whose oversight, authority, and responsibility also applies to the Panel. Ultimately, the Board is responsible for the adoption of environmental and social sustainability policies and for overseeing their full and faithful implementation by management. As a creation of the Board, the Panel plays a vital role in the process of ensuring that the Bank conducts its operations in compliance with Board-approved operational policies and procedures.

The commitment to independence and impartiality is also evidenced across the World Bank Group. For instance, the policy of the International Finance Corporation (IFC) and Multilateral Investment Guarantee Agency's (MIGA) IAM, the Compliance Advisor Ombudsman (CAO), emphasizes that "independence and impartiality are prerequisites to encourage stakeholders' trust and confidence in the CAO."[19]

The independence of the Panel is further bolstered by the process for appointing Panel members. While the President nominates the Panel members in consultation with the Board, their appointment rests with the Board itself. Similarly, when a request for inspection is received, the Chairperson of

19 World Bank Group, *IFC/MIGA Independent Accountability Mechanism (CAO) Policy* (June 28, 2021).

the Panel notifies the President and the Board. While management has the opportunity to respond to the request for inspection and the Panel may recommend an investigation, only the Board can authorize an investigation. If an investigation does go forward – either directly or after an opportunity for dispute resolution – the Panel's investigation report is limited to its findings on the Bank's compliance or non-compliance with the relevant operational policies and procedures of the institution. The 2020 Resolutions ensure a separation between the Panel's compliance role and the DRS. They clarify that the Panel has no role or opinion in the dispute resolution functions of the DRS and that the Panel independently performs its compliance functions. To further enhance the independence of the Panel, the role of the AM Secretary with respect to the Panel is limited to coordination with Panel members and the Chairperson. AM staff assigned to the Panel report to the AM Secretary only on administrative matters and to Panel members on the substance of technical matters.[20]

3.2 *The Role of the General Counsel and Legal Department*

The Bank's General Counsel (GC), and the Bank's Legal Vice Presidency more broadly, plays a key role in supporting the Bank's compliance with a wide range of policies, rules, and procedures across a wide range of operational and non-operational matters – including policies on environmental and social standards and accountability. Specifically, "[t]he Legal Vice Presidency …[helps] to ensure that all World Bank activities comply with the Institution's Articles of Agreement, policies, and procedures."[21] The General Counsel has a multi-faceted advisory role that covers the institution as a whole and is thus exercised independently of other functions and operations of the Bank in order to ensure objectivity and avoid undue influence.

Staff lawyers in the operational and policy units of the Legal Vice Presidency support teams across the institution to champion, strengthen, and faithfully comply with the institution's environmental and social policy framework and the accountability mechanism. They are responsible for drafting, reviewing, and negotiating financing agreements that require compliance with applicable environmental and social policies. They work with project teams and Bank management to ensure borrower compliance with applicable requirements during project planning and implementation. The lawyers also support task teams when addressing grievances raised by project-affected people, consistent

20 2020 AM Resolution, *supra* note 3, at Part II, para 8.

21 World Bank Group, *Legal Vice Presidency*, https://www.worldbank.org/en/about/unit/legal_vice_presidency (last visited Dec. 14, 2024).

with the Bank's environmental and social policies. In these respects, although the Legal Vice Presidency and the Panel have different roles, they share a common objective: supporting the Bank's compliance with its environmental and social policies and procedures across the full arc of project concept, design, preparation, implementation, and operation.

The Legal Vice Presidency advises the Panel and the AM Secretary "on matters related to the Bank's rights and obligations with respect to any request, whether it is addressed through dispute resolution or compliance review carried out by the Inspection Panel."[22] When the General Counsel advises the Panel or the Board on the Bank's obligations, the General Counsel's advice is available as needed but "with appropriate firewalls depending on the issue."[23] The "firewall" arrangement allows the General Counsel to advise the Panel with utmost impartiality and integrity, avoiding actual and perceived conflicts of interest. As my predecessor, Anne-Marie Leroy explained:

> Although the fact that the General Counsel is the legal advisor to both Management and the independent accountability and oversight entities does not ordinarily present a conflict of interest, there are situations in which other senior members of the Legal Vice Presidency are called upon to render legal advice in connection with such entities. For instance, a 'fire-wall' arrangement is usually observed in requests for advice on Inspection Panel matters. The General Counsel provides legal advice to the Inspection Panel and the Board on the Inspection Panel's scope, jurisdiction, and mandate. Another senior colleague in the Legal Vice Presidency assists Management in responding to requests for investigation by people claiming to have been harmed by Bank projects and addressing any legal or policy issues raised in them.[24]

The General Counsel's role differs from that of staff lawyers in several key respects. The General Counsel is the only senior management staff who has a direct line of responsibility to the Board of Executive Directors and is charged with supporting the Board's oversight, compliance, and accountability. As such, the Legal Vice Presidency and the General Counsel are important "lines

---

22 *Id.* at Part IV, para 17; *see also* 2020 Panel Resolution, *supra* note 1, at para. 16.

23 Anne-Marie Leroy, *The Institutional and Intellectual Role of the General Counsel: Perspectives from the World Bank*, in ASIF H. QURESHI & XUAN GAO, EDS., INTERNATIONAL ECONOMIC ORGANIZATIONS AND LAW: THE PERSPECTIVE AND ROLE OF THE LEGAL COUNSEL 51 (2012).

24 *Id.* at 58.

of defense" against the risks of non-compliance, risks that are further mitigated by a rigorous and effective accountability mechanism.[25]

The General Counsel's objectivity and integrity are further buttressed by the extraordinary requirement to publish the General Counsel's opinions:

> Management will also make available to the public opinions of the General Counsel related to Inspection Panel matters promptly after the Executive Directors have dealt with the issues involved, unless the Executive Directors decide otherwise in a specific case.[26]

Access to information policies of MDBs and IFIs, as well as national freedom of information laws and governmental rules routinely exempt legal opinions and advice from public disclosure in order to guide the free and candid flow of legal advice to facilitate compliance with policies and laws. In the accountability mechanism, however, the conscious decision was made that disclosure of the General Counsel's opinions will enhance stakeholder confidence and mitigate conflicts of interest – benefits that outweigh any risks to attorney-client privilege.

---

25 Compliance across a range of policies – including environmental and social safeguards policies – is buttressed by redundancies spread across different functions, project participants, and units. Each responsible party has an assigned role, and some of those roles intersect or overlap or – to some extent – duplicate the responsibilities of others. These successive "lines of defense" are created in order to take account of system complexity, risks of reliability, and the likelihood of failure or non-compliance. These lines of defense essentially presume that, at some point, some level of failure is inevitable, especially when considering the nature of the Bank's work, the jurisdictions where it conducts operations, and the capacity of clients, institutions, and systems involved. In the case of environmental and social safeguards, the first and primary responsibility for implementation and compliance rests with the borrowing client. The MDB takes steps to confirm the client's capacity to identify risks, to adopt and execute plans to avoid or mitigate those risks, and to maintain adequate systems to report and handle problems that arise despite those efforts and systems. In this ecosystem, the client is the "first line of defense" against policy failure. Bank operations teams can verify or provide assistance to enhance a client's capacity, advise the client on its responsibilities, and monitor the client's reporting and compliance during the loan term. In this sense, the Bank's team is a "second line of defense." If, notwithstanding these systems' redundancies, a failure to comply occurs, then the Panel, the Legal Vice Presidency, and the Board of Executive Directors fulfill additional roles, thereby providing additional "lines of defense" aimed at ensuring policy compliance or appropriate redress for harms. While duplications of overlapping responsibilities create obvious inefficiencies, the ESF reflects a considered decision that the benefits of reduced risk outweigh the costs of some redundancy.

26 2020 Panel Resolution, *supra* note 1, at para. 58.

3.3 *Greater Access While Safeguarding Confidentiality in the Age of Technological Disruption*

The Resolution establishing the Panel sets out a relatively low threshold to submit a request. It may be submitted by two or more individuals or "a community of persons such as an organization, association, society or other groupings of individuals," by the local representative of such party, or by another representative in the exceptional cases where the party submitting the request contends that appropriate representation is not locally available, and the Executive Directors so agree at the time they consider the request for inspection.[27]

However, even with this low eligibility threshold, indigenous communities and other vulnerable communities in places that lack access to technology may still face a challenge in accessing the Panel. In this context, such communities receive important support from accountability stakeholders such as NGOs that have historically paid close attention to the Bank's work and can lend vital support and advice to assist communities in navigating the IAM.

Effective use of information and communication technologies can play a vital role in the accountability process. Access to information, internet technologies, mobile phones, emailing, and teleconference services have strengthened the communication of requests, fact-finding, evidence-gathering, and other aspects of the accountability process. Today, the world is on the verge of a technological revolution with the advent of generative artificial intelligence (AI) that holds the potential to transform and accelerate development impact and organizational efficiency.

While AI technology offers potentially enormous benefits as its disruptive impacts increasingly reshape the digital world, it also poses risks that may not be understood fully. AI-generated opportunities for building awareness and enabling greater access for communities and individuals to accountability mechanisms also have underlying risks, such as compromising confidentiality and amplifying inequalities. Digital and technological advancement should therefore be approached as a new transparency and accountability challenge for the Panel and the Bank. Perhaps the question to ask for the future is to what extent technological measures and interventions will undermine accountability processes while enhancing their efficiency.[28] It is worth remembering that "technology use can only amplify existing human [and institutional] capacity

27 2020 Panel Resolution, *supra* note 1, at para. 13.

28 Francesco Gualdi & Antonio Cordella, *Artificial Intelligence and Decision-Making: The Question of Accountability*, Proceedings of the 54th Hawaii International Conference on System Sciences (2021).

and intent: it cannot act as a substitute where human [and institutional] capacity and intent do not exist."[29]

The 2016 World Development Report (WDR), *Digital Dividends*, notes that while technology promises to make the world more inclusive, technological opportunities and benefits remain "unavailable, inaccessible and unaffordable to a majority of the world's population."[30] It is therefore essential to ask how the Bank and the Panel can best maximize technological opportunities to reduce information inequality and empower the communities we work with, especially those facing the greatest geographical or social marginalization. The objective should always be to help such communities access information on Bank operations that have the potential to impact them. Information on the preparation, appraisal, and implementation of Bank operations is *sine qua non* to the effectiveness of the accountability mechanisms and for overall transparency and accountability in development.

3.4 *Harmonization and More Cooperative Approaches among MDBs and IFIs to Improve Development Outcomes and Address Harm*

MDBs and IFIs have differing memberships, institutional mandates, purposes, and strategies. The different regional focuses and shareholdings of different MDBs bring different viewpoints and priorities from stakeholders from different cultural, social, religious, economic, and development perspectives. And, while MDBs constantly confer and keep abreast of the policies and priorities of each other, each remains fiercely independent and best-positioned to determine what mix of policy prescriptions is best suited to their missions, regions, strategies, and clients' development priorities. Such an atmosphere breeds competition and innovation but makes efforts at harmonization vexing. This means that, while they share a common goal of financing development, their approaches to development financing and institutional accountability vary in scope, mandate, and operational procedures. However, over the past few years, MDBs and IFIs have pursued opportunities for harmonization to bridge gaps, enhance efficiency, and improve the effectiveness of international development financing and its results. At the same time, MDBs are working more determinedly than ever at finding more and better ways to collaborate, recognizing that, by joining forces and pooling resources, they can achieve results that are impossible to reach separately. Collaboration leverages

29 Kevin Hernandez & Tony Roberts, *Leaving No One Behind in a Digital World*, Emerging Issues Report, Institute of Development Studies, 6 (Nov. 2018).

30 World Bank, *World Development Report 2016: Digital Dividends*, 6–8 (2016).

strengths, fills knowledge gaps, and drives innovation that enables more and better outcomes.

The Paris Declaration on Aid Effectiveness (Paris Declaration) was adopted in 2005 and endorsed by the 2008 Accra Agenda for Action (Accra Agenda) by countries and other key stakeholders in international development cooperation, including the World Bank, as a partnership commitment to harmonizing development procedures, reducing duplication, and enhancing mutual accountability and transparency in development cooperation.[31] While the Paris Declaration and the Accra Agenda do not specifically address the role of accountability mechanisms, harmonization is needed across development work generally, including the handling of project-related grievances.

When MDBs and/or IFIs co-finance a project, they should actively explore the "common approaches" discussed below to environmental and social risk management as already envisioned – but not realized – in the ESF. Beyond that, MDBs and IFIs should continue to pursue harmonization of environmental and social standards, including those related to accountability.[32] Too often, borrowers – particularly borrowers in the poorest countries and in FCV situations or otherwise lacking capacity – struggle to understand, implement, and comply with environmental and social standards that vary between different IFIs co-financing a project. This also presents challenges for local communities in seeking access to the accountability mechanisms of these financiers. Harmonized standards, requirements, and processes would facilitate borrowers' understanding and therefore enhance compliance and the access of communities to grievance redress services, ultimately producing greater efficiency and better results for the lenders, borrowers, communities, civil society, boards of directors, and the goals of sustainable development generally.

Multilateral efforts to harmonize standards across a wide range of IFIs have yielded some progress over the past decade, but more work is needed. Under the ESF, for example, the borrower may apply a common set of environmental and social requirements agreeable to the government and the joint project lenders – known as a "common approach" – provided that this approach enables the project to achieve objectives materially consistent with the Bank's environmental and social standards.[33] Other mechanisms that have often allowed for even simpler approaches include trust funds, co-financing, or other agreements or accreditation mechanisms that allow the channeling of multiple

31 Organisation for Economic Co-operation and Development, *Paris Declaration on Aid Effectiveness* (2005) [hereinafter "Paris Declaration"].

32 *See* World Bank, *World Bank Environmental and Social Policy for Investment Project Financing, in* THE WORLD BANK ENVIRONMENTAL AND SOCIAL FRAMEWORK (ESF), 5 (2017).

33 *Id*; *see also* Paris Declaration, *supra* note 31, at para. 9.

sources of donor financing through a single MDB or IFI, and the application of the institution's single set of environmental and social standards to the entire co-financed project. More generally, as MDBs have updated their respective environmental and social policies, they have drawn inspiration from each other and organically coalesced around a common core of good international practice.

Still, greater efforts and faster harmonization are needed but are difficult to achieve, because, to a degree, different environmental and social requirements partially find their roots in each institution's specific structure and mandate, which can sometimes be difficult to align with those of other institutions. Short of a truly global and common set of standards, more pragmatic but meaningful reforms can be pursued. MDBs should sharpen their focus and renew their resolve toward cooperative approaches in order to meet the challenges of the *polycrises* and the need for more urgent and effective delivery with better compliance and accountability.

One such approach is the concept of "mutual reliance" by which two MDBs that are co-financing a project would agree among themselves and the borrower that the policies of one of the lenders – not both – would apply. The World Bank has agreed to use a mutual approach to the procurement systems in projects with the International Fund for Agricultural Development (IFAD), Asian Development Bank (ADB), Inter-American Development Bank (IADB), and Carribean Development Bank (CDB).[34]

Taking that concept forward, the World Bank and ADB agreed in February 2025 to launch a "Full Mutual Reliance Framework" (FMRF) under which the two banks and the borrower would agree that one bank – either the World Bank or ADB – would be designated "lead lender" and the other would be "trail lender." The lead lender would take the lead and be responsible for all aspects of project design, preparation, appraisal, supervision, completion, and evaluation of the co-financed project, and the lead lender's policy requirements would apply, including policies on procurement, anti-corruption, environmental and social standards, and accountability. While FMRF would not be suitable and would not be applied to all WB-ADB co-financed projects, the application of FMRF is expected to achieve significant benefits:

- FMRF would respond to borrowers' complaints that dealing with MDBs is cumbersome, time-consuming, and expensive – and more so when dealing with two or more MDBs in co-financings. FMRF would eliminate duplicative and potentially confusing policy requirements, assessments, instruments, monitoring, reporting, and integrity and accountability processes. It would

34 *See e.g.*, World Bank Group, *Joint Statement of IFAD and World Bank on the Signature of the Procurement Framework Agreement* (Sep. 25, 2023).

therefore enhance the quality of compliance and promote greater focus on development impact by facilitating the borrower's understanding of streamlined fiduciary obligations.
- FMRF would reduce processing times and overall project costs for borrowers, while maintaining the application of rigorous policy standards.
- FMRF would also refocus MDBs' efforts and resources toward more value-added efforts at development outcomes and eliminate unnecessary, duplicative work. The trail lender would invest less time and staff resources on the co-financed operations, thus reducing costs.
- FMRF would also address shareholders', borrowers', and stakeholders' calls for greater collaboration among development partners and better coordination among MDBs.
- FMRF would respond to the G20 Leaders Roadmap Towards Better, Bigger, and More Effective MDBs;[35] calls of the G20 Independent Experts Group for MDBs; the report to the Development Committee of the WB;[36] and the joint statement of ten MDBs, themselves, to "deepen collaboration" to deliver as an "MDB system."[37]
- FMRF would strengthen the concept of a global benchmark across a range of policies, set by two of the most widely respected development institutions in the world and thereby promote a "race-to-the-top" across MDBs to improve their policies and capacity in order to match best practices and enable participation in the "club" of mutual reliance.

But full mutual reliance works only where three preconditions are met:
- First, both institutions must have policies that are substantially aligned. The policies do not have to be fully harmonized in the sense that they are identical in every detail. But their policies must share the suite of principal objectives and include terms that ensure their application in similar fashion.
- Second, both lenders must have the institutional capacity to fully and faithfully implement those policies – meaning they have the staffing, expertise, and resources required.
- Third, both institutions must have a track record of implementation that instills stakeholder confidence – including the confidence of the two lenders and their Boards of Directors, borrowers, and civil society.

---

35 Council of European Development Bank, *G20 Leaders Roadmap Towards Better, Bigger, and More Effective MDBs* (G20, Brasil) Oct. 2024.

36 World Bank Inspection Panel, *Resolution No. IBRD 2020–0005 Resolution No. IDA 2020–0004* (Sept. 8, 2020).

37 World Bank, *Multilateral Development Banks Deepen Collaboration to Deliver as a System* (April 20, 2024).

Where applied, the trail lender in a co-financing under FMRF will still have an important role. The trail lender will have to review the proposed project to ensure it is aligned with the country partnership framework, meets the strategic needs of the borrower and the trail lenders' sectoral strategies and requirements, and permits the trail lender a "voice at the table" even though the decision-making remains with the lead lender.

All complaints related to the co-financed operation – including complaints about non-compliance with environmental and social policies, procurement policies, and allegations of fraud or corruption – would be handled by the lead lender in accordance with its policies and procedures, including through responsible independent accountability systems.

With respect specifically to the accountability mechanisms, the inspection function of the lead lender would apply because – logically – only the lead lenders' compliance function has the expertise to review the lead lender's compliance with its own policies. But, as with the role of the trail lender, the trail lender's inspection function would be expected to observe the implementation of the IAM by the lead lender's inspection function.

In any case, the main purpose of the IAMs must be ensured: that people and communities affected by the operations of the lenders have an independent, impartial, and expert forum where they can bring their concerns and be confident that those concerns will be handled through a reliably effective and efficient compliance and disputes resolution process.

Collaboration between the Bank's Accountability Mechanism and the IAMs of other IFIs is another area for enhancing accountability through cooperation and harmonization. Currently, there are approximately twenty-three AMs linked to different MDBs and IFIs, and together they are part of the Independent Accountability Mechanisms Network (IAMnet), a partnership dedicated to building institutional capacity on accountability and transparency;[38] since 2016, its Secretariat has been hosted by the World Bank.

Collaboration between AMs is an added-value for accountability, especially when a request for inspection relating to a co-financed project is simultaneously submitted to the Panel and the AMs of other MDBs and IFIs. In such circumstances, the Panel has in its Operating Procedures emphasized that it "will make its best efforts to coordinate with the accountability mechanism(s) of co-financier(s) to process the complaints in the most efficient and effective

38 World Bank, *Independent Accountability Mechanisms Network (IAMnet)*, https://www.worldbank.org/en/programs/accountability/iamnet (last visited Dec. 15, 2024).

way possible."[39] The Procedures recognize that this can only be realized if the activities in this area are based on principles of collaboration and cooperation; take place within the requirements and constraints of the Panel's purpose and mandate as set out in its Resolutions, rules, and procedures; and occur without affecting its independent and impartial compliance functions or the requirements of confidentiality and disclosure of information.

3.5 *Dispute Resolution and Compliance Functions*

While the Bank's focus on independent accountability through compliance dates back to 1993, its approach to accountability through dispute resolution is relatively new. In 2015, the Bank created and operationalized the GRS, a management-led process to enhance the Bank's commitment to transparency and accountability by providing "a clear entry point, process and platform for individuals and communities to raise concerns directly to Management on environmental and social issues related to Bank-financed Operations."[40] The GRS rests on the Bank's increasing recognition that genuine resolution of complaints is key to increasing accountability and credibility.[41] This broadly refers to the resolution of disputes in a timely, efficient, and effective manner, such as by encouraging the speedy handling of complaints at all levels – including through project-level grievance mechanisms and through corporate mechanisms such as the GRS.[42] This is meant to complement the Panel's work and to add value to accountability within the Bank by promptly responding to concerns that arise in the course of project implementation.[43]

While it is management-led, the GRS is functionally separate from the units that oversee Bank operations. This allows the GRS to provide dispute resolution support to Bank teams and a degree of independence and accountability to communities bringing their grievances to the attention of the Bank. The objective of the GRS is to facilitate communication between all parties involved in a complaint, including all relevant Bank units, Bank task teams, borrower implementing agencies, and complainants, "to determine the most

---

39 The World Bank Inspection Panel, *Inspection Panel Operating Procedures*. para. 72 (Dec. 2022).

40 World Bank, Bank Directive, *Grievance Redress Service* (GRS), (May 5, 2021) (setting out the mandate and functions of the GRS).

41 World Bank Group, *Safeguards and Sustainability Policies in a Changing World: An Independent Evaluation of World Bank Group Experience*, XVIII (2010) [hereinafter "2010 IEG study"].

42 The GRS is housed in the World Bank's Operations Policy and Country Services (OPCS) Vice Presidency.

43 *Id; see also* 2010 IEG study, *supra* note 41, at page XXIX.

adequate problem-solving approach (mediation, conciliation, fact-finding, etc.) to effectively and efficiently address the issues raised."[44] For the fiscal year ending June 30, 2023, the GRS received a total of 538 (admissible and inadmissible) complaints.[45] While this huge number of cases can be considered alarming, it is also an indication of the GRS's potential to receive and resolve issues – large and small – that arise in Bank-supported operations. It has also allowed Bank management to garner lessons and experiences from these grievances and to enhance Bank operations and accountability.

3.6 *Non-Compliance, Risk, and Harm*

Another challenge underscoring the AM processes is the misconception that an MDB will refrain from meaningful corrective action with respect to harm or the risk of harm in a community unless and until an inspection process produces a report that finds (1) a serious non-compliance by the MDB with its policies and procedures and (2) that such non-compliance resulted in or contributed to harm to affected parties. Experience has shown that MDBs generally take any allegations of harm seriously and take action, with or without the shadow of an independent accountability process looming.

At the World Bank, management makes considerable efforts through various mechanisms to minimize risks, prevent harm, and take corrective action where needed, including through regular project supervision, third party monitoring arrangements, requirements for borrowers to operate grievance mechanisms, and the aforementioned availability of the GRS. The recent creation of the DRS, as part of the World Bank's AM, introduced an additional independent avenue through which harm can be addressed without a finding of serious non-compliance.[46] Moreover, Management carefully considers necessary measures to mitigate the risk of harm or to identify corrective measures in relation to requests for inspection, even where the Panel does not end up making

---

44 2010 IEG study, *supra* note 41.

45 *See* World Bank, *Annual Report FY23 Grievance Redress Service* (2023) https://documents1.worldbank.org/curated/en/099543501102413057/pdf/IDU1dc5583d21f56b143ad19c4116 77673173c42.pdf (last visisted Jan. 26, 2025). A GRS complaint is admissible when it 1) relates to a World Bank-financed project that is under preparation, is active, or has been closed for less than fifteen months; 2) is submitted by individuals or communities affected by a World Bank-supported project, or by their authorized representative; and 3) alleges that the project has caused or is likely to cause harm. The GRS considers the complaint inadmissible if the complaint 1) is procurement-related; 2) alleges fraud and/or corruption; 3) pertains to IFC, MIGA, or other IFI-supported projects; 4) concerns employment or the pursuit of employment with the World Bank; or 5) is frivolous or anonymous.

46 2020 AM Resolution, *supra* note 3, at para. 11.

a formal finding of non-compliance. These "no-fault" mechanisms are utilized by the World Bank to respond to risks and harm that arise in its supported operations on a regular basis.

The assumption that a finding of non-compliance that is linked to harm is required for an MDB to take remedial action puts pressures on the MDB, the AM inspection function, and complainants that casts the compliance review process in an accusatory and unnecessarily contentious footing. This assumption can also give the compliance review function the appearance of a police and prosecution process and can drive MDBs' staff to assume a defensive mindset and posture – all of which can be exacerbated by legal concerns that a public finding by an institution's AM to the effect that the MDB's violations of policies caused harm is fraught with legal risk. The non-compliance/harm assumption also raises the bar for affected people and civil society, and may pressure an institution's AM to find links between non-compliance and harm that are not always obvious or practical. This, in turn, may raise MDB shareholder concerns that an AM may be pushing the boundaries of its mandate in order to meet a non-compliance/harm threshold. Worse, the adversarial atmosphere that sometimes surrounds the inspection process and the concerns regarding legal risks impede optimal levels of cooperation between MDB staff, the AM, and the affected communities.

In some situations, MDBs and IFIs may lack the means or mandate to enable redress of all harms that may occur in projects, especially those that arise from no fault or contribution by the MDB or IFI. However, in some cases of this nature, mechanisms similar to the Bank Management-led GRS or the recently created independent DRS may prove especially fruitful in going beyond such limitations and may enable the parties in conflict to find constructive and efficient avenues to redress harm.

In sum, MDBs and IFIs can and should establish multi-prong, multi-tool, and multi-institutional approaches to address harm and the risk of harm in order to deliver vitally and urgently needed projects in an environmentally and socially responsible way. Other MDBs that do not already have avenues like the World Bank's GRS and DRS, should continue to consider ways of addressing allegations of harm through "no-fault" approaches. A certain level of tension in the accountability processes is inevitable and can be healthy. But there may be an equilibrium between tension and contention that produces better results more efficiently.

4 Final Thoughts

Accountability in development is more important than ever, especially as calls are growing for the World Bank to evolve to tackle some of the world's toughest global challenges. Ongoing overlapping crises such as climate change, fragility, debt, and pandemics warrant action by both the public and private sectors and coordination across World Bank Group institutions and other MDBs.[47] At the same time, MDBs' expanded development priorities require operations that present higher degrees of risk in circumstances of fragility, conflict, violence, and low-capacity project counterparties. It is the perfect storm: polycrises and spillover effects, challenging projects and challenging circumstances, in an atmosphere of greater ambition to do more, do better, and do faster. This challenging landscape underscores the need for independent and effective AMs. As the Bank evolves its vision and mission to strengthen development financing and development impact, strategies and implementation plans will need to prioritize accountability.[48] What we have learned from the last thirty years can guide the evolution of the Bank and its AM. As we aim for the next thirty years of effective development financing and improved accountability, there is no doubt that independent accountability mechanisms remain a vital cornerstone of effective, transparent, and responsible sustainable development, but must continue to strive for greater effectiveness and efficiency to meet the challenges of an increasingly urgent development agenda.

Bibliography

Council Of European Development Bank. *G20 Leaders Roadmap Towards Better, Bigger, and More Effective MDBs*. Rio de Janeiro: G20 Brasil, October 2024.

Gualdi, Francesco, and Antonio Cordella. "Artificial Intelligence and Decision-Making: The Question of Accountability." *Proceedings of the 54th Hawaii International Conference on System Sciences*. Manoa: University of Hawaii, 2021.

Hernandez, Kevin, and Tony Roberts. "Leaving No One Behind in a Digital World." *Emerging Issues Report, Institute of Development Studies*, 6 (November 2018).

Leroy, Anne-Marie. "The Institutional and Intellectual Role of the General Counsel: Perspectives from the World Bank," *International Economic Organizations and Law: The Perspective and Role of the Legal Counsel*, edited by Asif H. Qureshi and Xuan Gao, 51. Netherlands: Kluwer Law International, 2012.

Organisation for Economic Co-operation and Development [OECD]. *Paris Declaration on Aid Effectiveness*. Paris: OECD, 2005.

Shihata, Ibrahim. "Issues Related to the Inspection Panel," in *The World Bank Legal Papers*. Leiden: Brill, 2001: 611.

47 World Bank Group, *Evolving the World Bank Group's Mission, Operations, and Resources: A Roadmap* (Dec. 18, 2022).

48 *Id.*

Umaña, Alvaro. *The World Bank Inspection Panel: The First Four Years (1994–1998)*. Washington DC: The World Bank, 1998: 3.

World Bank. *World Development Report 2016: Digital Dividends*. Washington DC: World Bank, 2016: 6–8.

World Bank. "World Bank Environmental and Social Policy for Investment Project Financing" in *The World Bank Environmental and Social Framework*. Washington DC: World Bank, 2017: 5.

World Bank. *Annual Report FY23 Grievance Redress Service*. Washington DC: The World Bank, 2023. https://documents1.worldbank.org/curated/en/099543501102413057/pdf/IDU1dc5583d21f56b143ad19c4116776731.

World Bank. *Independent Accountability Mechanisms Network (IAMnet)*. Accessed December 15, 2024. https://www.worldbank.org/en/programs/accountability/iamnet.

World Bank Bank Directive. *Grievance Redress Service (GRS)*. Washington DC: World Bank, May 5, 2021. https://www.worldbank.org/en/projects-operations/products-and-services/grievance-redress-service.

World Bank Group. *Safeguards and Sustainability Policies in a Changing World: An Independent Evaluation of World Bank Group Experience*, IEG Study Series. Washington DC: World Bank, 2010: xviii.

World Bank Group. *Report and Recommendations on the Inspection Panel's Toolkit Review*. Washington DC: March 5, 2020.

World Bank Group. *IFC/MIGA Independent Accountability Mechanism (CAO) Policy*. Washington DC: World Bank, June 28, 2021.

World Bank Group. *Evolving the World Bank Group's Mission, Operations, and Resources: A Roadmap*. Washington DC: World Bank, December 18, 2022.

World Bank Group. *Joint Statement of IFAD and World Bank on the Signature of the Proccurment Frameowrk Agreement*. Washington DC: World Bank, September 25, 2023.

World Bank Group. *Grievance Redress Service*. Accessed December 14, 2024. https://www.worldbank.org/en/projects-operations/products-and-services/grievance-redress-service.

World Bank Group. *Legal Vice Presidency*. Accessed December 14, 2024.

World Bank Group, *Report and Recommendations on the Inspection Panel's Toolkit Review* (March 5, 2020).

World Bank Inspection Panel. *Resolution No. IBRD 93–10 and Resolution No. IDA 93–6*. Washington DC: World Bank, September 22, 1993.

World Bank Inspection Panel. *Review of the Resolution Establishing the Inspection Panel: 1996 Clarification of Certain Aspects of the Resolution*. Washington DC: World Bank, May 9, 1996.

World Bank Inspection Panel. *The 1999 Clarification of the Board's Second Review of the Inspection Panel*. Washington DC: World Bank, October 17, 1999.

World Bank Inspection Panel. *Resolution No. IBRD 2020–0004 and Resolution No. IDA 2020–0003*. Washington DC: World Bank, September 8, 2020.

World Bank Inspection Panel. *Resolution No. IBRD 2020–0005 and Resolution No. IDA 2020–0004: The World Bank Accountability Mechanism*. Washington DC: World Bank, September 8, 2020.

World Bank Inspection Panel. *Inspection Panel Operating Procedures*. Washington DC: World Bank, December 2022: para. 72.

World Bank Inspection Panel. *Panel Cases Data*. Accessed December 14, 2024. https://www.inspectionpanel.org/panel-cases/data.

CHAPTER 22

IMF Human Rights Accountability: A Pragmatic Way to Break the Deadlock

*Aldo Caliari**

1 Introduction

In the three decades since the 1993 establishment of the World Bank Inspection Panel (the Panel), almost all international finance institutions (IFIs) have established analogous panels, ombudsperson offices, or other independent accountability mechanisms (IAMs) to allow people who believe they have been harmed by the IFIs' activities to directly trigger processes of fact-finding, dispute resolution, and, if applicable, redress. The primary exception has been the International Monetary Fund (IMF).

This article proposes the creation of an expert panel on the human rights dimensions of IMF programs, as an avenue similar to the IAMs of other IFIs for individuals affected by IMF policies. The article begins with a brief context on the history and debates surrounding the human rights obligations of the Bretton Woods Institutions, particularly the IMF. It then examines the relevance of human rights to a number of IMF areas of purview, whether the traditional ones or the expanded range of issues in member countries that the IMF covers today, including social spending, inequality, and climate change. The final part proposes an expert panel to address human rights impacts of IMF activities, designed to reflect differences between the IMF and other IFIs and serve as a practical means of advancing the deadlocked debate on the IMF's accountability for human rights.

2 The Debate over the IMF's Human Rights Obligations

In 2003, a group of experts drafted the *Tilburg Guiding Principles on the World Bank, IMF and Human Rights* to codify the obligations of the IMF and other

* Aldo Caliari is the Senior Director of Policy and Strategy at Jubilee USA Network. He previously served as the Senior Advisor at the Intergovernmental Group of 24 on International Monetary Affairs and Development (G–24) and directed the Rethinking Bretton Woods Project at the Center of Concern.

DOI:10.1163/9789004729735_029

Bretton Woods Institutions under international human rights law.[1] Twenty years later, none of the institutions, including the IMF, appear to be any closer to agreeing that they have such obligations.[2]

The scholarly work that attributes human rights responsibilities to the IMF rests on three main lines of argument.[3] First, as a subject of international law with its own legal personality, the IMF is bound by general rules of international law, including international human rights law. Second, international organizations are governed by their member countries, and these members are bound by international human rights law. They should not be allowed to do through their organizations what they are not allowed to do on their own. Third, the IMF is a specialized agency of the United Nations. The relationship agreement linking the institution to the United Nations emphasizes – as is the case for the World Bank – the independent status of the agency. However, this does not mean it is exempted from obligations arising from the UN Charter, including those relating to human rights.

Nevertheless, the IMF denies having such obligations. The closest reference to an official IMF definition regarding its obligations under human rights law is found in a 2005 paper by former IMF General Counsel Francois Gianviti.[4] Referring to the International Covenant on Economic, Social, and Cultural Rights, but on grounds that could extend to other human rights instruments, the paper contends that the Covenant does not apply to the IMF.[5] The three lines of argument are that:

> the IMF is not a party to the Covenant; the obligations imposed by the Covenant apply only to States, not to international organizations; and the Covenant, in its Article 24, explicitly recognizes that "[n]othing in the present Covenant shall be interpreted as impairing the provisions ...

1 WILLEM VAN GENUGTEN, PAUL HUNT & SUSAN MATHEWS, EDS., WORLD BANK, IMF AND HUMAN RIGHTS (2003).

2 UN Human Rights Council, *Report of the Special Rapporteur on extreme poverty and human rights*, A/HRC/38/33 (2018).

3 Daniel D. Bradlow, *The World Bank, the IMF and Human Rights*, 6 TRANSNATIONAL L. & CONTEMPORARY PROBLEMS 46 (1996); SIGRUN I. SKOGLY, THE HUMAN RIGHTS OBLIGATIONS OF THE WORLD BANK AND THE INTERNATIONAL MONETARY FUND (2001); MAC DARROW, BETWEEN LIGHT AND SHADOW: THE WORLD BANK, THE INTERNATIONAL MONETARY FUND AND INTERNATIONAL HUMAN RIGHTS LAW (2005); VAN GENUGTEN, *supra* note 1.

4 Francois Gianviti. *Economic, Social and Cultural Rights and the International Monetary Fund*. 3 CURRENT DEVELOPMENTS IN MONETARY AND FINANCIAL LAW (2009).

5 Yet, Gianviti argues, the IMF contributes to the conditions for the realization of rights set out in the Covenant. *Id.* at 43.

> of the constitutions of the specialized agencies which define the respective responsibilities ... of the specialized agencies in regard to the matters dealt with in the present Covenant."[6]

A main thread running through Gianviti's paper is that the IMF is a monetary, not a development, agency. Gianviti shares the story that, back in the 1950s when the UN Commission on Human Rights started the work that would lead to the Covenant, it invited the IMF to take part in the deliberations. The IMF "took the position that the questions raised in the elaboration of the Covenant were outside its own mandate."[7]

This may have been a defensible position in the early years of the IMF, when it limited its interventions to a few macroeconomic variables – money supply, inflation, budget deficits – in a context of fixed exchange rates.[8] But the transition to a flexible exchange rate system meant that multiple other variables could potentially have a bearing on how a country achieved stability. IMF monitoring, conditions, and policy advice could address – and over the years have addressed – issues such as *inter alia,* labor, agriculture, defense spending, corruption, poverty reduction, and health and social safety nets.[9]

3 Expansion of the IMF's Work on Inequality, Inclusiveness, and Climate Change

The last decade has seen a further expansion and codification of the IMF's remit beyond its core traditional areas. With the growing recognition that distributional issues affect sustainability of growth and macroeconomic stability, the IMF has expanded its work on inequality, inclusive growth, and jobs. In 2018, it issued a guidance note to operationalize inequality issues in country work, following more than forty country pilot experiences.[10]

In 2019, the institution released a strategy for engagement on social spending, reflecting its increased work on the subject. The strategy also responded to an IMF Independent Evaluation Office report on social protection that found the work had been uneven and needed strengthening.[11] One new strategy seeks

6 *Id.* at 6, fn 9.
7 *Id.* at 3–4.
8 Bradlow, *supra* note 3.
9 *Id.*
10 International Monetary Fund, How *to Operationalize Inequality Issues in Country Work* (2018).
11 International Monetary Fund, *A Strategy for IMF Engagement on Social Spending* (2019).

to help IMF member countries foster resilient and inclusive economies by supporting them in addressing gender gaps and improving women's economic empowerment. Although references to gender in IMF documents were rare before 2013, the recently adopted *IMF Strategy towards Mainstreaming Gender* seeks to systematize and provide a basis for the institution's rising involvement in gender-related projects during the last decade.[12] More recently, growing understanding of the macroeconomic implications of climate change and rising demand from the membership led the IMF to adopt, in 2021, its first-ever *Strategy to Help Members Address Climate Change Related Policy Challenges.*[13]

The establishment of the Resilience and Sustainability Trust further reflected the IMF's engagement in climate, as well as health and potentially other issues. The creation of this trust responds to the members' interest in finding ways wealthier members could re-channel Special Drawing Rights – an IMF-issued reserve asset – to poorer members.[14] One of the innovative features of this trust is that it aims to address longer-term structural challenges that pose macroeconomic risk, such as climate change and pandemics.[15] Notably, the IMF has made important contributions in the last three years toward covering elements of the pandemic response, including vaccines and therapeutics.[16]

The growing awareness within the IMF of the multiple social and environmental fields affected by its mandate is a positive development. It also erases any doubt that today's IMF has traveled a long way from the purely monetary agency that Gianviti's paper described – although it is debatable whether the IMF ever fit that description. What is more important for the purpose of understanding the IMF's current human rights responsibilities is that the environmental and social issues into which the IMF is lately venturing are all, to different but significant degrees, squarely within the scope of application of human rights principles and standards.[17]

---

12 International Monetary Fund, *Strategy Towards Mainstreaming Gender* (2022).

13 International Monetary Fund, *IMF Strategy to Help Members Address Climate Change Related Policy Challenges: Priorities, Modes of Delivery, and Budget Implications* (2021).

14 Special Drawing Rights are a reserve asset the IMF can issue to complement reserves of member countries, provided certain global conditions are in place. In 2021, the IMF created $650 billion in SDRs, the largest allocation in the institution's history, to help members withstand the pandemic shock.

15 International Monetary Fund, *Managing Director Welcomes the Creation of the Resilience and Sustainability Trust to Help Vulnerable Countries Meet Longer Term Challenges* (2022).

16 International Monetary Fund, *A Proposal to End the COVID-19 Pandemic*, IMF Staff Discussion Note, SDN/2021/4 (2019).

17 Although climate may superficially appear to be the exception, it has important human rights dimensions. In fact, the IMF strategy refers to the social costs of natural disasters

4 Human Rights within the IMF's Mandate and Expertise

The IMF is not the expert institution on climate change, public health, the gender gap, or other environmental and social issues; only where the issues are critical to a country's macroeconomic stability – that is, for example, where they significantly influence present or prospective balance of payments or domestic stability – are the issues relevant to its activities. The need to demonstrate such "macro-criticality" is a threshold condition discussed for each of the topics of the IMF's expanded agenda.[18] Where the IMF recognizes the existence of such a macro-critical issue – an issue relevant to its operations but in which the IMF does not have expertise – the IMF's most recent *Guidance Note on Surveillance* instructs staff to analyze the issue drawing on the expertise of, and in collaboration with, external partners, but the staff "are not expected to provide policy advice."[19]

This approach is problematic in several ways. The "macro-critical" filter seems to place a robust check on the number of issues extraneous to the IMF's expertise that staff address. But this may not in fact be the case. On social spending, for example, a survey of mission chiefs conducted to inform the engagement strategy found that social spending was macro-critical in nearly 80 percent of countries and that 70 percent of mission chiefs reported providing policy advice in this area, a ratio even higher for developing countries. The strategy on climate change considers it "one the most critical macroeconomic policy challenges that the IMF's membership will face in the coming years and decades,"[20] seemingly heralding much more IMF input on the issue. Moreover, the surveillance guidance states that the determination of macro-criticality is country-specific and will depend, *inter alia*, on the members' income level, structural characteristics, and institutional capacity.[21]

In other words, the determination of whether the IMF should or should not address matters that may be directly covered by human rights legal standards is left with the IMF itself, on a country-by-country basis. If the IMF decides to

---

and the need for a "just transition." *See, e.g.*, UN Office of the High Commissioner for Human Rights, *Human Rights and Climate Change* (2009).

18 International Monetary Fund, *Guidance Note for Surveillance under Article IV Consultations* (2022).

19 *Id.*

20 International Monetary Fund, *IMF Strategy to Help Members Address Climate Change Related Policy Challenges: Priorities, Modes of Delivery, and Budget Implications* (2021).

21 International Monetary Fund, *Guidance Note for Surveillance under Article IV Consultations* (2022).

address such matters, the choice of which partner agencies it should consult and how to incorporate their input, also rests with the IMF.

While these "new" areas of IMF interest provide the starkest examples of human rights relevance, the human rights implications of policies more obviously within the IMF's jurisdiction and expertise – that is, fiscal, macro-financial, monetary, external, and macro-structural – also deserve consideration. At present, there is no formal channel by which the IMF can receive input from human rights bodies when policies within its natural realm reach what could be called "rights-criticality" – including, for example, when IMF policies exacerbate climate change, gender gaps, or health crises.

5 A Path Forward

Twenty years after the *Tilburg Principles*, it is not easy to see a way out of the deadlocked exchanges of legal arguments for and against the human rights obligations of the IMF. But human rights were enshrined in law to protect the most vulnerable against abuse of power. The simple fact remains that the average person has a hard time digesting the notion that one of the most powerful international organizations does not feel bound by any sense of duty towards human rights. More so, that difficulty is exacerbated if that person lives in an IMF-program country where the institution is seen – justifiably or not – as having significant influence on the economic policies the government adopts. Given that the IMF recognizes environmental and social issues can be a result of macroeconomic policies and a barrier to macroeconomic stability, providing avenues for human rights assessments and accountability should not necessarily be driven by legal interpretations, but by a desire to lift the positive impact of the IMF's work in what it now recognizes is a more complex environment, and ensure the durability, legitimacy, and effectiveness of the policy reforms it promotes.

6 A Proposed Human Rights Panel for the IMF

In that spirit, the creation of an expert panel on the human rights dimensions of IMF programs could make a major contribution to embedding human rights in the policies and programs of the organization. The panel would be independent from the IMF and take complaints from individuals or groups who allege adverse human rights impacts from an IMF loan or program implemented by their government in contradiction with the human rights obligations of their country. The panel could also be available at the IMF's own initiative to identify and investigate such potentially adverse impacts.

Panel members would have economic and human rights backgrounds and examine the claims and potential alternatives that, in the context of that program, could better align with the country's human rights commitments. Its recommendations would be made public but would be non-binding. They would be provided to those staff with responsibility for the particular country. Every year, a compilation of cases would be presented to the Board along with recommendations that would give them the opportunity to consider implications for future programs and policies.

This pragmatic design sidesteps the need to take a position on the ongoing debate over whether the IMF has legal obligations under international human rights law. There is no illusion about the complexity of the many thorny issues that the creation of such a panel would still need to navigate, for example, composition, staffing, requirements for complaints, process, etc. In other respects, however, by explicitly making the institution non-binding and by staying anchored to concrete cases in a bottom-up way, it avoids the unending debate and wordsmithing that would dog attempts to come up with general definitions first. By staying focused on the obligations that a particular country already undertook, it would avoid the unwieldy task of having to define specific obligations applicable to the IMF and all its members.

The expectation is that such an approach would, over time, yield a number of cases that begin to form a body of knowledge on how to incorporate human rights into IMF policies. By helping flag prescriptions that are most commonly questioned from a human rights perspective, they could provide to the IMF a "heat map" of "rights critical" areas where more systematic work on making IMF policies compatible with human rights is needed.

It would also be a space for joint learning. Volumes have been written reflecting the many ways human rights and economic expert analyses differ;[22] this panel would break down the silos, offering a space where such experts can put their heads together to find solutions that might elude their different communities working alone. The requirement to collaborate could be an antidote to the group-think that otherwise inescapably pervades each discipline when addressing the other.

Amidst multiple crises and the reversals in development gains of the last few years, mechanisms to protect human rights of those most vulnerable to

---

22 *But see* International Council on Human Rights Policy, *Human Rights in the Global Economy: Report from a Colloquium* (2010).

IMF programs cannot wait for more decades of clever legal debate. It is time to break the deadlock.

Bibliography

Bradlow, Daniel. "The World Bank, the IMF and Human Rights." *Transnational Law and Contemporary Problems*, 6 (1996): 46.

Darrow, Mac. *Between Light and Shadow: The World Bank, the International Monetary Fund and International Human Rights Law*. Oxford: Hart Publishing, 2005.

Gianviti, Francois. "Economic, Social and Cultural Rights and the International Monetary Fund." *Current Developments in Monetary and Financial Law*, 3 (2009).

International Council on Human Rights. *Human Rights in the Global Economy: Report from a Colloquium*. Geneva: United Nations, 2010.

International Monetary Fund [IMF]. *How to Operationalize Inequality Issues in Country Work*. Washington DC: IMF, 2018.

IMF. *A Proposal to End the COVID-19 Pandemic*, IMF Staff Discussion Note, SDN/2021/4. Washington DC: IMF, 2019.

IMF. *A Strategy for IMF Engagement on Social Spending*. Washington DC: IMF, 2019.

IMF. *IMF Strategy to Help Members Address Climate Change Related Policy Challenges: Priorities, Modes of Delivery, and Budget Implications*. Washington DC: IMF, 2021.

IMF. *Guidance Note for Surveillance under Article IV Consultations*. Washington DC: IMF, 2022.

IMF. *Managing Director Welcomes the Creation of the Resilience and Sustainability Trust to Help Vulnerable Countries Meet Longer Term Challenges*. Washington DC: IMF, 2022.

IMF. *Strategy Towards Mainstreaming Gender*. Washington DC: IMF, 2022.

Skogly, Sigurn I. *The Human Rights Obligations of the World Bank and the International Monetary Fund*. London: Cavendish Publishing, 2001.

van Genugten, Willem, Paul Hunt, and Susan Mathews. *World Bank, IMF and Human Rights*. Nijmegen: Wolf Legal Publishers, 2003.

United Nations Human Rights Council. *Report of the Special Rapporteur on extreme poverty and human rights, A/HRC/38/33*. Geneva: United Nations, 2018.

CHAPTER 23

Ending Thirty Years of IMF Exceptionalism: A Call for an Accountability Mechanism at the International Monetary Fund

*Luiz Vieira**

1 Introduction

This year marks the 30th anniversary of the World Bank's Inspection Panel (the Panel), created as the result of grass-roots and international pressure on the Bank to address the well-documented negative impacts on marginalized communities by the Bank-financed Narmada Dam and similar projects.

The establishment of the world's first independent accountability mechanism (IAM) at the World Bank led to the creation of similar mechanisms at nearly all international financial institutions (IFIs), with the International Monetary Fund (IMF) an important exception. The establishment of the Panel and other IAMs was a step-change in accountability, as previously IFIs were only accountable to shareholders and borrowers – as opposed to communities affected by their investments. That said, at the 75th anniversary of the Universal Declaration of Human Rights and the establishment of the international human rights system, IAMs remain severely constrained in their ability to ensure IFIs 'do no harm' and contribute to, rather than negatively impact, the ability of citizens to avail themselves of their human rights.

2 Strengthening Accountability in an Increasingly Challenging World

The 30th anniversary of the Panel takes place as the world struggles to respond to the polycrisis, exacerbated by the Covid-19 pandemic, the worsening impacts of climate change, and the wars in Gaza and Ukraine. Even excluding long-standing calls from the Global South and marginalized communities, more recent calls for reform of the financial and international "development" systems predate the current post-pandemic difficulties and have not been

* Luiz Vieria is the Coordinator of the Bretton Woods Project.

 | DOI:10.1163/9789004729735_030

limited to those who might be considered the "usual suspects." IMF Managing Director Christine Lagarde underscored the need for a "new multilateralism" in a 2014 speech in which she stressed the similarities between 2014 and 1914, highlighting "massive dislocation," a "world ... rife with tension – rivalry between nations, upsetting the traditional balance of power, and inequality between the haves and have-nots."[1]

Criticisms of and cautions about the perils of the current system, strongly supported by the policies of the World Bank, IMF, and other IFIs, have also been voiced by other influential "establishment" thinkers such as Martin Wolf, the *Financial Times* Chief Economics Commentator. In his book, *The Crisis of Democratic Capitalism*, Wolf argues that, particularly after the Great Financial Crisis of 2008, the low economic growth, declining prospects, and rising inequality brought about by misguided policies conspired to threaten even "consolidated democracies" via the rise of populist far-right moments as evidenced by victory of Donald Trump in the United States.[2] The 2016 publication of an article titled *Neoliberalism Oversold?* in the IMF's *Finance and Development* publication further evidenced the gathering doubts about the effectiveness and consequences of the predominant market-based approach to development that gained force after the fall of the Berlin Wall and Soviet Union and the "end of history" in the late 1980s.

Concerns about political and social instability raised in the last decade are, if anything, more valid today. A May 2022 IMF assessment of global social unrest made clear that protests and social instability have once again gathered pace after a decline during the pandemic driven by curbs on mobility and mass gatherings. The assessment noted that while the causes of social unrest are complex, "steep price increases for food and fuel have been associated with more frequent protests in the past," adding that, "any rise in social unrest could pose a risk to the global economy's recovery, as it can have a lasting impact on economic performance."[3]

The IMF's concerns are shared by political risk consultancy Verisk Maplecroft, whose June 2022 report stressed that "middle-income countries will bear the brunt of social discontent" arising from the current economic conditions.[4] Additionally, a 2018 paper by Patricia Justino and Bruno Martorano found that

1 Christine Lagarde, *"A New Multilateralism for the 21st Century: the Richard Dimbleby Lecture" by Christine Lagarde, Managing Director, International Monetary Fund* (Feb. 3, 2014).

2 MARTIN WOLF, THE CRISIS OF DEMOCRATIC CAPITALISM (2023).

3 Philip Barrett, *Social Unrest is Rising, Adding to Risks for Global Economy* (International Monetary Fund) May 20, 2022.

4 Verisk Maplecroft, *Political Risk Outlook Report 2022* (2022).

"(w)elfare spending led to reductions in conflict in Latin America between 1970 and 2010," and that "increasing state capacity to provide social welfare programmes may improve political stability."[5]

The dynamics described above, which result from an exacerbation of previous economic and human rights challenges triggered by the unequal recovery from the Covid-19 pandemic, questions about vaccine equity, and the war in Ukraine, brought about revitalised calls for reform of the unjust international financial architecture, as evidenced by the Bridgetown Initiative.[6] Alas, the demands for substantive governance reforms have been largely met by "technical" and financial fixes, such as reforming multilateral development bank's capital adequacy framework, to meet a supposed development financing gap of trillions of dollars. Calls for the tripling of multilateral development finance to catalyze private sector co-financing – known as the Billions to Trillions agenda or "Cascade" approach reflected in the World Bank's Evolution Roadmap – evidence this drive, as outlined in a statement signed by seventy-four civil society organizations and academics highlighting the key issues with the renewed Cascade approach.[7]

The social and political consequences of an increased reliance on private sector "development" finance are particularly concerning in light of deepening within-country income and wealth inequality, which the 2022 World Inequality Report stresses "seem to be about as great today as they were at the peak of Western imperialism in the early 20th century," and related concerns about corporate capture of the states, the financialization of development finance, and the so-called Wall Street Consensus.[8] In October 2021, several UN human rights experts released a joint statement warning of the specific threat financial speculation poses to the enjoyment of a range of human rights.[9]

---

5 Particia Justino & Bruno Martorano, *Welfare spending and political conflict in Latin America, 1970–2010*, 107 World Development 98 (Jul. 2018).

6 The Bridgetown Initiative seeks to "address the immediate needs of countries facing debt distress and liquidity challenges," through a large-scale Sustainable Develop Goals Stimulus package and a reformation of international financial architecture. The United Nations, *With clock ticking for the SDGs, UN Chief and Barbados Prime Minister call for urgent action to transform broken global financial system* (Apr. 26, 2023).

7 CSO Joint Paper, *Civil Society calls for rethink of World Bank's Evolution Roadmap as part of wider reforms to highly unequal global financial architecture* (Bretton Woods Project), July 2023.

8 Lucas Chancel, et al., *World Inequality Report 2022* (World Inequality Lab) 2022, at 12; Francisco Cantamutto, *How IMF and World Bank Support for Financialisation Undermines Human Rights* (Bretton Woods Project), Apr. 6, 2022.

9 United Nations Human Rights Office of High Commissioner, *Joint Statement by Independent United Nations Human Rights Experts Warning of the Threat that Financial Speculation Poses to the Enjoyment of a Range of Human Rights* (Oct. 19, 2021).

3 IAMs Must Adapt to Address Long-Standing Concerns, Including those from Massively Increased MDB Financing

The proposed tripling of multilateral development bank (MDB) finance, principally focused on de-risking private sector investments, coupled with proposals to delegate project approval to management, can be expected to significantly impact the effectiveness and workload of already understaffed and under-resourced IAMs, particularly given the expected increased focus on large-scale, regional mega-infrastructure projects and indirect lending instruments. A *Proposal for an Evolution of the Accountability Roadmap* signed by organizations involved in supporting communities harmed by World Bank and other MDB projects clearly identifies the problem, stressing that, "[w]ithout reforms to the governance of WBG [World Bank Group] finance, new financing pursuant to the Evolution Roadmap risks not only continuing to cause the same environmental and social harm but also risks increasing that harm as more money in more areas is financed more quickly."[10]

The above-mentioned push for a dramatic expansion of MDB lending and private sector involvement in "development" must be considered within a broader historical context, which, the positive consequences resulting from the establishment of IAMs notwithstanding, is categorized by a persistent inability of accountability systems, as currently structured, to prevent and remedy human rights violations by MDBs, including the World Bank. The well-documented historic legacy of negative human rights consequences of World Bank and other MDB lending and programmes significantly predates the current proposed MDB "evolution" – as evidenced by the Narmada Dam and other grass-roots efforts to protect the rights of marginalised communities. Former UN Special Rapporteur on Extreme Poverty, Philip Alston, famously called the World Bank a "human rights-free zone" in 2015.[11] In 2019 Tunisia's Truth and Dignity Commission sent memoranda to the World Bank and the IMF, as well as to France, seeking reparations for Tunisian victims of human rights violations.[12]

---

10 Accountability Counsel, *Proposal for an Evolution to Accountability Roadmap,* 1 (July 25, 2023).

11 Philip Alston, *Report of the Special Rapporteur on extreme poverty and human rights,* 2 (Aug. 4, 2015).

12 Tunisia's Truth and Dignity Comission, *Mémorandum Relatif à la réparation due aux victimes tunisiennes des violations massives de droits de l'Homme et des droits économiques et sociaux dont la Banque Mondialeet le FMI portent une part de responsabilité* (IVD.TN), June 16, 2019.

The lack of systems within IFIs to meet their international human rights obligations, which arise from the *Universal Declaration of Human Rights* (UDHR), to provide remedy to affected communities can be expected to become more acute. The fact that the Evolution Roadmap foresees a major expansion in development policy finance (DPF), which has significant impact on countries' legislative and other regulatory and social service provision systems but falls outside the World Bank's environmental and social framework (ESF), is additional cause for concern. While progress in this regard could be made by bringing DPF and Program for Results lending within the ESF, the current Roadmap process fails to contemplate this urgently needed improvement in accountability.

4 Progress in IFI Accountability Requires the Establishment of an IAM at the IMF

The struggle for improved IFI accountability and compliance with international human rights obligations in the context of the 75th anniversary of the UDHR is significantly hindered by the fact that the IMF, a pivotal actor in the international architecture and response to multiple challenges currently facing the globe, lacks an IAM. This is particularly concerning given the expansion of the IMF's work to include, for example, gender and climate change, and the proliferation of its programmes in the context of increased debt burdens and a challenging global economic environment, where IMF-mandated austerity and other policies are having acute social impacts.

In 2021, as the consequences of the uneven recovery from the Covid-19 pandemic became increasingly apparent, Attiya Waris, UN Independent Expert on foreign debt, and other international financial obligations and human rights figures wrote a letter to the IMF Managing Director, Kristalina Georgieva, stressing that the IMF's role in the Covid-19 recovery and increasing leadership on climate change, "unavoidably raises important human rights considerations." Addressing the accountability issue directly, the Independent Expert noted that:

> [T]he IMF, like all actors engaged in addressing these complex challenges, inevitably operates on the basis of imperfect knowledge and in dynamic and complex environments. This suggests that, despite their best efforts, IMF staff … may sometimes err. While this is completely understandable, it raises concerns about the limited IMF accountability to those who may be adversely affected by its operations.

The Independent Expert concluded by emphasising the need for international organisations, including the IMF, to:

> [H]ave publicly available policies and procedures that can guide staff when dealing with complex environmental and social issues; and the need ... to have an independent accountability mechanism, like an independent ombudsman, that can provide non-state actors who claim that they have been harmed or threaten[ed] with harm by the organization's failure to comply with its own policies and procedures with a means to hold the organization accountable for this non-compliance.

As outlined by its advocates, one of the many benefits of the establishment of an IAM at the IMF is that it would require that the organization develop empirically robust and transparent policies to guide staff in undertaking what are undoubtedly complex and delicate operations. The development and publication of these policies would, in turn, greatly increase the IMF's legitimacy precisely at a time when its role is once again front and centre of global developments and in a context of the wider erosion of the multilateral system.

The call for the establishment of an IAM at the IMF is particularly pressing in light of a 2022 working paper by Isabel Ortiz and Matthew Cummings titled *End of Austerity: A Global Report on Budget Cuts and Harmful Social Reforms in 2022–25*, which warns of the "dangers of a post-pandemic austerity shock, far more premature and severe than the one that followed the [2008] global financial crisis."[13] The paper underscores in particular that "analysis of IMF expenditure projections shows that the adjustment shock is expected to impact 143 countries in 2023 in terms of GDP or 85% of the world population," and identifies eleven types of austerity measures being considered by governments, often with the support of or under the direction of the IMF that "will have negative social impacts on their populations, specially harming women."[14] Finally, of particular relevance to the discussion concerning accountability to communities and people impacted by IFI policy, the paper also details a number of specific policies that could be pursued instead of austerity, thus diminishing the negative human rights consequences of IMF programming.

Alas, despite some promising rhetoric and positive steps from the Fund on social protection floors, the evidence of the negative human rights consequences of IMF programming continues to be a well-documented trend,

13 Isabel Ortiz & Matthew Cummings, *End of Austerity: A Global Report on Budget Cuts and Harmful Social Reforms in 2022–25* (Initiative for Policy Dialogue), Sept. 2022, at 9.

14 *Id.* at Ex. Summ., 16.

with Human Rights Watch reporting in April 2022 that its analysis of sixteen countries, including of relief specific to the pandemic, "found that targeted programs excluded millions of people who were in need of social security to protect their rights, leaving them without adequate food and with other problems."[15] Similarly, a 2022 Oxfam analysis of IMF programming found that:

> 13 out of the 15 IMF loan programs negotiated during the second year of the pandemic require new austerity measures such as taxes on food and fuel or spending cuts that could put vital public services at risk. The IMF is also encouraging six additional countries to adopt similar measures.[16]

This analysis was complemented by other Oxfam research that demonstrated that "43 out of 55 African Union member states face public expenditure cuts totaling $183 billion over the next five years," greatly endangering the chances these states will achieve the UN's Sustainable Development Goals and, indeed, meet their international human rights obligations.[17]

The IMF's counter-productive and unnecessary surcharges policy, which imposes additional interest charges on IMF loans in accordance with their size and duration, has also been heavily criticised for its detrimental human rights consequences. In May 2021, former UN Independent Expert on Debt and Human Rights, Juan Pablo Bohoslavsky, published an open letter signed by the Independent Expert on Debt and Human Rights at the time, among others, stressing that the policy violates international human rights law because it discriminates against certain states without legitimate reason and "undermine[s] the borrower State's ability to respect, protect and fulfil its human rights obligations."[18] A subsequent August 2022 article in the periodical *Development* by Bohoslavsky, Cantamutto, and Clérico details how the policy threatens the right to development.[19]

The surcharges policy has been the target of a well-coordinated global civil society campaign, with an April 2022 letter signed by over 250 individuals and

15 Human Rights Watch, *IMF/World Bank: Targeted Safety Net Programs Fall Short on Rights Protection* (Apr. 14, 2022).

16 Oxfam International, *IMF Must Abandon Demands for Austerity as Cost-of Living Crisis Drives up Hunger and Poverty Worldwide* (Apr. 19, 2022).

17 *Id.*

18 Juan Bohoslavsky, *IMF Surcharges Punish Developing Countries* (Bretton Woods Project), May 2021.

19 Juan Bohoslavsky, et al., *IMF's Surcharges as a Threat to the Right to Development*, 65 DEVELOPMENT 194 (Aug. 13, 2022).

global civil society organizations calling for its immediate elimination.[20] Yet the policy persists. In fact, the IMF refuses to engage with the issue or respond to direct questions and concerns raised by the UN Human Rights Council. In August 2022, nine UN Independent Experts and Special Rapporteurs sent a letter under the Special Procedures of the UN Human Rights Council to IMF Managing Director Kristalina Georgieva requesting a response to specific apprehensions outlined in the letter.[21] The Managing Director has, to date, disregarded the letter.

Another pivotal area that would greatly benefit from the establishment of an IAM, related policy clarity, and transparency is the methodology used to conduct the IMF's Debt Sustainability Analyses (DSAs), which fundamentally impact the nature of debt relief granted, or not granted, to states under severe fiscal pressure and, thus, their capacity to meet their international human rights obligations. Prior to the significant fiscal pressures and increased debt resulting from the Covid-19 pandemic and recent capital outflow from the Global South, the UN Independent Expert on Debt and Human Rights noted, in his 2016 report, his concern that "a new global wave of austerity and debt vulnerabilities in many developing countries that challenges progress on human rights is again increasing …" and argued that "the current review of frameworks for debt sustainability analysis should be based on a more comprehensive understanding of debt sustainability, incorporating human rights and the social and environmental dimensions of sustainability."[22] The urgency of this call has significantly increased with the unequal recovery from the Covid-19 pandemic; a 2022 Oxfam report, for example, stressed that "Africa's debt servicing is almost three times as much as education spending, six times health spending, 22 times social spending and 236 times more than climate adaptation spending."[23]

The establishment of an IAM would provide the IMF an opportunity to heed long-standing civil society calls for the institution to develop a human rights

20 EURODAD, *IMF Surcharges are Unfair, Counterproductive and a Threat to an Equitable Global Economic Recovery. They Should be Eliminated Immediately* (DEBTGWA.NET), Apr. 7, 2022.

21 Attiya Waris, et al., *Mandates of the Independent Expert on the Effects of Foreign Debt and Other Related International Financial Obligations of States on the Full Enjoyment of all Human Rights, Particularly Economic, Social and Cultural Rights* (Office of Human Rights), Aug. 26, 2022.

22 Juan Bohoslavksy, *Effects of Foreign Debt and Other Related International Financial Obligations of States on the Full Enjoyment of all Human Rights, Particularly Economic, Social and Cultural Rights* 2 (Aug. 5, 2016).

23 Chelsea Hodgkins & Gerald Byarugaba, *Time to Deliver on Climate Finance: The Cost of a Just Transition* (Oxfam) Nov. 8, 2022.

policy to underpin all of its programming. An IAM could also ensure IMF policy and programmes are consistent with *The Principles for Human Rights in Fiscal Policy*[24] and benefit from the application of the UN *Guiding principles on human rights impact assessments of economic reforms*.[25]

As the shareholders of the World Bank, the IMF, and other IFIs celebrate the establishment of the international human rights system, they must go beyond words. Shareholders must demand that the World Bank, the IMF, and other IFIs establish human rights policies, integrate *ex ante* and *post hoc* human rights impact assessments into all of their programmes, and ensure their IAMs are adequately resourced and structured to enable them to meet their human rights obligations by providing remedy and accountability to communities affected by IFI projects, policy lending, and IMF programmes.

Bibliography

Accountability Counsel. *Proposal for an Evolution to Accountability Roadmap*. San Francisco: Accountability Counsel, July 25, 2023: 1.

Alston, Philip. *Report of the Special Rapporteur on extreme poverty and human rights*. Geneva: The United Nations, August 4, 2015: 2.

Barrett, Philip. *Social Unrest is Rising, Adding to Risks for Global Economy*. Washington DC: International Monetary Fund [IMF], May 20, 2022.

Bohoslavksy, Juan. *Effects of foreign debt and other related international financial obligations of States on the full enjoyment of all human rights, particularly economic, social and cultural rights*. Geneva: United Nations General Assembly, August 5, 2016: 2.

Bohoslavsky, Juan. *IMF Surcharges Punish Developing Countries*. London: Bretton Woods Project, May 2021.

Bohoslavsky, Juan Bohoslavsky. et al. "IMF's Surcharges as a Threat to the Right to Development." *Development*, 65. (August 13, 2022): 194.

Cantamutto, Francisco. *How IMF and World Bank support for financialisation undermines human rights*. London: Bretton Woods Project, April 6, 2022.

Chancel, Lucas. et al. *World Inequality Report 2022*. Paris: World Inequality Lab, 2022: 12.

CSO joint paper. *Civil Society calls for rethink of World Bank's Evolution Roadmap as part of wider reforms to highly unequal global financial architecture*. London: Bretton Woods Project, July 2023.

---

24 Initiative for Principles for Human Rights in Fiscal Policy, *Principles for Human Rights in Fiscal Policy*, https://derechosypoliticafiscal.org/images/ASSETS/Resumidos_ingls.pdf (last visited Dec. 2, 2024).

25 United Nations Human Rights Council, *Guiding principles on human rights impact assessments of economic reforms* (Dec. 19, 2018).

EURODAD. *IMF Surcharges are Unfair, Counterproductive and a Threat to an Equitable Global Economic Recovery. They Should be Eliminated Immediately.* DEBTGWA.NET, April 7, 2022.

Justino, Particia, and Bruno Martorano. "Welfare spending and political conflict in Latin America, 1970–2010." *World Development*, 107 (July 2018): 98.

Hodgkins, Chelsea and Gerald Byarugaba. "Time to Deliver on Climate Finance: The Cost of a Just Transition," Oxfam, November 8, 2022.

Human Rights Watch. *IMF/World Bank: Targeted Safety Net Programs Fall Short on Rights Protection.* Washington DC: Human Rights Watch, April 14, 2022.

Initiative for Principles for Human Rights in Fiscal Policy. *Principles for human rights in fiscal policy*. Accessed December 2, 2024.

Lagarde, Christine. *A New Multilateralism for the 21st Century: the Richard Dimbleby Lecture" By Christine Lagarde, Managing Director, International Monetary Fund.* Washington DC: IMF, February 3, 2014.

Maplecroft, Verisk. *Political Risk Outlook Report 2022*. Fleet: Maplecroft, 2022.

Ortiz, Isabel, and Matthew Cummings. *End of Austerity: A Global Report on Budget Cuts and Harmful Social Reforms in 2022–25*. New York: Initiative for Policy Dialogue, September 2022: 9.

Oxfam International. *IMF must abandon demands for austerity as cost-of-living crisis drives up hunger and poverty worldwide.* Nairobi: Oxfam International, April 19, 2022.

Tunisia's Truth and Dignity Commission. *Mémorandum Relatif à la réparation due aux victimes tunisiennes des violations massives de droits de l'Homme et des droits économiques et sociaux dont la Banque Mondialeet le FMI portent une part de responsabilité*. Sidi Boud Said: Tunisia's Truth and Dignity Commission, June 16, 2019.

The United Nations. *With clock ticking for the SDGs, UN Chief and Barbados Prime Min ister call for urgent action to transform broken global financial system*, new release. New York: United Nations, April 26, 2023.

United Nations Human Rights Council, *Guiding principles on human rights impact assessments of economic reforms*. Geneva: United Nations General Assembly, December 19, 2018.

United Nations Human Rights Office of High Commissioner. *Joint Statement by independent United Nations human rights experts warning of the threat that financial speculation poses to the enjoyment of a range of human rights*. Geneva: United Nation, October 19, 2021.

Waris, Attiya, et al. *Mandates of the Independent Expert on the effects of foreign debt and other related international financial obligations of States on the full enjoyment of all human rights, particularly economic, social and cultural rights*. Geneva: United Nations Office of Human Rights, August 26, 2022.

Wolf, Martin. *The Crisis of Democratic Capitalism*. New York: Penguin Random House, 2023.

CHAPTER 24

An Increased Normalization of IAMs Faces Ground Realities: Lack of Transparency Impedes Access to IAMs

*Hamid Sharif**

1 Introduction

The Asian Infrastructure Investment Bank (AIIB or the Bank) is the newest member of the multilateral development bank (MDB) fraternity. Established in December 2015 and commencing operations in 2016,[1] it is an MDB born in the 21st century, in the same year that the COP 21 concluded the Paris Agreement and the UN launched the Sustainable Development Goals.

AIIB's creation drew a lot of attention and some controversy. Its formation was led by China, which eventually became the largest shareholder. The US and Japan chose not to join AIIB. Whilst the US leaned on allies not to join, it failed to stop them; Germany, UK, South Korea, and Australia, among others, nevertheless joined. One rationale these countries offered for joining the bank was to influence it from the inside – paying particular attention to the Bank's governance.

2 Understanding the Institutional and Governance Context of AIIB's Independent Accountability Mechanism (IAM)

The AIIB opted for a non-resident board; a choice that harkened back to similar discussions at the genesis of the Bretton Woods Institutions, with Lord Keynes being a proponent for the idea. Chief negotiators were finally persuaded to take a more modern corporate governance approach, where the board plays

* Hamid Sharif served as the inaugural Managing Director of the Complaints-resolution, Evaluation, and Integrity Unit of the Asian Infrastructure Investment Bank (AIIB) and is a member of the Expert Committee of the China International Commercial Court under the Supreme People's Court of China.

1 *See* Asian Infrastructure Investment Bank, *About AIIB: Introduction*, https://www.aiib.org/en/about-aiib/index.html (last visited Dec. 15, 2024).

DOI:10.1163/9789004729735_031

a strategic and oversight role. The need for strong oversight, particularly by a non-resident board, is reflected in Article 26 of the Articles of Agreement of the AIIB:

> The Board of Directors shall be responsible for the direction of the general operations of the Bank and, this purpose, shall, in addition to the powers assigned to it expressly by this Agreement, exercise all the powers delegated to it by the Board of Governors, and in particular:
>
> (iv) supervise the management and the operation of the Bank on a regular basis, and establish and oversight mechanism for that purpose, in line with principles of transparency, openness, independence, and accountability.[2]

At first blush, this provision looks very similar to equivalent provisions in the charters of other MDBs. A closer reading, however, particularly when read together with the relevant minutes of the Report on the AIIB's Articles of Agreement by the chief negotiators, tells a different story:

> Representatives agreed that the oversight mechanism to be established by the Board of Directors under Article 26 (iv) would be designed in line with the principles of transparency, openness, independence and accountability, and would address such areas as audit, evaluation, fraud and corruption, project complains and staff grievances, and reflect the Bank's character as a multilateral financial institution focused on infrastructure development.[3]

Article 26(IV) goes well beyond the standard language found in charters of other MDBs that empower their respective board of directors to "supervise the management and operations" of the bank. It goes further and mandates the creation of an "oversight body" for that purpose, and the chief negotiators' minutes on this provision further explain that this body will be created in accordance with "the principles of transparency, openness, independence and accountability." Its functions would address such areas as audit, evaluation, fraud and corruption, project complaints, and staff grievances.

2 Asian Infrastructure Investment Bank, *Articles of Agreement*, Art. 26, 15–16 (June 15, 2019).

3 Asian Infrastructure Investment Bank, *Report on the Articles of Agreement of the Asian Infrastructure Investment Bank* 3 (June 6, 2015).

In 2019, the Board of Directors of AIIB approved a paper on the oversight mechanism.[4] This paper formalized the terms of reference of the AIIB's Complaints-Resolution, Evaluation, and Integrity Unit (CEIU), which deals with three of the five functions mentioned by the chief negotiators for the oversight mechanism, namely complaints-resolution, evaluation, and integrity (i.e., countering fraud and corruption). The paper formalized the "independent but engaged" model of the CEIU. Under this model, the Managing Director of the CEIU (MD-CEIU) is an observer at the Executive Committee and Management Committee of the Bank with the right to speak and participate. The MD-CEIU has no voting rights in these meetings. This is a move away from the puritanical notion of the "independence" of equivalent functions in other MDBs. The MD-CEIU is "engaged but independent" from management. This allows the MD-CEIU to provide the AIIB President independent inputs into decision-making at these committees. It also allows for meaningful engagement on issues relating to CEIU functions to ensure that a preventive approach is taken.

For a young bank like the AIIB, a traditional rigid and reactive structural independence model would mean that no positive feedback loops into policy making would be possible until the completion of evaluations or investigations into allegations of corruption or complaints regarding environmental or social policy compliance. During the Bank's nascent period, it was critical that real-time independent advice was provided to "keep it out of trouble" and for the institution to continuously learn and improve its practice.

This, however, could not be at the expense of independence granted to the MD-CEIU. This independence is, therefore, underscored by unique institutional arrangements such as the "Directors' Forum." The Directors' Forum empowers the board of directors to meet among themselves without the presence of management, providing an opportunity for board members "to share information and exchange views among themselves *and with* the MD-CEIU [emphasis added]." One specific function of the Directors' Forum is to assess the performance of the President of AIIB – another unique feature of AIIB governance. A Directors' Forum can be called by the Dean of the Board at the request of any board member, the MD-CEIU, or by the Dean acting on his or her own. A practice is evolving for the Directors' Forum to discuss CEIU's workplan and budget. The option of allowing the MD-CEIU to call a Directors' Forum is a safeguard to ensure that the CEIU is allowed functional autonomy in conducting its investigations, complaints-handling, and learning and evaluation activities. This is on top of the unique arrangements under which the MD-CEIU

4 *See* Asian Infrastructure Investment Bank, *Governance: Oversight Mechanism* (July 10, 2019).

reports on a quarterly basis to the Board in a face-to-face meeting – a practice unknown in other MDBs. This arrangement allows direct communication with the Board. In addition, any board member and the MD-CEIU can meet anytime they choose.

Uniquely, the CEIU is also responsible for leading policy formulation and any review of such policies in relation to its functions, including the Project-affected People's Mechanism (PPM) policy and its review. The final policy drafts proposed to the Board are still negotiated between the Board and Management, as in other banks, but the CEIU is the pen holder and has the initiative in making proposals. Furthermore, in each policy review carried out by Management, the CEIU is consulted for its input. In relation to policies that impact CEIU functions, the CEIU has advocated policy changes that were accepted during the review of the environmental and social policy, such as establishing project websites and time limits for disclosure of environmental and social assessments.[5]

Understanding these governance arrangements is critical to understanding AIIB's independent accountability mechanism, the PPM. The PPM is a part of the CEIU that comprises a large part of AIIB's oversight mechanism. This makes it unique among the IAMs at MDBs as it enables the MD-CEIU to directly influence policy making related to project-affected people and directly liaise with the management and the board on matters of policy and practice through regular interaction. Ready access to the board without presence of management through the Directors' Forum is a check on any management non-cooperation or interference with CEIU's independence. So far this has not been necessary. Regular contact with management and the board also militates against the possibility that the IAM or other functions of the CEIU are shelved and forgotten. The CEIU is, as a result, a mainstreamed feature of AIIB governance.

3 AIIB's PPM

The PPM was established by the board in 2019 after two rounds of consultation with stakeholders and shareholders. International advocacy non-governmental organizations and national-level civil society organizations participated, with lengthy submissions, in the design of the mechanism. Among the new features they pushed for were "remedies" for complainants like financial compensation by AIIB. This remedies proposal was not accepted on the basis that this

5 See Asian Infrastructure Investment Bank, *Environmental and Social Framework*, Section 66.2. (Feb. 2016, amend. Nov. 2022).

would detract from the responsibility of the client and create perverse incentives to pursue frivolous cases against AIIB, given its deep pockets. Shareholders expressed their concern that the mechanism should be one of last resort, allowing them to address the concerns of their own citizens. In the end, the mechanism was based on the principle of "subsidiarity," which allows a forum at each level to decide matters before a higher-level forum intervenes. In this sense, a project-level grievance redress mechanism (GRM) should be allowed to deal with matters before allowing higher level mechanisms to intervene. As with other IAM s, this means that PPM is a mechanism of last resort.

PPM policy formulation discussions considered the growing issue of "retaliation" against those who bring complaints. Borrowing from the "zero tolerance" concept adopted in anti-corruption policies of MDB s, the AIIB delegation at the IAM network meeting in 2018 in Thessaloniki suggested that a "zero tolerance" approach be adopted by all MDBs in relation to retaliation. Such an approach did not find its way into the final PPM policy that nevertheless adopted strong language relating to the risk of retaliation. A view prevailed that AIIB did not want to inadvertently convey that it had police powers to deal with the full consequences of retaliation by representing that it has a zero-tolerance policy. It is heartening to see that this phrase is now gaining currency.[6]

What is striking about the Board approval of the PPM is that no Board member contested the need for it. This is in sharp contrast to the acrimonious exchanges between developed and developing country board members in other MDBs when the proposal for establishing an IAM was first made. Unlike in many other MDB s, the establishment of the PPM at AIIB was not held up by threats from the developed members to withhold funds for "soft-window" lending such as in the International Development Association fund or the Asian Development Fund, to coax the management or developing country members to approve the PPM policy. By the time of AIIB's creation, the existence of IAM s was clearly normalized. During shareholder consultations (usually the external financing wing of a ministry of finance), it was refreshing to see that officials "owned" the problems of project-affected people, stating that they are "our citizens" first and solutions to their problems must be found. Again, this is in stark relief to the position of developing countries in the '90s, who saw the creation of IAM s as an imposition by the developed countries. Clearly much progress has been made since then, although much more remains to be done to ensure that the fine statements in IAM and environmental and social policy

6 Rabi Thapa, *Realizing Zero Tolerance Against Reprisals*, THE WORLD BANK GROUP: ACCOUNTABILITY MECHANISM (Jan. 19, 2023).

documents are translated into better lives for project-affected people (*see, e.g., infra* part 4: *Why So Few Submissions to IAMs?*).

After many discussions with the Board and Management, the PPM was finalized. Consistent with AIIB's lean philosophy, the PPM's flexible design allows the MD-CEIU to tap expertise appropriate for the task at hand rather than being stuck with a fixed panel with fixed costs. The PPM also introduced some unique features. Its structure recognizes that there may be a need to address issues during the design of a project without elevating them to full compliance review or a formal alternate dispute resolution process. So, in addition to the traditional compliance review and alternate dispute resolution, PPM allows for project-affected people to file a "Project Processing Query," relating to complaints about, for example, construction dust or failure to consult. The choice of any of these three avenues is for the requesters to make[7] and not the PPM secretariat, as has been misrepresented by even experienced commentators.[8] The PPM design also paid heed to the larger development debate where for years developing countries complained about having to deal with a multitude of MDB policies and procedures that sap their meager capacity.

The AIIB's charter includes as the Bank's purpose the promotion of "partnership" in addressing development challenges, by working in close collaboration with other multilateral and bilateral development institutions.[9] In designing its policies, the AIIB has deliberately set out to make it easier to work with development partners. Its environmental and social policy and the procurement policy contain provisions enabling AIIB to recognize and apply substantially equivalent policies of other MDBs or bilateral partners. The PPM

7 Rules of Procedure of PPM 6.4.5. *Screening for Eligibility; Registration*: (a) The PPM determines whether the submission meets the eligibility criteria set out above in Part 5.1 (*General Eligibility Criteria Applicable to all Submissions*). If the submission does not indicate a preferred PPM function to be pursued, or if it appears to indicate an inappropriate function, the PPM contacts the Requestors and recommends the most suitable processing option based on submission content, timing and eligibility criteria, taking the Requestor's proposal, if any, into account. The Requestors' decision on which process they wish to pursue is, however, final, subject to the submission meeting the applicable requirements of Part 4 (*Time Limits for Filing a Submission*) and Part 5 (*Eligibility of Submissions*).

8 *See* Korinna Horta, *Asian Infrastructure Investment Bank: A Multilateral Bank Where China Sets the Rules*, 52 PUBLICATION SERIES ON DEMOCRACY (Dec. 24, 2018).

9 *See* Asian Infrastructure Investment Bank, *Articles of Agreement*. Art. 1, para.1 (June 26, 2015) ("The purpose of the Bank shall be to: (i) foster sustainable economic development, create wealth and improve infrastructure connectivity in Asia by investing in infrastructure and other productive sectors; and (ii) promote regional cooperation and partnership in addressing development challenges by working in close collaboration with other multilateral and bilateral development institutions.")

takes the same approach. In a co-financed project, AIIB can agree to the lead co-financier's IAM handling all complaints or requests, provided that (1) the lead co-financier's environmental and social policy is applied by AIIB and (2) the lead co-financier agrees to the use of its IAM to handle all disputes, including those filed with the AIIB.

In most co-financed projects, the lead co-financier has agreed to the sole use of its own IAM rather than both the lead co-financier's IAM and the PPM. This makes sense. Firstly, it reduces the burden on the borrower in having to work with two independent accountability mechanisms. Secondly, it avoids putting the lead financier in an awkward position where its environmental and social policy is the subject of scrutiny by the PPM. Thirdly, it avoids the awkward results emanating from different IAMs coming to different conclusions on substantially the same assessment of compliance. Fourthly, this approach is consistent with the call for MDBs to work as a system.[10] Nonetheless, this approach to co-financed projects was criticized by international advocacy groups who view it as a reduction in choice of forum for project-affected people. Such views were brought to the attention of the AIIB board and management. In the end, the arguments for efficiency and simplicity prevailed. The approach taken by the PPM in co-financed projects was commended by the heads of MDBs.

Implementing interim measures to prevent irreparable harm pending an investigation has been problematic for IAMs. The PPM has made modest progress in this respect. Section 7.3 of the PPM Policy allows for some interim relief, where during a review of a submission the PPM concludes that "continued Project preparation or implementation may potentially result in irreversible material adverse impacts that have not been adequately addressed in accordance with the ESP."[11] In such a case, the PPM can bring the matter to the attention of management[12] to address the matter within a specified time (under Rule 7 of the PPM Rules of Procedure this is 60 Working Days). If management does not address the matter in this time, the MD-CEIU brings the matter to the notice of the president. If the matter is not addressed by the president in a specified time (30 Working Days under Rule 7 of the PPM Rules of Procedure),

10 Eminent Persons Group, *Making the Financial Global System Work for All: Report of the Eminent Persons Group on Global Finance Governance*, (Oct. 2018).

11 Asian Infrastructure Investment Bank, *AIIB Policy on the Project-affected People's Mechanism*, 8, Sec. 7.3 (Dec. 7, 2018).

12 "Management" for the purposes of PPM means the Vice Presidents concerned. See Part 1.3 of the PPM Policy.

the MD-CEIU can then bring the matter to the attention of the board. These provisions were heavily negotiated as the PPM was breaking new ground here.

Like many other IAM s, the PPM is the mechanism of last resort.[13] Part 5.1.8 of the PPM Policy provides that a submission is ineligible if "[t]he Requestors have not made good faith efforts to resolve the issues with the Project-level [Grievance Redress Mechanism][14] and with Management or have not indicated to the satisfaction of the PPM why they have been unable to do so."[15] This was based on the philosophy that the project-owner (especially in sovereign projects) must be given the chance to resolve issues at the local level. In case of sovereign lending, the complainants are also the borrower's own citizens. The provision also provides management a fair chance to resolve the issue (a practice followed by IAM s that do not have a requirement to first approach the GRM or management). This makes sense, as it is management and not the IAM that has the relationship and leverage with the client to resolve any alleged non-compliance. As mentioned above, this is also consistent with the principle of subsidiarity followed in modern governance systems such as the European Union.

The flip side of this is that the GRM must be functional and fully disclosed to project-affected people. Similarly, it also implies that project-affected people must know about the PPM and how they can approach it, including the requirement that they must first approach the GRM or management; in case that is not possible, then an explanation must be furnished as to why they could not approach them. Recognizing the importance of this, the Section 7.2 of the PPM policy allows the MD-CEIU to escalate the matter all the way to the Board of Directors if during an investigation of a submission, the PPM "identifies that the information about the Project-level GRM or the PPM has not been adequately disclosed or that the Project-level GRM has not been established or that it is ineffective."[16] The escalation procedure is the same as for interim measures described above in respect of Rule 7.3 of the PPM Rules of Procedure, and is set out in Rule 7.2 of the PPM Rules of Procedure. These provisions were designed to create incentives for the AIIB management and the client or borrower to establish GRM s and disseminate information about both the GRM and the PPM to project-affected people.

---

13 It is worth noting that even where an IAM allows a requestor to make a submission directly to it, in practice it refers the matter and the client to Management first.

14 A Grievance Redress Mechanism is a mechanism set up by the client at the project level that allows project-affected people to seek redress.

15 Asian Infrastructure Investment Bank, *supra* note 11 at 4, Sec. 5.1.8.

16 *Id.* at 8, Sec. 7.2.

To further underline the importance of this, the CEIU early on pushed for and succeeded in persuading management to present quarterly reports to the board on project implementation. Each project report includes information about GRMs. These quarterly reports are considered by the AIIB board in a face-to-face meeting with management. Alongside this, as civil society becomes more aware of the unique position of the MD-CEIU, submissions to management are also increasingly copied to the MD-CEIU. As management knows that the MD-CEIU interfaces with the board regularly, this creates further incentives for taking complaints seriously. Indeed, in consultation with CEIU, management has established an internal system to track all complaints. All these measures have raised the importance of implementation generally, and particularly the need for ESP compliance.

As in the case of IAMs in other MDBs, questions are raised from time to time whether PPM policy and procedures are adequate and effective.

4 Why So Few Submissions to IAMs?

Often over the years the board of each MDB has asked why so few submissions or cases are brought to their IAM. Management has often taken the self-congratulatory stance that this shows that environmental and social compliance is improving. The author, as a development practitioner with thirty years' experience in two MDBs can vouch that post-creation of IAMs, much greater attention is paid to environmental and social compliance, and to making projects "inspection-proof." The transparency of environmental and social documentation has improved, and each MDB has set up specialized units for better implementation and compliance of environmental and social requirements that are also better defined in revised policies and procedures. As part of MDB practice, the creation of GRMs was promoted. Initially this started as an informal practice; increasingly it is a requirement in the environmental and social policies of MDBs.

Like other MDB boards, the AIIB board frequently asks why there are not more complaints or submissions to the PPM. As a new bank with a modest portfolio, which is about 50% co-financed and to which the PPM is not applicable in most cases, it was relatively easy to explain the low number of submissions to the PPM. Considering the number of projects to which the PPM is applicable, the number of complaints received by the PPM is consistent with the experience of other MDBs. But why are the numbers of complaints to all MDBs so low?

The author's hypothesis is that the low number of submissions is related to issues of transparency. As in many other areas of citizens' rights, it goes to the issue of information asymmetry between project-affected people and project owners and financiers.

To test this hypothesis, the author looked at the active sovereign energy portfolio of the World Bank and the Asian Development Bank in Pakistan (AIIB has no stand-alone investments in the energy sector in Pakistan). The energy sector is pertinent, as both MDBs have decades-long engagement, having lent tens of billions of dollars to the sector. The sector at one point had just one utility that dealt with power generation, transmission, distribution, and water reservoirs. This utility was broken up in the nineties under the lead of the World Bank. Both MDBs have a history of being involved in the restructuring of energy utilities and working with the emerging entities that deal with different aspects of the sector. It can reasonably be assumed that with tens of billions of dollars invested through these entities, and massive amounts spent on their capacity building, the entities in these sectors would be the most capable in complying with the environmental and social policies of the MDBs.

There are sixteen total active projects in the energy sector for both banks. A survey of the published information about this portfolio on the banks' and project sponsors' websites, where they could be found, looked at the information on these projects from the point of view of an informed project-affected person or a civil society activist who wants to find out information about the GRMs or IAM for these projects. The survey results are summarized in the chart below (Figure 24.1), and the table of projects surveyed is appended at the end of this article (Table 24.1). The survey, of course, has its limitations, as it is possible that the client has done a lot more to make project-affected people aware of the GRMs and the applicable IAM than the information on these websites shows. The fact that less than 20 percent of the clients have websites and most of these do not have a project webpage or information about how to contact a GRM, however, may indicate otherwise.

While it is heartening to note that every project has its own webpage on the MDB's website – although this is not always so easy to find – information on the GRM and the applicable IAM is not found on that page; in fairness to both MDBs, they do disclose information about their IAM on their website. Client websites in most cases do not exist (80 percent have no websites), and even if they do, there is no ready information about the project or the GRM or applicable IAM. This means that a reasonably educated project-affected person cannot readily find information about the GRM or the applicable IAM on the project webpage of the MDB or the client's website even where these exist.

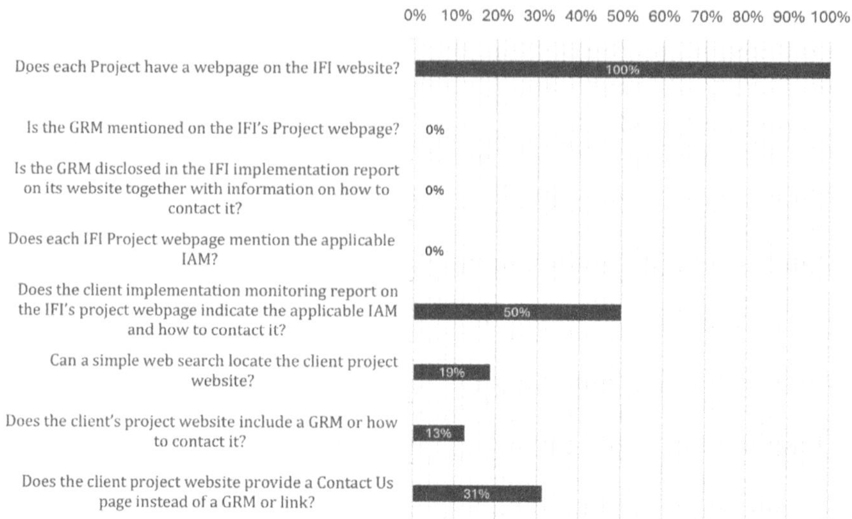

FIGURE 24.1 Online disclosures of GRM and IAM for active energy portfolio in Pakistan

This obvious information vacuum is surely part of the explanation why so few complaints are filed with the IAMs.

MDBs must do more to fill this gap. Both the MDBs and their clients can quickly fix this, at least in the digital space. Firstly, each client should be required to have a website for the project, where all relevant information, especially environmental and social assessments, implementation or management plans, and other documentation must be disclosed in local language(s) together with information about the GRM and how to access it. Information disclosure about the applicable IAM and how to approach it should also be compulsory; this information should also be disclosed on the project site. It is surprising that thirty years on, this is still not a mandatory requirement in MDB policies given its miniscule cost in the context of large infrastructure projects. It is also anachronistic in the digital age, especially amid the chest-thumping from some MDBs about being digitally aligned.

Most surprisingly, IAMs are still largely structured as passive or reactive bodies. This must change. IAMs should be mandated to proactively monitor and regularly report on environmental and social disclosures to the board, including disclosure of information about GRM and IAM. The MDB boards should further mandate IAMs to proactively monitor the working of GRMs, to confirm that these do not just exist on paper, and submit the relevant reports to them. These are *de minimis* requirements to ensure that project-affected persons have access to justice. The additional costs for this would be modest, as an

IAM would only carry out monitoring for a sample of projects. This would also create the right incentives for project teams and management to pay greater attention to GRM and IAM and to overall compliance.

It is worth noting that GRMs can vary in complexity; accordingly, project teams and clients must be given the flexibility to design these so that each GRM is fit for purpose for the relevant project. This is not to suggest that a GRM must be mechanically created *de novo* in each case. Indeed, existing arrangements in a project context, if assessed to be adequate, may serve as the GRM, or the GRM may be grafted onto an existing mechanism. Further, there may be an assessment that no GRM is required in the context of the project – for example a project with a low-risk environmental and social classification. In all such cases, it must be clearly disclosed whether a GRM exists and how it may be accessed. If no GRM is necessary, this should be explained, with arrangements for any project-affected person to contact the relevant client designated person in case a grievance does arise. This is surely not too much to ask for, as standard practice.

5 "It's All in the Implementation, Stupid!"

The prelude to the creation of the Inspection Function at the World Bank was public outcry about a series of projects and the massive environmental and social damage they caused or threatened to cause. This led to the World Bank setting up The Wapenhans Task Force[17] to investigate its portfolio. One of the task force's lasting observations is that the World Bank (and indeed each MDB) is driven by "an approval culture" that rewards new approvals and does not incentivize good design and implementation. It is ironic that, as shareholders of MDBs have rushed ahead to normalize creation of IAMs, relatively little attention has been paid to the implementation issues that lie at the heart of poor environmental and social outcomes of projects. Indeed, scrutiny of the implementation of the fine policies setting up IAMs, especially the implicit or explicit provisions on disclosure of information about the IAM or the GRM, is found wanting.[18] Shareholders must pay greater attention to ensuring that there

17 World Bank Group, *Record of the Portfolio Management Task Force (Wapenhans Report) and Follow Up*, Annexes (1992).

18 *See* AIIB Environmental and Social Policy (ESP), para. 72.1 ("The Bank requires the Client to establish, in accordance with the ESP and applicable ESSs, a suitable Project-level GRM to receive and facilitate resolution of the concerns and complaints of people who believe they have been adversely affected by the Project's environmental or social impacts, *and to inform Project-affected people of its availability (emphasis added)*; para. 42 (each

is full, timely, and appropriate disclosure in the relevant language about the GRM and IAM as part of the board's greater focus on project implementation.

AIIB's quarterly focus on implementation stands out in creating the right incentives for management and staff to take disclosure seriously. The quarterly reports' inclusion of a part on GRM s (as indeed is also the case with the World Bank implementation reports) is noteworthy, although there should be more explicit requirements on whether disclosure of information requirements about the GRM and IAM have been met. Realizing that there is a need to inform project-affected people about the IAM s, most MDB boards and IAM s have pursued "outreach" as a solution. This is simply a sinecure. The outreach sessions play well into the political economy of donor-funded civil society groups, allowing them all to claim victory. The real losers are the project-affected people who go largely uninformed. The language in MDB policies on GRM s and disclosure of information about them and the IAM is often ignored by the client and the MDB s (see footnote 12 for AIIB policy provisions). Clients and management are already required to disclose information, so MDB boards of directors must hold management to account for enforcing these provisions. As part of their oversight, they should strengthen the IAM s by giving them the powers to proactively monitor the implementation of these provisions. This will go a long way to ensure that project-affected people have ready access to justice at the project-level, especially as IAM s are designed as mechanisms of last resort. The periodic reviews of IAM and related environmental and social policies provide an opportunity for the MDB boards to act and make changes to improve access to remedial forums.

Finally, a word of caution on non-sovereign operations of IFI s. IFI management often makes a special case for different treatment of non-sovereign operations based on the commercial needs for confidentiality. They have largely succeeded in this argument, to the point that environmental and social information about the implementation phase of these projects is hardly in the public domain. A quick look at the IFC and other IFI s that undertake non-sovereign operations will confirm this. This is a serious issue, particularly in the context of financial intermediation operations that are increasingly a significant part of non-sovereign operations.

An interesting development is the increasing focus in domestic law on Environmental, Social, and Governance (ESG) and its requirements. For example,

---

Environmental and Social Management Plan includes "(e) provisions for the Project's GRM s, as well as a description of the PPM or other Bank-approved IAM and how they can be accessed"; *see also* notes 6 – 16 and accompanying text (discussing PPM Policy and Rules, 7.2 and 7.3 of the Rules of Procedure of PPM)).

several new regulatory requirements came into effect in 2023, such as the EU Corporate Sustainability Reporting Directive, the Sustainable Finance Reporting Directive and the German Supply Chain Due Diligence Act (LkSG). The regulatory requirements ratchet up reporting requirements for large firms and seek to provide remedies against exploitation and environmental damage. As these regulations further develop, it will be interesting to see how they also develop the requirements regarding disclosure for remedies. In the interests of credibility, IFIs cannot afford to be lagging the national requirements that they have traditionally led. Any foot-dragging in this respect will undermine the credibility and prestige of IFIs. It is imperative that IFIs develop and adopt such requirements to improve environmental social standards in their projects and regularly monitor their enforcement for continuous improvement.

TABLE 24.1 Surveyed active energy project portfolio in Pakistan

World Bank	**Asian Development Bank**
Electricity Distribution Efficiency Improvement Project https://projects.worldbank.org/en/projects-operations/project-detail/P170230	Second Power Transmission Enhancement Investment Program (Tranche 4) https://www.adb.org/projects/48078-006/main
Khyber Pakhtunkhwa Hydropower and Renewable Energy Development https://projects.worldbank.org/en/projects-operations/project-detail/P163461	MFF Power Transmission Enhancement Investment Program II Tranche 3 https://www.adb.org/projects/48078-005/main
Pakistan Community Support Project (CASA–1000) https://projects.worldbank.org/en/projects-operations/project-detail/P151075	Second Power Transmission Enhancement Investment Program – Tranche 2 https://www.adb.org/projects/48078-004/main
Additional Financing For Dasu Hydropower Stage I Project (Transmission Line) https://projects.worldbank.org/en/projects-operations/project-detail/P167843	Second Power Transmission Enhancement Investment Program – Tranche 1 https://www.adb.org/projects/48078-003/main
National Transmission Modernization I Project https://projects.worldbank.org/en/projects-operations/project-detail/P154987	Second Power Transmission Enhancement Investment Program https://www.adb.org/projects/48078-002/main

(*cont.*)

TABLE 24.1 Surveyed active energy project portfolio in Pakistan (*cont.*)

World Bank	Asian Development Bank
Additional Financing to PK: Tarbela 4th Extension Hydropower Project https://projects.worldbank.org/en/projects-operations/project-detail/P157372	Second Power Distribution Enhancement Investment Program – Tranche 1 https://www.adb.org/projects/47190-003/main
Dasu Hydropower Stage I Project https://projects.worldbank.org/en/projects-operations/project-detail/P121507	Second Power Distribution Enhancement Investment Program https://www.adb.org/projects/47190-002/main
Tarbela Fourth Extension Hydropower Project https://projects.worldbank.org/en/projects-operations/project-detail/P115893	Jamshoro Power Generation Project (47094-001; Pakistan; Energy) https://www.adb.org/projects/47094-001/main

Bibliography

Asian Infrastructure Investment Bank [AIIB]. *Report on the Articles of Agreement of the Asian Infrastructure Investment Bank*. Beijing: AIIB, June 6, 2015: 3.

AIIB. *Articles of Agreement*. Beijing: AIIB, June 26, 2015: Art. 1, para.1.

AIIB. *Environmental and Social Framework*. Beijing: AIIB, February 2016, amended November 2022: Section 66.2.

AIIB. *AIIB Policy on the Project-affected People's Mechanism*. Beijing: AIIB, December 7, 2018: 8, Sect. 7.3.

AIIB. *Articles of Agreement*. Beijing: AIIB, June 15, 2019: Art. 26, 15–16.

AIIB. *Governance: Oversight Mechanism*. Beijing: AIIB, July 10, 2019.

AIIB. *About AIIB: Introduction*. Accessed December 15, 2024. https://www.aiib.org/en/about-aiib/index.html.

Eminent Persons Group. *Making the Financial Global System Work for All: Report of the Eminent Persons Group on Global Finance Governance*. Global Finance Governance, October 2018.

Horta, Korinna. "Asian Infrastructure Investment Bank: A Multilateral Bank Where China Sets the Rules." *Publication Series on Democracy*. (December 24, 2018): 52.

Thapa, Rabi. *Realizing Zero Tolerance Against Reprisals*. Washington DC: World Bank, January 19, 2023.

World Bank Group. *Record of the Portfolio Management Task Force (Wapenhans Report) and Follow Up*. Washington DC: World Bank, 1992.

CHAPTER 25

The River of Accountability Mechanisms: Then and Now

Suresh Nanwani[*]

1 The Source and the Flow of the River

In 1993, the river of international accountability mechanisms (IAMs) commenced from its source: the World Bank Inspection Panel (the Panel). In its journey, the river was fed by the tributaries of similar accountability mechanisms from other development institutions, including four regional development banks – the Inter-American Development Bank (IADB) in 1994, the Asian Development Bank in 1995, the European Bank for Reconstruction and Development (EBRD) in 2003, and the African Development Bank (AfDB) in 2006. It also welcomed other entities – bilateral institutions like the Japan Bank for International Cooperation (2003) and Proparco (2018), and others like the United Nations Development Program (2014), the Green Climate Fund (2017) and the Asian Infrastructure Investment Bank (AIIB) (2018).[1]

Thirty years on, the river is still navigating several winding courses to manage its flow while fulfilling the IAMs' purpose as people-driven mechanisms. The International Accountability Mechanisms Network (IAMNet) was established under the auspices of the Panel in 2004 to enhance coordination among the IAMs.[2] Initially, the IAMNet included entities like the citizen submission unit of the North American Agreement on Environmental Cooperation, but later IAMNet membership was clarified and limited to public institutions that provide or support development finance. The IAMNet states that while the IAMs "differ in nature and structure, collectively they share a common mission to independently assess people's complaints and seek a response to their concerns."

* Suresh Nanwani is Professor in Practice at Durham University, United Kingdom and Honorary Research Fellow at Birkbeck University of London.

1 Information on these and other IAMs can be found at the website of the Independent Accountability Network (IAMNet). *See* World Bank Inspection Panel, *About Us: International Accountability Mechanism Network*, https://www.inspectionpanel.org/about-us/independent-accountability-network (last visited Dec. 9, 2024).

2 *Id.*

From its inauguration in 2004 with a handful of organizations, it grew to eleven in 2012; as of August 2023, the network has expanded to over twenty IAMs.

These mechanisms are viewed as "independent" in assessing people's complaints and in seeking a response to their concerns. They are independent from management, they report to the board of directors, and they are able to take measures that effectively enhance the development outcomes of their organizations. This assumption is a central theme in this essay. I also include my views and experiences with IAMs; share my experience teaching this subject to students in various countries and obtaining their responses and reactions as future leaders; present an examination of the Jamuna New Multipurpose Bridge Project request, its impact then, and how some barriers have been removed; review the claimant's needs in a citizen-driven mechanism; and suggest best practices for accountability mechanisms moving forward.

Despite the proliferation of IAMs to address claims by project-impacted communities and the periodic reviews of many institutional accountability mechanism policies, there is still room for improvement in each mechanism and in the overall direction of the IAMs. While there were positive aspects in the setup of these mechanisms, there have also been shortcomings. Overall, the landscape has changed over the years to better serve the needs of project communities. Still more needs to be done to achieve the lofty goal of independently assessing people's concerns and seeking responses to these.

My views are based on my work with IAMs in different capacities, including as one of the two co-drafters of the ADB accountability mechanism policy (2003); Associate Secretary of the ADB Compliance Review Panel; Acting Head of the Office of the Compliance Review Panel; Secretary of the ADB Board of Directors' Compliance Review Committee; accountability practitioner; and lecturer. My views are also shaped by many interactions with civil society members, including those championing advocacy and good governance in development finance.

2 My Views and Experiences – Including Teaching Students

The Panel's early years were fraught with many issues, including Panel independence and access.[3] In teaching the topic of accountability mechanisms in a course on international development finance, I have found that having case studies of actual project claims provides students with a wider mindset on

3 Lori Udall. *The World Bank Inspection Panel: A Three Year Review*, Bank Information Center (Oct. 1997).

various issues raised in these claims, and how the accountability mechanism has addressed them, while learning how complex organizations work at the project level. Overall students' reactions are a mixed bag:

- Surprise at the idea that individuals have a voice, at the international level, to articulate their grievances on projects supported by development financial institutions;
- Dismay that the remedies available to the project affectees are limited so no damages can be offered or injunctions enforced, and that the process can be politicized within the institution, including by management and staff, the Board of Directors, and shareholder member countries;
- Wonder that the mechanism with its central theme of accountability (and its multifaceted meanings) and good governance is critical to many contexts, such as public disclosure policies and environmental, social, and governance frameworks for the organization;
- Added wonder that the case studies remind students of similar cases in their own experience that they may see anew through the lens of a more informed perspective; and
- Hope that the current climate change regime, with its impact on the world and on development, will allow far more openness, transparency, and discussion around accountability, and with more participatory outcomes for project affectees and civil society organizations (CSOs) that were officially not part of the Bank's development business forty years ago.

In my teaching, students' insights in their discussions on claims filed with accountability mechanisms have been candid and insightful:

- When claimants file again on the same project with repeated concerns such as involuntary resettlement, the legacy projects are not managed more effectively by the institutions to enhance their organizational development effectiveness (such as the Southern Transport Development Project in Sri Lanka[4] and the Bujagali hydropower plant project in Uganda[5]).
- Despite the purpose of the mechanisms to address project concerns by citizens, the immunity of the organizations is viewed as an impediment in delivering effective remedies for project communities; the immunity should be seriously reconsidered by the institutions if they wish to effectively address project concerns.

4 Asian Development Bank, *Sri Lanka: Southern Transport Development,* https://www.adb.org/projects/26522-013/main (last visited Dec. 9, 2024).

5 *See* Centre for Public Impact, *The Bujagali Dam Project in Uganda* (July 28, 2017) https://centreforpublicimpact.org/public-impact-fundamentals/the-bujagali-dam-project-in-uganda/, (last visited Jan. 25, 2024).

- The institutions should take active steps by setting aside funds to defray for non-compliance as the projects are prepared and financed in accordance with their procedures and policies.

The students have varying views in the rich debate and they realize that development is a gradual process. Importantly they gain awareness that much more can be done by the institutions to prevent the design and implementation of poorly-designed projects.

3 The Jamuna New Multipurpose Bridge Project Request

I am also struck by students' reactions when they discuss the Jamuna New Multipurpose Bridge Project request[6] (1996) as a case study in class, particularly as they consider improvements in the project that could avoid harmful impacts on marginalized communities. The *Jamuna* claim, which was early in the World Bank Inspection Panel, was significant because it empowered about 3,000 char (island) people in the Jamuna River – the poorest and most vulnerable people in Bangladesh. They signed the request through signatures and thumb prints, and authorized the director of Jamuna Char Integrated Development Project (JCDP), a local CSO, to represent them. The Panel conducted an assessment of the claim and management's response but did not recommend an investigation of the claim on the basis that management would follow through on its commitments under the Erosion and Flood Policy (EFP) agreed with the government of Bangladesh.

THE EFP was a milestone because it provided the people in Bangladesh – including the char dwellers who had been excluded from the project's design and appraisal phases, such as the environmental and resettlement plans – the right to compensation for losses from river erosion. JCDP had working relationships with international CSOs such as International Rivers Network and Center for International Environmental Law. In 1996, JCDP did not have access to the Internet, and it also lacked information or guidance based on other requests that had been filed with the Panel. Additionally, it encountered difficulties in filing a claim in English, as the panel procedures and other documents were not available in Bengali and most of the claimants had no formal education. I also highlight this claim in the matters below.

6 The World Bank Inspection Panel, *Jamuna New Multipurpose Bridge Project* (last visited Dec. 9, 2024) https://www.inspectionpanel.org/panel-cases/jamuna-new-multipurpose-bridge-project.

3.1 *A Powerful Tool for Voices to Be Heard*

The Panel achieved a powerful result even in its early years: from remote areas in Bangladesh, the 3,000 disenfranchised char dwellers had their voices heard at the World Bank's headquarters in Washington, D.C. The claim caught considerable international media attention, partially as a result of the number of claimants; few later claims at other accountability mechanisms were brought by so many. Many IAMs have since published their communications materials in languages other than the institution's official languages, and the Panel information brochure is available in many languages including Bengali. Claims may now be filed in languages other than English, and local languages can now be used in almost all the mechanisms.

3.2 *Forum Shopping*

The claimants are free to forum shop if the project is supported by institutions with accountability mechanisms. The claimants in the Bangladesh project had the option to file a claim with the then fledgling ADB Inspection Function (1995), as ADB was also a co-financier. However, the claimants chose to access the Panel because it attracted more international attention, and the World Bank was the lead agency among the lending institutions.

Forum shopping allows claimants to approach their IAMs of choice for various reasons, including a better functioning mechanism with experience and visible public attention (in the case of the Bangladesh project) and where there had already been claims filed with the key institutional lender, Asian Development Bank (the Southern Transport Development Project)[7] instead of the Japan Bank for International Cooperation, which provided parallel financing – in this instance many project matters were left to ADB including the application of ADB's safeguard policies. In another example, the claimants chose to use two mechanisms at the same time – the World Bank Inspection Panel[8] and AfDB's accountability mechanism[9] in the Private Power Generation Project (Bujagali hydropower plant). The claimants wanted to know how their requests for compliance review would work out at both institutions, as each institution would investigate following their own operational policies.

7 Asian Development Bank Compliance Review Panel, *Sri Lanka Southern Transport Development Project*, https://lnadbg4.adb.org/dir0035p.nsf/alldocs/BDAO-7XVBSH?OpenDocument (last visited Dec. 9, 2024).

8 The World Bank Inspection Panel, *Uganda: Private Power Generation Project*, https://www.inspectionpanel.org/panel-cases/private-power-generation-project (last visited Dec. 9, 2024).

9 African Bank Development Group, *RQ 2007/1 (Uganda)*, https://www.afdb.org/en/independent-review-mechanism/management-of-complaints/registered-requests/rq-20071-uganda (last visited Dec. 9, 2024).

Many project claims have since been filed with two or more mechanisms, such as the Pando Montelirio Hydropower Electric project (Panama)[10] claim filed with IADB's Independent Consultation and Investigation Mechanism (ICIM) and the International Finance Corporation's Compliance Advisor Ombudsman (CAO) Office, and the Baku-Tbilisi-Ceyhan pipeline project (Azerbaijan, Georgia, Turkey)[11] filed with the CAO Office and EBRD's accountability mechanism.

3.3 *Gradual Progress on Better Access*

Another development is that IAMs have made themselves more accessible over time by gradually removing barriers to access, such as eliminating requirements that claims only be filed in English and that they must cite the specific policies alleged to have been violated. As part of this, IAMs have extended the period within which a claim can be filed – the Panel, for example, replaced its rule barring claims on projects after 95 percent of the loan has been disbursed to a rule permitting claims until 15 months after closure of the loan financing the project,[12] which is more aligned with the rule at other IAMs (for example, two years after the loan closing date at the ADB Accountability Mechanism[13] and fifteen months after termination of the financing, investment, or guarantee period at the IFC and MIGA).[14]

It is surprising, given that the Panel is the fountainhead of all accountability mechanisms, that there has not been as much progress with the others in two key areas. First, the Panel does not automatically monitor the outcome of the decisions by the Board of Directors based on the Panel's findings report. This is an area where some mechanisms such as THE ADB accountability mechanism, EBRD Independent Project Accountability Mechanism (IPAM), and AfDB Independent Recourse Mechanism (IRM) fare far better in moving forward.

10 InterAmerican Development Bank. Independent Consultation and Investigation Mechanism, *Pando-Monte Lirio Hydroelectric Power Project*, https://www.iadb.org/en/project/PN-L1054 (last visited Dec. 9, 2024).

11 Compliance Advisor Ombudsman, *Georgia: BTC Pipeline-09/Tetriskaro*, https://www.cao-ombudsman.org/cases/georgia-btc-pipeline-09tetritskaro#:~:text=Synopsis&text=The%20Baku%2DTbilisi%2DCeyhan%20 (last visited Dec. 9, 2024).

12 World Bank Inspection Panel, *Resolution No. IBRD 2020–0004 and Resolution No. IDA 2020–0003*, para. 15 (c) (ii) (Sept. 8, 2020).

13 Asian Development Bank, *Accountability Mechanism Policy 2012*, para. 142(iv) (Mar. 22, 2012).

14 Compliance Advisor/Ombudsman, *IFC/MIGA Independent Accountability Mechanism (CAO) Policy* (June 28, 2021).

Second, the Panel allows groups of two or more private citizens who believe that they or their interests have been or could be harmed by Bank-financed activities to present their concerns through a request for inspection. This is also the position taken by the ADB Accountability Mechanism.[15] However, other mechanisms have gone much further in allowing CSOs or individuals to file claims. The CAO Office at IFC/MIGA was the first to incorporate this claimant eligibility, which has since been emulated by other mechanisms including the EBRD's IPAM.

The fear of the "floodgate principle" behind the World Bank Inspection Panel's or ADB accountability mechanism's threshold does not hold any water, as there has been no deluge of claims in the many other mechanisms allowing individuals to file claims. Upholding the right of individuals to file claims makes the mechanisms more friendly and accessible, as citizen-driven mechanisms, without the rigid requirement of a group of two or more persons.

3.4 *What Does a Claimant Really Want?*

Despite the platitudes found in the communications of many accountability mechanisms – for example, "[t]he Inspection Panel is an independent complaints mechanism for people and communities who believe that they have been, or are likely to be, adversely affected by a World Bank-funded project"[16] – the reality of the IAM's ability to truly be a mechanism that can actually meet the claimant's needs is far different. IAMs reflect the principle of "citizen-driven accountability," which aims to give greater voice and rights of recourse to people with respect to actions that affect them.[17] Yet, when it comes to the crunch, the avenues afforded to the claimants are essentially still driven by the institutions.

An example is the 1995 ADB Inspection Function (IF) policy, using the term "inspection" from the World Bank Inspection Panel. ADB received responses from civil society objecting to the exclusion of private sector operations from the scope of the IF policy. ADB's response was that this concern would be visited as part of the general review of the policy. In 1998, ADB reviewed the IF policy on the application of the inspection procedures to private sector operations, as was required by the 1995 policy. However, ADB produced only a working paper,

15 *Id.* at para. 138.

16 The World Bank Inspection Panel, *Home* (last visited Dec. 9, 2024) https://www.inspectionpanel.org/.

17 Kristen Lewis, *Citizen-driven Accountability for Sustainable Development: Giving Affected People a Greater Voice—20 Years On. A contribution to Rio+20 by the Independent Accountability Mechanisms Network,* World Bank Inspection Panel (June 2012).

not a final Board-approved paper, after the review. In 2003, after a two-year extensive consultation process, both internal and external, ADB replaced its IF policy with an Accountability Mechanism policy that not only allowed both problem-solving and compliance review, but also expanded to cover private sector operations. The review process was a marked 180-degree turnaround from the 1995 IF policy, which had no public consultation review. A representative from Bank Information Center, USA in the Washington, D.C. workshop in 2002 stated that "this was the best consultation that ADB has done in its working with NGOs" and that the full impact "is not there as yet, but almost."[18] The extensive engagement made by ADB with civil society was critical to the delivery of a credible new policy where CSOs felt their voices were heard if not always incorporated.

Thirty years on, the avenues for responding to complaints have shifted gear since the Panel's sole focus on compliance review in 1993. Most mechanisms now encompass three broad functions: compliance review, problem-solving, and advisory. Problem-solving and compliance review, as dual options applicable to the whole institution, were introduced in 2003 by the ADB. At the time, Panel member Marta van Putten considered "the ADB model a vanguard amongst the accountability mechanisms."[19] (The initial examples of problem-solving were found in the CAO, which only covered the private operations of the World Bank Group – i.e. the IFC and MIGA). The CAO was also the first IAM to include Advisory Services, and today many other IAMs have incorporated the advisory function to enhance the development effectiveness of the operation of their respective institutions.[20]

3.5 *Need to Be More Responsive to Claimants*

The public consultations carried out by many IFIs in enunciating a new policy or in updating their accountability mechanisms have demonstrated the need to be more responsive to claimants, who are still largely left out of the equation. And accountability mechanisms are still seen as internal governance tools of the IFIs. This stance is at odds with the principle of citizen-driven mechanism, as at the end, the decision on any complaint rests within the institution and its member shareholders.

18 Asian Development Bank, *Summary of Proceedings Report: External Consultations to Review the Inspection Function* (2002).

19 Maartje Van Putten & Maria Jeanette Anna Putten, Policing the World: Accountability Mechanisms for Multilateral Financial Institutions and Private Financial Institutions 129 (2006).

20 *See, e.g.,* U.S. International Development Finance Corporation, *Independent Accountability Mechanism* https://www.dfc.gov/our-impact/transparency/independent-accountability-mechanism (last visited Dec. 9, 2024).

In recent years, there has been a widening of the ambit to allow "redress" for claimants; the Green Climate Fund's IRM is required to be "cost-effective and expeditious in the delivery of just redress"[21] in line with its mandate "to address complaints from affected people and provide recourse in a way that is fair, effective and transparent, and enhance the performance of GCF's climate funding."[22] The term redress is defined in the Procedures and Guidelines of the Independent Redress Mechanism as:

> to set right or remedy an adverse impact that has been or may be caused by a GCF funded project or programme. When such a project or programme has been found to be not in compliance WITH GCF operational policies and procedures, redress includes bringing the project or program into compliance.[23]

The definition of redress is wider here than merely bringing the project back into compliance.

The debate on reinforcing remedy stems not just from project communities – who are effectively shut out from the mechanism process at many stages – but has been given voice by many practitioners. Civil society groups, including Accountability Counsel, also reinforce advocacy for the effective functioning of IAMs. They advocate for providing "remedy for environmental harm and rights abuses."[24] The reality is that these mechanisms were not designed for judicial remedies, as they were internal administrative tools for the institutions.

4 Best Practices Moving Forward

There have been many proposals suggesting the best criteria for an accountability mechanism. As early as 2003, Hunter[25] proffered three basic criteria:

---

21 The Green Climate Fund, *Annex II: Updated terms of reference of the Independent Redress Mechanism* (Sept. 25, 2017).

22 The Green Climate Fund Independent Redress Mechanism, *About the IRM*, https://irm.greenclimate.fund/about#:~:text=The%20IRM%27s%20mission%20is%20to,performance%20of%20GCF%27s%20climate%20funding (last visited Dec. 9, 2024).

23 Green Climate Fund, *Procedures and Guidelines for Independent Redress Mechanisms* (July 14, 2021).

24 Komala Ramachandra, *Civil Society in the Independent Accountability Community of Practice*, in OWEN MCINTRYE & SURESH NANWANI (EDS.), THE PRACTICE OF INDEPENDENT ACCOUNTABILITY MECHANISMS: TOWARDS GOOD GOVERNANCE IN DEVELOPMENT FINANCE 291–307 (2019).

25 David Hunter, *Using the World Bank Inspection Panel to Defend the Interests of Project-Affected People*, 4 CHICAGO J. OF INT'L L. 201–211 (2003).

independence from bank management, transparency, and participation by the local communities affected by the bank's projects. These critical criteria have given rise to other useful lists. Since 2005, academics and practitioners have recommended benchmarks in designing an accountability mechanism, including Bradlow,[26] Weiss,[27] Bridgeman and Hunter,[28] and Bissell and Nanwani.[29] The standards are broadly similar and in sync with the benchmarks of the United Nations Guiding Principles' effectiveness criteria, with a significant emphasis on business and human rights, including addressing the provision of effective remedies and reprisal.

There is no perfect recipe for an ideal accountability mechanism. In my view, the best practice lies in adapting to the needs of the project communities, including the need for protection from retaliation, in recognition of the crucial role played by CSOs as independent development actors under the Accra Agenda for Action;[30] and highlighting of the work by the UN Office of the High Commissioner for Human Rights (OHCHR) on its Accountability and Remedy Project (ARP) from 2014 to 2022, including its publication on Remedy and Development Finance: Guidance and Application.[31]

This forward-looking approach is in line with current thinking on expanding the accessibility of accountability mechanisms to users and addressing their needs, in addition to enhancing institutional development effectiveness. But before expanding this access, the issue of independence has to be settled. One clear instance is the 2012 ADB Accountability Mechanism,[32] where the Special Project Facilitator is appointed by and reports to the President. CSOs were not satisfied that there was no change to ensure the independence of the mechanism during the public consultations leading to the 2012 ADB accountability

26 Daniel Bradlow, *Private Complainants and International Organizations: A Comparative Study of The Independent Inspection Mechanisms in International Financial Institutions*, 36 GEORGETOWN JOURNAL OF INTERNATIONAL LAW 405–494 (2005).

27 Fourth Meeting of Principals of Independent Accountability Mechanisms in International Financial Institutions held in June 2007 in EBRD, London.

28 Natalie Bridgeman & David Hunter, *Narrowing the Accountability Gap: Toward a New Foreign Investor Accountability Mechanism*, 20 GEORGETOWN INT'L ENVTL. L. REV. 188–236 (2008).

29 Richard Bissell & Suresh Nanwani, *Multilateral Development Bank Accountability Mechanisms: Developments and Challenges*, 3(2) CENTRAL EUROPEAN JOURNAL OF INTERNATIONAL AND SECURITY STUDIES 154–197 (2009).

30 Organization of Economic Cooperation and Development, *Accra Agenda for Action* (2008).

31 Office of High Commissioner for Human Rights, *Remedy and Development Finance: Guidance and Application* (Feb. 23, 2022).

32 Asian Development Bank, *supra* note 18.

mechanism; as a result, three CSOs disengaged from the consultations – Both ENDs, the NGO Forum on ADB, and Oxfam Australia. This was in stark contrast to the more constructive CSO engagement during the previous consultations that resulted in the 2003 ADM accountability mechanism (noted above).

The Panel experience, to which Bissell attests, remains valid today for many accountability mechanisms – Panel independence is only partial at best with the Board of Directors divided in supporting the statutory independence of the Panel, and the grim reality that both the Board of Directors and Management, in their own ways and from different perspectives, are uncomfortable with the Panel being independent.[33] De Silva identifies two fatal flaws in the IAM system in his article on *Fixing a Broken Accountability System at MDBs and DFIs*:[34] the Board and President are not impartial or independent as they are political by nature, and there is a break in the chain of accountability.

Panel independence still remains a vexing and unresolved issue in terms of operational independence. The Panel and other IAMs are all independent (with many mechanisms incorporating "independent" in their names, such as EBRD's Independent Project Accountability Mechanism).[35] This independence is crucial to the nomenclature of the *Independent* Accountability Mechanisms. These mechanisms should not be viewed as independent as a façade because they incorporate yardsticks as credible mechanisms by their users. The conditions for IAM members to have not immediately previously worked as staff members, to have fixed term appointments, and to be permanently barred from employment in the organization after serving the term are pivotal; but more needs to be done to ensure non-politicization by the institution through its Board of Directors and Management. Representation from civil society needs to be firmly entrenched – and not for window dressing – in the appointment and selection process to ensure credibility for the independent mechanism.

With the climate change regime now taking precedence over the "right to development" agenda of the 1990s, as well as the ongoing transformational change on the review of the World Bank Evolution Roadmap, we are at a turning point for institutions that are either contemplating accountability

33 Richard Bissell, *Institutional and Procedural Aspects of the Inspection Panel*, in G. Alfredsson & E. Ring, eds., The Inspection Panel of the World Bank: A Different Complaints Procedure 107–125 (2001).

34 Lalanath de Silva, *Fixing a Broken Accountability System at MDBs and DFIs*, LinkedIn (Oct. 26, 2022).

35 European Bank for Reconstruction and Development, Independent Project Accountability Mechanism, *About IPAM*, https://www.ebrd.com/ipam (last visited Dec. 9, 2024).

mechanisms such as the New Development Bank[36] or seeking to update their accountability mechanisms. In 2024, at least four multilateral development banks – World Bank, ADB, EBRD, and Asian Infrastructure Investment Bank – are reviewing their accountability mechanism policies and procedures, and IAN and civil society can seize this occasion by contributing to modernize them with best global practices. The IAMNet can also serve as a collective platform to discuss effective ways of addressing citizen complaints on legacy projects, as these projects involve institutional lenders. It would serve citizens as well as the institutions in establishing how these legacy projects can be addressed by all to avoid repetition and to enhance development outcomes, as in the cases of the Bujagali hydropower plant project in Uganda and the Baku-Tbilisi-Ceyhan (BTC) pipeline project.

As the mechanisms are citizen-driven, the role of civil society cannot be ignored. Civil society can and continues to play a pivotal role in empowering accountability mechanisms to serve their purpose by managing the currents and rapids as the river meanders to the sea as a truly people-driven mechanism.

Bibliography

African Development Group. *Independent Recourse Mechanism.* Accessed December 9, 2024. https://www.afdb.org/en/about-us/organisational-structure/independent-review-mechanism-irm.

Asian Development Bank [ADB]. *Summary of Proceedings Report: External Consultations to Review the Inspection Function.* Manilla: ADB, 2002.

ADB. *Accountability Mechanism Policy 2012.* Washington DC: ADB, March 22, 2012.

ADB. *Accountability Mechanism.* Accessed December 9, 2024. https://www.adb.org/who-we-are/accountability-mechanism.

ADB. *Sri Lanka: Southern Transport Development.* Accessed December 9, 2024. https://www.adb.org/projects/26522-013/main.

Asian Infrastructure Investment Bank [AIIB]. *Project-Affected People's Mechanism: How We Assist You.* Accessed December 9, 2024. https://www.aiib.org/en/about-aiib/who-we-are/project-affected-peoples-mechanism/how-we-assist-you/index.html.

36 New Development Bank, *New Development Bank General Strategy for 2022–2026: Scaling up Development Finance For a Sustainable Future*, 25 (July 28, 2024) ("To adequately address grievances arising out of its expanding operations and to collect feedback from clients as well as individuals, communities, and civil society organizations (CSOs), the Bank will establish well-designed mechanisms that will supplement clients' own grievance redressal mechanisms.").

Bissell, Richard. "International and Procedural Aspects of International Law," in *The Inspection Panel of the World Bank: A Different Complaints Procedure*, edited by Gudmundur Alfredsson and Rolf Ring, 107–125. Leiden: Brill, 2001.

Bissell, Richard, and Suresh Nanwani. "Multilateral Development Bank Accountability Mechanisms: Developments and Challenges." *Central European Journal of International and Security Studies*, 3, no. 2 (2009): 154–197.

Bradlow, Daniel. "Private Complainants and International Organizations: A Comparative Study of The Independent Inspection Mechanisms in International Financial Institutions." *Georgetown Journal of International Law*, 36 (2005): 405–494.

Bridgeman, Natalia, and David Hunter. "Narrowing the Accountability Gap: Toward a New Foreign Investor Accountability Mechanism." *Georgetown International Environmental Law Review*. (2008): 188–236.

CAO. *IFC/MIGA Independent Accountability Mechanism (CAO) Policy*. Washington DC: CAO, June 28, 2021.

Centre for Public Impact. *The Bujagali Dam Project in Uganda*. Washington: Centre for Public Impact, July 28, 2017.

de Silva, Lalanath. *Fixing a Broken Accountability System at MDBs and DFIs*. LinkedIn. October 26, 2022.

European Bank for Reconstruction and Development [EBRD]. *Fourth Meeting of Principals of Independent Accountability Mechanisms in International Financial Institutions*. London: EBRD, June 2007.

ERBD. Independent Project Accountability Mechanism. *About IPAM*. Accessed December 9, 2024, https://www.ebrd.com/ipam.

The Green Climate Fund. *Annex II: Updated terms of reference of the Independent Redress Mechanism*. Songdo: Green Climate Fund, September 25, 2017.

The Green Climate Fund. *Procedures and Guidelines for Independent Redress Mechanisms*. Songdo: Green Climate Fund, July 14, 2021.

The Green Climate Fund. *Independent Redress Mechanism*. Accessed December 9, 2024. https://irm.greenclimate.fund/.

Hunter, David. "Using the World Bank Inspection Panel to Defend the Interests of Project-Affected People." *Chicago Journal of International*. 4, no. 1 (2003): 201–211.

Inter-American Development Bank, Mechanism: Independent Consultation and Investigation. *Home*. Accessed December 9, 2024. https://mici.iadb.org/en.

Japan Bank for International Cooperation. *Summary of Objection Procedures Based on Guidelines for Confirmation of Environmental and Social Considerations*. Accessed December 9, 2024. https://www.jbic.go.jp/en/business-areas/environment/disagree.html.

Lewis, Kristen. *Citizen-driven Accountability for Sustainable Development: Giving Affected People a Greater Voice—20 Years On. A contribution to Rio+20 by the Independent Accountability Mechanisms Network*. Washington DC: World Bank, June 2021.

New Development Bank. *New Development Bank General Strategy for 2022–2026: Scaling up Development Finance For a Sustainable Future*. Shanghai: New Development Bank, July 28, 2024: 25.

Office of the United Nations High Commission of Human Rights [OHCHR]. *Remedy and Development Finance: Guidance and Application*. Geneva: OHCHR, February 23, 2022.

Organization of Economic Co-Operation and Development. *Accra Agenda for Action*. Parish: OECD Publishing, 2008.

Proparco. *Environmental and Social Independent Complaints Mechanism (ICM)*. Accessed December 9, 2024. https://www.proparco.fr/en/icm.

Ramachandra, Komala. "Civil Society in the Independent Accountability Community of Practice," in *The Practice of Independent Accountability Mechanisms: Towards Good Governance in Development Finance*, edited by Owen McIntyre and Suresh Nanwani, 291–307. Leiden: Brill Nijoff, 2019.

Lori Udall. *The World Bank Inspection Panel: A Three Year Review*. Washington DC: Bank Information Center, October 1997.

United States International Development Finance Corporation. *Independent Accountability Mechanism*. Accessed December 9, 2024. https://www.dfc.gov/our-impact/transparency/independent-accountability-mechanism.

The United Nations Development Programme. *UNDP Accountability*. Accessed December 9, 2024. https://www.undp.org/accountability/audit/social-and-environmental-compliance-review-and-stakeholder-response-mechanism.

Van Putten, Maartje, Maria Jeanette, and Anna Putten. *Policing the World: Accountability Mechanisms for Multilateral Financial Institutions and Private Financial Institutions*. Tilburg: Tilburg University, 2006: 129.

The World Bank Inspection Panel. *Home*. Accessed December 9, 2024. https://www.inspectionpanel.org/.

The World Bank Inspection Panel. *The Inspection Panel*. Accessed December 9, 2024. https://www.inspectionpanel.org/.

The World Bank Inspection Panel. *Jamuna New Multipurpose Bridge Project*. Accessed December 9, 2024. https://www.inspectionpanel.org/panel-cases/jamuna-new-multipurpose-bridge-project.

The World Bank Inspection Panel. *About Us: International Accountability Mechanism Network*. Accessed December 9, 2024. https://www.inspectionpanel.org/about-us/independent-accountability-network.

CHAPTER 26

A Proposal for One "Super" Independent Accountability Mechanism

*Daniel D. Bradlow**

1 Introduction**

One of the most significant developments in international affairs since the Second World War has been the expanding role of international organizations. They were designed to act with restraint, out of respect for the sovereignty of their member states, and in support of their member state's efforts to promote international peace and security, international economic cooperation, and human welfare.[1] However, some of them are now actively engaged in performing such functions in their member states as peacekeeping; managing refugee camps; reviewing the performance of national financial sectors; financing and monitoring the implementation of development projects and programmes; giving policy advice; and providing technical assistance.[2] This means that these organizations are making decisions that are directly affecting the lives of the citizens of their member states.

This evolution in their operations has implications for the relationship between individual international organizations and their member states and for their accountability to those who are affected by their operations.

The Multilateral Development Banks (MDBs) provide a good illustration of these changes in the role of international organizations. They have evolved from institutions focused on merely funding specific projects into entities involved in a range of development financing and advisory activities in their member states. They have also become leaders in formulating, interpreting, and applying standards for dealing with the environmental and social impacts of development projects. Consequently, their decisions are directly affecting

---

* Professor/Senior Research Fellow, Centre for Advancement of Scholarship, University of Pretoria and Professor of Law Emeritus, American University Washington College of Law.

** This article was originally published in 11 Indian Journal of International Economic Law (2019).

1 Jan Klabbers, An Introduction to International Organizations Law (3rd ed. 2015).

2 *Id.*

the societies in which the projects and programmes they fund are located. These developments have raised concerns about how those communities or groups that are adversely affected by their operations can hold the MDBS accountable for their decisions and their impacts.

This essay will discuss how the MDBS[3] – for example, the World Bank Group, the African, Asian, and Inter-American Development Banks, and more recently the European Bank for Reconstruction and Development, Asian Infrastructure Investment Bank, and the New Development Bank – are dealing with the issue of accountability. It will argue that, although the MDBS have been leaders in promoting international organizational accountability, their mechanisms of accountability are not keeping up with the evolution in their operations. In the interests of promoting new and creative thinking about these issues, it will also make an ambitious proposal for how the MDBS jointly can more effectively meet the accountability challenge that they face while also respecting the sovereignty of their member states and protecting an appropriate level of immunity for the MDBS.

The paper is divided into two parts. The first part will provide some background on the MDBS and their current approach to accountability. The second part discusses the proposal for improving MDB accountability.

2 Background on the MDBS

The oldest MDB, the International Bank for Reconstruction and Development (IBRD or Bank), was created at the Bretton Woods conference in 1944 and

3 These are the most prominent MDBS and the most significant either globally or in their regions. Consequently, they are the focus of this article. For more information on these banks see generally The World Bank, https://www.worldbank.org/ (last visited Dec. 18, 2024); The African Development Bank [AfDB], https://www.afdb.org/en/(last visited Dec. 18, 2024); The Asian Development Bank [ADB], https://www.adb.org/(last visited May 11, 2019); The Inter-American Development Bank [IADB], https://www.iadb.org/en(last visited Dec. 18, 2024); The European Bank for Reconstruction and Development Bank [EBRD], https://www.ebrd.com/home (last visited Dec. 18, 2024); The Asian Infrastructure Investment Bank [AIIB], https://www.aiib.org/en/index.html (last visited Dec. 18, 2024); The New Development Bank, https://www.ndb.int/ (last visited Dec. 18, 2024). For more information on the international law relating to the MDBS, see generally DANIEL D. BRADLOW & DAVID HUNTER, INTERNATIONAL FINANCIAL INSTRUCTIONS AND INTERNATIONAL LAW (2010). However, it is important to note that there are other MDBS, such as the Islamic Development Bank and sub-regional MDBS like the Corporación Andina de Fomento and the East African Development Bank.

opened for business in 1946.[4] It has been the model for all the major MDBs created thereafter. Consequently, the points made below are applicable to all the MDBs listed above, even though the discussion focuses on the IBRD, which is the largest part of the World Bank Group.

When a state[5] joins the IBRD, it is authorized to buy a certain number of shares in the Bank. The number of shares is determined by a formula that takes into account the size of the country's economy and its contribution to the global economy. The member state is only required to pay a small portion of the price of each share and to commit to provide the rest of the price if called upon to do so. Each member state's vote depends on the number of shares that it owns. This means that the Bank operates with a weighted voting system in which the member states do not have equal votes.[6]

At the time of its creation, the IBRD was a bold innovation in global finance. There had never been an institution like it. Consequently, there was considerable uncertainty about how effectively it would function. The first source of uncertainty was that the member states were sovereign states, but they were joining an organization that would operate on the basis of weighted voting and not on the principle of the sovereign equality of states. This suggested that a state could find itself bound by a decision or action that it had specifically opposed.[7]

The drafters of the Bank's Articles of Agreement sought to assure member states that the Bank would respect their sovereignty by stipulating that its staff would operate in a fair and objective way. They were specifically prohibited from being influenced by the political character of the member state and were instructed that their decision-making should only be based on economic considerations, which should be evaluated impartially.[8] The Articles also stipulate that the IBRD staff owe their loyalty to the Bank and that they cannot show any favour to any individual state.[9] These arrangements suggested that the Bank

4 Articles of Agreement of the International Bank for Reconstruction and Development (July 22, 1944) [IBRD Articles of Agreement].

5 Only sovereign states that are members of the International Monetary Fund can join the IBRD. *See* IBRD Articles of Agreement, Art. II (1).

6 DANIEL D. BRADLOW, *International Law and the Operations of the International Financial Institutions*, in DANIEL D. BRADLOW & DAVID HUNTER, INTERNATIONAL FINANCIAL INSTRUCTIONS AND INTERNATIONAL LAW (2010).

7 EDWARD S. MASON & ROBERT E. ASHER, THE WORLD BANK SINCE BRETTON WOODS (1973); DEVESH KAPUR, JOHN P. LEWIS & RICHARD WEBB, THE WORLD BANK: ITS FIRST HALF CENTURY (1997).

8 IBRD Articles of Agreement, Art. IV (10).

9 IBRD Articles of Agreement, Art. V (5)(c).

would focus their loan conditions on the economic and financial aspects of the projects they were funding and would defer to the borrower's decisions that many states saw as part of their sovereign prerogatives, regarding the project's social, political, cultural, and environmental implications.

A second source of uncertainty related to the fact that the IBRD would be operating within the territory of each of its member states. This created a risk that each member state could assert its jurisdiction over the Bank and interfere with its operations.[10] In other words, member states could use their sovereignty to undermine the multinational character and mission of the Bank and interfere with its ability to protect its rights as a creditor. In order to protect against this risk, the Articles granted the IBRD full immunity from the jurisdiction of its member states unless the Bank specifically waived its immunity.[11]

Over time, confidence in the IBRD and the other MBDs grew and these concerns were allayed. Slowly their role began expanding beyond merely providing finance for infrastructure projects in qualifying member states. They also began providing policy advice, technical assistance, and funding for a broad range of development activities. Additionally, they started playing a more active role in the design and implementation of the projects and programmes that they financed. Their more active role created the possibility that their decisions could directly impact, and therefore cause harm to, the communities and social groups affected by their operations.[12]

These developments coincided with a growing general awareness of the need for project sponsors to account for all the significant social and environmental impacts of their projects.[13] This means that they should assess these impacts in advance and should address them in their project design, implementation, and management plans. It also means that their funders should make sure that the project sponsors have adequately assessed and addressed all these impacts before they commit to funding the projects. This pushed the MDBs to assume an active role in overseeing their borrowers' assessments of the social and environmental impacts of the projects that they funded. They also formulated more detailed operational policies and procedures (OPs) to help their borrowers and staff understand each particular MDB's approach to these issues.[14]

10 KLABBERS, *supra* note 1.

11 IBRD Articles of Agreement, Art. VII.

12 Kapur, *supra* note 7; Bradlow, *supra* note 6.

13 Daniel D. Bradlow, *Development Decision Making and the Content of International Development Law*, 21 SOUTH AFRICAN J. HUMAN RIGHTS 47–85 (2005).

14 The World Bank, *Policies and Procedures: Operations Manual,* https://policies.worldbank.org/en/policies/operational-manual (last visited Dec. 14, 2024).

The MDBs faced a challenge when they took on this new role. There were only a few universally accepted principles that were applicable to these environmental and social issues. The most accepted requirement was that each project sponsor must conduct an environmental and social impact assessment (ESA) before deciding to undertake the project.[15] However, there were not internationally agreed and universally accepted standards on how to allocate the costs and benefits associated with the identified impacts. Historically, this decision was viewed as a sovereign prerogative.

It is important to note that there are international legal standards that are widely accepted and are applicable to the management of some of these issues. For example, almost all the MDB member states have signed and ratified international human rights conventions.[16] These conventions stipulate what rights individuals have. They also make clear that the ultimate obligation to respect, protect, and promote human rights rests with the state. However, they are stated in general terms, and they do not clarify how the responsibilities to deal with human rights in a particular project or transaction should be managed. They also do not address, with any specificity, how these responsibilities should be shared between the state, the borrower, the project sponsor, and the funder in a particular project or transaction. This means, in effect, that each state, each borrower, each project sponsor, and each funder must exercise its own discretion in determining whether to support a particular project, based on their assessment of the social and environmental impacts and how they will be managed. It also means that there is a high risk in complex projects with substantial social and environmental impacts that key project decision makers will be accused of making decisions that are not compliant with the applicable international standards. This is because the decisions are unavoidably being made in conditions of imperfect knowledge, and they are inherently controversial.

---

15 *See* DAVID B. HUNTER, *International Law and Public Participation in Policy-Making at the International Financial Institutions, in* INTERNATIONAL FINANCIAL INSTITUTIONS AND INTERNATIONAL LAW 199 (2010); DAVID HUNTER, ET AL., INTERNATIONAL ENVIRONMENTAL LAW AND POLICY (5th ed., 2015).

16 *See* The United Nations, Human Rights, https://www.un.org/en/global-issues/human-rights (last visited Dec. 14, 2024); Office of the High Commissioner for Human Rights [OHCHR], *The Core International Human Rights Instruments and their Monitoring Bodies*, https://www.ohchr.org/en/core-international-human-rights-instruments-and-their-monitoring-bodies [last visited Dec. 14, 2024); The United Nations, International Covenant on Economic, Social and Cultural Rights, Dec. 16, 1966, 993 U.N.T.S. 3; The United Nations, International Covenant on Civil and Political Rights, Dec. 16, 1966, 999 U.N.T.S. 171.

It is therefore not surprising that the MDBs' engagement with these environmental and social issues generated tension between their rich member states and borrower member states.[17] The former group were strong advocates for implementing high environmental and social standards in MDB-funded projects. It should be noted that it was easy for these states to take this position because they do not borrow from the MDBs and so the MDBs would not be applying these standards to their projects.

The borrower member states, who would have to assume the burden of complying with whatever standards the MDBs adopted, were more cautious. They argued that it was their sovereign prerogative to decide how much environmental and social risk they would assume in their development projects and how they would allocate and manage these risks. They also contended that, pursuant to their Articles, the MDBs were required to only consider economic factors in their decision-making. They maintained that managing environmental and social issues requires making political judgments and so should be treated by the MDBs as political concerns. This meant that, from their perspective, the MDBs were exceeding their mandates by commenting on these issues.

This tension was exacerbated by the advocacy of both local and international civil society groups who opposed certain projects on environmental and social grounds. Since there was no obvious forum in which these groups could take their concerns and have them addressed on their merits, they tended to take their campaigns to the media and to lobby their own countries' governments, politicians, and World Bank Executive Directors. As a result, these campaigns became politicized and the source of serious reputational risk for the World Bank. This was demonstrated in the 1980s by the handling of such controversial World Bank projects as the Narmada Dam in India and road projects in the Amazon area of Brazil.[18]

---

17 Most of the MDBs divide their member states into categories indicating which states are eligible to borrow from the MDB and which are not. For example, the World Bank Group divides member states into different groups for purposes of determining eligibility to borrow based on GNI per capita; in general, member states with an annual GNI per capita below US$12055 (2017 dollars) are eligible to borrow from the World Bank Group and those with an annual GNI per capita above US$12056 (2017 dollars) are not eligible to borrow. See, World Bank Country and Lending Groups, https://datahelpdesk.worldbank.org/knowledgebase/articles/906519-world-bank-country-and-lending-groups (last visited Dec. 14, 2024).

18 Bradford Morse & Thomas R. Berger, *Sardar Sarovar- Report of the Independent Review*, International Environmental Law Research Centre, http://ielrc.org/Content/c9202.pdf (last visited on May 12, 2019); BRUCE REICH, THE WORLD BANK AND THE POLITICS OF ENVIRONMENTAL DESTRUCTION (2013).

To its credit, the World Bank responded creatively to this challenge by establishing the Inspection Panel.[19] This was the first mechanism in an international organization that non-state actors could utilize to hold the organization directly accountable for the consequences of its conduct.

The Inspection Panel is an independent three-member panel that is authorized to investigate complaints from any two or more people who claim they have been harmed or threatened with harm by the failure of the World Bank to comply with its OPs. They are independent of the management of the Bank. Panel members are appointed for one non-renewable five-year term by the Bank's Board of Executive Directors (the Board), and they report directly to the Board. In addition, they can only be fired for cause by the Board.

The Panel is authorized to receive any request for an investigation from any two or more persons who allege that they have been harmed or threatened with harm by the Bank's failure to comply with its own OPs. Based on a recommendation from the Panel, the Board decides whether to approve the request and authorize the Panel to investigate. If the investigation is approved, the Panel, after conducting an independent investigation, submits its findings to the Board that can accept or reject these findings. The Board will publicly release the Panel report and the management's response to the report after its deliberations. The management is expected to develop an action plan for addressing any issues of non-compliance identified by the Panel.

It is important to note that the Panel only investigates the compliance of the Bank staff with the OPs and does not look into the conduct of the borrower or of any other actor in the project. Since the Panel does not investigate its member states, it does not implicate their sovereignty.

After the World Bank established the Inspection Panel, the other MDBs created their own independent accountability mechanisms (IAMs).[20] They all have the same basic approach to independence and to investigating

19 The World Bank Inspection Panel was established on Sept. 22, 1993, by IBRD Res. No. 93–10 and IDA No. Res. 93–6 of the Bank's Board, as reviewed, clarified and supplemented by the Board on October 17, 1996 in the "Review of the Resolution Establishing the Inspection Panel – 1996 Clarification of Certain Aspects of the Resolution", and April 20, 1999 in the"1999 Clarification of the Board's Second Review of the Inspection Panel"; IBRAHIM F. I. SHIHATA, THE WORLD BANK INSPECTION PANEL: IN PRACTICE (2nd ed., 2000); Daniel Bradlow, International Organizations and Private Complaints: The Case of the World Bank Inspection Panel, 34(3) VIRGINIA J. INT'L L. (1994).

20 *See, e.g.*, AfDB, *Independent Recourse Mechanism* https://www.afdb.org/en/about-us/organisational-structure/independent-review-mechanism-irm (last visited Dec. 14, 2024); ADB, *Accountability Mechanism*, https://www.adb.org/who-we-are/accountability-mechanism (last visited Dec. 14, 2024); IADB, *Independent Consultation and Investigation Mechanism*, https://mici.iadb.org/en (last visited Dec. 14, 2024); AIIB Project, *Affected*

non-compliance by their staff with the applicable OPs.[21] Over time, cooperation between the IAMs has grown. They have now formed a network that meets once a year to share information and experiences.[22] As part of this meeting, they also meet with a counterpart network that consists of civil society groups that have an interest in these mechanisms.

More than twenty-five years have passed since the first IAM was established. Consequently, there has been sufficient time to assess the IAMs' strengths and weaknesses.[23]

The most obvious contribution of the IAMs is that they provide a means for holding those with authority accountable for the way in which they exercise their authority.[24] Thus, they have encouraged the management and staff of the MDBs to place greater emphasis on complying with their institution's OPs as a way of demonstrating that they are exercising their decision making authority responsibly. This is sometimes expressed in the World Bank as "Panel proofing" a project.[25] This increased focus on OP-compliance should help ensure that the MDBs are performing their mandates as effectively as possible.

The IAM's also help the MDBs learn all the lessons that they can from their operations. In this regard, the IAMs offer the MDBs a unique opportunity. They are the only entity within the MDBs whose work is initiated by groups or communities that have been adversely affected by the projects that the MDBs fund. Consequently, they are able to offer the MDBs unique insights into their

---

People's Mechanism, https://www.aiib.org/en/about-aiib/who-we-are/project-affected-peoples-mechanism/how-we-assist-you/index.html (last visited on Dec. 14, 2024).

21 However, in addition to investigating compliance with the applicable OPPs, the IAMs at the other MDBs – but not the Inspection Panel – also undertake dispute resolution. This means that they use their good offices to deal with disputes between affected communities and the MDB's borrower. These dispute resolution procedures are entirely voluntary.

22 World Bank, *Independent Accountability Mechanisms Network,* https://accountability.worldbank.org/en/iamnet (last visited Dec. 14, 2024).

23 This paper will not focus on their substantive work that would require an analysis of their cases, which is beyond the scope of this paper. For examples of cases in which Inspection Panel has produced benefits for requesters see, Chapter 3 and 4 relating to the Jamuna Bridge project and the Uganda Hydropower project in World Bank, *Accountability at the World Bank* (2003). However, cases before the Inspection Panel do not always bring satisfactory results for requesters; for instance, see DANA CLARK, ET AL., DEMANDING ACCOUNTABILITY: CIVIL SOCIETY CLAIMS AND THE WORLD INSPECTION PANEL (2003).

24 Daniel Bradlow & A. Naude Fourie, *The Operational Policies and Procedures of the World Bank and the International Finance Corporation: Creating Law-Making and Law Governed Institutions,* 10 INT'L ORGS. L. REV. 3 (2013).

25 Jonathan A. Fox, *The World Bank Inspection Panel: Lessons from the First Five Years*, 6(2) GLOBAL GOVERNANCE 279, 310 (2000).

operations and the impact they have at a community level. It is important to recognize in this regard, that in many cases, the cause of the MDB staff's failure to comply with the OPs is that they are operating in complex environments with imperfect knowledge. As a result, the risk that, despite acting with great professional responsibility and judgement, they will make decisions that turn out to be sub-optimal, is not insignificant. The lessons-learned function of the IAMs helps reduce this risk. It also helps the Bank staff and management learn how well their OPs are functioning and to identify any weaknesses in the OPs. The IAMs therefore should help the MDBs ensure that their OPs are fit for their intended purpose.

Third, the IAMs contribute to making the MDBs more transparent. In order for the IAMs to function effectively, it is necessary that the banks make their OPs publicly available. As a result, it is easier for outside stakeholders to learn more about the way in which the MDBs operate. In fact, in recent years, some MDBs have engaged in extensive public consultations about their OPs.[26]

The IAMs are also facing some challenges. The first is that the tension that the IAMs created between borrower and creditor member states has persisted.[27] This is due in part to borrower states' ongoing concerns that the IAMs are unwittingly contributing to undermining their sovereignty and are causing problems for their governments. One reason is that complaints to the IAMs can lead to the requesters getting additional project benefits that are not available to communities and groups that have been adversely affected by non-MDB funded projects. Another is a concern that the government's political opponents may use the IAMs to embarrass the government. This issue is important for the efficacy of the IAMs because one of their key contributions should be that they help to depoliticize disputes arising from MDB funded projects.

There are two reasons to think that these tensions may now be more amenable to resolution. The first is that in a recent US Supreme Court case, *Jam v IFC*,[28] the Court ruled that, at least in US courts, international organizations have the same restricted immunity as states. The decision leaves many unanswered questions about the scope of MDB immunity and so increases the risk of litigation against MDBs with a presence in the US or in states that may choose to adopt a similar approach. This means that borrower countries now face the real possibility that their MDB-funded projects could end up in foreign courts,

26 World Bank, *Environmental and Social Framework*, https://www.worldbank.org/en/projects-operations/environmental-and-social-framework (last visited Dec. 14, 2024).

27 *See, e.g.*, A. Ebrahim and S. Herz, *Accountability in Complex Organizations: World Bank Responses to Civil Society*, Working Paper 08–027, Harvard Business School (2007).

28 *Jam v. International Finance Corp*, 586 U. S. __ (2019).

with unpredictable and potentially embarrassing outcomes. Based on the limited available jurisprudence[29] and international human rights standards, the best way for them to avoid this unfortunate possibility is for the MDBs to provide those adversely affected by their operations with a meaningful remedy that courts could view as equivalent to a judicial remedy.

The second is that because of climate change, there is a growing appreciation around the world of the importance of accounting for the environmental and social impacts of projects.[30] Consequently, there should be increased willingness from all states to have the MDBs that are generally seen to have state of the art OPs, comply with these standards.

Another important and complex challenge pertains to the situation in which the IAM's investigation confirms that the relevant MDB has failed to comply with the applicable OPs and that this has caused harm. In this case, the MDB management develops an action plan that is intended to correct or mitigate the harm caused by the MDB.[31] However, the cost of implementing this plan in effect is either paid by the borrower or the other borrowing member states even though the problem was caused by the MDB. The reason is that, unless the borrower pays for the implementation itself, the MDB's action plan will be financed either by increasing the size of the borrower's loan or, by the MDB itself paying the costs. In either case these resources will be drawn from the MDB's existing pool of available funds, thereby diminishing the amount available to other borrowing member states. Unfortunately, under existing arrangements it is hard to avoid this situation because there is no other readily available pot of money that can assist the adversely affected community.

A fourth challenge for the IAMs is that in recent years the MDBs have increased the scale of their collaborations with each other.[32] As a result, there are now more projects that are being jointly funded by two or more MDBs. In many cases, these projects are governed by the OPs of the project's lead MDB. This creates a risk that more than one IAM could receive a request for investigation from an affected community. In principle, each IAM will only investigate compliance with its own MDB's operational policies. The different IAMs

29 *See, e.g.*, Waite and Kennedy v. Germany, App. No. 26083/94Eur. Ct. H.R. (1999).

30 *See, e.g.*, Network for Greening the Financial System, *First Comprehensive Report: A Call for Action Climate change as a Source of Financial Risk* (Apr. 17, 2019).

31 See World Bank, *The Inspection Panel*, https://www.inspectionpanel.org/ (last visited Dec. 14, 2024); ANDRIA NAUDE FOURIE, THE WORLD BANK INSPECTION PANEL CASEBOOK (2014).

32 *See*, World Bank, *Development Banks Working Together to Optimize Balance Sheets* (Dec. 22, 2015); World Bank, *Multilateral Development Banks (MDBs) Announced a Joint Framework for Aligning their Activities with the Goals of the Paris Agreement* (Dec. 3, 2018).

might, therefore, either base their investigations and findings on different OPs or on their own views of the lead MDB's OPs. Either approach will increase the risk of inconsistent findings being made by the different IAMs in jointly funded projects.

The IAMs, the MDBs, and their member states need to address these challenges without unduly restricting the MDBs ability to implement their mandates or undermining either the member states' sovereignty or the accountability of the MDBs. The next part discusses a proposal that achieves these objectives.

3 A Proposal for Improving MDB Accountability

In brief, the first part of this two-part proposal is for all the MDBs to create one combined IAM that has the authority to receive requests for investigations from people who allege that they have been harmed by the failure of any MDB to comply with its own policies and procedures. The second part is to create an assistance fund that can provide support to help communities and individuals who are found by the IAM to have been harmed by a non-compliant MDB funded project. Each aspect of this proposal is discussed in more detail below.

3.1 *One IAM for all MDBs*

The proposal is that there should be one "super-IAM" (S-IAM) that can serve all the MDBs.[33] This S-IAM, which would be created by agreement between all participating MDBs and would be free-standing, meaning that it would be independent of all the MDBs. Since it would provide an accountability service to all the MDBs, each of them would contribute to its budget on a pro rata basis according to the number of cases arising from each participating MDB. The MDBs' boards of directors would all vote to approve the members of the S-IAM.

33 All the existing IAMs except the World Bank Inspection Panel offer requesters the possibility of engaging in a voluntary dispute resolution process or a compliance review. This proposal only deals with compliance review. In principle, the proposal is compatible with either leaving each institution free to conduct its own dispute resolution process or with incorporating a dispute resolution process into the "super-IAM." However, the appropriate structuring of a dispute resolution process in an IAM is a complex issue, and it is not possible to do it justice within the space constraints of this paper. Consequently, dispute resolution is not discussed in this paper. *See*, Joshua M. Javits, *Internal Conflict Resolution at International Organizations*, 28(2) ABA J. LAB & EMP. L. 223–253 (2015) for more information on dispute resolution in an IAM.

Each MDB would agree to second staff to it for a stipulated period, for example three years.

This S-IAM would operate according to similar compliance review procedures as all currently functioning IAMs. This means that it would be authorized to accept requests for investigation from any two or more persons who allege that they have been harmed or threatened with harm because of the failure of the MDB or MDBs funding a particular project to comply with the applicable OPs. The S-IAM would determine for itself the eligibility of the request and, if found eligible, would investigate the issues raised in the request based on the applicable OPs. The reports of the investigation would be submitted to the board of executive directors of the relevant MDB. The Board would be required to either accept the findings of the S-IAM and ensure that the management develops an action plan that is designed to resolve the cases of non-compliance identified in the report or to issue a public explanation of their reasons for rejecting the findings. As is the practice in almost all the current IAMs, the report would also be made available to the requesters at the same time as it is provided to the relevant board. The S-IAM would also monitor the implementation of the action plan in order to ensure that it in fact resolves the problems that it identified in its investigation report.

It is not unprecedented for one review mechanism to have the authority to deal with cases applying the rules of different international organizations. The International Labour Organization (ILO) Administrative Tribunal is authorized to decide cases based on the human resource policies of each of the organizations that have accepted its authority to hear employment disputes. Currently, fifty-seven organizations have agreed to use the ILO Administrative Tribunal for this purpose.[34]

This S-IAM offers a number of advantages. First, it clearly demonstrates that the MDBs are offering those who have been harmed by non-compliant projects a meaningful alternative to a judicial remedy. This should help reduce the risk of litigation created by the *Jam v IFC* case and thereby also help preserve the appropriate level of immunity for the MDBs. Second, because the S-IAM is gathering information from investigations at all the MDBs, it will develop a rich database of information on the implementation of the OPs of the MDBs. This will contribute to the lessons-learned function of the IAMs. The additional knowledge about how to assess and manage the social and

34 For information on the ILO Administrative Tribunal, see: International Labor Administration, *The ILO Administrative Tribunal*, https://www.ilo.org/tribunal/lang--en/index.htm (last visited Dec. 14, 2024).

environmental impacts should lead to improvements in the design and implementation of MDB-funded projects and the formulation and interpretation of their OPs. Third, it would mitigate the risk of inconsistent decisions in cases of jointly-funded projects.

The S-IAM will have some costs. Most significantly, there is a cost associated with the fact that the IAM will not be located in any MDB. This means that it will lose the familiarity with the MDB that the current IAMs can gain from interacting with the MDB staff and management on a regular basis. There are two factors that suggest that this cost may not be significant. The first is that the staff of the S-IAM will be officials seconded from the various MDBs. Consequently, they will understand their own MDB well and can help educate and inform the members of the S-IAM about the culture and operating practices of the MDB. In addition, many of the members of the current IAMs do not serve on a full-time basis and so do not interact on a regular basis with the staff and management. In addition, since they only serve for a fixed term and only after not being employed in any capacity by the MDB for a set period before appointment, they are unlikely to have great familiarity with the MDBs staff and management when they join the IAM. They are also unlikely to develop it during their tenure.

A second potential cost is that the S-IAM will have a large number of cases and will therefore need a large budget and staff. There is no doubt that the S-IAM will need a larger staff and more resources than any one of the currently existing IAMs. However, it is reasonable to expect that the S-IAM will need a smaller staff than the sum of the total staff at the existing IAMs. The reason is that the S-IAM will have a full-time panel. The current arrangements at the IAMs involve part-time panel members. Thus, a smaller number of S-IAM staff members than the sum of the current total of IAM members should be possible. It is also possible that the more effective learning process that the S-IAM offers all the MDBs could result in fewer cases of non-compliant projects being brought to the S-IAM than the total being brought to the current IAMs.

While the S-IAM will be larger than that at any of the existing IAMs, it will not result in a large permanent bureaucracy. The S-IAM staff will consist of panelists who have been appointed for fixed non-renewable terms and experts who are seconded for fixed periods of time from the various MDBs. Thus, the staff will all be temporary and will work with the expectation that they will be returning to their home MDB. It is important to note that the creation of the S-IAM need not lead to additional financial costs for each MDB. The reason is that the creation of the S-IAM will allow each MDB to shut down its own IAM and use the funds for the S-IAM.

3.2 An Assistance Fund

The second part of this proposal is that all the stakeholders in the MDBs should create an independent Assistance Fund (the Fund) that can accept contributions from individuals, corporations, foundations, states, and international organizations. This Fund will provide assistance to communities that the S-IAM finds have been harmed by an MDB's failure to comply with the applicable OPs. All the categories of potential contributors have expressed an interest in promoting both accountability at the MDBs and concern for the groups that have been harmed by the MDBs' failure to comply with their OPs. Consequently, they should be willing to contribute to a Fund that is independent of the MDBs and that can assist individuals and communities who the S-IAM has found were harmed by the relevant MDB's failure to comply with its own OPs. Any award made by this Fund will not require a finding that any particular party is to blame for the harm that they have suffered. Instead, it will be premised merely on the finding that they have suffered harm and need assistance.

It is important to note that independent international funds that can raise funds from both state and non-state actors to support specific purposes are not unprecedented. The following international funds allow for contributions by non-state actors:

- The Trust Fund for Victims at the International Criminal Court allows for individuals to contribute to the Trust Fund;[3735]
- The Global Alliance for Vaccines and Inoculations (GAVI) accepts contributions from states, foundations, civil society organizations (CSOs), corporations, and individuals;[36]
- The Global Fund to Fight AIDS, TB, and Malaria allows states, corps, foundations, and CSOs to contribute;[37]
- The Global Partnership for Education accepts contributions from governments, international organizations, foundations, and the private sector.[40]

35 *See* Donations to the Trust Fund for Victims, *Make a Donation,* https://www.trustfundforvictims.org/index.php/en/your-support/make-a-donation (last visited Dec. 14, 2024); *see also* Frederick Megret, *Justifying Compensation by the International Criminal Court's Victims Trust Fund: Lessons from Domestic Compensation Schemes*, 36 BROOK J. INT'L L. (2010). *But see*, David Scheffer, *The Rising Challenge of Funding Victims' Needs at the International Criminal Court*, JUST SECURITY (Dec. 3, 2018) https://www.justsecurity.org/61701/rising challenge-funding-victims-international-criminal-court/.

36 *See* The Global Alliance for Vaccines and Inoculations, *Funding,* https://www.gavi.org/investing-gavi/funding (last visited Dec. 14, 2024).

37 *See* The Global Fund to Fight AIDS, TB and Malaria, *Home,* https://www.theglobalfund.org/en/ (last visited Dec. 14, 2024).

The Fund will be overseen by a Board of Directors. The board members will participate in their individual capacity and will be elected by all contributors to the Fund. The Board will outsource the investing of the corpus of the Fund and the management of its financial transactions to a fund manager.

The Board will also receive all requests for assistance. Any requester who submitted a request for investigation to the S-IAM and was found to have been harmed by the non-compliance of the relevant MDB will be eligible to file a request with the Fund. The request for assistance would include a copy of the report of the S-IAM finding that the requester has suffered harm because of the failure of the MDB to comply with its own OPs and a motivation for the amount of assistance being requested. In no case can the request exceed the amount that the requesters would have received under the relevant MDB's OPs. The decision to provide assistance will be made by the Fund's Board. In determining the amount of assistance, the Board will consider the severity of the harm suffered and the amount of funds available that year for assisting requesters.

The rationale for the Fund is that it is not inherently unreasonable for a society to decide that since a particular project will produce benefits for the whole society over time, the social, environmental, economic, and financial costs of the project should be shared by the whole society. However, a problem arises when there has been a finding that a non-compliant MDB has contributed to the costs falling disproportionately on a particular group or community in the society. In this case, there is a basis for the international community providing the group or community with special assistance to deal with its "disproportionate" share of the costs.

The Fund enables the requesters to receive this assistance while avoiding the problems that would arise if the funds used to assist the affected group were contributed only by the relevant MDB. As indicated above, this could mean that the funds are ultimately paid by the borrower through an increase in the size of its loan or by the other borrower member states through reduced availability of financing. After all, this would be another way of imposing a disproportionate cost on one group of stakeholders in the MDBs.

4 Conclusion

This paper has argued that the world in which the MDBs must operate has changed dramatically since the first MDBs were created. They now have detailed OPs to deal with the social and environmental impacts of their operations that inform interested stakeholders about how they can expect the MDBs to deal with these impacts. In addition, based on international law and the evolving case law, the MDBs need to provide those who claim they have been harmed by the failure of the MDBs to act in compliance with these OPs with a meaningful means of holding these MDBs accountable for their own failings. It therefore proposes that the MDBs create a super-IAM to replace their individual IAMs. This S-IAM would be authorized to receive and investigate claims from any of the MDBs. Its findings would be binding on the relevant MDB unless the board of that MDB provides a specific public explanation for their rejection of the findings.

In addition, in order to ensure that any community or group who has been harmed by the non-compliant acts of the relevant MDB is assisted to address its harm and that the assistance does not come at the expense of the relevant MDB's member states, the MDBs should create an independent Assistance Fund. The Fund should be authorized to receive contributions from any state or non-state actor. It should only be able to provide assistance in cases where there has been a finding of MDB non-compliance.

If the MDBs implement these two proposals, they will have created a structure that respects the sovereignty of their member states and the rights of all project affected groups and communities. It will also provide the basis for courts and member states governments to provide MDBs with an appropriate level of immunity.

Acknowledgements

The author thanks Mallika Sen for her excellent research assistance with this article.

Bibliography

African Development Bank. *Home*. Accessed December 18, 2024. https://www.afdb.org/en/.

African Development Bank. *Independent Recourse Mechanism*. Accessed December 18, 2024. https://www.afdb.org/en/about-us/organisational-structure/independent-review-mechanism-irm.

The Asian Development Bank. *Accountability Mechanism*. Accessed December 14, 2024. https://www.adb.org/who-we-are/accountability-mechanism.

The Asian Infrastructure Investment Bank Project. *Affected People's Mechanism*. Accessed December 14, 2024.

https://www.aiib.org/en/about-aiib/who-we-are/project-affected-peoples-mechanism/how-we-assist-you/index.html.

The Asian Development Bank. *Home*. Accessed December 18, 2024. https://www.adb.org/.

The Asian Infrastructure Investment Bank. *Home*. Accessed December 18, 2024. https://www.aiib.org/en/index.html.

Bradlow, Daniel. "International Organizations and Private Complaints: The Case of the World Bank Inspection Panel." *Virginia Journal of International Law*, 34, no. 3 (1994).

Bradlow, Daniel. "Development Decision Making and the Content of International Development Law." *South African Journal of Human Rights*, 21 (2005); 47–85.

Bradlow, Daniel, and David Hunter. *International Financial Institutions and International Law*. Netherlands: Kluwer International Law, 2010.

Bradlow, Daniel. "International Law and the Operations of the International Financial Institutions," in *International Financial Institutions and International Law*. Netherlands: Kluwer International Law, 2010.

Bradlow, Daniel, and A. Naude Fourie. "The Operational Policies and Procedures of the World Bank and the International Finance Corporation: Creating Law-Making and Law Governed Institutions." *International Organizations Law Review*, 10 (2013): 3.

Clark, Dana, Jonathan Fox, and Kay Treakle. *Demanding Accountability: Civil Society Claims and the World Bank Inspection Panel*. Laham: Rowland & Littlefield, 2003.

Donations to the Trust Fund for Victims. *About Us*. Accessed December 14, 2024. https://www.trustfundforvictims.org/en/about/vision

Ebrahim, A., and S. Herz, *Accountability in Complex Organizations: World Bank Responses to Civil Society* Working Paper 08–027, Harvard Business School (2007).

The European Bank for Reconstruction and Development Bank. *Home*. Accessed December 18, 2024. https://www.ebrd.com/home.

Fourie, Andira Naude. *The World Bank Inspection Panel Casebook*. Washington DC: World Bank, 2014.

Fox, Jonathan. "The World Bank Inspection Panel: Lessons from the First Five Years." *Global Governance*, 6, no. 2 (2000): 279, 310.

The Global Fund to Fight AIDS, TB and Malaria. *Home*. Accessed December 14, 2024. https://www.theglobalfund.org/en/.

The Global Alliance for Vaccines and Inoculations. *Funding*. Accessed December 14, 2024. https://www.gavi.org/investing-gavi/funding.

Hunter, David. "International Law and Public Participation in Policy-Making at the International Financial Institutions," in *International Financial Institutions and International Law*. Netherlands: Kluwer Law International, 2010: 199.

Hunter, David, James Salzman and Durwood Zaekle. *International Environmental Law and Policy*, 5th ed. Goleta: Foundation Press, 2015.

The Inter-American Development Bank. *Home*. Accessed December 18, 2024. https://www.iadb.org/en.

The Inter-American Development Bank. *Independent Consultation and Investigation Mechanism*. Accessed December 14, 2024. https://mici.iadb.org/en.

International Labor Administration. *The ILO Administrative Tribunal*. December 14, 2024. https://www.ilo.org/tribunal/lang--en/index.htm.

Network for Greening the Financial System. *First Comprehensive Report: A Call for Action Climate change as a Source of Financial Risk*. Paris: Network for Greening the Financial System, April 17, 2019.

The New Development Bank. *Home*. Accessed December 18, 2024. https://www.ndb.int/.

International Bank for Reconstruction and Development. *Articles of Agreement*. Washington DC: World Bank, July 22, 1944.

Javits, Joshua M. "Internal Conflict Resolution at International Organizations." *ABA Journal Labor Law and Employment*, 28, no. 2 (2015): 223–253.

Kapur, Devesh, John P. Lewis, and Richard Werb. *The World Bank: Its First Half Century*. Washington DC: Brookings Institute Press, 1997.

Klabbers, Jan. *An Introduction to International Organizations Law*, 3rd ed. Cambridge: Cambridge University Press, 2015.

Mason, Edward, and Robert Asher. *The World Bank Since Bretton Woods*. Washington DC: Brookings Institute Press, 1973.

Megret, Frederick. "Justifying Compensation by the International Criminal Court's Victims Trust Fund: Lessons from Domestic Compensation Schemes." *Brookings Journal of International Law*. 2010: 36.

Morse, Bradford, and Thomas R. Berger. *Sardor Sarovar- Report of the Independent Review*. Geneva: International Environmental Law Research Centre, June 18, 1992.

Reich, Bruce. *The World Bank and the Politics of Environmental Destruction*. 2013.

Scheffer, David. *The Rising Challenge of Funding Victims' Needs and the International Criminal Court*. New York: Just Security, December 3, 2018. https://www.justsecurity.org/61701/rising challenge-funding-victims-international-criminal-court/.

Shihata, Ibrahim F. *The World Bank Inspection Panel: In Practice*, 2d ed. Washington DC; World Bank, 2000

United Nations. *International Covenant on Civil and Political Rights*. S. Treaty Doc. No. 95–20, 6 I.L.M. 368 (1967), 999 U.N.T.S. 171. Geneva: Washington DC, December 16, 1966.

United Nations. *International Covenant on Economic, Social and Cultural Rights*. S. Treaty Doc. No. 95–19, 6 I.L.M. 360 (1967), 993 U.N.T.S. 3. Geneva: Washington DC, December 16, 1966.

United Nations. *Human Rights*. Accessed December 14, 2024. https://www.un.org/en/global-issues/human-rights.

United Nations Office of the High Commissioner for Human Rights (OHCHR). *The Core International Human Rights Instruments and their Monitoring Bodies.* Accessed December 14, 2024. https://www.ohchr.org/en/core-international-human-rights-instruments-and-their-monitoring-bodies.

World Bank. *Accountability at the World Bank: The Inspection Panel.* Washington DC: World Bank, 2003.

World Bank. *Development Banks Working Together to Optimize Balance Sheets.* Washington DC; World Bank, December 22, 2015.

World Bank. *Multilateral Development Banks (MDBs) Announced a Joint Framework for Aligning their Activities with the Goals of the Paris Agreement.* Washington DC: World Bank, December 3, 2018.

World Bank. *Independent Accountability Mechanisms Network.* Accessed December 14, 2024.

https://accountability.worldbank.org/en/iamnet.

World Bank. *Environmental and Social Framework.* Accessed December 14, 2024. https://www.worldbank.org/en/projects-operations/environmental-and-social-framework.

World Bank. *Policies and Procedures: Operations Manual.* Accessed December 14, 2024. https://policies.worldbank.org/en/policies/operational-manual.

The World Bank. *Country and Lending Groups.* Accessed December 14, 2024. https://datahelpdesk.worldbank.org/knowledgebase/articles/906519-world-bank-country-and-lending-groups.

World Bank Inspection Panel. *The World Bank Inspection Panel.* Accessed December 14, 2024. https://www.inspectionpanel.org/.

PART 6

Conclusion

Conclusion

Daniel Bradlow, David Hunter, Nick Paul, and
Vishna Iyengar Rameswamy

The diverse perspectives presented in this book reflect the unique and somewhat disruptive position that the World Bank Inspection Panel (the Panel) and other international accountability mechanisms (IAMs) hold in the structure and governance of international finance institutions (IFIs). By providing a formal process for bringing the concerns of affected people to the attention of the IFIs' senior management and boards of executive directors, the IAMs opened up unprecedented opportunities for communities to be heard in the international development process. By promoting IFI compliance with internationally agreed environmental and social standards, the IAMs help ensure that the interests and concerns of affected local communities receive appropriate attention in IFI-funded projects and programmes. The IAMs challenged the executive directors to reflect on the impacts of IFI lending and, in some instances, to exercise more rigorous oversight over how the bank management implements projects. In so doing, the IAMs disrupted some basic presumptions of how IFIs operate. The IAMs' disruption of the status quo partly explains why so many different stakeholders have an interest in their performance and why they are contested and continue to attract so much diverse commentary from both academics and practitioners, including the diverse perspectives reflected herein.

Despite their different perspectives, the contributors largely appear to share the view that creation of the Panel and the subsequent spread of IAMs to so many other institutions has been an important development in the evolution of IFIs – but there is less agreement on the direction or purpose of that evolution. Moreover, whether the contributors view the achievements of the Panel and other IAMs as a "glass half empty, or half full," appears to depend on their expectations about the primary purposes of the IAMs. This is complicated because the primary purpose of the IAMs is itself conflicted terrain. Consider the different purposes attributed to the IAMs, as reflected by different contributors to this volume:

- To create a predictable channel for the voice of affected people to be heard in the development process;[1]
- To improve the development effectiveness of IFI lending;[2]

1 *See* Eduardo Abbott, *supra* Chapter 5; Dilek Barlas, *supra* Chapter 6.

2 *See* Christopher H. Stephens, *supra* Chapter 21.

- To assist the executive directors in managing the IFIs by providing credible information from the 'last mile' of development;[3]
- To demonstrate the possibility and value of democratizing international law and organizations;[4]
- To prevent or reduce the environmental and social costs and impacts visited on local communities of IFI development decisions;[5]
- To ensure IFI compliance with applicable environmental and social standards;[6]
- To hold IFIs institutionally accountable for their environmental and social impacts, filling the gap created by their immunity from suit;[7]
- To provide a neutral forum for the resolution of disputes involving local communities, the IFIs, and in some cases the project sponsors;[8]
- To provide a remedy for complainants for the harms caused by the IFI activities;[9]
- To channelize dissent into a professional, technical process that 'accountability washes' a destructive development model.[10]

The IAMs have succeeded in meeting some of these expectations better than they have others. For example, since the onset of Panel "proofing" in the early days of the Panel, the IAMs have enhanced compliance of the IFIs with the environmental and social policies of their banks. The IAMs have had also had considerable success in identifying gaps and catalysing improvements in IFI policies. The IAMs have also been relatively successful in creating predictable procedural opportunities for the engagement of locally affected people not only at the IAMs but also in project-level and management-led grievance redress systems.

On the other hand, the IAMs have been decidedly less successful in being a regular source of remedy for claimants. Questions of providing effective remedy quickly raise questions of who pays for the remedy and what is the standard for when remedies are expected. But the remedy question is somewhat existential for the IAMs, because if they do not hold any promise for remedy, why should communities take the somewhat risky decision to file

3 *See* David Hunter, *supra* Chapter 8 (quoting Mr. Broder the first Panel Chair).
4 *See* Daniel D. Bradlow, *supra* Chapter 4; David Hunter, *supra* Chapter 8.
5 *See infra* sec. 3.
6 *See* Christopher Stephens, *supra* Chapter 21.
7 *See* Susan Park, *supra* Chapter 2; Christopher Stephens, *supra* Chapter 21.
8 *See* Gina Barbieri, *supra* Chapter 16; Christopher Stephens, *supra* Chapter 21.
9 *See* Dilek Barlas, *supra* Chapter 6; Richard Bissell, *supra* Chapter 10; Natalie Bridgeman Fields, *supra* Chapter 18.
10 *See* Schaefer, *supra* Chapter 19.

a claim? In too many cases the complainants have not been satisfied with the outcome, even when the IAMs have found the IFI violated its own policies. Success in bringing a complaint to the IAMs has also tended to depend on the complainants having access to expert legal and technical advice. This disadvantages communities that do not have links to technical experts or relations with organizations offering such expertise raises questions about the accessibility, complexity, and effectiveness of the IAMs in serving the most vulnerable communities.

1 Insights on Outcomes

One point that comes through, particularly from the historical contributions, is that many constraints on the IAMs' ability to deliver acceptable outcomes today are rooted in the original design of the Panel, reflecting the tensions between those who welcomed the disruptive potential of community voices in international development and those who were trying to curb the ultimate impact of that engagement. Recurring challenges to the IAMs' independence, eligibility decisions, authority to make recommendations, or ability to monitor outcomes, are all linked to a basic underlying tension: having decided to create a potentially disruptive force within the IFIs, how could that force be managed and directed.

The discussion of expected outcomes dates back to the Panel's beginnings.[11] When the Panel was established, its function was clearly limited to undertaking compliance reviews – that is, to investigate whether or not the Bank staff and management had complied with the applicable Bank policies in regard to the issues raised in the complaint. It was never explicitly stated whether the ultimate purpose of the investigation was to improve Bank compliance with its own policies and procedures, or to provide remedy to the complainants who were found to have been harmed by the Bank's non-compliance. What was clear is that the Panel, itself, was never allowed the power to ensure that the Bank changed its behaviour or that the complainants received remedy beyond validation of their allegations. The Panel could only make findings of non-compliance; other parts of the Bank's accountability system (i.e. the Bank Management and Executive Directors) were responsible for fashioning any systematic changes or remedies. The failure to consistently provide

11 *See, e.g.*, Richard Bissell, *supra* Chapter 10.

positive outcomes is thus not a failure of the IAMs alone but of the accountability system as a whole.

1.1 *Providing Complainants with a Remedy*

As several of the contributors point out, the Panel had significant design flaws if it were intended to provide remedy for harms to the complainants, at least beyond the public validation of their claims. The expectation was clearly that Bank Management had the responsibility to correct any non-compliance – and thus implicitly to provide remedy – through its preparation of a management action plan in response to the Panel's findings. Several of the contributions remind us of Bank management's efforts in early cases to avoid investigations by pre-emptively issuing action plans.[12] Ironically, this meant that the management offered a form of remedy as an alternative to a compliance review. The debate then was not *whether* the Bank should provide a remedy, but *when* it would be provided. It also became a question of *who* should pay for a remedy, because management's action plans in these early cases usually required the borrower to take on more debt to address the problem. This was particularly unpopular with borrowers and their representatives on the Bank's board, given that the compliance review the Bank was avoiding was supposed to be focused only on Bank non-compliance. Once the Board streamlined its review of the Panel's eligibility recommendations, management's incentive for pre-emptively developing action plans disappeared–and they became decidedly less proactive in fashioning remedial plans.

The challenge remains that the IAMs are typically able to make findings only on the IFI's compliance and cannot explicitly investigate the borrowers' behaviour. While this is consistent with the IAMs' purpose of improving IFI performance (for example, improving its project supervision or environmental screening processes), it is problematic for providing remedy because the non-complying IFI does not have dedicated funds available for purposes of remedy. The IFIs would either have to shift the cost onto the borrower in the particular project, or get the funds from their own general account, effectively spreading the costs of IFI non-compliance across all their borrowers (because less money would be available to other borrowers). Given that these other borrowers are represented on the boards of the banks, it is not surprising that the banks are reluctant to provide compensation to complainants. Moreover, the borrowers are particularly reluctant to bear the costs of providing a remedy when the cause of the identified problem has been the non-complying acts

12 *See* Eduardo Abbott, *supra* Chapter 5.

or omissions of the IFI, and where there has been no such finding against the borrower.

Although the remedy debate swirls on with what seems like little progress, it should be noted that the lack of available remedies generated through the Panel's compliance review process led – indirectly, at least – to new opportunities for communities to engage in dispute resolution (DR) with project sponsors. Since the creation of the Compliance Advisor/Ombudsman (CAO) office by the IFC and MIGA, almost every IFI has added a DR function to its compliance review function.[13] The DR function is primarily focused on facilitating a satisfactory outcome for all parties, including the complainants. Although as some of the contributions to this volume note, DR does not always result in an agreement, it has focused a brighter spotlight on the complainants' harms and expanded their opportunities for negotiating remedies with project sponsors.[14]

Many IFIs have expanded DR opportunities even further; some IFI's, like the World Bank Group, have created a complaints window for affected people to raise project concerns directly with Bank Management. Such corporate-level grievance redress mechanisms (GRMs) are designed in part to give staff an opportunity to resolve problems and complaints before they are elevated to the IAM. Consistent with the principle of subsidiarity, some IFIs also require project-level grievance mechanisms (PLGMs), reflecting the view that many disputes can and should be handled at the local level. As several contributors note, this trend toward multiple, decentralized avenues for raising concerns about specific IFI-financed projects holds some promise for remediating community impacts.[15] With greater transparency and procedural regularity, these decentralized efforts could be an important opportunity for harmed communities. The lack of transparency and insufficient markers of independence, however, make it difficult to assess whether these mechanisms ensure effective community engagement in the same way as the IAMs' DR processes – not to mention that they are partly designed to avoid compliance investigations that could enhance Bank accountability.

13 MDBs that have created separate dispute resolution and compliance functions include the ADB and the World Bank. MDBs that have authorized their one IAM to perform both compliance review and dispute resolution functions include the IFC and MIGA and the AfDB.

14 *See, e.g.*, Suzan Nada, *supra* Chapter 11; Gina Barbieri, *supra* Chapter 16; Natalie Bridgeman-Fields, *supra* Chapter 18.

15 *See, e.g.*, Charles Di Leva, *supra* Chapter 7.

1.2 *Improving IFI Performance*

Unlike the case for providing remedies for complainants' harms, there is almost complete consensus among the contributors that the IAMs were intended to improve the accountability, and ultimately the performance, of the IFIs. Nonetheless, the Panel and most other IAMs face similar structural obstacles for translating their findings of non-compliance into better performance by the IFIs as they do for remedying harm done to the complainants. Formally, the Panel has the authority only to undertake investigations and make factual findings regarding whether the Bank is in compliance. Even in those cases where the IAMs have been authorized to make recommendations on what would be required for the IFI to come back into compliance, changes in IFI behaviour requires the cooperation of bank management and attention by the boards.[16] In none of the IAMs are the recommendations binding on the IFI staff, as noted in da Silva and Giacoma's contribution.[17] IFI staff do not have to take any steps recommended by the IAMs, or for that matter to take any action at all. The projects can remain out-of-compliance going forward; for change to occur in the IFI's behaviour takes a decision by the project implementing agency, the IFI management, or its executive directors. The likelihood of changes in performance can be increased through public attention or pressure from the governments, but it rarely results only from a constructive engagement between the IAM and IFI staff. Despite some notable, high-profile exceptions – for example, World Bank actions taken regarding gender issues after the Uganda case,[18] the IFIs' record in engaging constructively with their respective IAMs varies significantly across different IAMs and over time. Many in IFI management, even those whose responsibilities include ensuring environmental and social compliance, do not view the IAMs as allies in addressing environmental and social risks.

2 Understanding the IAMs Impact as Law-Makers

Although IAMs have little authority to compel changes directly in the specific project that is being investigated, they have the potential to indirectly change behaviour in future cases if, for example, their interpretations of IFI policies

16 For examples of IAMs with the authority to make recommendations see AfDB, *Independent Recourse Mechanism: Operating Rules and Procedures* para. 67(III) (July 2021); *see also* EBRD, *Project Accountability Policy* para. 2.7 (D)(II) (April 2019).

17 Lalanath Da Silva & Giada Giacomo, *supra* Chapter 20.

18 *See* Elana Berger, *How a Community-Led Response to Sexual Exploitation in Uganda Led to Systemic World Bank Reform*, Bank Information Centre (June 2018).

are considered precedent-setting and are followed by MDB staff and management in future cases and projects. The responsibility of IAMs to make findings and recommendations about compliance necessarily requires them to apply and interpret relevant bank policies. By interpreting the policies consistently over time, the IAMs can signal that they consider their decisions as precedents to be applied by the IFI in similar situations going forward. At the very least, the IAM's interpretations of the policies should be influential in how policies are interpreted in future projects.

The IAM decisions also have some legal effect – or at least some persuasive power – over decisions outside of their own specific institutional context, both through their deliberate actions and indirectly as their respective decisions circulate. The establishment of the IAMNet mentioned by several contributors is a deliberate effort by the IAMs to create a community of practice that shares experiences and either implicitly or explicitly works toward harmonizing best practice at all the IAMs. This is one way that progress (e.g., a policy change) can be spread to other IAMs and their respective financial institutions. Gregory Berry's contribution on how the IAMs have collaborated and discussed their response to reprisals collectively is one example where the IAMNet and the community of practice has pushed the adoption of harmonized policies at several IAMs. Beginning with the Panel, several IAMs have adopted similar zero-tolerance policies for reprisals to protect those courageous enough to file a complaint with them. Several IAMs are also currently promoting a "responsible exit" policy at their IFIs, modelled after the policy recently adopted by the IFC.

Regardless of whether an IAM report has any formal precedential impact in their own institution, IAM interpretations have the potential to harmonize the interpretation of environmental and social policies across a variety of IFIs. This is particularly evident in the rules governing the operation of the IAMs themselves; these rules are continually revised with an eye toward benchmarking and harmonizing across the various IAMs. But it is also true more generally across the environmental and social policies of many IFIs, which have long explicitly valued harmonization, for example to facilitate co-financing arrangements. Other policies present similar gaps and ambiguities that raise similar questions of interpretation. Well-supported and analysed IAM reports on these issues may thus influence the development of the policies outside the context of their particular IFI.

Ultimately, the extent and impact of the IAMs' law-making role varies considerably across different IAMs and in different institutional contexts.[19] This

19 See David Hunter, *Contextual Accountability, the World Bank Inspection Panel, and the Transformation of International Law in Edith Brown Weiss' "Kaleidoscopic World,"* 32 GEORGETOWN ENVTL. L. REV. 439–466 (2020).

is somewhat in each of the IAM's control, because they can decide how much they cite past reports and how much they feel constrained by their own previous decisions. If the IAM does not treat its decisions as being meaningful interpretations of the policies, it can hardly feel slighted if other parts of the institution do not feel compelled to follow those interpretations. Certainly, since the early days of the Panel, the IAMs have taken a legalistic approach to the interpretation of eligibility and procedural requirements in their own policies. As several of the contributors note, most of the early Panel cases sparked legalistic exchanges between Bank Management and the complainants. The outcome is made first by the IAM's "judgment" and then ultimately by the Board, the decision of which is binding for that case and persuasive for future cases. This process has led to consistent interpretations of eligibility requirements across both time and IAMs. The same process has not been as evident, or at least not as well documented, with respect to the substantive interpretations of similar environmental and social policies over time and between institutions.

3 Prioritizing Community Impact in Development

The debate about whether IAMs should provide remedies to local communities reveals a more fundamental tension often raised by the IAM's community-facing work. The majority of cases at the IAMs raise issues regarding environmental and social policies that are intended to prevent, minimize or mitigate harms on affected people. Viewed as a technical investigation into compliance, an IAM finding of non-compliance means that the project planners and financiers did not internalize all the relevant costs and benefits in their project preparation and implementation. Some costs were externalized and imposed on the complainants, without them having been consulted or having received the consideration that the IFI's own policy actually required. In this sense, all the complainants are asking is that when an IAM makes a finding of non-compliance, the IFI (or the project sponsor) corrects the misallocation of costs and benefits and accurately allocates them among the various stakeholders. In this sense, the issue is about the technical allocation of the costs and benefits of the project so that the local community does not suffer more than it *should* have under the policies.

The IAM's entry into this discussion is only through the complaints filed by affected people. Giving weight to such a request in the development process immediately raises fundamental questions about who are "affected" people? Who are the intended beneficiaries of MDB-funded projects? The possible beneficiaries could include the communities in which the projects are located and which directly experience their impacts, positive or negative–but they also frequently include people throughout the region, all the citizens of the borrowing state, or even the state itself. This inquiry is important for two reasons with respect to IAM projects: (1) the risks of harm borne by the community may have been planned and warranted for the common good; and (2) the voices complaining about the project may be a vocal, but small, minority in the community. The IAMs are only mandated to investigate whether or not the particular complainants have been harmed by the IFI's non-compliance with its policies. Whether the complainants represent the majority or minority views of an affected community or whether they are seeking special treatment compared to their neighbors is not relevant to the IAM's view of eligibility.

4 The Changing Expectations of IFIs

Viewing an IAM from this perspective begins to reveal how IAM compliance reviews are not always simply technical exercises akin to the IFIs' supervision missions. To the extent complaints are raising questions about the burden an affected community (or a minority of an affected community) is bearing, they are implicitly raising questions about the government's choice to pursue the project–and the development effectiveness of the benefit/cost trade-offs inherent in that decision. Historically, the assumption was that this decision was the prerogative of the sovereign, as expressed through its law and decision-making processes.[20] The IFI was expected to accept these decisions and limit its decision-making to the financial and technical aspects of the operation. However, the existence of the IAMs reflects a changing perspective on the role of the IFIs. The IFIs, through their safeguard policies, now have environmental and social responsibilities that they must fulfil regardless of the decisions and actions of their borrowers or member states.[21] These responsibilities flow to the benefit of the local communities and other non-state actors in the borrower state, resulting in a more intensive engagement with member states and with the member state's citizens in the case of the IAMs.

Put another way, by creating a process that asks the IFIs to investigate how their actions may have impacted the local community, the IAMs arguably

---

20 *See generally The Challenges Facing the International Financial Institutions,* in DANIEL D. BRADLOW, THE LAW OF THE INTERNATIONAL FINANCIAL INSTITUTIONS (2023).

21 *See* Daniel D. Bradlow, *Differing Conceptions of Development and the Content of International Development Law*, 21(1) SOUTH AFRICAN J. ON HUMAN (2005).

challenge the borrowing country's sovereign right to allocate the costs and benefits of development within their own country. As Natalie Bridgeman Fields notes, some of the most difficult IAM cases with some of the largest negative impacts did not result from *operational flaws* in the project, but from *design features.*[22] A decision to place a project on Indigenous territories or in an area requiring mass resettlements is a political decision within the sovereign rights of the borrowing country. The IFIs (and their constituent parts, including the IAMs) are supposed to provide financial and technical support to the borrowing member states' chosen path of development. An IAM's investigation into whether local communities have been adequately consulted or compensated is not just an investigation into *technical* issues of how the IFIs mitigated the environmental and social costs of the project, it is a process that invites the highest level of the IFI's management to revisit the borrower's *political* decision of whether the development benefits to the country warranted the disproportionate harms imposed on the communities.

Moreover, the seemingly benign question of whether a local community is suffering more than it *should* have under the IFI policies becomes, when asserted by the community to an IAM, an inquiry into whether the rights of the borrowers' residents were violated. To be sure, the IFIs have always been enmeshed in the human rights of their borrower state residents–but always because they had been invited in by the State on the State's terms. Through the complaints to their IAMs, however, the IFIs are enmeshed in their member state's human rights issues by invitation of the affected local people and on the people's terms. This may be valued by communities, but may also help explain some borrowing country government's antipathy toward the IAMs.

5 Conclusion: the Future of the IAMs

The contributors to this volume are clear-eyed about the potential and the limitations of IAMs. Nevertheless, they all seem to agree that, despite their limitations, the IAMs have contributed to the operations of the IFIs in at least three ways. First, they have enhanced the focus of the IFI's and the member states on the 'last mile' of development–including those often overlooked 'miles' comprising communities that bear the costs of development and never figured as beneficiaries of the project. This focus and the associated increased understanding of these development-driven impacts have contributed to

22 Natalie Bridgeman-Fields, *supra,* Chapter 18.

improving their policies and compliance with them. Second, although to a less satisfactory extent, the IAMs have created a welcoming space in the development process for affected people to raise their concerns or seek resolution of their disputes. Third, the IAMs reflect a norm in development finance that the IFIs themselves have responsibilities that run directly to affected people, and by interpreting IFI policies have contributed to making them more subject to the rule of law, or at least a dynamic set of standards that safeguard the rights of affected people.

The contributions to this volume also make clear that the IAMs and the accountability of the IFIs are still works in progress, with many forces affecting their future. The long-term increase in the number of institutions that have adopted IAMs is likely to continue. CSOs are continuing to demand the adoption of IAMs by additional institutions, including the International Monetary Fund (IMF), as two contributors note.[23] In addition, pressure is mounting from IFIs and other financial institutions that require their co-financing partners, borrowers, or grantees to have an accountability mechanism in place. These vertical funder conditions are not dissimilar to the use of guarantees to ensure that minimum environmental and social standards are met in manufacturing supply chains. This is certainly true for the emergence of new IAMs among UN agencies–at least nine have established or are considering the establishment of an IAM. New accountability mechanisms have also been emerging at conservation groups (World Wildlife Fund (WWF) and Conservation International (CI)) as well as bilateral financial institutions (like the US Development Finance Corporation). But the fact that more financial institutions seek IAMs does not necessarily mean the next years will see an expansion of IAMs.

Significant forces are pushing for the consolidation of the IAMs as well. As the IAMs coordinate and cooperate more, the IFIs may find that sharing a mechanism or coordinating one or more of their functions provides sufficient cost cutting and efficiencies that they consider consolidating further–perhaps even to the extent of establishing the single IAM envisioned by Bradlow in the final chapter.

Most importantly, given the dominance of donor countries in the creation of the Panel, current shifts in geopolitical power or engagement with the IFIs may have significant impacts on the future of the IAMs. In this regard, it is important to note that historically it is the high-income member states that pushed for the creation of the IAMs and have supported them when they have come under attack. The borrower member states have tended to oppose the

23 Aldo Calieri, *supra* Chapter 22; Luis Vieira, *supra* Chapter 23.

IAMs and view them as an imposition from the rich world onto developing countries. The fact is that now some of the borrower member states have become richer and more powerful actors in the global economy. It is unclear if the rising powers will provide the same support to the IAMs or will demand changes in their powers and operating capacities.

However, even in a world where the acceptance of the IAMs is potentially undermined by the changing balance of geo-political power, the underlying rationale for the IAMs as vehicles for improving development effectiveness by integrating the concerns of local communities has not changed. Nor have other forms of accountability emerged as sufficiently strong alternatives for ensuring IFI accountability.[24] Despite the different perspectives on the overall track record of the IAMs, most contributors believe the IAMs are here to stay. The demand for them has not waned nor will it, particularly if the role of the IFIs continues to expand to address complex socio-economic and environmental issues like climate change, the loss of biodiversity, and the challenge of achieving the SDGs. The unfortunate aspect is that no other forms of accountability for communities currently exist that would replace the IAMs in enabling affected people to hold accountable those who have the power to affect their lives, including the IFIs. In that spirit, the editors hope that this volume will contribute to improving the performance of the IAMs – and that it will inspire a new generation to work on improving the accountability of the IFIs so that they are better able to fulfil their developmental potential.

---

24 *See* Charles DiLeva, *supra* Chapter 7; Athialy, *supra* Chapter 13; Stephens, *supra* Chapter 21.

Index

www.ingramcontent.com/pod-product-compliance
Lightning Source LLC
LaVergne TN
LVHW012051011026
849162LV00017B/140
9789004687578